SPIDER
BLUES

SPIDER BLUES

ESSAYS ON
MICHAEL ONDAATJE

EDITED BY
SAM SOLECKI

Véhicule Press

Montréal, Canada

The publication of this book was assisted by a Block Grant from the
Canada Council.

Cover design: JW Stewart
Book design: Simon Dardick
Production: Margaret Christakos
Manuscript pages courtesy of Michael Ondaatje
Typeset by Zibra Inc.
Printed by Les Editions Marquis Ltée

Véhicule Press, P.O.B. 125, Place du Parc Station,
Montreal, Canada H2W 2M9

Canadian Cataloguing in Publication Data

Main entry under title:
    Spider Blues: essays on Michael Ondaatje

Bibliography: p.
ISBN 0-919890-66-0

1. Ondaatje, Michael, 1943- —Criticism and interpretation—Addresses,
essays, lectures.
I. Solecki, Sam, 1946-

PS8529.N283Z88 1985   C818'.5409   C85-090181-2
PR9199.3.063Z9 1985

Printed in Canada.

CONTENTS

ABBREVIATIONS

DM   *The Dainty Monsters.*
Toronto: Coach House Press, 1967.

mst   *the man with seven toes.*
Toronto: Coach House Press, 1969.

CW   *The Collected Works of Billy the Kid.*
Toronto: House of Anansi, 1970.

RJ   *Rat Jelly.*
Toronto: Coach House Press, 1973.

CTS   *Coming Through Slaughter.*
Toronto: House of Anansi, 1976.

TK   *There's a Trick with a Knife I'm Learning to Do.*
Toronto: McClelland and Stewart, 1979.

RF   *Running in the Family.*
Toronto: McClelland and Stewart, 1982.

SL   *Secular Love.*
Toronto: Coach House Press, 1984.

INTRODUCTION

Now it is understood that a critic resembles a poet to a hair;
he only lacks the suffering in his heart and the music upon
his lips.

(Soren Kierkegaard, *Either/Or*)

The reviews and essays in this collection should be seen as a first and
very tentative attempt to describe, interpret, evaluate and situate a
writer very much in mid-career who, as Margaret Atwood noted in her
introduction to *The New Oxford Book of Canadian Verse*, evades "easy
categorization." This is especially true if, like Atwood, one is trying to
describe a specifically Canadian tradition of writing "from there to
here" that will include and see relationships among figures as different
as Roberts, Pratt, F.R. Scott, Purdy and Atwood herself. There's a
very important line there but it doesn't and, for obvious reasons, can't
include Ondaatje whose characters, landscapes, stories and themes resist
any taxonomies based on an overtly Canadian thematics. Every attempt
in the next generation to define and trace a Canadian tradition — analogous, say, to an American one — will have to deal with
Ondaatje's anomalous status within our literary culture. Like Aimé
Césaire, V.S. Naipaul, Derek Walcott and Salman Rushdie he compels
a rethinking of the notion of a national literary tradition. My own
hunch is that future Canadian literary historians will acknowledge Ondaatje's stature as a major writer but will probably end by offering a
paraphrase of Atwood's perceptive comments. J.E. Chamberlin's suggestive essay in this anthology anticipates this to some extent by argu-

ing that "the poetry of Ondaatje is centred around questions of traditions" without being rooted in or originating from any single tradition or cultural identity.

The best introduction to Ondaatje's life is his own fictionalized autobiography, *Running in the Family*. Deliberately ignoring many facts and dates it nevertheless provides, as Ernest MacIntyre's essay confirms, an accurate and moving image of the Ceylon/Sri Lanka phase of Ondaatje's past. Other than that, perhaps it's enough to say that Ondaatje was born in 1943, moved to England at the age of 11, and emigrated to Canada in 1962. Having studied at Bishop's College, the University of Toronto and Queen's University, he taught for a brief time at the University of Western Ontario before joining Glendon College of York University in 1981 as a professor of English. *The Dainty Monsters*, his first volume of poems, appeared in 1967. Since then he's gone from strength to strength, with each new book a start in a direction none of his readers could have foreseen. Looking back over his twenty year career we can see continuity and development, even the shape of an evolving body of work but I doubt if anyone can predict where Ondaatje will venture after *Secular Love*.

Every collection of this kind attempts, as I mentioned, to place and evaluate an artist. Often the evaluation is implicit in the simple existence of such a volume, in the fact that critics have chosen to write about a contemporary artist; we usually write about our contemporaries out of conviction that their work is important enough to be interpreted and evaluated. Interpretation itself often has a tacit evaluative dimension since it assumes a depth and complexity of art and vision in a poem, novel or body of work necessitating and justifying interpretation; if these don't exist then all that our criticism can offer is a redundant higher remedial reading. Perhaps, then, this is also one way of distinguishing between minor and major work: we intuitively recognize the strong writer and the essential text because they require not only an extended engagement between self and text but among several readers and critics. To paraphrase one of Freud's essay titles, minor writing requires only a brief and terminable analysis; major writing is a lifetime engagement. Ondaatje's poetry and prose, I'm suggesting, belong in the latter category.

In "Spider Blues," for example, one of his most engaging yet challenging poems, Ondaatje imagines the artist as a skillful if deadly spider practicing his ambiguous art on the common fly. One of the poem's enriching ambiguities—generated by shifts in tone, ambivalence and symbolism—lies in the way it allows us at one and the same time to admire Ondaatje's (and the spider's) artistry—evident here in the fact of the poem—while raising large and disturbing questions about the nature of the creative act and the emotional consequences for the artist involved in it. Part of my conviction that Ondaatje is an important and potentially major writer (which is something different from "a major *Canadian* writer") stems from his astonishing ability to enact two often powerfully contradictory attitudes or two aspects of a single thematic structure within one lyric or within a single dramatic moment. There is in his work a complexity and profundity of art and vision that makes rereadings inevitable. There is also, of course, the sensual pleasure in lingering over Ondaatje's brilliant tricks with the verbal knife: the wit, the unexpected shifts in tone, the evocative imagery and the brilliance of his metaphors.

The essays in this collection offer various approaches: Stephen Scobie, George Bowering and J.E. Chamberlin present very different arguments about influence and tradition; Sheila Watson and Dennis Lee examine the large implications of *The Collected Works of Billy the Kid*; Linda Hutcheon and Dennis Cooley read Ondaatje within the context of postmodernism; the essays by Susan Glickman, Tom Marshall and myself attempt to define Ondaatje's central concerns and myths. Instead of offering the customary introductory precis of these and other essays I would like to say something, briefly and perhaps paradoxically, about the approaches to Ondaatje's work not included because not yet written. Interesting to read would be an essay on Ondaatje as dramatist and on the relationship between the book and stage versions of *the man with seven toes, The Collected Works of Billy the Kid* and *Coming Through Slaughter*. Also worthwhile would be an essay on Ondaatje's humour; as George Bowering and Tom Marshall mention, Ondaatje can be a very funny writer. Too many essays, my own included, tend to leave the impression of a solemn and pervasively dark writer. *That* dimension is certainly there but anyone who has read "After shooting Gregory," "War Machine," "Moving Fred's Outhouse/Geriatrics of Pine," and "The Passions of Lalla" (from *Running in the Family*) realizes that Ondaatje has a range of humour extending from whimsy and wit to farce and grotesque. Third, there's a need for analyses of Ondaatje's style or

9

styles: whether these take their point of departure from Cleanth Brooks or Michael Riffaterre is irrelevant so long as they deal with the nuts and bolts of Ondaatje's poetry and prose and discuss *how* these work as verbal artifacts. Louis Dudek once suggested in a polemical and curmudgeonly moment that most contemporary poets are "technically incompetent." Perhaps the best way of dealing with this provocative claim would be to offer technical analyses of central contemporary poems like Ondaatje's "White Dwarfs" and "Letters and Other Worlds." Among other things, such analyses would tell us whether our critics are any more technically competent than our writers.

An essay on Ondaatje as a film maker was commissioned but didn't appear on time. Like many writers of his generation Ondaatje grew up on films, and it would be interesting to have essays not only on his three films but also on the influence that film as a medium or as an art form has had on his work. To what extent is *Billy the Kid* a script in search of a film? How have film techniques, especially various kinds of montage, influenced the structuring of Ondaatje's longer works? To what extent has Ondaatje's interest in film form influenced his notions about literary genres?

For obvious reasons this volume includes no biographical or psychoanalytical criticism although there are hints of the former in the essays by Glickman, Marshall and myself. Considering the centrality of the father, both absent (*Billy the Kid* and *Slaughter*) and present (*Running in the Family*), and of triangular relationships in what Eli Mandel would call Ondaatje's "family romance," some sort of psychoanalytical criticism seems inevitable. At this point, however, it strikes me as premature, intrusive, and presumptuous. Still, I suspect it's only from that direction that someone will deal adequately with the radical darkness at the heart of Ondaatje's vision, that emotional and spiritual maelstrom embodied in the often luminous metaphors, verbal prestidigitations and other tricks which simultaneously reveal and conceal it. Such a criticism, taking its cues from Freud and Harold Bloom, would also explore the relationship between creativity and the death instinct in Ondaatje and would ask why in Ondaatje's iconographic bestiary the artist is sometimes a killer or a spider.

But far more important than any of the above is the inevitably missing engagement between Ondaatje's work and the strong critic who, in his own field, is Ondaatje's equal in stature. Such an engagement

10

will occur only if the next generation sees the appearance of a Canadian critic with a voice sufficiently original and powerful to engage the strongest literary voices of this era in a creative dialogue. Of our critics to date only four have had the chance to fill such a role: Northrop Frye arrived too early on the scene and had to turn his attention elsewhere; Robert Kroetsch, Eli Mandel and Margaret Atwood, divided between art and criticism, chose for understandable reasons to devote most of their energies to art. Among our academic critics none can be even remotely compared to Lionel Trilling, Leslie Fiedler, and Harold Bloom, just to cite some major figures in American literary criticism. The presence of a strong critic will also mean the arrival of a confident *negative* criticism lacking in most of our writing. We have lacked negative comment either because, following Frye, we rightly judged that most Canadian literature produced before 1950 was mediocre and therefore unable to sustain any fully engaged critical commentary; or, because caught up in the necessary cultural nationalism of the past 25 years we tacitly regarded negative criticism as ultimately unpatriotic. The larger reasons for the disparity between the quality of our best contemporary literature and our best criticism lie somewhere in literary history, in the formation of our departments of English and in the whole related sets of problems arising out of a colonial and post-colonial culture.

Restricting ourselves simply to Ondaatje's case this means that like Atwood (his only peer among the poets of their generation), he is just beginning to receive the challenging criticism he deserves.

Sam Solecki,
St. Michael's College,
University of Toronto

11

Sam Solecki
AN INTERVIEW WITH MICHAEL ONDAATJE (1975)

The interview took place on Friday September 27th, 1974 in Michael Ondaatje's office at Glendon College, York University, Toronto. This was only the second time that I had met Ondaatje; on the first he had given a reading to a class of mine and I had used the occasion to ask whether he would be willing to do an interview for *Rune*, a magazine I was editing at the time with E.J. Carson and Brian Henderson. Ten years later, I remember the framed Uccello print with the shattered glass (see *Rat Jelly*, 39), the sunshine on the Glendon lawns outside Ondaatje's office window, and my impression that Ondaatje disliked giving interviews as much as I disliked doing them.

You recently completed a new film, The Clinton Special, *which is concerned with the Theatre Passe Muraille's* Farm Show. *How did you become interested in making films?*

About 5 years before the making of *Sons of Captain Poetry* (1970), I'd been involved in a film by David Secter, who'd made *Winter Kept Us Warm*, called *The Offering*, which wasn't very good. I'd volunteered my services one summer and . . .

. . . You were an extra in it.

I had a small part.

As a reporter?

You mustn't mention this; it was a terrible thing. That was the worst scene in the film. I'd always been interested in film and I love movies. But working with Secter I hated the experience, not because of him so much but the idea of working in a feature film with 20 or 30 other people and a very large crew which meant that you worked at other people's speeds, and that turned me off film-making for quite a while. I decided that if I was going to make films it was going to be a very small crew that I would work with, 2 or 3 people. So when I made the film on Barrie Nichol it was just me and a guy named Bob Fresco and we shot the film and edited that film together and that was fine; with Nichol that made 3 of us and it involved 2 weeks of shooting and 2 months of editing.

Why did you want to make a film specifically about Nichol?

At that time I was very interested in the possibilities of concrete poetry and I'd just finished the actual writing of *The Collected Works of Billy the Kid* and there was a real sense of words meaning nothing to me anymore, and I was going around interpreting things into words. If I saw a tree I just found myself saying tree: translating everything into words or metaphors. It was a very dangerous thing for me mentally and I didn't want to carry on in that way. I just felt I had to go into another field, something totally visual. The film was quite a help cos it freed me from going around and doing this kind of thing.

So the film was worth doing both because of artistic reasons as well as psychological ones?

Yes, psychologically, personally, and artistically. Also I had wanted to write something on Nichol and I'd realized you couldn't really *write* about concrete poetry, that it had to be expressed in another form.

What about The Clinton Special? *How did it get started?*

That began when I went and saw *The Farm Show* when it was first put on. I'd known Paul Thompson for quite a while; he'd done a dramatic version of *the man with seven toes* 2 or 3 years earlier. So I knew him and his wife, the actress Anne Anglin, when I went to see *The Farm Show* — although I wasn't really interested in theatre at all, you know; I kind of thought theatre was a dead art, one that had been dead for quite a while. This play, however, this play really turned me around. I began to think of all the possibilities that were in the theatre; the whole of documentary drama, the possibilities of finding your own mythology in your own landscape; and it was, again, a very freeing thing, for me, in the same way that Nichol's aesthetics had been. So that I didn't want to make a film right then. Next spring Paul was talking about going on a tour of the auction barns and back to the same farming community in which the play had originated. I thought that was a wonderful idea. I was also very interested in the reactions of the people to seeing themselves on stage; so I decided to make the film at the time of the tour.

Did you approach Paul Thompson?

Yeah. We'd kind of talked about working on something together before.

I didn't notice any mention of a script in the credits. Was there one?

Whatever script there is, is the play itself. Whenever the actors are doing the play that's *their* script. But documentary film has no real script or director. Talking about the director of a documentary film strikes me as invalid cos I find that you have a situation in which everything is left up to the camera-man, the lighting man, the actors and the people you are actually interviewing. I think it's very dangerous to try to over-control that; when you try and control it into a certain point of view then you get the CBC kind of documentary which knows what it's going to say before the actual filming begins. I had no idea what form the film would take before I began to make it. I just knew that somewhere there would be a discussion of how a play like this was made, and the plot-line of the tour, and also the plot-line of an actual performance: you know, *Henry V*.

Did you have a sense of how the film was going to evolve emotionally, ending

15

on that scene of the wife's monologue about her injured husband?

I didn't have that sense of development at the time.

What about when the editing began?

With the actual editing that's when the director moves in. That's when you decide the film's structure. You remake the whole film.

What about episodes such as the Lobb's discussion of their rural life, or the Merrill's; did you determine the format and the particular shots?

Yeah. Very much so. I worked with the camera-man, in terms of framing. I'm very interested in photography.

Yes, that came through in several episodes, where I had the feeling that you were looking for a photo-effect yet you didn't want simply to reproduce stills.

I think I was very annoying to the camera-man. Cos he kept saying that the camera should be moving in and out, that it should be zooming, or the film would be very dull. But I wanted that sense throughout the film that each shot would almost be a static photograph. Thus throughout the film the camera doesn't move very much at all except in the scene where Miles does the hay-baling. It's talking photography. I envisioned, to some extent, the cutting back and forth and that would have meant that the film would be quite busy already and so I didn't want too much business within the individual shot. In that sense it's very different from the Nichol film which is much more rhythmic in terms of a certain kind of beat or rhythm in his poetry. In this film it was very important to let people take their time, you know, and to give a sense of the pauses. I think I only had 2 or 3 cut-aways, where in the Nichol film there must have been 5,000. I just became really fascinated with *the way* that people talk, not just what they're saying, but the way they kind of choose a word or think it up. Something that people like Ray Bird — the fellow who gave the company the barn — did; he would really think out, and think out on film. That was a nice element I wanted to save.

Did you direct any of the local people in the filmed interviews?

No, it was just a case of getting them to talk, and sometimes asking them to expand a certain thing which was either very personal to them or to me.

Another interesting technical aspect was the way the film used colour, black-white and sepia effect. Was it your decision which determined what kind of film would be used?

Yeah, right. Also it's financial. With interviews you never know when someone is going to say something that you're going to use. So you have to use black and white because of the cost; but with something like *The Farm Show* it was valid that the source of the play should be in black and white while the actual play itself in performance would be in colour, though at times I wish some of the interviews had been in colour; I wish Les Jervis's scene at his sanctuary had been in colour cos it was very difficult to cut back and forth for that scene. And then with the sepia-effect for the old Charlie Wilson scenes I did want to make it look like an old photograph so that only after a couple of seconds would you notice that the trees are moving.

Also the film's pace is deliberately, and I think appropriately, slow in that it matches rhythm or pace of the subject matter. And within the film's overall rhythm the different colour effects point to different emphases.

I think you need that for a film of this length. Unfortunately because of television we've become used to seeing films in blocks of 28 or 58 minutes and I think it's affected us physically in how we look at film. I think we tend to become irritable toward the end of *The Clinton Special* when we find that there's still 10 more minutes left. So one does need something to kind of keep the film physically awake, you know, and that is why music was also important in the film, as a kind of adrenalin.

You mentioned Charlie Wilson. That particular episode, together with the David Fox interview in which he articulates his fears that the movie and the play may be simplistic representations of the rural experience served to deflate my own anxieties about whether or not the film was simply going to do a ver-

sion of Canadian pastoral or gothic. The two occur well into the movie and serve to introduce a differing note, one of complexity, which, in a sense, alerts the viewer to the fact that this is something more than a pastoral interlude. The Charlie Wilson episode strikes me as one of the film's most impressive.

We were looking for photographs of him when we were shooting, but I'm glad, really glad, that we didn't find any cos he becomes more detailed just cos he is so abstract. It's the kind of thing, you know, where it's left up to the imagination and it's preferable that way. It's funny, there were 2 or 3 sequences I knew just how I'd film and that was one of them.

Charlie seems to be a character out of your own poems. A man who has made what in The Collected Works of Billy the Kid *you call "the one altered move" that has made him almost "maniac."*

The Charlie Wilson scene was one that obsessed me from the first time that I saw the play. One of the things that knocks me out every time I see that scene is where somebody is talking about Charlie's coming every Saturday night to watch *Bonanza*, you know, totally unaware that he himself is a myth and that *Bonanza* is third rate mythology.

Paul Thompson remarks in the film that "You have to create your own mythology" and surely one thing The Farm Show *discovered in Clinton is an indigenous mythology. Do you have a sense of* The Clinton Special *as recording and recreating that mythology on film?*

Right. I think it does and perhaps that's why I got interested in it in the first place. Not so much of saying this is an important form of mythology, but, highly subconsciously the idea of making stories, you know, out of normal incidents and making them mythic.

Is that why the play and the movie focus to such an extent on the Lobb family?

Yes. But once again it's Passe Muraille's emphasis, not mine. They made this whole thing with the dynasty, which is just wonderful.

How long did the filming take?

18

About a week on trail with the company which included 4 nights of performance. The problem was that we began with no money at all, about $500 and we got cameras when we could. One of the cameras got broken and in the auction barn, for example, a lot of the stuff from the barn was ruined. So we shot one week of the tour and filmed the interviews with the actors themselves — that was in April '73 — then in August we went back to Clinton and met the actual characters in the play in their real settings cos I really wanted to get the film outside into the fields and actual homes somehow. CBC has done a television version of *The Farm Show* in the studio and I just found that terrifying because I think the play is a powerful thing in the theatre but on film I think it has to move out otherwise it becomes too enclosed . . .

. . . especially when the troupe emphasizes the close relationship between the area and the play. This was also evident in the way a farm audience reacted to the play.

Right. I saw the play several times with a rural audience, and they would always get the jokes about 5 seconds faster than an urban one. It was really the equivalent of everybody's idea of an Elizabethan theatre. And cos we had lights on to shoot the audience, the actors could see it and its reactions. David Fox said it was the first time that he was so conscious of the audience as a presence.

I suppose it's an Elizabethan play in that it is serious yet entertaining to all kinds of audiences.

Yes. I find that idea that art should not forget to be entertainment really important.

This comes across in your poems "War Machine" and "Bad Taste," both of which indicate a suspicion of people who treat art too solemnly. Let's talk about an entertainment movie which you admire, Leone's Once Upon a Time in the West.

That's one of my favourite movies.

Why?

19

I'm not quite sure that there's an intellectual reason, but emotionally I like that film's expansiveness and I find it a very moving film in the way it deals with the destruction of social violence by the violence of outsiders — something that interests me. And, ah, well I don't really like to intellectualize that film; it is delightful. It also contains the whole history of the western: there's a scene where just before the family is shot all the birds fly off which Leone has literally taken from John Ford's *The Searchers*; the shooting through the boot is from a Gene Autry film and so on. I don't know how Leone gets away with it without seeming too self conscious but he does. Luckily I saw the film after I had finished *Billy the Kid* because here was an Italian film-maker making this western, in many ways the best western, where with *Billy the Kid* I was trying to make the film I couldn't afford to shoot, in the form of a book. All those B movies in which strange things that didn't happen but could and should have happened I explored in the book.

In talking about your work we've touched on myth several times. In your article on Howard O'Hagan's Tay John *you define that work's mythic qualities as being "biblical, surreal, brief, imagistic." I would certainly apply these adjectives, with the exception of "biblical," to your second book* the man with seven toes. *How did you come to write that book?*

There's a series of paintings by Sidney Nolan on this story and I was previously interested in Nolan's Ned Kelly series. I got fascinated by the story of which I only knew the account in the paintings and the quote from Colin MacInnes. That's how it grew. It had to be brief and imagistic because the formal alternative was to write a long graphic introduction explaining the situation, setting, characters and so on. All the geographical references in the book are probably wrong and I'm sure all Australians think that the book is geographically ridiculous, just as the people of the south-west might think *Billy the Kid* is. I was putting geographical names into the latter cos I liked the sound of them. Chupadero Mesa, Punta de la Glorieta. The sound of words was something that concrete poetry woke me up to at that time.

Did you reject many poems from the man with seven toes?

Lots. Same with *Billy the Kid. the man with seven toes* was twice as long in the original manuscript. I find the editing of a manuscript to be like the editing of a film, that's when you determine the work's shape, rhythmic structures etc. You know you asked earlier about the rhythm of *The Clinton Special*, well I knew I wanted it to go in one direction and then bend off into another which would preferably be darker. There was another ending to the film which I loved but which would have been too much for an audience to take. After the applause at the end everyone stands up and we cut to old Mrs. Lobb who proceeds to tell us a long, long, long, very long story of some wedding; the film runs out but the sound keeps on and on; but that would have made the point as to where the source of the play and the film lies, in the raw material of stories told to the actors.

You indicated you edit your own books very carefully; what part do you play in the actual design of the books?

This is something that I find personally very interesting. The presentation of the poem is very important to me, and one of the reasons that I work with Coach House so much — and they've designed all my books — is that with Stan Bevington I can talk for several days about design; for example I don't like having to turn over a page in order to finish a poem, so that becomes a consideration in the actual design. Certainly with *The Collected Works of Billy the Kid* design was very important. We had to determine the type, the paper design, the paper texture, where the photographs would go, things like the first page on which Billy's photograph doesn't appear. I find it very difficult to write while a finished book is in the process of being printed, cos the printing itself is an art form and I'm deeply involved in it.

In an interview with Manna *you mentioned that George Whalley and Wayne Clifford helped you to organize the poems in* The Dainty Monsters. *In what specific way did they help you?*

Well I had lots of stuff, it was a first book, and they helped me to structure it by suggesting which poem follows which; all this relates to how a book looks and feels. This kind of structuring involves presenting something to the reader in a certain way. Dennis Lee was a great help in structuring *The Collected Works of Billy the Kid*. With *Rat Jelly* I tried patterning the book on the basis of certain images recurring in each section in totally different ways.

Another reference in the Manna *interview concerns your days at Bishop's University, where you say that a teacher named Arthur Motyer introduced you to poetry "in the best possible way." What do you mean by "the best possible way"?*

It was a very theatrical thing or presentation of a poem. He also taught drama and he read beautifully. He'd come into class and read a Browning poem and the poem became an acted thing, a passionate thing. He aroused an enthusiasm for literature. I think in teaching it's not so important that a student learn anything specific but that an enthusiasm be communicated; and Motyer had that real love of literature.

How do you teach poetry?

It's a terrible thing to admit after having been a teacher for x number of years but I don't really know, I don't think anybody knows — oh, I suppose there's someone. But with each poem it's a different process. I have to teach Ezra Pound's "Near Perigord," for example, and in the middle of the class I'll probably focus on the visual images of the hand and the five cities — an image that isn't really spelled out. But it's there all the way through the poem.

Let's turn to your own work; do you rewrite a great deal?

Yes, all my poems grow through a great deal of revision. "Letters and Other Worlds" in *Rat Jelly*, which was probably the most difficult poem for me to write, was about 4 or 5 times as long as it is in the finished version. I cut it down so that it would be suggestive as well as descriptive, suggestive of things that aren't or can't be said. My first drafts always seem horrendously awful and I've always been amazed how I get from the first draft to the finished product. I'm a great believer in rewriting. I suppose this is the effect of film on me because no one can make a totally unconscious film. All art, for that matter, is self-conscious. One has to admit that; one has to be on the border where that craft meets the accidental and the unconscious, as close as possible to the unconscious.

Hitchcock's point that "most films are slices of life, mine are slices of cake," is just one extreme.

Several of your poems, "Burning Hills" for example, as well as many of your epigraphs to sections of your books, contain reflections on the degree to which art in general and your poems in particular are truthful. Are these lines/epigraphs warnings to the reader?

Yes, but to myself as well. There's a great deal of lying in poetry, by necessity. It's not a case of being tactful or misrepresenting something but of making art; art is, to a certain extent, deceit. And what disturbs me in having my work interpreted as either physically or biographically right or wrong is that there's an emotional or psychological rightness which, for me, is more important than the other two. The epigraph in *Rat Jelly* from Melville's *The Confidence Man* is like the one at the beginning of John Newlove's *Lies*, "accidentally telling the truth."

This awareness of different viewpoints and possibilities is also apparent in another aspect of your work which appears in poems as different as "Postcard from Piccadilly," "Burning Hills," and "Lovely the Country of Peacocks." In the last poem for example, your tone is deliberately sentimental for the most part yet in the midst of the sentimentality you write, "we wear sentimentality like a curse." The very fact that you show an awareness of sentimentality in this way is a kind of judgement on it. I find this kind of interplay between opposed viewpoints, moods and ideas throughout your work; the David Fox interview in The Clinton Special *is another example.*

That's interesting because I didn't see that many connections. I suppose in writing you have to get all the truth down — the qualifications, the lies, the uncertainties — I had a quarrel with Paul Thompson as to whether or not that scene of David worrying about how close they are getting to the truth of these people should be in the film. But in many ways it's the greatest defence their point of view can have because if they raise the issue of veracity or accuracy, then nobody else can. They made the play themselves and that kind of awareness — David Fox's — is a sign of their integrity as a creative company. That's why I can't see *The Farm Show* as being done by any other company; it's their own personal voice.

23

Are you at all aware of having been influenced by any other writers? For example, I think Auden's "In Memory of W.B. Yeats" echoes in "Dates"; similarly I think Yeats' "No Second Troy" and "The Second Coming" stand somewhere behind "The Inheritors" and "Come to the Desert."

I think that a line in "Dates" — "no instruments/ agreed on a specific weather" — is my most conscious borrowing from anyone. I don't think that I've been influenced, or at least I'm not aware of it. In *the man with seven toes*, I guess that book was influenced in a lot of ways, though not in theme, by Phyllis Webb's *Naked Poems*, somewhere where she talks about a narrative form as a kind of necklace in which each bead-poem while being related to the others on the string was, nevertheless, self-sufficient, independent, lyrical. That got me really interested in the form for *the man with seven toes*.

Yes, the formal/structural difference between this book and your others is clear but I think that thematically, in its central concern with what the closing ballad calls "Green wild rivers in these people / running under ice that's calm" one can see the book's place in your body of work. For example, "The Republic," "Near Elginburg," "Gorillas," "Tink, the Summer Rider," and "King Kong Meets Wallace Stevens" all are concerned with the relationship between the calm surface of a landscape or a person and the dream or surreal aspect which lies underneath. I hesitate to call it an obsession...

...Yeah, it's probably an obsession. I'm interested in that part of human experience but the interest isn't formal. I mean I don't read books on psychology.

Like Freud's The Interpretation of Dreams?

No, no. I avoid reading books on philosophy, psychology, politics. It's a funny thing, political theses I find impossible to read. I have to be affected emotionally or in a sensual way before something hits me.

Which means you can read Stuart MacKinnon's The Intervals *or some other political poetry.*

Yes, I think *The Intervals* is a marvelous book because it starts from the

24

personal and moves out. The whole political thing has been obsessing me in the last year but I find it impossible to read someone like Trotsky, no . . . what's his name?

Marx?

Yes, Marx. I can't sit down and read them but I can read someone like Tom Wayman and envy that kind of poetry which is about himself and yet also political: he talks about politics, about history as it happens to himself. The book that really affected me in the last year was Marquez's *A Hundred Years of Solitude*, then I read his article on the death of Allende and that really knocked me out; it became even more powerful because I had been previously affected by the book.

You mention Stuart MacKinnon's The Intervals *in your poem "Burning Hills." Do you read friends' work in manuscript and have them read yours? What kind of comments do you invite/offer?*

The Intervals was a really infuriating book to read; he asked me to read it in manuscript. I told him it was "fantastic." He rewrote the whole thing again. I said, "This is even better. Don't change a word." And I think he's rewritten it once since then.

But what kind of specific comments would be made? Would you point to a line or a word and suggest an alternative?

Yeah. Victor Coleman did that with *The Intervals* too. He's a strange editor in the kind of marvelous associations or connections he makes between lines, words, sections. I usually give my manuscripts to people a long time after I've finished them; but then I'm quite happy to change something if I agree with the proposal. I tend to write a poem in a vacuum and then to leave it alone for a long time before rewriting it and submitting it to a friend. With *The Collected Works of Billy the Kid* I wrote the whole thing before telling anyone about it or letting anyone see it.

But they knew you were working on it?

Well, my wife and friends knew I was working on something and towards the end she guessed that obviously it was about Billy the Kid although I didn't admit it and then when I finished it I gave her the manuscript and went for a very long walk while she read it. I had no idea at that point what it was like, whether it was good or whether it was garbage. That's why I don't like talking about what I'm writing right now. I don't want to be influenced during the actual writing by anyone. I want to climb all the possible branches.

Did you have a preconceived notion of Billy the Kid *before you began?*

I really don't plan anything and this is what makes me very frightened while writing. With *Billy* I began with a couple of poems I had written about Billy the Kid and moved from these to being dissatisfied with the limits of lyric; so I moved to prose and interviews and so on. Right now I'm working on some prose but if I mention it people say that I'm working on a novel and I'm not. To me the novel is a 100 yard hurdles which you have to plan, prepare etc. And what I'm doing doesn't have a preformed shape. That's why I'm very nervous about what I'm doing right now because it's finding its shape and I've been working on it for 3 or 4 years and there's always the chance it won't work out.

A final question: I know that among film directions you admire Hitchcock and Leone . . .

That's one side of my taste. I also love Louis Malle's films, and films like *The Pedestrian* and *Mean Streets*.

Are there any writers whose work particularly interests you?

I like Stephen Crane very much — the epigraph in "Billboards": "Even his jokes were exceedingly drastic" — is somebody's description of Crane. I'm really fascinated by Crane and for me he's a really mythic figure. Partly I suppose because I'm reading his life by way of Ford Madox Ford who turns him into an angel. I love Crane's short stories. We were talking earlier on about how to teach a poem. One of the interesting things about Crane for me was that I could never get close to his poetry until I read an article on it by John Berryman that really got me interested in it. Like a good teacher, Berryman got you onto what Crane was trying to do emotionally and intellectually. That article stands out for me as a touchstone of what criticism and teaching should be and do. And I can't even remember a word of it.

The Poetry

~~between intervals, anthems, in time~~
~~they all hled together on the page he was writing on.~~
The summers were layers of civilisation in his memory
they were old photographs he did not look at anymore
for girls in them were chubby, not as perfect as in his mind,
his hair ~~was~~ (ungovernable) ~~and so~~ shaved to the edge of skin.
And he and friends, leaning on bicycles or posing ~~in the sand~~
were 16 and tried to look 21 with cigarettes
~~which looked~~ too big for their faces.
Townspecific. He could read ~~each~~ characters
~~too well~~, like wedding photographs
~~they shoved the undisguised flesh of history.~~
He could now hardly remember their names
though they had talked all day and exchanged styles
~~each of them from~~ ~~~~
~~~~ ~~the neutral vacuum of summer.~~
~~Armed with bicycles, cigarettes, swimming trunks,~~
one dangled a catapult ~~off his handlebars, one the historical camera.~~

~~Cycling through the rain, playing~~ ~~~~
~~with the girls (who rode horses not bikes)~~
~~which had simple plots.~~ ~~~~
~~something to do~~ ~~that gave you the~~ ~~to kiss anyone~~
~~any such~~ ~~then passed on,~~ ~~cold.~~
Sex a game ~~of~~ targets, of throwing firecrackers
at a couple in a field who were locked in hand-made orgasms.
Singing or mouthing dramatically with the record in someone's ear,
"How do you think I feel/You know our love's not real,
The girl you're mad about/Is just a gad-about
How do you think I feel."
He saw all that complex tension the way his children would.
~~Something on the level of these photographs:~~
A jigsaw of 5 summers that fused to one picture --
eight of them are leaning against a wall
~~some sitting,~~ arms around each other
looking into ~~the~~ camera and the sun
trying to smile at the unseen adult ~~taking the picture.~~
Trying against that glare to look relaxed, 21, and confidant
that the summer and friendship would last forever.

Except one who was eating an apple. That was him,
~~Somehow~~ accidently oblivious to the significance of the moment.
Looking at the picture now he hungers to have his arm around ~~someone.~~
As it is he is half alone, the wretched apple looks fresh and white.

Since he began burning hills
the Shell Vapona Strip has taken effect.
A wasp is crawling on the floor
tumbling over, its motor fanatic.
He has smoked 5 cigarettes.
He has written slowly and carefully, with great love,
with great coldness.
When he finishes it, he will go back
hunting for the lies that are obvious.

Manuscript page for "Burning Hills" from *Rat Jelly*

J.E. Chamberlin
LET THERE BE COMMERCE BETWEEN US:
THE POETRY OF MICHAEL ONDAATJE

Michael Ondaatje is a poet of contradictions. There are some obvious
ones, such as juxtaposition of the familiar and the surprising: "I have
been seeing dragons again." It is part of poetic convention, from the
seventeenth century ("I saw Eternity the other night") to the nineteenth century ("I like a look of Agony")' but it is always refreshing.
And there are some less obvious but equally significant contradictions:
a classical decorum balancing a romantic desire, for example; such as
when Sallie Chisum describes how Billy the Kid taught her to smoke
cigarettes: "Showed me how to hold it and how to want it." Then
there is another set of contradictions less easy to delineate, contradictions that involve a sense of what we sometimes refer to as the poet's
traditions, by which we usually mean inheritances that somehow are
less powerful than conventions and yet more binding than obligations.
Or maybe it is the other way around. Whatever the case, we accept that
poets are not only the unacknowledged legislators of the world but also
its great conveyancers, arranging for the passing on of things from one
to another. They are the middlemen of inheritances, and any contradictions in what they are doing must be taken seriously. The difficulty is in
recognizing these contradictions, for although they bedevil and inspire
those contemporary poets who have a heightened sense of the distance
between their literary and their cultural inheritances, they are hidden
behind our superficial understanding of the idea of tradition.

The poetry of Ondaatje is centred around questions of tradition. He
almost masks this with, among other things, his romantic fascination
for those Wordsworthian foster-parents, beauty and fear; and those
Coleridgean children, love and hate. But these fascinations are ultimate-

ly subsumed in Ondaatje's work into an even more ambivalent preoccupation with exactly what assumptions the poet can or should make about his function as the agent of complex inheritances. "Tradition" has usually been the portmanteau word for these complex arrangements; but it needs some closer attention than we usually give it. We understand the workings of individual talent much better than we do those of tradition.

Tradition refers to the passing of things from one to another. In its early use, the word accounted for the informal ways in which property changed hands, which is to say the ways in which it was either inherited or conveyed. Its informality was its hallmark, especially in legal or religious contexts, which is why we retain a sense of traditions as things that cannot be written down, but are passed on orally, or in other customary ways that do not conform to codified procedure. There was always an alternative, the ceremonies according to which certain things of particular importance in society were handed over. In Roman law, such things were called *res mancipi*; and the ceremony was called a "mancipation." Among the things that fell under this procedure, the most important tended to be land, and that which was necessary for its cultivation — usually horses, oxen, and slaves. We have long since lost a precise sense of the distinction between mancipations and traditions, but retain something of it in the difference between the strict legal procedures followed in the transfer of land, the adoption of children, or the conferring of citizenship; and the much more casual procedures that in most cases apply when presents are exchanged at festivals, when regulations governing the hours of opening of taverns are handed down, or when the truths of religious texts are inherited by priests and conveyed through sermons.

Inheritance and conveyance: they have always been what life is all about. Ask any lawyer, or any legislator. Perhaps contracts fit in there as well; the Latin word first used for a contract was *nexum*. The languages of commercial transaction and of inheritance and conveyance have long been languages used to talk about the poet and about poetry. It may be useful to take this language seriously.

It was a legal scholar in the nineteenth century who more than anyone before or since explained the differences between traditions and mancipations, and delineated the ways in which conveyances and contracts were at the centre of social and cultural activity. His name was

Henry Maine and the title of his book was *Ancient Law*. It was first published in 1861, and by the 1870s, Oxford and Cambridge were teaching Maine and Mill as the great modern thinkers. Maine's reputation has slipped over the years, but his arguments are worth attending to. He proposed that in the early stages of civil society certain things which were central to its functioning could only be passed on through very formal processes called mancipations. Compared to mancipations, what became known as traditions would not stand up under much scrutiny, though they tended to have the advantage of economy and efficiency, and were increasingly used as societies became more comfortable with their arrangements. But they were still casual, part of the scheme of things when more precise arrangements seemed to be too— well, too much trouble. The American Civil War, which was being fought just when Maine's book appeared, became eloquent testimony to the significance of mancipations, and to the way in which the word had come to refer to those conveyances about which society needed strict arrangements. One could change a thousand traditions, and still not emancipate one slave, still not release a slave from the strict conditions governing his or her status as a thing to be passed along. Not, at any rate, when one part of society saw things one way, and the other saw them quite differently.

This distinction between mancipations and traditions admittedly has an antique character about it; and so-called legal "fictions" by which law moves along with society were often used to give to such simple traditions as the straightforward delivery of something to someone else, or simple "possession" of New World land by Old World sovereigns, all the effective authority without the formal rigamarole of a mancipation.

But the distinction still has a compelling kind of application, especially to the question of poetic traditions. The delivery of a text from author to reader is part of the story. The other part has to do with the terms of the transaction between author and reader, and it is a difficult part to talk about these days. The nervousness that surrounds the discussion of such matters as the relationship of the poetic subject to tone of voice or to the role of the speaker in the poem is a nervousness that confirms the contemporary anxiety about the nature of tradition in poetry.

Michael Ondaatje is continually aware that the poet is responsible for

33

conveying beauth and truth, and continually unsatisfied by comfortable transactions. He returns us to the stringencies of *res mancipi*, things — such as the beautiful and the true — which require a mancipation, a more precise and codified form of succession, in order to be passed on from one to another.

> This is for people who disappear
> for those who descend into the code
> and make their room a fridge for Superman
> — who exhaust costume and bones that could perform flight,
> who shave their moral so raw
> they can tear themselves through the eye of a needle
> this is for those people
> that hover and hover
> and die in the ether peripheries
>
> There is my fear
> of no words   of
> falling without words
> over and over   of
> mouthing the silence
> Why do I love most
> among my heroes those
> who sail to that perfect edge ("White Dwarfs," *RJ*, 70)

That perfect edge is where things are in balance. What things? In practice there are three sets of them; we can call them different names, but the terms I have used are chosen to coincide with the sets of things that determine the character of social contracts and conveyances. There is land, and the instruments of its cultivation; there is the group that uses and occupies and may even own — but more importantly that inherits and conveys — the land; and there is the livelihood that binds together (or breaks apart) the group and its land. In literary terms — and my analogues are merely convenient here — there are also three sets. There is the language of discourse; there are the readers of texts, with their proprietary interest in the language; and there is the author of a text, and his relationship to the reader and to the reader's language.

And so I suggest that those elements — land, group, and livelihood — which govern inheritances and conveyances in civil society have an analogy in language, reader (in relationship to language) and author (in relationship to reader) in the sphere of poetry. It is here that the poet

34

legislates; and it is here that the distinctions between the comfortable conveniences of tradition and the strict observances of mancipation become an issue. At least they do so for the poet who is radically uncertain about what he is conveying, and what he has inherited.

This uncertainty generates several responses on the part of the poet Ondaatje. One is to admire those who giggle a lot. Another is to acquiesce in the inheritance of his language, and leave the first category all but alone. He does this by using a language that is ostentatiously familiar, a language that *does not need* the formalities of a mancipation because it has already been inherited according to the strict laws of cultural succession, laws whose authority Ondaatje recognizes. The language Ondaatje uses is the language of conventional late-twentieth-century discourse. Neither in its diction nor in its syntax is it a language for which Ondaatje needs to feel responsible. It is neither intensified nor clarified nor set in contrast to another kind of language, or to language raised or lowered to different degrees. Nothing depends on the language, the way it does for example in the poetry of Seamus Heaney or Derek Walcott. And nothing needs to be done about the language to ensure that it is passed on in an appropriate way or is a fit instrument. It is already in the hands of the next generation, of Ondaatje's audience. So the first element of Ondaatje's cultural world, the poetic equivalent of land if you will, is looked after willy-nilly. Its inheritance is easy, and its conveyance is accommodated within the laws of conversation.

But this is not at all the case with the second element, the relationship of the reader to the poet; or with the third, the relationship of the poet to his reader. It is not the case, that is to say, with matters regarding the tone of poetic voice, and the role of the poet within the poem and his relationship to the world outside the poem. In these areas, Ondaatje is engaged in a process of trying to purify not the dialect of the tribe—that was presumably done by the modernists—but the ways in which the author and the reader reach agreement that what is said is, to use conventional terminology, beautiful and true. Perhaps the most obvious manner in which Ondaatje engages the issue is to make the voice of his poems an affront: the voice of violence, or deviousness, or clumsiness; the voice of Philoctetes or of Pat Garrett, or the voice of the poet of ''Farre Off,'' who has been reading in the Renaissance company of Wyatt and Campion, and then translates into the rural company of dogs and lightning, all of them apparently

> aroused by Wyatt's talk of women who step
> naked into his bedchamber
>
> Moonlight and barnlight constant
> lightning every second minute
> I have on my thin blue parka
> and walk behind the asses of the dogs
> who slide under the gate
> and sense cattle
> deep in the fields (TK, 80)

Now in a sense this is familiar confusion. There is a deliberate subversion going on here, a deliberate confounding of any easy inheriting of things said or done, either literary or cultural. But there is something else as well, a more complex subversion. In my experience one of the first reactions of readers of this poem is to ask, "Why does he put in that line about his thin blue parka? It ruins the tone; and besides, it is irrelevant." They usually don't mind the asses of the dogs nearly as much. But that thin blue parka is central to Ondaatje's strategy, his use of shifting tones and unexpected voices. This happens several times in the final stanzas of "For John, Falling," where the shifts between what Walter Bagehot once called the pure, the ornate and the grotesque are obvious, and wonderful.

> Arched there he made
> ridiculous requests for air.
> And twelve construction workers
> what should they do but surround
> or examine the path of falling.
>
> And the press in bright shirts,
> a doctor, the foreman scuffing a mound,
> men removing helmets,
> the machine above him
> shielding out the sun
> while he drowned
> in the beautiful dark orgasm of his mouth. (DM, 48)

One way of accommodating this kind of tonal collage is to say that Ondaatje is more a maker of imaginative things than a mirrorer of real things. That said, he does not, as poets for the past hundred years have

36

done, play upon the fine line between art and life. Instead, he entertains the magical possibilities of *another* life, as Billy the Kid or Philoctetes, say — or as himself. It is this last pose that is his most important. It provides him with his most significant and most subversive tone of voice, for it ensures that his poetry does not inherit and does not convey the familiar conditions of lyric expression, the dramatic monologue. He moves in and out of his poems — especially the most explicitly autobiographical ones — with unnerving arbitrariness, as though he were determined to undermine the authority of the conventional phrase he employs: I thought, I gaze, I recall (from "The Hour of Cowdust") or I walk, I am alone (from "The Palace") or I thought, I found, I disturbed, my tongue (from "Pig Glass"). This last poem is a nice example because its shifts are more than usually erratic, beginning with a colloquial "Bonjour," to the recognizable pun on "eye/I" and the ambiguities of "lie," to the finely tuned ambivalence of its final generalization: "Determined histories of glass." It is not the poet's history; but it *is* in his pocket. He is passing it on to us, apparently a found object, which he has made a significant form. But it is uncertain at the end whether it may not be the other way around, a significant form that he has made a found object; and the uncertainty is generated out of the shifting location of the voice within the poem, inside and outside its actions, participating in and commenting on its implications, committed to and disengaged from its meanings. It is a poem specifically about inheriting and conveying, but inheriting and conveying that cannot be trusted to the convenient modes of poetic tradition. Its awkwardness is its defence; what then is its alternative? It is not exactly in confusion. It is in bearing witness, the poet's and mankind's, subtlest obligation.

Poets speak in particular times and places. They bear witness to these times and places, and to themselves. The act of bearing witness is the contemporary poet's central commitment, and provides an alternative to unscrupulous or compromised traditions. Ondaatje takes its inheritance very seriously indeed.

The concept of witness has a long history. The Greek words for which witness, witnessing or bearing witness are the usual Biblical translation form a group from which comes our English word martyr. Its cognates include a group of Indo-European words clustering around the notion of being mindful of, or remembering. The English word witness has its source in notions of wisdom or knowledge. The origins of witness are within a legal frame of reference and turn around questions of giving an accurate account, or of telling the truth. In classical times, there was an additional element in which the testimony given by a witness was assumed to incorporate subjective moral or philosophical conviction as well as objective data; and so the Stoic regarded his conduct in adverse circumstances as testimony to the truth of his ideas and doctrines. So did the martyr.

It is at this point that the New Testament idea of witness comes to the fore, along with a considerable ambivalence. It is in the Gospel according to St. John, the Gospel of the Word, that the concept of witness is most prominent; bearing witness becomes less a substantiation of verifiable events, less a way of seeing, than a way of saying, a proclaiming. Not a mirroring, but a making. It is here that the uneasy question of truth or falsehood — of fact or fiction — arises. One of the central discussions in John concerns the truth of that which Jesus testifies about himself. On the one hand, there is his comment that "if I bear witness of myself, my witness is not true" (5:31). On the other, when the Pharisees put that comment back to him, his response is that "though I bear record of myself, yet my record is true: for I know whence I came, and whither I go" (8:14).

The authority of Ondaatje's witness to the congregation is equally uncertain. It is the uncertainty inherent in making, or making up, a story about what happened. Parables are a problem in this way. So are confessions. What Ondaatje does is invite the expectations of confession and the exhilarations of parable, but leave the identity of the speaker hovering between himself and another. He is most himself when he is Philoctetes, say, and when Philoctetes is a spider; or Paris, when Paris is a heron — as in "The Goodnight."

> With the bleak heron Paris
> imagine Philoctetes
> the powerful fat thighed man,
> the bandaged smelling foot
> with rivers of bloodshot veins
> scattering like trails into his thighs:
> a man who roared on an island for ten years,
> whose body grew banal
> while he stayed humane
> behind the black teeth and withering hair.

38

Imagine in his hands—black
from the dried blood of animals,
a bow of torn silver
that noised arrows loose like a wild heart;

in front of him—Paris
darting and turning, the perfumed stag,
and beyond him the sun
netted in the hills, throwing back his shape,
until the running spider of shadow
gaped on the bandaged foot of the standing man
who let shafts of eagles into the ribs
that were moving to mountains. (*DM*, 58)

A spider—especially a Swiftian spider—is a maker of webs,—"in his
loathing / [he] crucifies the victims in his spit / making them the art he
cannot be" ("Spider Blues"); and poets are makers of songs and pictures and stories. But Ondaatje won't let them be, won't let a song sustain its magic of sound—the opening song of "Letters and Other
Worlds" shifts into narrative. Nor will he let a picture maintain its precision—"Kim, at half an inch" slips into song. And a story becomes
something to be suspicious of, or to disintegrate into picture and song.
Take "Walking to Bellrock."

But there is no history or philosophy or metaphor with us.
The problem is the toughness of the Adidas shoe
its three stripes gleaming like fish decoration.
The story is Russell's arm waving out of the green of a field.

The plot of the afternoon is to get to Bellrock
through rapids, falls, stink water
and reach the island where beer and a towel wait for us.
That night there is not even pain in our newly used muscles
not even the puckering of flesh
and little to tell except you won't
believe how that river winds and when you
don't see the feet you concentrate on the feet.
And all the next day trying to think
what we didn't talk about.
Where was the criminal conversation
broken sentences lost in the splash in wind.

Stan, my crazy summer friend,
why are we both going crazy?
Going down to Bellrock

recognizing home by the colour of barns
which tell us north, south, west,
and otherwise lost in miles and miles of rain
in the middle of this century
following the easy fucking stupid plot to town. (*TK*, 83)

What Ondaatje is doing is making his act of bearing witness transparently an act, with the testimony no less important but needing a much more radical scepticism, and a much more stringent code to give authority to what it conveys, than any easy notion of tradition would accommodate. And through his testimony Ondaatje proposes that self and voice and audience and subject be returned to the formal arrangements of the literary equivalent of mancipation, to a more ordered code of conveying things, rather than be allowed to remain within the functional efficiencies of tradition. The English poet Charles Tomlinson has a meditative poem on the painter John Constable which concludes,

> The artist lies
> For the improvement of truth. Believe him.

Ondaatje contradicts this in "Country Night," and says instead, with a surprise that conveys the shift in authority that is going on,

> The sofa calls the dog, the cat
> in perfect blackness walks over the stove.
> In the room of permanent light
> cockroaches march on enamel.
> The spider with jewel coloured thighs the brown moth
> with corporal stripes
> > ascend pipes
> and look into mirrors.
>
> All night the truth happens. (*TK*, 73)

Believe the poet? Leave that to other poets, or to lunatics and lovers. Ondaatje is much more interested in making believe, in a mirroring that requires its own, new authority as a mode of passing things on to their true inheritors. It is an admirable ambition, and he has taken on the obligations of an unacknowledged legislator of rules of conveyances and contracts, in order to write new laws of succession. He does not take the modernist way, the way of parody, but instead moves to a new point of balance between mirroring and making, between seeing and saying, a point at which neither standards of truth nor ideals of beauty can be assumed. Ondaatje is in a curious position as a poet, but a position that is close to that of other contemporary poets writing out of situations that define essentially colonial predicaments, where language or audience or the identity and role of the poet are indeterminate. It is good company to be in, for it is the company of some of the best contemporary poets writing in English—in the West Indies, say, or Nigeria, or Ireland, or Detroit. Canada offers Ondaatje a geography, but no inheritance; Sri Lanka offers him a family history, but no tradition, no way of passing things on; the English language offers him both an inheritance and a history, but no time and place. Ondaatje's success as a poet has been to subject the conditions of his craft to relentless scrutiny, to ensure that his inheritances are indeed his, and to ensure that they can be ours. The scrutiny is mediated by his personality, which is why we read his poetry. This scrutiny is not finished, which is why we will continue to read it. I just hope he does not leave the language alone too much longer. It has a habit of disinheriting those who take it for granted.

Stephen Scobie
HIS LEGEND A JUNGLE SLEEP:
MICHAEL ONDAATJE AND HENRI ROUSSEAU

Having to put forward candidates for God
I nominate Henri Rousseau and Dr Bucke.
"The Vault"

The choice, for this exalted position, of Richard Maurice Bucke (1837–1902), psychiatrist, intrepid wanderer in the Rocky Mountains, superintendent of the London insane asylum, author of *Cosmic Consciousness*, friend, pallbearer, and literary executor of Walt Whitman,[1] may come as something of a surprise to the reader of Michael Ondaatje's poetry, for he is not, with this exception, a prominent figure in it. On the other hand, there is nothing at all surprising about the choice of the Douanier, *"gentil Rousseau," artiste-peintre*, since Ondaatje's fascination with him is visible throughout his poetry.

The Dainty Monsters contains one complete poem, "Henri Rousseau and Friends," and Rousseau also turns up, appropriately enough, in the zoo poem "You Can Look But You Better Not Touch." In *Rat Jelly*, the poem already quoted, "The Vault," proceeds to a discussion of Rousseau's last great painting, *The Dream*, a postcard of which is also to be found on the poet's desk in "Burning Hills." Earlier in the book, Ondaatje uses as the text for a found poem the famous letter "To Monsieur le Maire," in which Rousseau, with his usual unsettling blend of naïveté and shrewdness, offers *The Sleeping Gypsy* for sale to the citizenry of Laval, the home-town which he shared with the author of *Ubu Roi*, Alfred Jarry.[2]

There is of course no mention (at least no direct mention: the presence may still be felt indirectly) of Henri Rousseau in *The Collected Works of Billy the Kid*: in 1881, the year of Billy's death, Rousseau was still an obscure employee of the Paris octroi, who had not yet painted a picture. Only his apocryphal incarnation (in the legend fostered by Guillaume Apollinaire) has visited Billy's part of the world, playing clarinet in Mexico for the army of the doomed Maximilian, whose ruined palace haunts the opening chapter of *Under the Volcano*. After the manner of Alfred Hitchcock, who in his later films put in his famous "personal appearance" as early as possible so that audiences could stop waiting for it and get on with watching the movie, Ondaatje inserts the Rousseau reference on the first full page of *Running in the Family*: "I sat up on the uncomfortable sofa and I was in a jungle" (*RF*, 21; see below the discussion of Rousseau's *The Dream*).

Rousseau's entire life and work present a fascinating complex of paradoxes and contradictions. His genius was largely instinctive, yet he was a painstaking craftsman; unable to detect irony, he accepted praise and abuse alike as evidence of his own greatness; a committed admirer of the official, academic school of painting, he nevertheless exhibited with the most radical and anti-academic groups of painters, and may indeed have contributed to the naming of one of them: the Fauves. The kindliest and most humanitarian of men, he was twice imprisoned for larceny. Personal anecdotes delight in exposing his naïveté, yet in many ways he was very shrewd—shrewd enough, even, to play up to his own naïve image. Dora Vallier comments:

> One day, in his lawyer's office, he made a telephone call. "Suddenly I heard him shouting," Maître Guilhermet tells us. "Surprised, I asked him why he was speaking so loudly, and he replied, 'The people I'm talking to are so far away.'" Rousseau was trying so hard to appear naïve that he occasionally overacted the part. This was a form of self-defense, but the naïveté with which he approached the part made him seem much more naïve than he really was—hence, the distorted image that those who knew him passed on to us.... On another occasion he was handed an invitation to a party being given by the President of the Republic [by friends as a joke]. When he came back, he told a long story: the guards had refused to admit him, he had insisted, and the President in person had come out and, patting him on the shoulder, said, "It's a pity, Rousseau, that you're in everyday clothes. You see, everybody is in evening dress. Come back some other time." But did he ever really go to the Elysée? (Vallier, 82–83)

The Mexican legend is another case in point. Apollinaire, and most of Rousseau's friends in the last years of his life, may have been all too ready to believe in it because it provided a suitably exotic source for Rousseau's exotic pictures. "When questioned about this period in his life," Apollinaire's version runs, "he seemed to remember only the fruits which he had seen there, which the soldiers were forbidden to eat. But his eyes had preserved other memories: tropical forests, monkeys, and strange flowers.... " Historically, it appears certain that Rousseau did not go to Mexico: at best, he may have had the opportunity to talk to survivors of the expedition. The forbidden fruits, and the "tropical forests, monkeys, and strange flowers" actually had humbler, more domestic sources: the Jardin des Plantes, and the international displays from the Paris World's Fair of 1889.

But to some extent, Rousseau had to invent a past for himself. "A curious phenomenon occurred," writes Dora Vallier: "his paintings provided him with the raw materials for a past. Since he excelled in exotic landscapes, his obscure years of military service became a fabulous journey to Mexico." Rousseau was forty years old before he began to paint, but from that time on he devoted himself to his art, and to his conviction (naïve? shrewd? laughable? correct?) of his own greatness, with an intensity which blotted out and transformed almost everything about his early years. His art became his life, and in the Mexican legend his life learned, in a Wildean manner, to imitate his art. Asked once if it was not uncomfortable to have to sleep in his cramped and crowded studio, Rousseau replied: "You know, when I wake up I can smile at my canvases."

In his life as in his work, Henri Rousseau was one of the most bizarre, and ultimately mysterious, of all artists. This alone might well account for Ondaatje's interest, for Ondaatje's own work shows a lively interest in the bizarre. What, for example, could be more like an Ondaatje narrative—the shifting of tone between absurdity and profundity of, say, "Letters & Other Worlds"—than the many stories which surround the famous Rousseau Banquet held in Picasso's studio at the Bateau Lavoir?

The banquet was held in November 1908, in honour of Picasso's acquisition of a Rousseau portrait, sold to him for five francs by a dealer who said that he might be able to make use of the canvas. In fact, it remained to the end of his life one of the treasured paintings in Picasso's personal collection. The gathering of those who came to honour this most unsophisticated of painters reads like a roll call of the Parisian avant-garde: Pablo Picasso and Fernande Olivier; Georges Braque; Guillaume Apollinaire and Marie Laurencin; Gertrude Stein, Leo Stein, and Alice B. Toklas; Max Jacob, André Salmon, Maurice Raynal, and Maurice de Vlaminck. Picasso ordered the food for the wrong day but still had fifty bottles of wine; Apollinaire caught up on his correspondence and improvised a poetic tribute to Rousseau; André Salmon and Maurice Cremnitz chewed soap and foamed at the mouth in an elaborate impersonation of delirium tremens for the bemused benefit of the Americans. Gertrude Stein, writing of course in the person of Alice B. Toklas, records that "Guillaume Apollinaire solemnly approached myself and my friend and asked us to sing some of the native songs of the red indians. We did not either of us feel up to that to the great regret of Guillaume and all the company."

Throughout all this, Rousseau was seated on a makeshift throne consisting of a chair placed on top of a packing crate, directly beneath a lamp which "with remarkable regularity," according to Raynal, "let fall drops of burning wax on his head." Fernande Olivier's account perhaps improves on the story, but in its bizarre simplicity and juxtapositions it certainly reflects the centre of the Rousseau legend:

> Rousseau was so happy that, throughout the evening, he received on his head drops of wax from a large lamp that hung above him, without flinching. They ended by forming a small eminence on his head like a clown's hat which he kept right up to the moment when the lamp caught fire. He was made to believe that this was his final apotheosis. Afterwards he started to play a short piece on the violin which he had brought with him.

Gertrude Stein's version, however, shows that Rousseau was still assiduously propagating his own versions of legend: "Rousseau blissful and gentle played the violin and told us about the plays he had written and his memories of Mexico."

But it is not just this quality of the bizarre which accounts for Ondaatje's interest in Rousseau. They are in many ways very different artists—Ondaatje, obviously, works at a level of sophistication and self-consciousness entirely alien to Rousseau—but nevertheless there are areas of affinity between their works. I use the word "affinity"

45

rather than "influence," because the latter would suggest too direct a causal relation. There are aspects of Rousseau's work towards which Ondaatje is drawn, but the poet does not treat them in the same way as the painter. This essay will explore two such areas of affinity: in each case, the use of Rousseau's paintings as an approach to Ondaatje's poems is not to be seen as limiting our understanding of the poems but as opening up possibilities, and showing how the self-conscious development of theme in Ondaatje inevitably raises questions which Rousseau's naïveté stops short of. It is, of course, the glory of Rousseau's work that he *does* stop short: it is the limitation of his imagination which produces those inimitable qualities which fascinate us still in the irreducible pictorial vision of the gentle toll-collector who never went to Mexico.

> ... a postcard of Rousseau's *The Dream*. ("Burning Hills")

The Dream is a large painting (80½" by 117½"), depicting one of Rousseau's characteristic jungle scenes: thick foliage with spiked leaves in intricate crisscross patterns, exotic pink and blue flowers, oranges. One painter is reported to have counted more than fifty shades of green in the painting. An orange-breasted bird sits on a branch; an elephant hides in the undergrowth; two playfully drawn lions stare around them in a rather baffled manner; a large black snake with a pink belly glides towards a charmer playing his pipe. And plumped down in the middle of this, dominating the left side of the composition, is a large red couch with a naked woman reclining on it, stretching out her hand toward the scene.

The couch had long been in Rousseau's studio — all his friends recognized it — but its presence in this painting proved a sore trouble to the literal minded. Rousseau courteously and patiently explained it to the art critic André Dupont:

> I am answering your kind letter immediately in order to explain to you the reason why the sofa in question is included. The woman sleeping on the sofa dreams that she is transported into the forest, hearing the music of the snake charmer's instrument. This explains why the sofa is in the picture. . . . I end this note by thanking you in advance for the article you will write about me. Please accept my best wishes, and a hearty and cordial handshake.

(To the poet André Salmon, Rousseau gave a slightly different version: "The sofa is there only because of its glowing, red colour.") Attached to the frame was the following poem:

Yadwigha dans un beau rêve
S'étant endormie doucement
Entendait les sons d'une musette
Dont jouait un charmeur bien pensant.
Pendant que la lune reflète
Sur les fleuves, les arbres verdoyants,
Les fauves serpents prêtent l'oreille
Aux air gais de l'instrument.

Yadwigha, peacefully asleep,
Enjoys a lovely dream:
She hears a kind snake charmer
Playing upon his reed,
On stream and foliage glisten
The silvery beams of the moon
And savage serpents listen
To the gay, entrancing tune. (Vallier's translation)

Describing the painting in "The Vault," Ondaatje emphasizes the intimate connection between the dreaming lady and the landscape she has created for herself in her dream: she

has been animal and tree
her breast a suckled orange.
The fibres and fluids of their moral nature
have seeped within her frame.

The hand is outstretched
her fingers move out in
mutual transfusion to the place. (67)

The identity between the dreamer and the dreamed is complete, a "mutual transfusion" has taken place. The red sofa belongs in the imaginary jungle; the enchanter's pipe plays in the small studio on the Rue Perrel.

This, then, is the first area of affinity between Rousseau and Ondaatje: the coexistence, amounting to interpenetration, of a domestic scene and a jungle. Ondaatje's poetry reaches towards the

47

kind of balance found in the visual composition of *The Dream*, but for him it is more difficult to attain. Rousseau's jungle is more exotic than violent; but for Ondaatje, violence is the essence of the jungle, and time after time it breaks through his poems with disturbing effect.

Not that violence is entirely absent from Rousseau's paintings, though in *The Dream* it is held in check: Yadwigha's dream is not a nightmare but *"un beau rêve,"* and the charmer is *"bien pensant."* Similarly, with regard to *The Sleeping Gypsy*, the letter to the Mayor of Laval insists that *"A lion wanders by, detects her and doesn't devour her."* Indeed, the absence of any footprints in the sand, in an otherwise meticulously realistic picture, has led some critics to suggest that *The Sleeping Gypsy* may also represent a dream. But in other Rousseau paintings, violence does erupt, as is shown by such titles as *The Jungle, Tiger Attacking a Buffalo, Tiger and Buffalo Fighting, Negro Attacked by a Jaguar, Horse Attacked by a Jaguar, Scouts Attacked by a Tiger, The Repast of a Lion* (a lion eating a jaguar), and the famous *Hungry Lion*, the painting which may have contributed to the naming of the Fauves, with its straight-faced commentary by Rousseau: "The hungry lion throws himself on the antelope and devours it; the panther waits anxiously for the moment when it too will have its share. Carnivorous birds have pecked out a piece of flesh from the back of the animal, which weeps. Sunset."

The extraordinary understatement of these final words (like the "effect of moonlight, very poetic" in the description of *The Sleeping Gypsy*) may be deliberately ironic, or simply naïve, on Rousseau's part; Ondaatje's use of this kind of comment is more clearly ironic, as in "Application for a Driving License":

> Two birds loved
> in a flurry of red feathers
> like a burst cottonball,
> continuing while I drove over them
>
> I am a good driver, nothing shocks me. (*DM*, 35)

The irony, and absence of shock, are constants in Ondaatje's poetry, even if they do not always emerge quite as blatantly. Within the domestic scene, violence is always liable to erupt, and irony is frequently a way of dealing with the intensity of this perception.

48

The dog in "Biography" is "tacked to humility all day" by the children who are "unaware that she/tore bulls apart, loosed/heads of partridges, / dreamt blood" (*DM*, 16). But if the children see only Yadwigha asleep on the familiar red couch, the poet sees also the jungle, the dreams of blood.

Such dreams intrude all the time: a summer badminton net becomes tangled with dragons, and "My mother while caressing camels/had her left breast bitten off" ("Over the Garden Wall," *DM*, 30). For Ondaatje, the problem is to achieve some sort of equilibrium, or "mutual transfusion." It will not do simply to repress such knowledge — "In spite of this I've no objections / to camels" — although this is undeniably what the social structure will attempt — "a vulture calmly resting at a traffic light / would undoubtedly be shot, very messily, / by the first policeman who spotted him." Here again the ironic tone — the comic understatement of "I've no objections," the more chilling understatement of "very messily" — is reminiscent of the distancing Rousseau achieves by his naïve description.

Ondaatje's responses to the irruption of the violent into the domestic are rarely phrased as direct statements: at their best, the statement is indirect, controlled by tone, by what is not said. Often this emerges not as "*un beau rêve*" but as various kinds of nightmare: the tight hysteria of "War Machine," the surreal but savage humour of "Rat Jelly" itself. Occasionally the terms are reversed: "After shooting Gregory," Billy finds his carefully controlled world of violence disrupted by the intrusion of a domestic element, the chicken, which pushes the scene to a height of surreal horror before Ondaatje, reasserting the poet's control of tone if not Billy's control of death, dissolves the scene in laughter.

Most of these illustrations, both in Rousseau and Ondaatje, have centred on the role of animals. Ondaatje's fascination with animals is too well known to require much comment: what is remarkable is the way that they retain their integrity and absolute identity *as animals* at the same time as they provide an almost continuous commentary on what is done in human society. From the dog's dream in "Biography" through to the terrifyingly detailed observation of the porcupine quills in "Dashiell,"[3] the violence of the jungle is immanent in the most domestic of pets; the mad cracked eyes of Livingstone's mongrels are reflected in the one-eyed owls of Sallie Chisum's menagerie. Introducing his anthology of animal poems, *The Broken Ark,*[4] Ondaatje wrote that he was not interested in pretty pictures of animals as pets, but rather that he wanted the reader to "imagine yourself pregnant and being chased and pounded to death by snowmobiles." Ondaatje's vision reaches to levels of harsh reality which the Douanier's gentle exoticism never accounted for.

But if the violence is harsh, vivid, and uncomfortably convincing, the domestic scene is no less real. Rousseau's sofa, whose "glowing, red colour" provides the necessary visual counterbalance to the fifty greens of the jungle, was also the most familiar and affectionately regarded of the objects of his daily life. In *The Dream* it provides a fully adequate, and even humorous, image of the domestic security in which Yadwigha's dream is based. In the same way, Ondaatje's poetry is full of images which establish the warmth, reality and humour of the domestic scene. One such image, that of the Chisum ranch, is, as I have pointed out elsewhere,[5] lovingly built up in direct contradiction to the acknowledged source material.

In *Rat Jelly*, the first section "Families," is dominated by the evocation of that small circle — "wife kids dogs couple of friends" — which forms the necessary complement to the jungle of "Live Bait." It is often more difficult to present a convincing portrayal of happiness than of unhappiness; but Ondaatje is a master at this — as, indeed, is Rousseau. There is a skillful use of small details, observed with the most intimate affection, out of which the reader can reconstruct the fabric of a whole relationship:

> I am writing this with a pen my wife has used
> to write a letter to her first husband.
> On it is the smell of her hair.
> She must have placed it down between sentences
> and thought, and driven her fingers round her skull
> gathered the slightest smell of her head
> and brought it back to the pen. ("Billboards," *RJ*, 14)

The centre of this section is the group of joke poems — "Notes for the legend of Salad Woman," "Postcard from Picadilly Street," "The Strange Case" — which are marvellous jokes but even better poems. Their humour is not there just for its own sake, but plays a functional role in establishing the tone and the credibility of the domestic image. If Rousseau smiled at his canvases, Ondaatje must surely smile at these poems.

The finest poems in this section, however, are those in which, as in *The Dream*, the red sofa is firmly set in the jungle. In "White Room," the image of the woman's body as "cool fruit" gives way to an image of her "stray bones" as "scattered fragments / of a wrecked aircraft." Ondaatje's descent, "like helicopters onto the plain," may be taken as the arrival of rescue helicopters at a crash site; but it also carries uncomfortable evocations of the Vietnamese television war. The final line, "within the angles of the room," remains ambiguous: these angles may provide the security of a solid structure, but they are set harshly against the "collapse" of human "flesh."

In "Letters & Other Worlds," the domestic scene — again evoked by affectionate detail and the masterful narration of comic incident — becomes the scene for an intensely private struggle with an interior jungle. This is one of Ondaatje's finest poems: the control of tone, as the poem moves from comedy to deeply moving simplicity, is breathtaking. It is one of Ondaatje's fullest realizations of that "mutual transfusion" between the jungle and the sofa; but here, continuing the metaphor of blood, the transfusion is deadly: the "blood screaming in / the empty reservoir of bones" so that "he died in minutes of a new equilibrium."

"Equilibrium" is here a key word. (One is reminded again of Robert Kroetsch's description of Canadians as "fascinated with problems of equilibrium."[6]) As I mentioned earlier, the jungle dream cannot be repressed: a balance must be sought, and maintained in the control of the poem's tone, whether it be ironic distance, surreal or affectionate humour, or the highly sophisticated manipulation of various tones in "Letters & Other Worlds." At any rate, equilibrium is the task of the artist. Rousseau, not Yadwigha, is the real dreamer; and it is Ondaatje's dream which must attempt to mediate between "Families" and "Live Bait."

> Breavman loves the pictures of Henri Rousseau,
> the way he stops time.
> (Leonard Cohen, *The Favourite Game*[7])

Rousseau always had trouble with feet. One of the points of technique that the naïve self-taught painter never mastered was the natural perspective by which feet appear to be placed squarely and firmly on the ground. Frequently, Rousseau avoids this problem by hiding the feet behind low vegetation; but when he cannot do this, the deficiency is obvious—as, most obviously, in his famous *Myself: Portrait-Landscape* (note, in passing, the similarity in title to Klein's great poem), in which he seems to be standing on tip-toe on the banks of the Seine, or else gently floating, like a ghost oblivious to land subsidence, a few inches off the ground. Although Rousseau was very concerned with the interaction between a figure and its setting, and was proud of having "invented" the genre of "Portrait-Landscape," in most of his portraits there is a curious dislocation between figure and ground. Rousseau's people all seem to float in space, cut off from its normal continuum. One consequence of this is that they are also dislocated in time.

Rousseau's technique is an extraordinary combination of primitive, child-like naïveté in the modelling, and high polish and exactness in the finish. The effect is to give his own awkwardnesses in space and time a very precise, fixed quality. He was capable of painting swift impromptu sketches of a scene which in manner and execution would stand with the best of the Impressionists; yet these were always painstakingly transformed into the precisions of his own style, all the rough edges made hard, all the sweeps of colour clarified to exact forms. Curiously, the eye accustomed to Monet sees these sketches as far more "realistic," at least in their sense of perspective and illusion of depth, than the finished works. Compare, for example, the sketch and the final version of *Path in Parc Montsouris* (Vallier, plates 60, 61). This is what lies behind Rousseau's famous comment on the Cézanne exhibition of 1907: "You know, I could finish all these pictures."

A good example of this aspect of Rousseau is *The Football Players*. Four men with identical moustaches are playing football (rugger) in a neat little field framed by trees whose trunks seem to rest on the ground like stage-props rather than grow out of it. The men's positions are drawn as if they had been frozen in the middle of a rather jolly ballet; their feet, of course, have no solid connection with the ground on which they supposedly stand. One man is about to catch the ball, which hangs suspended in the air above him, surrounded by a haze in which the leaves of the background trees are less precisely drawn than anywhere else in the painting. Rather than watching the ball which he is trying to catch (and probably therefore won't) this man—like all the four-square, straight-on faces in Rousseau's portraits—stares directly out at the viewer. The effect is, totally, one of suspension. Shattuck writes: "The figures move... in total stillness.... They appear to have no location, to float in air" (*The Banquet Years*, 95). The players stand as awkwardly in the temporal continuum as they do in the spatial. The eyes staring straight at the viewer induce an intense awareness of the artificiality of the situation: they stare out of the canvas and out of time, out of the whole temporal-spatial situation of Henri Rousseau in 1908 into the timelessness of art.

This approach—through the naïveté of the technique, seeing the paintings' temporal dislocation as the result of their naïve handling of space—is, I believe, the most profitable way of understanding that quality in Rousseau which Leonard Cohen eulogizes in the first section of Book II of *The Favourite Game*. Cohen, however, approaches it entirely through subject-matter:

> Always is the word that must be used. The lion will always be sniffing the robes of the sleeping gypsy, there will be no attack, no guts on the sand: The total encounter is expressed. The moon, even though it is doomed to travel, will never go down on this scene. The abandoned lute does not cry for fingers. It is swollen with all the music it needs.
>
> (*The Favourite Game*, 58)

This sounds very much like Keats addressing his Grecian Urn, and indeed, when the young Breavman is being lionized (excuse the pun) by literary Montreal Cohen comments that "Canadians are desperate for a Keats" (*The Favourite Game*, 101). One of Breavman's obsessions, throughout the book, is with the stopping of time—most notably in the midnight car-ride with Krantz—and this is associated with the vision he has in the brass foundry, of the "liquid metal" which was "the colour gold should be.... The arch of liquid came to represent an intensity he would never achieve"(*The Favourite Game*, 104-6).

This is an aspect of *The Favourite Game* which Michael Ondaatje does not deal with in his book on Leonard Cohen. He does comment, briefly, on Cohen's reference to the other Rousseau, Jean-Jacques,[8] but there is nothing at all about Henri. This is very curious, considering Ondaatje's interest in Rousseau, and considering that this whole theme of "the way he stops time" is as central to Ondaatje as it is to Cohen. In "Taking" Ondaatje does pick up the associated image of the arch of liquid metal:

To learn to pour the exact arc
of steel still soft and crazy
before it hits the page. (*RJ*, 55)

The obsession with fixing moving things in time is most clearly announced in the opening of *The Collected Works of Billy the Kid*: under the empty frame of the "picture of Billy" is the quotation from L.A. Huffman describing the progress made in photographing moving objects: "I am able to take passing horses at a lively trot square across the line of fire — bits of snow in the air — spokes well defined — some blur on top of wheel but sharp in the main — men walking are no trick." This states, at the outset, one of the main themes of the book: *fixing* the image of Billy, a character constantly in motion both literally (the finger exercises) and ontologically (as his image shifts between historical fact, legendary accretion, and the creations of Ondaatje's personal imagination). I have already discussed[9] the differences between Ondaatje's fixing of Billy in legend, and bp Nichol's evocation of Billy as rumour: here it should be noted that Ondaatje's Billy, while constantly in motion, can in fact be frozen, as in Huffman's photographs (or Rousseau's paintings), to a much greater extent than Nichol's.

This concern is also present in the early poems of *The Dainty Monsters*, and interestingly, it is directly associated with Rousseau. In the zoo poem, "You Can Look But You Better Not Touch," Ondaatje comments:

ROUSSEAU wisely eliminated
leopards from his follies
A mistake to imagine them static (*DM*, 32)

The leopard is too much a creature of movement, Ondaatje says, to be frozen into the static image of Rousseau's paintings, and Rousseau was wise to recognize this. (In fact, Rousseau managed to incorporate lions, tigers, and jaguars, so there seems no reason why he couldn't have included leopards as well: but the interesting point is Ondaatje's insistence on the static nature of Rousseau's art.)

The motif is associated with all of Ondaatje's major themes. In "The Sows," the "immobile" animals "categorize the flux around them." In "The Time Around Scars," one of the results of the sudden eruption of violence into a domestic scene is to "freeze irrelevant emotions / and divide us from our present friends." The task of the artist in "Four Eyes" is to "freeze this moment... and in immobilized time / attempt to reconstruct." He can do this, in "The Respect of Landscapes," only by "translating" himself and "taking the egoism" of birds, "becoming like them the centre."

In *Rat Jelly*, the idea is most thoroughly explored in " 'The gate in his head,' " a poem written for Victor Coleman. The poem celebrates the beauty of things in motion: "not clarity but the sense of shift." A book left in a fishbowl opens "like some sea animal / camouflaging itself," and the "clarity" of the typeface letters acquires a new beauty, "going slow blonde in the sun full water." Ondaatje sees his own mind as "pouring chaos... onto the page," in the same way as the liquid metal is poured. But these movements / moments are also caught and fixed in time: the chaos is poured "in nets." Coleman provides the climactic image with "a blurred photograph of a gull. / ... The stunning white bird / an unclear stir." Again, this is a "Caught vision," and the same word is repeated in the final stanza:

> And that is all this writing should be then.
> The beautiful formed things caught at the wrong moment
> so they are shapeless, awkward
> moving to the clear. (*RJ*, 62)

This is, in another form, the "equilibrium" which I spoke of earlier. The balance to be struck here is between the essential beauty of movement, the "sense of shift," and the artist's "catching" of that movement. The resulting image is simultaneously a fixed moment abstracted from time, and a moment which implies and contains the continued "moving to the clear." It is a clear, unmoving image of a blurred movement towards clarity.

This kind of paradox is also implicit in "Dates," Ondaatje's portrait of Wallace Stevens writing:

> his head making his hand
> move where he wanted
> and he saw his hand was saying
> the mind is never finished, no, never (*RJ*, 21)

Stevens creates a clarity, a fixed moment under his control, which im-

55

mediately and uncontrollably generates a further movement towards a further clarity. Another poem says that Stevens "is thinking chaos is thinking fences" ("King Kong Meets Wallace Stevens"). The lack of punctuation equates the two activities, runs them together into one; it could also be read that what Stevens is thinking is that "chaos is thinking fences," and in a circle, fences are thinking chaos. The artist performs these impossibilities; under Stevens' hand, the page is "becoming thought where nothing had been," just as the spider-poet "thinks a path and travels / the emptiness that was there" ("Spider Blues").

The effect is always to stop time: in "Taking," Ondaatje speaks of how he has "stroked the mood and tone / of hundred year dead men and women," and thus, for himself "removed them from historical traffic." It could be said of all Ondaatje's images, and also for the figures in Rousseau's paintings, that "Their idea of the immaculate moment is now."

There is a distinction to be made, however, here as always, between the poems and the poet. The poems may aspire towards the timelessness of the sleeping gypsy, the Grecian urn, or the blurred white bird; but the poet is still caught in flux and change, and so is the reader. Art may achieve moments of equilibrium, but these cannot be entered into by the artist or the spectator: the experience of them must pass. Ondaatje's description of *The Dream* suggests that this is anticipated even within the painting itself. The reason that Yadwigha "looks to her left" is that "that is the direction we leave in / when we fall from her room of flowers." (This is, incidentally, factually correct for the present hanging of the painting in the Museum of Modern Art, New York.) Time is stopped in the "room of flowers," but both artist and spectator must sooner or later "fall" out of it.

The perfect moments when the intensity of "the exact arc" is achieved may go some way towards mediating between "Families" and "Live Bait," but they cannot go all the way. Rousseau died in despair when the petite bourgeoise Léonie refused to become Yadwigha for him, even when Robert Delaunay pleaded with her to visit the painter's deathbed. The artist does not escape from the destructive movement of time: indeed, he may feel called upon to immerse himself in it.

The Huffman quotation which sets out the image of caught movement in *The Collected Works of Billy the Kid* closes by insisting that "many of the best [were] exposed when my horse was in motion," in other words, when the artist himself partook of the nature of the subject. The relationship between Ondaatje and his persona in this book is a very complex one: although Ondaatje has to stand back at times in his familiar ironic pose, he cannot totally separate himself from the outlaw personality. Ondaatje as artist moves towards Billy as outlaw, and vice versa. It is Billy himself who stops time to replay the scene preceding his death which "I would have seen if I was on the roof looking," and who prolongs the moment of death itself with "the bullet itch frozen in my head." When the blank frame is finally filled, it is not with a photograph of Billy, but with one of Michael Ondaatje.

The image of the artist projected in many of the poems in the "White Dwarfs" section of *Rat Jelly* is a self-destructive one: the herons who find "ways of going/physically mad" ("Heron Rex"), those who commit "Our suicide into nature" as insects eat the brain ("Near Elginburg"), the unwinding body from Vaughn-James' *The Projector* which "will be consumed before ever reaching the ground," Icarus "fished. . . from this Quebec river" ("Fabulous shadow"), and above all the "heroes" of "White Dwarfs" itself. "White Dwarfs" is a hymn to self-destruction, to those who are — returning for a moment to the terminology of Leonard Cohen — beautiful losers. The artists are "those who disappear," those who "die in the ether peripheries," the outcasts who "sail to that perfect edge/where there is no social fuel." The artists can "understand their altitude" only by the "Release of sandbags" to take them higher from the ground. The artist moves into silence: the lonely "silence of the third cross," the silence of mules with their tongues cut out, the silence of the "perfect white between the words." Participating in the very movement which their art cancels, immersing themselves in the destructive element which their words have transcended, they become like stars gone nova, collapsing in on themselves, imploding into that silence which Eliot proclaimed words could reach into, "beyond speech."

Ondaatje understands this type of self-destructive artist, or beautiful loser (as is shown, in fact, by his interest in Cohen); but he is not himself one of them. Neither indeed was Rousseau, and though Ondaatje's main poem on a Rousseau painting ("The Vault") is included in the "White Dwarfs" section of *Rat Jelly*, his major poem about Rousseau's personality ("To Monsieur le Maire") is not.

57

Rousseau is live bait rather than white dwarf, at least in the pathetically vulnerable naïveté which the letter displays. But if we remember that Rousseau's naïveté may well have been fully as calculated as it was genuine, and if we note that the price that Rousseau asks for his painting in this "naïve" letter is considerably higher than any he had up till that time been paid, the same letter may be seen as demonstrating an intelligence and ironic control of tone not too far removed from Ondaatje's. When Ondaatje uses the Rousseau text as a "found poem," it is hard to tell which of them has the last laugh.

There is a clear distinction, then, between the misery of Rousseau's last days, which he certainly did not seek to bring upon himself, and the obsessive self-destructiveness of his friend, sponsor, and fellow townsman of Laval, Alfred Jarry. Having created the monstrous role of Ubu in his work, Jarry came to adopt it in his life to such an extent that he broke down all barriers between the two. The result was what Roger Shattuck calls "Suicide by hallucination": Jarry died at the age of 34, becoming in the most literal sense one of those who "died in the ether peripheries." In *The Banquet Years* (the book which Ondaatje acknowledges as his source for Rousseau's letter), Shattuck writes:

> The willfulness with which [Jarry] kept himself saturated with ether was no longer a form of drinking or alcoholism; he was simply killing himself. . . . One of his last writings, a chapter called "*Descendit ad infernos*" intended for *La dragonne*, contains this visionary description of the hero's approaching death: "But soon he could drink no more, for there was no more darkness for him and, no doubt like Adam before the fall. . . he could see in the dark." (*The Banquet Years*, 221)

These are of course the lines which Ondaatje uses, without identifying their source, as the epigraph to "Letters & Other Worlds"; the source adds yet another dimension to this rich and complex poem. Ondaatje's father, in the terrible isolation of the room where he "stayed. . . until he was drunk / and until he was sober," is also the artist immersed in self-destruction, yet "moving to the clear." His tragedy is the failure of equilibrium: he "balanced and fell," so that in death he is only human, "without metaphor." For him as for Jarry, the self-destruction of alcohol provided a new vision; but unlike Jarry, what he created—the "gentle letters. . . of the most complete

58

empathy'' — were expressions of love rather than of contempt. When Jarry died, he became completely Ubu; when Ondaatje's father died, he became completely himself.

"White Dwarfs," then, despite its climactic position in the book, does not seem to me to be Ondaatje's ultimate word on the nature of the artist. Rousseau and not Jarry must continue to serve as the paradigm: Rousseau who stops time, not Jarry who is destroyed by it. The maintaining of equilibrium is a matter of control, and Ondaatje is himself, always, a highly controlled artist. He is of course aware of the dangers of control, as "Spider Blues" shows — "Spiders like poets are obsessed with power" — but this does not mean that he will endorse the surrender of control, the dissolution of personality, as completely as Cohen does in *Beautiful Losers*. The poet in "Burning Hills," who has the Rousseau postcard on his desk, and who prizes "one picture that fuses... 5 summers," is described in the final lines of the poem as writing "slowly and carefully / with great love and great coldness." It is precisely *that* equilibrium which Ondaatje at his best — as in "Letters & Other Worlds" — so triumphantly displays.

So perhaps a more profound statement is to be found not in the last poem of the "White Dwarfs" section but in the first: "We're at the graveyard." It is a moment frozen in time, a moment of that small circle of friends — "Stuart Sally Kim and I" — preserved against the unfriendly world. Above their heads there are both mobility and immobility, together — "still stars... sliding stars" — which form "clear charts," a "geometry of moving." The stars provide an "intricate" form within which movement and clarity coexist; this form is paralleled "down here" by "friends / whose minds and bodies / shift like acrobats to each other." Only the presence of such friends can give expression to the clarities of the stars — "When we leave, they move / to an altitude of silence" — but the human limitations of these friends are clearly if unobtrusively indicated by the graveyard setting. At the same time, Sally is pregnant.

(If this poem is reminiscent of any Rousseau painting, it is *Un Soir de Carnaval*, with the lucid ordering of its night sky, the clown's / acrobat's costume, and the mysterious pale mask hung on the wall.)

The human function, which *is* here the artistic function, is as always to give form, to exercise control, to maintain equilibrium, to "shape/and lock the transient." The image used here is that of "bats/who organize the air/with thick blinks of travel" — like the spider poet who "thinks a path and travels/the emptiness that was there," like Wallace Stevens' page "becoming thought where nothing had been." In the closing lines, Ondaatje offers another such image, a shape to lock the transient. Insofar as it achieves this, it is certainly fashioned with "great coldness" and control on his part; but it is also, just as certainly, fashioned like his father's letters, "with great love":

> Sally is like grey snow in the grass.
> Sally of the beautiful bones
> pregnant below stars.

1 This information is derived from the article on Bucke by Robert W. Cumberland in *A Standard Dictionary of Canadian Biography*, ed. Charles G. D. Roberts and Arthur L. Tunnell, Toronto, 1934.

2 The best short biography of Henri Rousseau is to be found in the book which Ondaatje acknowledges as his source: Roger Shattuck, *The Banquet Years*, first published 1958, Vintage edition 1968. The most useful full length study is Dora Vallier, *Henri Rousseau* (Abrams, 1960). Most of the biographical information in this essay is derived from these two sources.

3 Michael Ondaatje, "Dashiell," *Canadian Forum* (March 1975), p. 26.

4 Michael Ondaatje, ed., *The Broken Ark: A book of Beasts* (Ottawa: Oberon, 1971).

5 "Two Authors in Search of a Character: Michael Ondaatje, bp Nichol, and Billy the Kid," first published in *Canadian Literature* No. 54 (Autumn 1972), 37-55.

6 Kroetsch makes this comment in Donald Cameron's *Conversations With Canadian Novelists* (Toronto: Macmillan, 1973), Vol. I, p. 85.

7 Leonard Cohen, *The Favourite Game* (Toronto: New Canadian Library, 1970), p. 58.

8 Cohen, p. 33; Michael Ondaatje, *Leonard Cohen* (Toronto: McClelland & Stewart, 1970), p. 34.

9 See footnote 5, above.

George Bowering
ONDAATJE LEARNING TO DO

Most of the Canadian poets whose work I admire have been published at some time by Coach House Press, the poets' house that became habitable in the same year that its predecessor, Contact Press, closed its door. As a Vancouver writer I have been cheered for years by the fact that this fine press in the middle of Toronto's university district should publish the works of the best non-U poets from my bailiwick. I am thinking of a list of names that has grown surprisingly long, and includes Fred Wah, Daphne Marlatt, Lionel Kearns, Robert Hogg, Frank Davey, and Gladys Hindmarch.

Sometimes we facetiously refer to Coach House as the Toronto arm of the West Coast movement, even citing the fact that bp Nichol and Victor Coleman have at various times lived in the Vancouver region. But Coach House is, we admit from time to time, there for reasons other than our own, and for poetry that stems from different traditions. David McFadden is there, not at all hip but the material that the hip love. D.G. Jones and Sheila Watson we enclose because of their interest in matters linguistic rather than thematic. There are the young Toronto poets who plunge into and out of the speedy multiface glistening of Toronto. And there is the peculiar case of Michael Ondaatje, most of whose books have been published or printed by Coach House.

The development of Ondaatje's poetry, from his early years in this country to the present, resembles the development of the main currents of Canadian verse over a period perhaps twice as long. Unlike the Vancouver poets with their advocation of open-ended, process form, Ondaatje emerged from the school that believes the poem to be an artifact, something well-made and thus rescued from the chaos of contemporary world and mind. If the Vancouver poets might loosely be said to descend from Duncan, and Victor Coleman from Zukofsky, Ondaatje might be said to descend from Yeats and Stevens.

But over the course of his first fifteen years as a Canadian poet, Ondaatje has come to seek a less British and more American poetic. Having come by way of England from colonial Ceylon, and once here through UEL universities to the Coach House Press, he had many skins to rub off. In his fourth book, *Rat Jelly* (1973), he arrived at a poem called " 'The gate in his head,' " and dedicated to Victor Coleman. It finished with a passage that may not open that gate but at least points to its location, that signals the way out and in:

> My mind is pouring chaos
> in nets onto the page.
> A blind lover, dont know
> what I love till I write it out.
> And then from Gibson's your letter
> with a blurred photograph of a gull.
> Caught vision. The stunning white bird
> an unclear stir.
>
> And that is all this writing should be then.
> The beautiful formed things caught at the wrong moment
> so they are shapeless, awkward
> moving to the clear. (*RJ*, 62)

It is a departure, if not in form at least in intention, from his earlier predilection for preserving his objects in the amber of his directed emotions. In his poetry since 1973, and more so in his non-lyric works, we have seen him seeking the unrested form he requires, and the realization that it is in form that we present what we deem the real. All content is, as William Carlos Williams pointed out, dream; and while dream is interesting, it is interesting only when it is not volitional.

In his earlier poems Ondaatje had a habit, that is, of intensifying the world, of fashioning artifice, as I have said. In them we found steady images of brutality, especially of the suffering of beasts, as in the verse of Pat Lane. I was slow to respond favourably to the poems in *The Dainty Monsters* (1967), attractive as they might have seemed with all their violence, because they were, by the time I the reader got to them, over with; there was no mystery left, no labour for the reader, just puzzle or rue. No mystery for writer *or* reader, that is. Observe the lightbulb in

"Gold and Black":

> In the black Kim is turning
> a geiger counter to this pillow.
> She cracks me open like a lightbulb. (RJ, 12)

You see, black instead of dark, because it is emotionally more intense. Geiger counter, dangerous and scary because out of place in that context. And the simile: it is intended to set your teeth on edge. Really, I don't know what happened there, because the dream was not meant for me; it did not come up out of my funnel into the universal memory. On the other (left) hand, though I clearly remember Ondaatje's Billy the Kid sitting among the animals in a real unpainted barn.

On reading the first two books of lyrical poetry (though on reading the selected poems at the end of the decade I was to change my view to my gain) I saw the poems as anecdotal, really Canadian, and considered them to be exercises written between sessions of work on Ondaatje's more serious and larger concerns, such as Billy and Buddy Bolden. The shorter pieces were poems for enjoyment, and I enjoyed them. They were, in my view, well cut and shaped, but not risky.

An exception was his famous poem about his father, "Letters & Other Worlds." It does take risks, and for most of its three pages it is a world rather than a picture of one. But at the last, in getting out, Ondaatje the son trips over a Figure of Speech which contains "blood screaming." That sort of thing the reader can only accept or reject as a *mot* performed by the author; he cannot experience it.

One consequence of fashioning ordered, unified, palpable poems is that one makes anthology numbers. A reader often re-encounters Ondaatje's poems, or thinks that he does. More than a usual number of them stand up well after an elapsed time as notable set-pieces, such as the snake poem, "Breaking Green," which ends with a flourish:

> The head was narrower now.
> He blocked our looks at it.
> The death was his. He
> folded the scarless body
> and tossed it like a river into the grass. (RJ, 33)

The maiming and torture of animals is either an obsession or secure access to effect. He psyches it and we squirm if we are so bent, we death-dealing Canadians. One animal poem, "A bad taste," out-Rosenblatts Joe and out-Lanes Pat, but is wisely left out of the selected poems. It is about rats, Ondaatje's favourite animals. In the poem, which I too will leave in the book it lies in, the author is perverse as he must be, saddled, let us say, with that central metaphor. You will go and look it up. But I mean if the animal have dreams, as Margaret Atwood has said, we are their dreams.

Rat Jelly was an improvement on *The Dainty Monsters*, rather than an advance, for the most part. But it was and is that rare kind of collection nowadays, a book of poems to enjoy, not to be dislocated or awed by. The poems are, I suspect, among the last id-haunted remnants from an ex-English boyhood. The aforementioned poem addressed to Victor Coleman probably satisfies the essentially neo-Georgian literary people who make up the Eastern establishment, but the aim it announces, when totally realized, will turn them right off and thus conserve energy, and we will use the reserve to warm the house for the invited not the commanded muse.

On the cover of Michael Ondaatje's selected shorter poems, *There's a Trick with a Knife I'm Learning to Do* (1979), there is a photograph of a seated man using his *left* foot to throw knives around the body of a woman who looks like Dorothy Livesay. Whether or not that says anything about the course of Canadian poetry, it does suggest the nature of Ondaatje's wit: among other things (especially while we notice that the title of the book is nowhere to be found among the poems), the poet's "trick" is to use an edge that seems to miss its target, barely.

When Ondaatje, while learning, comes closest to his boundary, there is a great deal to admire in his performance of these left-footed poems. The newest ones, in a section of the book called "Pig Glass: 1973-1978," are intent upon not quite that dislocation I looked for earlier, but a dislocating settlement, a resolute oddity. The last line of each poem sounds like your most adept friend's final smack of his hammer on his fifteen-story birdhouse, or the last knife thudding into the board above your own pate. Observe the ironic pastoral, "Farre Off":

There are the poems of Campion I never saw till now

64

and Wyatt who loved with the best
and suddenly I want 16th century women
round me devious politic aware
of step ladders to the king

Tonight I am alone with dogs and lightning
aroused by Wyatt's talk of women who step
naked into his bedchamber

Moonlight and barnlight constant
lightning every second minute
I have on my thin blue parka
and walk behind the asses of the dogs
who slide under the gate
and sense cattle
deep in the fields

I look out into the dark pasture
past where even the moonlight stops

   my eyes are against the ink of Campion (*TK*, 80)

Subtitled "Poems 1963–1978," the book is made up of Ondaatje's selections from *The Dainty Monsters* and *Rat Jelly*, plus thirty-five pages of "Pig Glass." We see just over a hundred pages of work of the lyric poet from the age of twenty to the age of thirty-five, a bracket that always seems interesting in the careers of Canadian poets.

That Ondaatje has always been interested in animals as figures is apparent from the three titles just mentioned (as well as his anthology, *The Broken Ark*, published originally in 1971 and reprinted in 1979 as *A Book of Beasts*). In his twenties he explored and exploited the violence implied in the confrontation between people and animals, but as I now read it, with a spectral uneasiness rather than the advantageous exposition of Pat Lane's lyrics. Lane tells us that man is naturally murderous toward his fellow beasts, but Ondaatje is interested in the experiential philosophy developing from a paradox pronounced early in his verse:

Deep in the fields
behind stiff dirt fern
nature breeds the unnatural. (*DM*, 21)

So did Ondaatje, especially in his first poems. Here is a typical example of his early predilection for the wry metamorphosing of the Anglo-

65

American academic poets in the post-Eliot age, the sort of exterior
design then found in the Donald Hall anthologies:

> I have been seeing dragons again.
> Last night, hunched on a beaver dam,
> one clutched a body like a badly held cocktail;
> his tail, keeping the beat of a waltz,
> sent a morse of ripples to my canoe. ("Dragon," *TK*, 4)

That figuring was carved while Ondaatje was still a British immigrant
student, at the Waspy English departments of Sherbrooke and
Queen's. His poetic during that time might be characterized by a
stanza from another poem:

> I would freeze this moment
> and in supreme patience
> place pianos
> and craggy black horses on a beach
> and in immobilized time
> attempt to reconstruct. ("Four Eyes," *DM*, 46)

But then came the association with the poets at the Coach House
Press, and a poetics that espoused a non-Euclidian order. One need only
compare the above passage with the later poem addressed to Victor
Coleman, with its "blind lover" and "caught vision." There is a concomitant change in the music, from deliberate manipulation to more
subtle and patient rime. In "Pig Glass" there is a wonderful poem
addressed to Christopher Dewdney, another Coach House poet. It
begins with a quotation from Dewdney: "Listen, it was so savage and
brutal and powerful / that even though it happened out of the blue I /
knew there was nothing arbitrary about it" (*TK*, 100). That message is
obviously as important as the photograph that Coleman had earlier sent
from Gibson's.

So the younger Ondaatje's poems deliver a diction that is formalized,
literary, or British; at least it signifies an elevation into printed
language. But from the beginning the poet shows us a sure comprehension of what a line is, not just a length, not only a syntactic unit, but a
necessary step in knowing and surprise. It is telling that when he comes
to contemplating a painter's work, it is the work of Henri Rousseau,
with his sharply defined wonderment. Thus, even while the subject is
eerie or terrible, the words suggesting the man's observations of them

are "exact," "exactness," "order" and "freeze."

In *Rat Jelly* there appear some family poems, with constructed metaphors; *i.e.,* what is this (thing, experience, feeling) like? It's like a _____ . It is still a geocentric world, in which the poet's invention is the earth, albeit an unusually interesting one. But "Billboards," the opening poem of the selection from *Rat Jelly* in *Trick With a Knife* seems deliberately to exhibit a promising progression of the poet's means, from fancy to phenomenological imagination. Its two pages end this way:

> Nowadays I somehow get the feeling
> I'm in a complex situation,
> one of several billboard posters
> blending in the rain.
>
> I am writing this with a pen my wife has used
> to write a letter to her first husband.
> On it is the smell of her hair.
> She must have placed it down between sentences
> and thought, and driven her fingers round her skull
> gathered the slightest smell of her head
> and brought it back to the pen. (*TK*, 35)

The last few lines, delivered not on stage but in dressing room, might seem to be tacked on, but they are really the emerging achievement of the poem. They hug to contours not their own.

Other poems, such as the oft-remembered "Notes for the legend of Salad Woman," enact wonderful images without any academic super-structure, though perhaps Laytonic exaggeration, and lots of robust humour. The last is a feature of Ondaatje's writing that deserves an extended study. There are, in *Rat Jelly*, still some laconic poems about men's mistreatment of wild animals, as well as the poet's amused admiration for his dogs. But Ondaatje is still there looking for a magically charged world, a world with Margaret Atwood's immanent peril and Gwendolyn MacEwen's legerdemainous nature. "Burning Hills," an important piece, suggests on the other hand the self-reflexive narrative put to such good use in Ondaatje's most important books, *The Collected Works of Billy the Kid* and *Coming Through Slaughter.*

> There is one picture that fuses the 5 summers.

Eight of them are leaning against a wall
arms around each other
looking into the camera and the sun
trying to smile at the unseen adult photographer
trying against the glare to look 21 and confident.
The summer and friendship will last forever.
Except one who was eating an apple. That was him
Oblivious to the significance of the moment.
Now he hungers to have that arm around the next shoulder.
The wretched apple is fresh and white. (*TK*, 60)

"Pig Glass" is a collection of lyrics that benefit from the practice of *Billy* and *Slaughter*, partaking of their concern with the ironies inherent in the act of composition, the acknowledgement that a writer who participates in motion cannot "freeze" a scene for the universal literary museum. In "Country Night" (73) the poet notes the liveliness of the unseen creatures of the farmhouse while people are abed. He finishes by saying, "All night the truth happens." A pretty clear statement of poetic. But when is he composing this? During the continuous present of the poem's night-time verbs, or out of bed in the daytime? Is this poem truth, that is, and is that last line from it?

The poems in "Pig Glass" are as the previous lyrics are, usually one page filled, a regularity suggesting that the author is working on a contract, as both entertainers (see title, *There's a Trick With a Knife I'm Learning to Do*) and bridegrooms (see cover photograph) do. The last section sports some travel-to-roots poems, some family poems, but most important, some departures from the regular observing occasional poem, in the direction of his peculiar pamphlet from Nairn Press, *Elimination Dance* (1977). There is, for example, "Sweet like a Crow," two pages of outrageous similes, in which the addressed one's voice is "Like a crow swimming in milk, / like a nose being hit by a mango" etc. And there is "Pure Memory," the non-sequential meditations on Chris Dewdney, and there is the poem of Sally Chisum's recollections of Billy the Kid thirty-seven years later, the heartening evidence that Ondaatje does not consider *Billy* to be a polished artifact, over and closed. These are all good signs that Ondaatje is bringing to his shorter verse the engaging fabrication of his longer works: that the nature of invention has met and bested the culture of mastery.

In his career to this date, Michael Ondaatje has been a poet who makes art that is like the best of Canadian poetry. As a novelist he

68

writes stuff most of our respected novelists do not begin to dream of. As a fiction writer he is superior; as a poet he is one of our most proficient.

Susan Glickman
FROM "PHILOCTETES ON THE ISLAND"
TO "TIN ROOF":
THE EMERGING MYTH OF MICHAEL ONDAATJE

Michael Ondaatje's earliest book of poetry, *The Dainty Monsters* (1967), was an exceptionally strong first collection and introduced readers immediately to the Ondaatje universe teeming with creatures at once grotesque and beautiful. The batik reproduced on the cover, with its reptilian birds and mineral flowers, provided a visual analogue for the poems inside. Being Ceylonese, it also signalled the elusive autobiographical element in Ondaatje's work, hinting at the poet's exotic background which also glinted here and there between the covers. Amidst all the glamour of the book, its occasional graduate-student bravado, its echoes of Yeats, Stevens, and Auden, we recognized the distinctive Ondaatje voice. The poet's *vision* was confident and individual from the start, but his language and syntax were less secure than they were to become with time. But in pieces like "A House Divided," "Signature," "Biography," "For John, Falling," and "The Time around Scars" the casual diction, startling imagery, and colloquial rhythms of Ondaatje's mature voice were already present.

Ondaatje chose to reprint only eighteen of *The Dainty Monsters'* forty-five poems in his 1979 volume of selected work, *There's a Trick with a Knife I'm Learning to Do*, principally those in his demotic voice. If we compare the table of contents of *The Dainty Monsters* with that of the selected poems, we can see Ondaatje editing himself, retelling his story, making his first book into a chapter of his larger oeuvre which clarifies its continuing themes and interests.

order in
Trick   *The Dainty Monsters*

OVER THE GARDEN WALL

'Description is a Bird'
1   Birds for Janet — The Heron
     Pigeons, Sussex Avenue
     The Sows
7   Biography
     Song to Alfred Hitchcock and Wilkinson
2   Dragon
     Gorillas
8   The Republic
3   Early Morning, Kingston to Gananoque
4   The Diverse Causes
5   Signature
6   Henri Rousseau and Friends
     The Martinique
     The Trojan War Goes to Japan
     Over the Garden Wall
     Sows, One More Time
     You Can Look But You Better Not Touch
9   In Another Fashion
10   Application for a Driving License
     A Toronto Home for Birds and Manticores
     As Thurber Would Say — C*ws
13   A House Divided
     Eventually the Poem for Keewaydin
     Tink, Summer Rider
11   'Lovely the Country of Peacocks'
     She Carries a 'Fat Gold Watch'
     Coming Home
     The Moving to Griffin
     Christmas Poem 1965
12   Four Eyes
     The Inheritors
15   For John, Falling
14   The Time Around Scars
     The Respect of Landscapes
     Come to the Desert

TROY TOWN

Pyramid
Prometheus, With Wings
Lilith

71

The general structure of *The Dainty Monsters* is reproduced in the *Trick with a Knife* selection. The first section, "Over the Garden Wall," as its title suggests, and as poems like "The Republic" and "The Diverse Causes" make clear, represents the domestic world as an ineffectual attempt to shut out the exuberant natural world which surrounds it. "Nature" and "Civilization" are held in balance, however, because the "monsters" are primarily "dainty" — pigeons, sows, dogs, and cows. Even those who are truly wild, the herons, gorillas, beaver, are treated somewhat anthropomorphically: the other exotic beasts are caged (see "You Can Look But You Better Not Touch").

The second section of the book, "Troy Town," comprises more ambitious and "literary" pieces, in which details of the poet's own life are woven into the shifting tapestries of myth and legend. The epigraph from Dostoevsky which introduced the section in the original book invites us to search for Ondaatje in the guilty Paris, for his wife Kim in Helen, the stolen bride. Here, the poet appropriates exotic *characters*, rather than magical beasts, to be the carriers of personal symbols.

Rat Jelly (1973), is represented in *Trick with a Knife* by twenty-six of its forty poems. Ondaatje's editorial method here is more radical — he dispenses with the book's original division into three sections ("Families," "Live Bait," and "White Dwarfs"), although he maintains the overall progression from domestic anecdote, to sardonic analysis of the animal side of man, to cosmic meditation.

order in *Trick*	*Rat Jelly*
	FAMILIES
12	War Machine
3	Gold and Black
	Letter to Ann Landers
1	Billboards
2	Kim, at half an inch
	Somebody sent me a tape

72

Nonetheless, a striking change of *tone* results from the way in which the book is retold. By beginning with "Billboards," one of the strongest and one of the most personally explicit poems in the book, rather than with "War Machine," a much slighter piece of rhythmical grumbling, Ondaatje places himself directly before the reader as a *character* instead of an attitude. The confessional quality of "Billboards" articulates the themes of the book and shows us the poet at a point of equipoise between two conflicting ways of being—engagement and detachment. At the moment of writing the poem he is alone; the situation he is exploring, however, is that of involvement in a complex network of family responsibilities. He recognizes wryly, as from a distance, what a contrast his present circumstances make to his life before marriage:

> Here was I trying to live
> with a neutrality so great
> I'd have nothing to think of,
> just to sense
> and kill it in the mind. (*TK*, 35)

He offers us his bemusement that he has become the man he now is: husband, father, stepfather—that he has stepped off the island of self into the marine chaos of community.

By placing this poem first in the *Rat Jelly* section of *Trick with a Knife*, Ondaatje acknowledges the man behind the poems and places him squarely in our field of vision. The poems which follow are about his love for his wife—the catalyst for his change in lifestyle—and his love for his son, his father, his friends. We shift into the "Live Bait" mode of bitterness, for which "War Machine" serves as an introduction, only after experiencing the profound and intimate world of loving relationships. The poet's simultaneous attraction to and repulsion from the world outside the self is clearly polarized in this new order.

The menagerie in *Rat Jelly* is more hostile than that of *The Dainty Monsters*; man is at war with nature here because he is at war with the nature in himself. (This theme is more overt in the complete *Rat Jelly*.) The mysterious otherness of the animal kingdom is now perceived as threat and challenge, rather than as consolation and delight. In fact, it is the *self-sufficiency* of the animals that man envies ("Loop," "Sullivan and the iguana"), and this envy goads him to destroy them ("Breaking Green," "Philoctetes on the island"). Man's interactions with animals show him up as graceless and clumsy ("Stuart's Bird") and reveal his need of them as symbols of unexpressed parts of himself ("King Kong"). At the same time, man insists on identifying what is destructive in himself *as* bestial—hence the characterization of man as rat ("Rat Jelly," "A bad taste").

74

The relationship between Sullivan and his iguana most poignantly exemplifies the way animals function as carriers of myth for dream-starved men. In Ondaatje's bestiary it is not the "social animals," the caged performers like his comical family dogs, but "the one / who appears again on roads / One eye torn out and chasing" ("Loop," 64) who escapes our nets of language, and lopes on. The autonomy of the animal world continues to fascinate the poet, especially the silence of its suffering in the face of our inexplicable behaviour: "after such cruelty what could they speak of anyway," ("White Dwarfs, " 71).

What is most unexpected in Ondaatje's reorganization of his earlier poems in *Trick with a Knife* is the unacknowledged displacement of "Philoctetes on the island" from *Rat Jelly* (where it was really published), to *The Dainty Monsters*. Both in style and content this poem shows affinities to the "Troy Town" section of the first book, so the reordering is apt—an editorial "trick with a knife." The poem was probably written at the same time as the other mythological pieces and, for some reason, missed the boat when they were published, appearing as a kind of coda in the later book. Nonetheless, this is the only example of editorial prestidigitation in *Trick with a Knife*, and so it calls attention to itself, and makes us focus on the poem as a kind of link between the first two books.

The story of Philoctetes is familiar to us from post-Homeric legend, most notably, Sophocles' play of 409 B.C. Philoctetes was the Achaean hero who was abandoned on the island of Lemnos by Agamemnon and Odysseus when he became crippled and delirious from snakebite. The serpent attacked him in divine reprisal for his violation of the shrine of Chryse on the island; the Gods had decreed, however, that the Trojan war could not be won without him, and after nine years the Greeks returned for him. With his bow and arrows, which originally belonged to Hercules, he killed Paris — and thus helped to end the war.

In Sophocles' bleak and powerful drama, Philoctetes is a lonely man, driven to suicidal madness in ephemeral fits of pain, but otherwise gentle. He hunts only for survival, and feels a deep love for the creatures of the island who are his necessary victims. *Rage* is directed only at the men who abandoned him, and at the cruelty of his fate. Ondaatje reinvents this figure as a mad hunter, at war with "the beautiful animals." His insane logic is clear—he must

> ...kill to fool myself alive
> to leave all pity on the staggering body
> in order not to shoot an arrow up
> and let it hurl
> down through my petalling skull
> or neck vein, and lie
> heaving round the wood in my lung.
> That the end of thinking.
> Shoot either eye of bird instead
> and run and catch it in your hand. (*TK*, 22)

To resist the temptation to commit suicide, he must commit murder. To escape the torment of his own suppurating foot, he has to break the foot of an animal

> so two run wounded
> reel in the bush, flap
> bodies at each other
> till free of forest
> it gallops broken in the sand,
> then use a bow
> and pin the tongue back down its throat. (23)

This last grotesque image reminds us of the mutilation of the Malayan mules Ondaatje tells us about in "White Dwarfs"; guilty man has to silence the victims of his violence. As we have seen, the way man compensates for his own indignities by defiling the natural world is a central theme of *Rat Jelly*; it is Ondaatje's reinterpretation of Sophocles' benign outcast which makes him the mythological centre of the book, and explains why "Philoctetes on the island" does not appear out of place in it.

Because it depicts the outcast hero at war with the world of animals, "Philoctetes on the island" also serves as a transition from *The Dainty Monsters* to the more dangerous worlds of *the man with seven toes* (1969), and *The Collected Works of Billy the Kid* (1970). Ondaatje tells us in his afterword to *Rat Jelly* that it comprises poems "written before during and after" these two other books, "when the right hand thought it knew what the left hand was doing." Both of the longer works expand upon the themes of "Philoctetes on the island." Both concern lawbreakers who survive in the wild places of the earth through cunning and instinct and in both, the heroes are wounded in the legs. Billy's are badly burned in a fire (*CW*, 33-35), and he is symbolically buried in

76

leg irons (*CW*, 97); Potter too wears ankle manacles (*mst*, 22).

Actually, the figure of the wounded hunter in Ondaatje's work predates Philoctetes; we first meet him in "Peter" of *The Dainty Monsters*. A later incarnation is Bellocq, the crippled photographer who "shoots" the Storyville prostitutes in the novel *Coming Through Slaughter* (1976). The identification of hunter with artist, and the artist with the frustrated lover, implicit in *Billy the Kid*, is explicit in Bellocq, who stalks women with his camera and slashes their captured images as a way of penetrating them. More violently, Peter rapes Tara, the innocent daughter of those who crippled him. After years of making "golden spiders for her / and silver frogs, with opal glares" he "shaped her body like a mould" and "poured loathing of fifteen years on her" (*DM*, 76-7) in revenge for his torment and her inaccessible beauty and youth.

The predatory nature of the artist is explored with black humour in "Spider Blues," like "Philoctetes on the island," one of the *Rat Jelly* poems which shows us that not all monsters are dainty.

> And spider comes to fly, says
> Love me I can kill you, love me
> my intelligence has run rings about you
> love me, I kill you for the clarity that
> comes when roads I make are being made
> love me, antisocial, lovely. (*TK*, 62-3)

Being rejected, "the spider in his loathing / crucifies his victims in his spit / making them the art he cannot be."

Bellocq is clearly a spider, living "at the edge of the social world" (*CTS*, 64). Buddy Bolden, the gregarious improviser of Storyville life, follows him there, into silence and madness. Bellocq's physical and Bolden's spiritual suicides may be seen as a concession to the fact that we live in "an age of afternoon men," and therefore cannot expect "a Joycean or Homeric hero to clatter up the steps with the pay" ("The Inheritors," *DM*, 47). The frontier has been conquered, the jungle planted; there is no escape from the "cell of civilized magic" that is the domestic world ("The Diverse Causes," *DM*, 22) except into the *self*, into the unexplored terrain at the very border of consciousness. Buddy Bolden explains his fascination with Bellocq in exactly these terms: "We were furnished rooms and Bellocq was a window looking out"

(*CTS*, 59). His retreat to Webb's cabin at Pontchartrain puts Bolden into an equal and opposite situation:

> Here. Where I am anonymous and alone in a white room with no history and no parading. So I can make something unknown in the shape of this room. Where I am King of Corners. (*CTS*, 86)

The room becomes a hall of mirrors, however, when Bolden goes mad. Trapped in the self and deprived of "social fuel" ("White Dwarfs," *RJ*, 70), he can only rehearse the limits of his prison.

> In the room there is the air
> and there is the corner
> and there is the corner and there is the corner
> and there is the corner. (*CTS*, 146)

This entrapment makes him realize "if you don't shake, don't get no cake" (146).

This is the artist's continuing dilemma, usually displaced into fiction, but occasionally enacted directly, as we have seen in "Billboards," and in other poems like "Burning Hills" in *Rat Jelly*, "Light" in *Trick with a Knife* and, most sublimely, in *Tin Roof*. He needs to place himself *outside* the social world to write about it; a "blind lover, dont know / what I love till I write it out" (" 'The gate in his head,' " *RJ*, 62). But once he removes himself from the entanglements *of* that world, he understands more and more clearly his ties to it—and his need of it.

> In dark bound rooms
> the lost men imagine
> paths of biography
> on their palms ("Moon Lines, after Jiménez," *TK*, 74)

"Letters and Other Worlds," Ondaatje's elegy for his father sets forth this situation most tenderly, and it is Ondaatje's father, drinking himself to death, sending love letters to those he has shut out of his pain, who is ultimately the source of the Philoctetes figure in the poet's work. Until the memoir *Running in the Family* (1982), we didn't know much about this man, but he is evoked continually in Ondaatje's work. For example, speaking of his apprenticeship to jazz, Buddy Bolden declares

> My fathers were those who put their bodies over barbed wire. For me.
> To slide over into the region of hell. Through their sacrifice they seduced
> me into the game. (*CTS*, 95)

And in his own acknowledgments to the book Ondaatje explains "While I have used real names and characters and historical situations I have also used more personal pieces of friends and fathers."

Bolden is drawn to Bellocq because the photographer, like Bolden's adopted "fathers" and like Bolden himself, is

> drawn to opposites, even in the music we play. In terror we lean in the
> direction that is most unlike us. Running past your own character into
> pain. (*CTS*, 96)

This "running" is enacted by Ondaatje's father in *Running in the Family*—periodically he retreats into what the elegy calls "the terrible acute hatred / of his own privacy" (*TK*, 46). Like Bolden, Ondaatje's father is depicted as "a weatherbird arcing round in the middle of [his] life to exact opposites and burning [his] brains out" (*CTS*, 134). He becomes one of those "people who disappear" whom "White Dwarfs" commemorates; one of those "who sail to that perfect edge / where there is no social fuel" (*TK*, 68).

But, as Webb tells Bolden, "All suicides all acts of privacy are romantic" (*CTS*, 101). It is Ondaatje's recognition of the adolescent fatuity of the code "White Dwarfs" addresses, its spurious glamour, which makes him deflate it even as he continues to explore its romance. The code insists that man is an island and that woman is a threat, that the existential hero is necessarily a loner.

> What has he to do with the smell of ladies
> can they eat off his skeleton of pain?

But in "Late Movies with Skyler" the poet identifies his restless twenty-one-year-old companion with the heroes of his childhood movies and recognizes that they

> after skilled swordplay and moral victories
> leave with absolutely nothing

to do for the rest of their lives. (*TK*, 97)

And in the long poem *Tin Roof*, Ondaatje sardonically acknowledges that he was "educated / at the Bijou," and projects a suite of poems

for Bogart   drunk
six months after the departure at Casablanca.
I see him lying under the fan
at the Slavyansky Bazar Hotel
and soon he will see the truth
the stupidity of his gesture
he'll see it in the space
between the whirling metal. (See also *SL*, 40)

It is because "Love, the real / terrifies / the dreamer in his riot cell" ("Gold and Black," *RJ*, 12) that the dreamer shrinks from it. Paris says of Helen "by calming me she removes my dreams" ("Paris," *DM*, 59). Love is both a release from solitude and potential madness, and a threat to individual consciousness. The artist needs to hone his edge, to keep himself painfully separate and aware — but the *man* longs for affiliation and comfort and family. He dreads being devoured, and at the same time longs for it, like Buddy Bolden when he feels "the home of his wife's mouth coming down on him" (*CTS*, 122).

If Philoctetes represents the artist's ambivalent relationship to the world of nature, another crippled hunter, Adonis, is the unacknowledged archetype for his relationship with women. In Greek mythology Adonis was a beautiful youth devoted to Diana, goddess of chastity and the hunt. Venus became enamoured of him, but he fled her embraces to pursue an equally dangerous antagonist, the wild boar, only to be gored in the thigh and to die of his wounds. This injury is usually seen as a symbolic castration — an appropriate punishment for a man who refuses to fulfill his sexual (and hence social) nature. Adonis's preference for solitary mastery of the hunt over union with a woman, his fear of *losing* himself in love, can be read as a subtext for Ondaatje's wounded heroes (see *Tin Roof*: "Burt Lancaster / *limping* away at the end of *Trapeze*," my emphasis).

Tin Roof "places" this figure as self-deluded, a loser. The poem admits the poet's continuing fascination with him but punctures his glamour. Moreover, the poem provides a resolution to the poet's ongoing discussion with himself about his place in nature and society not only in its explicit content but in its dramatic situation, for now it is the poet himself, in his own person as Michael Ondaatje, who is on an island (Waikiki). By calling the poem *Tin Roof*, however, he reminds us that he is housebound, civilized, and that the island is ultimately a metaphor for the artist's necessary position as observer. It is a lush green retreat, yes, but he still needs a roof to protect him. The poet can go away, but his memories of the social world come with him. More strikingly, in *this* poem, the only animal present is the tiny Gecko lizard who peers through the window, and a beloved woman is invited to break into the poet's isolation.

Ondaatje's most confessional poem to date, *Tin Roof* follows, perhaps inevitably, his coming-to-terms with his ancestors in *Running in the Family*. Having placed the past firmly *in* the past, Sri Lanka on *its* side of the Pacific, Ondaatje writes from the edge of North America of himself, in the present tense. He also faces his personal mythology head on; *Tin Roof* presents the poet, "joyous and breaking down" (*SL*, 28) "drowning / on the edge of the sea" (25) but ultimately saved from "the tug over the cliff" (28) by "the warmth in the sleeve"—by his own hand, that is, its familiar life, its innate knowledge of how to hold on.

Rainer Marie Rilke is the tutelary spirit invoked by *Tin Roof*, and the *Duino Elegies* are proposed as the model of a poetry undistracted, transcendent, able to live "by the heart and nothing else." But the *Duino Elegies*, for all their inwardness, swoop over a dazzlingly varied landscape of human experience and emotion. Therefore the fact that Rilke at Duino Castle has replaced Philoctetes on the island as an analogue for the poet's internal exile suggests that Ondaatje now sees that exile as an inevitable part of the poetic process rather than as a tragic "fate." *Tin Roof* acknowledges, for the first time, the possibility that

...solitude...
is not an absolute
it is just a resting place. (*SL*, 37)

81

Tom Marshall
LAYERING:
THE SHORTER POEMS OF MICHAEL ONDAATJE

It occurred to me when I was asked to write this article that if I was going to find anything more to say about the poems of Michael Ondaatje I would have to try to forget that I had known the poet since the summer of 1965, at which time the early poems that he showed me both puzzled and (intermittently) impressed me. So I have tried to look anew at long-familiar poems, to look at them analytically without (except in one case) reference to my own first experience of them as part of a very immediate exchange of poems, ideas and personalities with a fellow poet.

The poetry has matured a great deal; my puzzlement has never entirely vanished. In the early poems brilliant and sometimes bizarre imagery often co-existed with what I thought rhythmic and idiomatic awkwardness or oddity. Sometimes the oddity grew on me or seemed eventually to justify itself in terms of a brilliant concept that had escaped me on first reading. Sometimes it did not.

Re-reading the poems, I want to ask certain questions of them, as if I were a high-school textbook. These are perhaps naïve (like all the best questions) but they constitute a beginning. Many early poems reveal the poet's aestheticism, and Ondaatje's whole work in poetry and prose reveals an obsession with art and the artist, yet he claims to "hate art."[1] Why? In "Billboards" he speaks of "trying to live / with a neutrality so great / I'd have nothing to think of" (*TK*, 35). Why does the poet want this "neutrality"? Is this desirable or even possible for a poet? Poems like "Gold and Black" present bizarre images of loss of self and disintegration (as does *The Collected Works of Billy the Kid*), and in "Burning Hills" the poet writes: "Every summer he believed would be his last" (58). (In context this may mean simply the last summer he would write, not imminent death, though the larger significance cannot be dismissed. And in his most recent book, *Tin Roof*, Ondaatje announces on the first page: "This last year I was sure / I was going to die.") Why does the poet believe this? In "Walking to Bellrock" he himself asks: "Stan, my crazy summer friend, / why are we both going crazy?" (83). Well, if they are, why are they? Does the poem offer any clue? Should the reader be especially concerned about or perhaps even put off by these unsupported suggestions of authorial precariousness or melodrama?

Naïve questions perhaps deserve naïve answers. But I am not interested in answering them in terms of the particular strains and changes of Ondaatje's personal life (which are not in any case so very different from those of more ordinary mortals). I would like to say, however, that I believe that these questions arise for me because the persona or artist-figure revealed in the poems seems to me to be a rather different person from the sensible, capable, well-balanced, considerate, shrewd, determined, healthily ambitious and competitive, good-humoured (he once, at my suggestion, fed to his book-eating pigs a battered old copy of *Animal Farm*), somewhat shy, interestingly tricky and only moderately high-strung, volatile and moody individual also named Michael Ondaatje whom I know. (Similarly, "Stan" is one of the saner people I have known in or out of Kingston.) All artists are no doubt divided selves (as in Yeats's formulation of "self' and "anti-self"), but the alternative self or life of Ondaatje's work is often a remarkably dramatic and even bizarre one that has had considerable appeal to those readers who have made *Billy the Kid* in particular a long-time best-seller.

Stephen Scobie, Sam Solecki and others have commented on the author's identification with his historical-fictional personae William Bonney and Buddy Bolden. Both author and reader live vicarious or alternative lives through these figures. I think there is a sense in which the "I" (or sometimes, as in "Burning Hills," a poem more obviously autobiographical than most, the "he") of the shorter poems is also a fictional construction, an anti-self or an exaggeration of certain (sometimes violent) human feelings and possibilities. (The other day I heard filmmaker David Cronenberg explain on the radio that when someone's head literally explodes in his film it is a dramatization of the sensory overload that makes one feel as if one's head "is exploding":

83

Ondaatje, nobody need be surprised to learn, likes horror films just as much as westerns and old swashbucklers like *Scaramouche*.) This is the naïve and no doubt obvious answer to my series of naïve questions: Ondaatje the artist exaggerates.

The earlier Ondaatje's myth or fiction is often bizarre and, I think, somewhat arbitrary. It is one in which an artist-figure lives on the brink of disaster. He is a killer-spider ("Spider Blues") or a persecuted and deformed monster ("Peter") who hates the world as much as he loves it. Art and the making of beauty, indeed all communication, are for him inseparable from psychic rape or murder or, ultimately, suicide. The artist is both killer and victim in his participation in the processes of an almost wholly predatory universe. Art is for him necessarily exploitation of reality. Thus the poet suspects himself at all times.

I am, as I have indicated before, neither temperamentally nor philosophically inclined to assent wholly to such a world-view. But I can assent in part, I can suspend my disbelief while experiencing the poem, and I can easily admire the brilliance with which the myth is often executed (so to speak). All of the above remarks have been by way of introduction and to get some general comments and views (or perhaps prejudices) of my own out of the way. What follows is the result of my re-examination of the poems.

It occurs to me in re-reading the poems that the dominant metaphor in Ondaatje's work is "layering" or merging itself. Palimpsest perhaps. His reality involves "billboard posters / blending in the rain" ("Billboards," 35) and "coloured strata of the brain" (" 'The gate in his head,' " 64). "The summers were layers of civilisation in his memory," we are told in "Burning Hills" (59). Almost all of his earlier poems involve the laying or layering of one landscape, one geographic or temporal or psychic reality, and in the marriage poems even one person, on another. (Even the epigraph of "The Dainty Monsters" section in *There's a Trick With a Knife I'm Learning to Do* projects a human face on the sky, and suggests the necessity of this layering or integration of fact and dream, world and self, for psychic survival.) This process perhaps begins with the "laying" of Ceylon on Canada. In the early poems the mythic past, whether personal or historical, is laid on the mundane Canadian present: new women are projected for the fields between Kingston and Gananoque ("Early Morning, Kingston to Gananoque").

84

In "Birds for Janet — The Heron," the first poem in Ondaatje's selected poems, a suicidal king is superimposed or projected rather arbitrarily upon a heron (a notion elaborated on later in "Heron Rex"). In "Dragon," the second poem, a dragon is superimposed on a beaver (and, behind the poem, on Tom Marshall, since it was I — I confess — who ran into the badminton net while playing hide-and-seek at dusk and thus lost my breath — though not, obviously, forever). In subsequent poems reflection imagery blends the seasons, the worlds of sleeping and waking, of nature and human dwelling ("The Diverse Causes"); Gary Snyder and his mountains are superimposed on a hospital scene while the poet is imaginatively spread all over Ontario ("Signature"); Henri Rousseau's dream landscape is laid on the world of society ladies ("Henri Rousseau and Friends"); wild nature and man's (not to mention the dog's) savage dreamlife are laid on his domesticity ("Biography," "The Republic"); passion and instinct are laid on reason and mechanism (and vice versa), as in *Billy the Kid*; art is frequently laid on life. Indeed, "layering" may be another way of saying metaphor, and it may be that, at some level, these poems are "about" the mind's poetic process itself. This makes the poet's later objections to "metaphor" and "art" somewhat ironic.

In many poems beauty is laid on violence, or violence on beauty. Layering is sometimes a violent or aggressive transgression of a boundary, even an internecine war within the poet (as in Dennis Lee's reading of *Billy the Kid* in *Savage Fields*). "Philoctetes on the island" presents the aggressive artist:

> Sun moves broken in the trees
> drops like a paw
> turns sea to red leopard
>
> I trap sharks and drown them
> stuffing gills with sand
> cut them with coral till
> the blurred grey runs
> red designs (*TK*, 22)

A predatory sun laid on sea, and the hunter who kills, making "red designs": here is Ondaatje's world and his subtext of the wounded and wounding artist in a nutshell.

In "Elizabeth" there is historical layering (as there is in *Billy the Kid*

85

and *Coming Through Slaughter*). The presumed twentieth century of "Daddy," "Uncle Jack" and "Mrs. Kelly" is gradually merged with the story of Elizabeth, her sister "Bloody" Mary, Mary's husband Philip of Spain, the unfortunate or perhaps very foolish Tom Seymour, who was thought to have had a sexual dalliance with the young princess and was later executed for political reasons, and her late favourite the Earl of Essex (also, of course, executed — an irony not made explicit in the poem itself). The lively little girl who had an adventure with a snake at the zoo is, by this somewhat suspect poetic trickery, revealed eventually as the aged, already legendary queen. Thus the poem seems to support Gwendolyn MacEwen's assertion that all times and worlds are one. (I expect the young Ondaatje saw Jean Simmons and Stewart Granger in *Young Bess*, as I did.)

In more personal and domestic poems a complex family situation is laid on the poet's "virgin past," the poet's interpretations are laid on his wife's past ("Billboards"), body is laid on brain, numbing it ("Kim, at half an inch"), and wife, "Love, the real," is laid on poet, "the dreamer in his riot cell" ("Gold and Black"). Here fact (flesh) is laid on dream (imagination), but this works the other way around too, as we have seen.

Ondaatje merges with his dog ("The Strange Case"), with his son ("Griffin of the Night"), with Henri Rousseau ("The Vault"), with Darwin ("Charles Darwin pays a visit, December 1971"), with King Kong and Wallace Stevens ("Dates," "King Kong meets Wallace Stevens"). In "Letters and Other Worlds" he attempts to recover his lost father and his first world as he does at greater length in *Running in the Family*. The search for his father in himself as much as in the world of recoverable fact is analogous to the search *in himself* for Billy or for Buddy. And he assimilates and takes unto himself those he admires and needs:

It is the formal need
to suck blossoms out of the flesh
in those we admire
planting them private in the brain
and cause fruit in lonely gardens.

To learn to pour the exact arc
of steel still soft and crazy

86

before it hits the page.
I have stroked the mood and tone
Of hundred year dead men and women
Emily Dickinson's large dog, Conrad's beard
and, for myself,
removed them from historical traffic.
Having tasted their brain. Or heard
the wet sound of a death cough.
Their idea of the immaculate moment is now. ('Taking,'' 57)

In "Letters and Other Worlds" Ondaatje credits his father with "complete empathy." The father's life and fate can, of course, be seen as tragic. Nevertheless, "complete empathy" is a rather more positive characterization of the poetic process so often seen in earlier poems as predatory or cannibalistic or suicidal. Perhaps this may even indicate the possibility of a new identification with the real that is now so close that it is no longer an imposition of his private myth of the world or a "suicide into nature" (54) but a reconciliation with the world—a balance that transcends the two poles of destruction and self-destruction. In "Pig Glass," the closing section of the selected poems, something like this may be happening. (And perhaps it was foreshadowed in such earlier poems of relative balance and harmony as "The Diverse Causes" and "We're at the graveyard.")

In "Pig Glass" there is perhaps a new departure or direction for Ondaatje's poetry. Beyond the self-destructive silence of "White Dwarfs," the powerful last poem of *Rat Jelly*, is a new apprehension of the world simply as it is immediately experienced without obvious "layering" or metaphor. (I am not quite so naïve as to say "simply *as it is.*")

Ondaatje quotes Italo Calvino:

> Newly arrived and totally ignorant of the Levantine languages, Marco Polo could express himself only with gestures, leaps, cries of wonder and of horror, animal barkings or hootings, or with objects he took from his knapsacks — ostrich plumes, pea-shooters, quartzes — which he arranged in front of him.... (*TK*, 71)

The poems that follow make such assertions as "All night the truth happens" ("Country Night") and "There is no metaphor here" ("Walking to Bellrock"). "Country Night" describes the small events (including small dreams) of the night. "The Agatha Christie books by the window" celebrates avocados and other concrete objects on Vancouver Island. "Buying the dog," "Moving Fred's Outhouse / Geriatrics of Pine" and "Buck Lake Store Auction" are also predominantly poems of fact. In "Walking to Bellrock," the most expansive and impressive of these poems, the poet and his friend Stan seek relief from their unparticularized human craziness in the immediate physical reality of walking in the river to Bellrock, so that "all thought / is about the mechanics of this river" which are then presented vividly and effectively. There is no "history or philosophy or metaphor" here, and instead of myth there is the simple "plot" to get to Bellrock. (Though, of course, the archetypal critic might want to argue that all journeys on a river signify the attempt to get through life itself—here a purely physical existence—more or less intact.) Other poems describe very directly Ondaatje's renewed impressions of Ceylon (now Sri Lanka), give Sallie Chisum's commonsensical late thoughts about Billy the Kid ("He was a fool"), and arrange the concrete fragments of Ondaatje's experience of fellow poet Chris Dewdney. Indeed, in all of these poems we get the sort of arrangement of objects indicated in the epigraph from Calvino.

But the earlier Ondaatje "layering" formula does not altogether disappear. The erotic poems of Wyatt and Campion are laid on the present in "Farre Off." There is perhaps archeological layering in "Pig Glass" itself. In "Sweet Like a Crow" all Ceylon is laid on a eight-year-old girl's raucous voice. In "Late Movies with Skyler" the Stewart Granger version of *The Prisoner of Zenda* (plus the poet's past involvement with it) is laid on footloose young Skyler. Even Billy is projected on the night sky in Sallie's mind. Most importantly (since it brings us in a sense back to the starting gate, and also looks forward to *Running in the Family*), in the beautiful "Light," the last poem of the selected poems, Ceylon and the past (more particularly, the poet's late mother and her family) are laid on a stormy summer night in Canada. The electric storm makes the trees appear to be walking away from the speaker, but in truth they, and by implication the mother and her world, haven't "moved an inch" from him. He is in process here, as in *Running in the Family*, of recovering that lost world and, in thus healing an old rupture, recovering a lost self as well.

For these are poems notably more gentle than most of those in *The*

Dainty Monsters or *Rat Jelly* (let alone those in *Billy the Kid*). It seems as if the process of "layering" of past and present, of Ceylon and Canada, of disturbed imagination and Canadian landscape, of inner and outer, has led, eventually, to a degree of self-realization, self-integration, and reconcilitation of these and other polarities that makes possible a new kind of poetry, and perhaps a new anti-mythic "myth" for the poet.

Does the recently published sequence *Tin Roof* bear this out? Well, it seems to me to be a transitional poem, sharp in local detail but perhaps a little incoherent in overall structure. We find the poet once again posed on the brink of an unspecified disaster, unspecified, that is, except for the opening remark, already quoted, about dying. He is waiting for "wisdom," a "solution" to his unspecified problem, and perhaps simultaneously for poetic inspiration (like Rilke, whom he eventually addresses), whether it comes as "seraphim or bitch." (*SL*, 23) He watches for "cue cards/blazing in the sky." But he finds no wisdom thus projected or "layered" on the world, only the specifics of the place, a cabin on the Pacific beside

sea,

        the unknown magic he loves
    throws himself into

            the blue heart (*SL*, 25)

The poet tells us

how he feels now
everything passing through him like light (*SL*, 28)

He is literally on the edge here, "joyous and breaking down" into the world — yet he remains distinct, intact, within this union. It is not, I think, "suicide into nature." Simple physical sanity (plus humour) is once again his salvation:

Good
morning to your body
hello nipple
and appendix scar like a letter
of too much passion
from a mad Mexican doctor (*SL*, 32)

There is sometimes a lady present, and they live for the moment. Their

89

imaginations interact with America (Kansas and Missouri) and with old movies like *Casablanca*; Ondaatje imagines the Bogart character after the movie's end bitterly regretting the noble renunciation of his lover (Ingrid Bergman). Finally the poet both identifies with and distinguishes himself from Rilke, whom he addresses directly, making reference to the poems of Phyllis Webb (to whom *Tin Roof* is dedicated), and concludes:

> I wanted poetry to be walnuts
> in their green cases
> but now it is the sea
> and we let it drown us,
> and we fly to it released
> by giant catapults
> of pain loneliness deceit and vanity (*SL*, 43)

I'm not sure quite what to make of this conclusion. Obviously the poet accuses himself of certain common human faults, yet these seem to be the mainspring of his surrender to a poetry of the world itself in flux — not a poetry imposed on the world, as in the past. My sense of the whole poem is that, despite the announcement of crisis, there is here a degree of acceptance, though not without "pain" and "loneliness," of the world and self; the poem embodies that growing sense of balance I have found in the poems of "Pig Glass," rearranging as it does a number of long-familiar Ondaatje themes and materials. Crises are also opportunities for growth.

This is perhaps the place to remind myself and other readers that Ondaatje's highly developed sense of humour has always provided a certain counterweight to his violent melodrama and to the Byronic romanticism that cause him to announce from time to time that he is going crazy or that he feels he may not survive this or that year or summer. Humour helps to create the complex artistic balance of *Billy the Kid* and *Coming Through Slaughter*. And in the shorter poems too it can accompany and to some extent lighten the grotesque or violent. "Letters and Other Worlds" is one good example of this. In other, non-violent poems Ondaatje makes comic instead of tragic art from the conflict of intellect and instinct, art and life. "The Strange Case" is one example:

> My dog's assumed my alter ego.

90

Has taken over — walks the house
phallus hanging wealthy and raw
in front of guests, nuzzling
head up skirts
while I direct my mandarin mood.

Last week driving the baby sitter home.
She, unaware dog sat in dark back seat,
talked on about the kids' behaviour.
On Huron Street the dog leaned forward
and licked her ear.
The car going 40 miles an hour
she seemed more amazed
at my driving ability
than my indiscretion.

It was only the dog I said.
Oh she said.
Me interpreting her reply all the way home. (*TK*, 40)

As we have seen, the notion of "alter ego" is extremely important throughout Ondaatje's work. Here the passionate and reckless "other" Ondaatje is laid not on Billy the Kid or Buddy Bolden or his tragic father but, comically, on the well-hung dog. This leaves the "I" of the poem free to be his more "ordinary" self.

As I suggested in my opening paragraph, some Ondaatje poems have impressed me much more than others. For the record these are: "Paris" (which he chose to discard, leaving it out of his selected poems), "The Diverse Causes," "Peter," "Burning Hills," "We're at the graveyard," "White Dwarfs," "Walking to Bellrock," and "Light." (A near-miss might be "Letters and Other Worlds," which is certainly thematically central in Ondaatje's work and development, but which I find as rhythmically and grammatically awkward as it is powerful.) To say just why, and examine each of these favourites closely, would take another essay, but I must add that when a contemporary poet has written eight or more poems I admire very much then his batting average is (with this reader) a good one. Obviously, I "like" numbers of other Ondaatje poems, but these seem to me to be the best — for their qualities of sound, rhythm, diction and imagery as well as for sensuous immediacy and emotional strength and depth. Ondaatje's work, exploring as it does a psychological reality, does not, I think, have the kind of social or historical or metaphysical scope and

91

range that one finds in the best poems of Al Purdy or Margaret Avison. It *does* have brilliant effects, wonderful immediacy and impressive emotional depth. Moreover, as the artist has matured, his work has become increasingly relaxed (in the best sense) and accomplished as he has moved beyond shock tactics (or what a witty novelist of my acquaintance has called "special effects") and obvious "layering" or metaphor.

But there is, of course, in all poetry (and civilization) an inevitable and inescapable "layering": man imposes his own "myth" on the world, on empirical reality, in inventing, using and living within language at all. Thus Italo Calvino writes: "This world I see, the one we ordinarily recognize as *the* world, presents itself to my eyes — at least to a large extent — already defined, labeled, catalogued. It is a world already conquered, colonized by words, a world that bears a heavy crust of speech."[2] Man is the "language animal" as George Steiner (I think) once said.

Still, I have believed that poetry at its highest power (which is language at its highest power) is that musical use of language that may transcend the apparent limitations as well as the tyranny of language: it is the language the poet finds both within and beyond himself, the language that is, in his physiological processes of sense-perception, his and the world's together, words caught and disposed within that larger sound and rhythm of things, that contains poet and external landscape and language alike as eternally related parts of its ceaseless continuing. More simply, it is shaped by, even becomes, the rhythm of the organism (mind and body) interacting with the rhythm of environment / universe: here metaphor may be important but it is *sound* that is primary. At his best Michael Ondaatje, a true poet, has been part of that large flow.

---

1 "War Machine," *There's a Trick With a Knife I'm Learning to Do*, p. 48. All references are to the selected poems or to *Tin Roof*, which is unpaginated.

2 "The Written and the Unwritten Word," *The New York Review of Books*, May 12, 1983.

Sam Solecki
NETS AND CHAOS:
THE POETRY OF MICHAEL ONDAATJE

My mind is pouring chaos
in nets onto the page.[1]

Michael Ondaatje is a poet of reality. In applying this phrase to
Ondaatje, I wish to call attention to the fact that in his poetry the fundamental or essential nature of experience is consistently being described and examined. The entire thrust of his vision is directed at
compelling the reader to reperceive reality, to assume an unusual angle
of vision from which reality appears surreal, absurd, inchoate, dynamic,
and, most importantly, ambiguous. His poetic world is filled with mad
or suicidal herons, one-eyed mythic dogs, tortured people, oneiric
scenes, gorillas, dragons, creative spiders, and imploding stars. These
extraordinary images function as a kind of metaphoric shorthand to
disorient the reader, to make him enter a psychological or material reality which has been revealed as almost overwhelmingly anarchic or
chaotic. What is at issue in Ondaatje's poetry is the existence not of an
alternate reality but of different perceptions of one which the reader has
always assumed to be clear, patterned, and meaningful. To use Wallace
Stevens' apt phrase, Ondaatje is often a "connoisseur of chaos"; and
whether his poems depict an unconscious mode of being similar to
Freud's primary process ("Biography," "King Kong," "King Kong
meets Wallace Stevens") or simply the ordinary phenomenal flux of life
("Loop," "We're at the graveyard"), the central formal and thematic
concern in his work has been the description of internal and external
reality as dynamic, chaotic, and ambiguous.[2]
  But his major poems not only redefine our sense of reality; they also

create an awareness of the extent to which the mind distorts reality in any act of perception and description. In the period between *The Dainty Monsters* (1967) and *Rat Jelly* (1973), Ondaatje has shown an increasing awareness of the epistemological difficulties involved in the relationship between the "nets" of the perceiving and recreating mind and the "chaos" of life. Not content to raise just the usual issue about the limitations of language as a representational medium, Ondaatje has shown more concern for the possibility that poetry might not be able to do justice to the existential complexity of reality because of the inevitable tendency of the mind to see pattern and clarity where life offers only flux and ambiguity. This tension between mind and chaos is at the centre of Ondaatje's poetry; and its implications can be seen in the dualistic nature of his imagery, in the deliberate thematic irresolution of his major lyrics, and in the complex structuring of his two longer poems, *the man with seven toes* and *The Collected Works of Billy the Kid*. Without resorting to what R.P. Blackmur has called the fallacy of expressive form,[3] one variant of which can be seen in some of the work of the Black Mountain school and in Victor Coleman's poetry, Ondaatje has written poems describing the fundamentally chaotic nature of experience.

In his first collection, *The Dainty Monsters*, most of the poems simply reflect the assumption that a lyric can recreate any aspect of reality or re-enact any experience which the poet chooses. Only in the poems about poetry—"Four Eyes," "The Martinique," and "Eventually the Poem for Keewaydin"—is the question raised—but only implicitly—to what extent is such an assumption valid and, if it is valid, what are the problems involved in transfiguring life into poetry? Many poems describe life dualistically in terms of a suggestive dialectic between a dark oneiric or surreal world and a daylight one. The former is shown as co-existent with the latter ("The Republic"), vaguely threatening to it ("Gorillas"), or in danger of being extirpated by it ("Dragon"). As is usual in his work, Ondaatje is primarily concerned with the relationship between kinds of reality or modes of being. "The Republic" is a representative poem:

This house, exact,
coils with efficiency and style.
A different heaven here,
air even is remade in the basement.

94

The plants fed daily
stand like footmen by the windows,
flush with decent green
and meet the breeze with polish;
no dancing with the wind here.

Too much reason in its element
passions crack the mask in dreams.
While we sleep
the plants in frenzy heave floors apart,
lust with common daisies,
feel rain,
fling their noble bodies, release a fart.
The clock alone, frigid and superior,
swaggers in the hall.

At dawn gardenias revitalize
and meet the morning with decorum. (*DM*, 20)

In the day this is a world of "reason" and order, but at night the Dionysian world of primal vitality reasserts itself and establishes the republic of the title. But the point of the poem is that this world is there unperceived all the time. It is a necessary counter-balance to a world of "too much reason." The final couplet even suggests that its vitality and chaos "revitalize" the realm of order and light. It is typical of Ondaatje that the relationship between the two worlds is presented as a complex one and that no simplistic resolution is offered. Thus although "decorum" is restored at the end of the poem, the verb "revitalize" serves as a disturbing reminder of the anarchic frenzy of the nighttime. The final couplet subtly reiterates the emotional tension created by the central juxtaposition of two opposed realities. This tension, as it relates to the theme, works against the formal closure which arises inevitably with the last word of any poem, and, in doing so, it implies a deliberate thematic irresolution which gives the poem the open-endedness characteristic of Ondaatje's best work.

While "The Republic" is primarily concerned with the description of a scene or an event, "Four Eyes" is more concerned with an examination of the actual process by which a poet transforms a lived, dynamic moment into poetry. The speaker, choosing to see only what is within his companion's field of vision, breaks from the moment in order to record it:

95

Naked I lie here
attempting to separate toes
with no help from hands.
You with scattered nightgown
listen to music, hug a knee.

I pick this moment up
with our common eyes
only choose what you can see

a photograph of you with posing dog
a picture with Chagall's red
a sprawling dress.

This moment I broke to record,
walking round the house
to look for paper.
Returning
I saw you, in your gaze,
still netted the picture, the dog.
The music continuing
you were still being unfurled
shaped by the scene.

I would freeze this moment
and in supreme patience
place pianos
and craggy black horses on a beach
and in immobilised time
attempt to reconstruct. (*DM*, 46)

In its focus on the act of creation, the poem anticipates that group of difficult and ambitious lyrics in *Rat Jelly* which deal explicitly with this theme. "Four Eyes" does not examine the problem as perceptively as those more mature poems do, but it is nevertheless exploring a similar area of creative experience. Ondaatje is concerned here with what happens when a poet tries to "reconstruct" a lived moment into art. In "Four Eyes" the first consequence of such an attempt is the poet's necessary separation from the experience itself. In order to write about it, he must leave it: "This moment I broke to record." With its double meaning of separating and breaking, "broke" questions the quality of the writer's departure and suggests that ultimately he values art over life. Instead of being a participant, he becomes a detached observer who prefers searching for a verbal equivalent of a lived moment to life itself.

While "record" indicates the probability of a point by point imitation, the final stanza reveals that the reconstruction will be metaphoric. The writer will use "pianos / and craggy black horses on a beach," images not present in the original scene. The poem ends by suggesting that the essential qualities of a scene "still being unfurled" can only be captured in metaphor. But Ondaatje's final lines simultaneously point to the possibility that even this reconstruction may misrepresent the original moment. The connotations of "freeze" and "immobilized time" imply that the poet will ultimately fail to do justice to life's temporal dimension and its dynamic quality. If my reading is correct, then "Four Eyes" offers both a solution to the problem it poses and a searching critique of that solution. It is not the best poem in Ondaatje's first volume—"Dragon" and "The Time Around Scars" are better—but, together with "The Martinique" and "Eventually the Poem for Keewaydin," it is the one in which he most profoundly questions the possibilities of the kind of poetry he is writing.[5]

In his second book, the long narrative poem *the man with seven toes* (1969), the very form and texture of the poem attempt to recreate for the reader the sense of an unpredictable and often chaotic experience "being unfurled" in the actual body of the poem. Without resorting to formlessness, Ondaatje nevertheless conveys the sense of a descent into a psychological and material chaos. The book is concerned with the response of an anonymous civilized woman to a landscape and culture completely different from her own. Like Margaret Atwood's Susanna Moodie, she is placed in a world whose reality is ostensibly unrelated to her own. The poem is the account of the confrontation with and gradual acceptance of the darker and more chaotic aspects of life which, by the end of the book, are recognized as not only outside the self but within it as well.

Each of the brief self-contained lyrics vividly re-enacts a stage in her development.

> goats   black goats, balls bushed in the centre
> cocks rising like birds flying to you   reeling on you
> and smiles smiles as they ruffle you open
> spill you down, jump and spill over you
> white leaping like fountains in your hair
> your head and mouth till it dries
> and tightens your face like a scar

97

> Then up to cook a fox or whatever
> goats eating goats heaving the bodies
> open like purple cunts under ribs, then tear
> like to you a knife down their pit, a hand in the warm
> the hot the dark boiling belly and rip
> open and blood spraying out like dynamite
> caught in the children's mouths on the ground
> laughing collecting it in their hands
> or off to a pan, holding blood like gold
> and the men rip flesh tearing, the muscles
> nerves green and red still jumping
> stringing them out, like you (*mst*, 16)

The syntax, imagery, and rhythm, the very texture of the verse, re-enact her complex response to an experience which, prior to becoming lost, she had not even imagined. The violent rape evokes a curiously ambivalent response; some of the similes — "like birds," "white leaping like fountains" — have quite positive connotations, but their hint of beauty suddenly disappears in an image — "a scar" — which begins the comparison of the rape and the cutting up of a fox. Her confusion and terror are brilliantly caught in a simile which, because of the deliberate absence of punctuation, has a double reference: "open and blood spraying out like dynamite / caught in the children's mouths on the ground." Because of the syntactical ambiguity, both the blood and the dynamite are "caught in the children's mouths"; this occasion of violence, sexuality, and innocence stunningly registers the woman's own shocked response. But the similes in this lyric also fulfill another function: they indicate her attempt to appropriate, in terms of analogous or more familiar images, certain experiences which she finds almost indescribable. In describing the tearing apart of a fox in terms of a rape, for example, she is able to articulate her reaction to what has happened to herself as well.

Yet, despite her suffering throughout the journey — and "goats black goats" is a typical instance — she is described at the end of the book as lying on a bed and

> sensing herself like a map, then
> lowering her hands into her body. (41)

This suggests that an increased awareness of herself has been gained from her experiences. The poem continues with the following stanzas:

> In the morning she found pieces of a bird
> chopped and scattered by the fan
> blood sprayed onto the mosquito net,
> its body leaving paths on the walls
> like red snails that drifted down in lumps.
>
> She could imagine the feathers
> while she had slept
> falling around her
> like slow rain.

The violent death of the bird is a clear reminder of the world from which she had recently escaped. Her change in attitude to that world, however, is indicated in her ability to imagine the death of the bird in terms of "feathers / while she has slept / falling around her." Again, like Atwood's Moodie, she has achieved a new awareness of herself and of aspects of reality about which she had been previously ignorant.

A similar but even more developed and complex reperception of reality takes place in *The Collected Works of Billy the Kid* (1970), the events of which are consistently ambiguous in their significance and in which the two central characters are both paradoxes. Billy the Kid is a murderer and "the pink of politeness / and as courteous a little gentleman / as I ever met (*CW*, 87). Pat Garrett, the ostensible representative of law and order, is a "sane assassin sane assassin sane assassin sane assassin sane assassin sane" (29) with the final stress falling on "—in sane." In the world of *The Collected Works of Billy the Kid*, peace and violence, sanity and insanity, order and chaos, and darkness and light are almost inextricably confused. It is as if the key characters have all made "the one altered move" (41) to remove themselves from the normal expectations and moral judgments taken for granted by the reader.

Ondaatje's handling of the story subjects the reader to a process of defamiliarization in which the standard western made familiar by Burns, Penn, and Peckinpah is deliberately "made new." Every aspect of Ondaatje's version emphasizes both the difficulties inherent and the artistic problems involved in recreating that reality in art. As in *the man with seven toes*, Ondaatje achieves this by making the reader experience many of the episodes as if he were a direct witness to them, a temporary insider in the events themselves. But then in his normal position as an objective reader, inevitably outside the text, he must also stand back, organize and evaluate these "collected" but still, so to speak, disorganized "works" which are told from a variety of viewpoints and which lack a summarizing judgment by an omniscient narrator. The effect is similar to that achieved in Robbe-Grillet's fiction where the reader also enters a confusing fictive world knowing that there will be no ostensible authorial guidance. Both authors compel the reader to become both a surrogate character and a surrogate author in order to make him implicitly aware of the difficulties involved in the perceiving and describing of reality. The initial disorientation leads ultimately to a new awareness.

The allusions to Billy's non-picture (5) and the episodes which emphasize that the apparent is not the real serve a similar function. John Chisum's story of Livingstone, the mad breeder of dogs, is a case in point. Chisum says that Livingstone "seemed a pretty sane guy to me. I mean, he didnt twitch or nothing like that" (60). This "pretty sane guy" "clinically and scientifically" (61) bred a race of mad dogs on his farm. Sallie Chisum reacts to the story by telling her bassett Henry, "Aint that a nasty story Henry, aint it? Aint it nasty" (62). The story may be "nasty," but its significance is not summed up in that judgment. The story is a reminder that we should refrain from assuming that the apparent is the real. If Livingstone was able to deceive John Chisum about his sanity, then what kind of final judgment can the reader make about the sanity or insanity of Billy the Kid or Pat Garrett? Ondaatje's point is that the task of art is to present the reader with the "collected works" so that he can experience them in their total complexity. Sallie Chisum's final judgment of Billy and Pat seems authoritative because it preserves their ambiguities and contradictions:

> I knew both these men intimately.
> There was good mixed in with the bad
> in Billy the Kid
> and bad mixed in with the good
> in Pat Garrett.
>
> No matter what they did in the world
> or what the world thought of them
> they were my friends.
> Both were worth knowing. (89)

Despite Billy's death, the book remains thematically open-ended. One of its last prose pieces suggests that Billy's story will be written again, interpreted again:

> Imagine if you dug him up and brought him out. You'd see very little. There'd be the buck teeth. Perhaps Garrett's bullet no longer in thick wet flesh would roll in the skull like a marble. From the head there'd be a trail of vertebrae like a row of pearl buttons off a rich coat down to the pelvis. The arms would be cramped on the edge of what was the box. And a pair of hand cuffs holding ridiculously fine ankle bones. (Even though dead they buried him in leg irons). There would be the silver from the toe of each boot.

> His legend a jungle sleep (97)

The metaphor in the last line is almost oxymoronic, containing within itself both peace and a potential violence, Billy's gentleness and his killing. The image has an undefined but thoroughly disturbing and haunting quality which leaves the reader with a sense of anticipation and even anxiety. It is as if the violence in Billy and the story is only temporarily quiescent. Ondaatje has managed to summarize within a single sensuous complex the unresolved tensions and ambiguities of the book.

While Ondaatje was writing his two longer works, he was also working on those poems in *Rat Jelly* which as a group constitute his most explicit exploration of the relationship between poetry and reality: "King Kong meets Wallace Stevens," "Spider Blues," "Taking," "'The gate in his head,'" "Burning Hills," and "White Dwarfs." In its concern with the creative mind's "fencing" of chaos, the first of these is representative of the group:

> Take two photographs —
> Wallace Stevens and King Kong
> (Is it significant that I eat bananas as I write this?)

> Stevens is portly, benign, a white brush cut
> striped tie. Businessman but
> for the dark thick hands, the naked brain
> the thought in him.

> Kong is staggering
> lost in New York streets again
> a spawn of annoyed cars at his toes.

101

The mind is nowhere.
Fingers are plastic, electric under the skin.
He's at the call of Metro-Goldwyn-Mayer.

Meanwhile W.S. in his suit
is thinking chaos is thinking fences.
In his head the seeds of fresh pain
his exorcising,
the bellow of locked blood.

The hands drain from his jacket,
pose in the murderer's shadow.[8] (RJ, 61)

The poem is structured upon a series of antitheses; the primary contrast
is between Stevens, the businessman whose "thought is in him," and
Kong, whose "mind is nowhere." But, as so often in Ondaatje's
poetry, the opposed terms are ultimately related. Kong, after all, is
more than just a suggestive photographer's image of directable energy;
he is also, as the poem's structure and imagery suggest, an aspect of
Stevens himself, and the meeting between them occurs not only in the
juxtaposing of their photographs but also within Stevens' mind. This is
established by the presentation of analogous situations in the third and
fourth stanzas: MGM directs Kong; Stevens fences the chaos and blood
within himself. No comma or conjunction appears between the two
clauses of "is thinking chaos is thinking fences" because the poem is
suggesting the problematic simultaneity of both the "chaos" and the
"fences" in the "thinking" of Stevens. If, as I have suggested, Kong
and "chaos" or "blood" are synonymous, then the entire fourth stanza points to Kong's presence within Stevens himself: both the containing form and the contained energy are within the mind of the
businessman who is also a poet. This connection between the two is
also present in the image of Stevens' "dark thick hands" which, at the
poem's end, "drain from his jacket, / pose in the murderer's shadow."
The poem closes on the alarming association between Stevens and "the
murderer's shadow" which can only be his own. He is a murderer
because he has subdued his "chaos" or "blood," his unconscious self.[9]

But the poem also suggests, almost too casually, that Stevens is not
the only poet with a shadow self. After all, the writer-speaker of the
poem asks humorously in the opening stanza, "Is it significant that I
eat bananas as I write this?" In view of the almost symbiotic relation-

ship between Stevens and Kong, there can only be one answer. Despite the parenthetical nature of the question, the image of the "bananas" functions as a comic allusion to the speaker's Kong-like aspect. Thus the poem indicates that both of the poets within it are in creative contact with everything that the ostensibly antithetical Kong represents; but they are able to transform, control, and shape this "chaos" within the self into an aesthetic construct, into "King Kong meets Wallace Stevens." There is also a lingering suggestion, however, that some of the "chaos" will resist and even escape the poet's act of transformation. Both "the *bellow* of locked blood" and "hands *drain* from his jacket" (my italics) raise this possibility.[10]

The notion that the poet pays a price for creating a poem — "In his head the seeds of fresh pain / his exorcising" — reappears in "Spider Blues" in which the poet is seen as an admirable, because dextrous, spider:

> I admire the spider, his control classic,
> his eight legs finicky,
> making lines out of the juice in his abdomen.
> A kind of writer I suppose.
> He thinks a path and travels
> the emptiness that was there
> leaves his bridge behind
> looking back saying Jeez
> did I do that?
> and uses his ending
> to swivel to new regions
> where the raw of feelings exist. (RJ, 63-64)

The spider as creative artist is a cartographer of the unknown, and, as the image in the last line reveals, he brings back a message about some essential or primal reality. But, like the speaker in "Four Eyes," he can only do this by separating himself from that reality. The spider may be more talented than the fly; yet, in terms of the allegory of the poem, the fly, because it is closer to life, is the necessary subject matter of art:

> And spider comes to fly, says
> Love me I can kill you, love me
> my intelligence has run rings about you
> love me, I kill you for that clarity that

comes when roads I make are being made
love me, antisocial, lovely
. . . .
And the spider in his loathing
crucifies his victims in his spit
making them the art he cannot be.

Mind distinguishes Wallace Stevens from King Kong, and ''intelligence'' the spider from the fly; but the cost of the distinction is registered by the title of the poem, ''Spider Blues'': it is sung by Ray Charles, not Anne Murray. But the poem is also a blues song because in the relationship between the spider and the fly, the former creates ''beauty'' by ''crucifying'' the latter. It is not clear what alternative modes of creation are possible, but the suggestion is nevertheless felt that this is not an ideal relationship between art and life.

If a poem is a mediation between mind and experience, then the ultimate poem for Ondaatje is the one which transforms reality into poetry without ''crucifying'' it. '''The gate in his head''' is not that poem, but it is Ondaatje's most emphatic statement about what poetry should be:

My mind is pouring chaos
in nets onto the page.
A blind lover, dont know
what I love till I write it out.
And then from Gibson's your letter
with a blurred photograph of a gull.
Caught vision. The stunning white bird
an unclear stir.

And that is all this writing should be then.
The beautiful formed things caught at the wrong moment
so they are shapeless, awkward
moving to the clear. (RJ, 62)

The ''chaos'' here is syonymous with whatever reality the poet has chosen to describe. It is the basic life stuff or substance out of which he shapes a poem. The central tension of the poem is between this ''chaos'' and the mental ''nets'' of language within which the poet represents it. The ''nets'' recall the ''fences'' in ''King Kong meets Wallace Stevens'' and the ''webs'' in ''Spider Blues'' and *The Collected Works of Billy the Kid*[11]: they are the actual medium — film or words —

104

in which the vision is recreated or caught. Although "caught" is Ondaatje's word, it does not really do justice to either his essentially heuristic assumption about poetic creativity — "A blind lover, dont know / what I love till I write it out" — or his concern with registering as sensitively as possible the dynamic quality of a moment or of an image. His concern is that the poem describe "the unclear stir" made by "a beautiful formed thing" perceived "at the wrong moment." This last detail is particularly important if the poetic perception is to yield a new, unexpected awareness of the image and, consequently, of reality. Yet, as I pointed out earlier, the poem must deal with motion, flux and formlessness within the confines of poetic form. Ondaatje's poem achieves this by hinting at forms — the page, the photograph — and then subtly, through oxymoron, syntax, and an inter-weaving of sounds — n's and r's — recreating the reality, the image of the bird.

The photograph is by Victor Coleman and the entire poem is an *hommage* to a writer whose extremely difficult poems reveal

> ... the faint scars
> coloured strata of the brain,
> not clarity but *the sense of shift*. (my emphasis)

The "faint scars" are metaphors for Coleman's poems (*One Eye Love, Stranger*) which, in a mode much more radical than Ondaatje's, attempt to give the reader a sense of life as pure process, as "shift" and "chaos."[12] But the "scars" are also literally scars. Here, as elsewhere in Ondaatje's work, a physical scar represents caught motion, just as a mental scar or an emotional scar is caught memory.[13] In other words, the scar literally incorporates and memorializes an emotion, an act, or an experience. In terms of the imagery of "The Time Around Scars," a scar is a "medallion" or "watch" which records a violent and revealing event. One could even say that a scar is finally analogous to an ideal, because nonverbal, poem in which the distinction between word and thing or state of being has finally disappeared. I shall return to this idea when discussing "White Dwarfs."

The very fact that in comparing his work to Coleman's Ondaatje writes "that is all this writing *should be* then" (my emphasis) is a reminder of an ideal which he feels he has not yet achieved. I would suggest that it is a mark of Ondaatje's integrity as a poet that his most successful poems raise this kind of question. He has said in an interview that "in writing you have to get all the truth down — the qualifications, the lies, the uncertainties — ."[14] And if " 'The gate in his head' " voices his doubts about the possibility — or impossibility — of an adequate linguistic representation — "all the truth" — of external or objective reality, "Burning Hills," one of his finest personal poems, indicates an awareness that any attempt to come to terms with an emotionally charged complex of memories carries with it its own difficulties:

> Since he began burning hills
> the Shell strip has taken effect.
> A wasp is crawling on the floor
> tumbling over, its motor fanatic.
> He has smoked five cigarettes.
> He has written slowly and carefully
> with great love and great coldness.
> When he finishes he will go back
> hunting for the lies that are obvious. (*RJ*, 58)

Unlike most of Ondaatje's personal poems, this one is written, almost over-insistently ("He has... / He has"), in the third person. The repetition of the pronoun suggests the attempted, but not completely realized, distancing of his personal memories. The "burning hills," the wasp, and the five cigarettes are not random details; their cumulative significance is to point to how difficult it is for him to achieve an attitude of "great love and great coldness." Yet this is how he must write in order to achieve a successful, because objective, recreation of his personal experiences. In this poem his "coldness," both emotional and tonal, is evident in the ending's unsentimental and deliberately monotoned voice "hunting for the lies that are obvious." In what sounds like a line from Cohen's *The Energy of Slaves* (but isn't), Ondaatje is indicating that, despite his attempts at objectivity, his poem may be a misrepresentation or lie. And if the lies to be sought out are the "obvious" ones, there is the disturbing implication that the "unobvious" lies will remain. In either case, the reader has been warned about the poem and the poet's limitations in getting "all the truth down."

Ondaatje's most radical gesture in the direction of indicating that there are times when "all the truth" cannot be stated, described, or reenacted is the final poem in *Rat Jelly*, "White Dwarfs." Here the poet

106

confronts not just the unconscious, or process or chaos, but events that in their total human significance seem to demand a response of awed silence. A variation on T.W. Adorno's "No poetry after Auschwitz,"[15] the poem is a profound meditation on both life and art. It is a tribute to those who have gone beyond "social fuel" and language:

This is for those people who disappear
for those who descend into the code
and make their room a fridge for Superman
—who exhaust costume and bones that could perform flight,
who shave their moral so raw
they can tear themselves through the eye of a needle
this is for those people
that hover and hover
and die in the ether peripheries (RJ, 70)

The key word here is "moral," which, although slightly ambiguous, does seem to be synonymous with life-meaning or mode of being. Those who "shave their moral... raw" live in a condition in which their character or self exists without a social persona, "where there is no social fuel"; consequently, they come in touch with the very ground of their being, which is here quite subtly associated with heaven ("through the eye of a needle").[16] Like Ondaatje's outlaws (Billy), alienated loners (Pat Garrett and Charlie Wilson), and sufferers (Philoctetes, his father), they are the ones who can provide a glimpse of what the terrifyingly brilliant poem about his father calls the "other worlds"[17] lying beyond either consciousness or social forms.

In "White Dwarfs" the speaker admires those people whose achievement or experience in patience or suffering is beyond him:

Why do I love most
among my heroes those
who sail to that perfect edge
where there is no social fuel
Release of sandbags
to understand their altitude—

that silence of the third cross
3rd man hung so high and lonely
we dont hear him say
say his pain, say his unbrotherhood

> What has he to do with the smell of ladies
> can they eat off his skeleton of pain? (*RJ*, 70)

Himself afraid of "no words   of / falling without words," he loves those whose language is an expressive and deafening silence: for them the experience and their expression of it are one. Silence is here a final poetry — like the earlier image of a scar — which cannot be improved upon by the poet's facility with words. This is a supreme fiction in which the dualities of nets and chaos, Wallace Stevens and King Kong, art and life, words and objects have been finally dissolved — but only at a price which the traditional poet cannot pay. Even as he suggests that poetry in such a context would be superfluous and perhaps blasphemous, he is nevertheless writing a poem. Like other poets who interrogate the validity of language — Rózewicz and Celan, for example — Ondaatje inevitably uses language to conduct that interrogation.[18] This dialectic of language and silence leads finally not to despair about poetry but to an affirmation. The confrontation with a reality which at first seemed resistant to the "nets" of verbal representation has not silenced the poet; rather it has provoked him into an even more ambitious poetry. In the final movement of the poem, he attempts to describe the unknown:

> And Dashiell Hammett in success
> suffered conversation and moved
> to the perfect white between the words
>
> This white that can grow
> is fridge, bed,
> is an egg — most beautiful
> when unbroken, where
> what we cannot see is growing
> in all the colours we cannot see
>
> there are those burned out stars
> who implode into silence
> after parading in the sky
> after such choreography what would they wish to speak of   anyway
> (*RJ*, 71)

The poem ends by pointing hauntingly to a beauty ("an egg") and a human profundity (the personified "star") which are beyond more explicit description and discussion. The tentative metaphoric gestures of

108

the poem are all that can be expected of poetry in such a situation. Yet Ondaatje's willingness to risk these inevitably anti-climactic lines ("after such choreography"), to explore "the perfect white between the words" and "the colours we cannot see," is a paradoxical attestation of his belief in poetry.

Ondaatje's work as a whole can be described as an attempt to make us aware of aspects of reality — surreal, oneiric, dynamic, chaotic — which we normally "cannot see" or perhaps do not want to see. Sheila Watson has written that Ondaatje "is as intelligent as Auden but less afraid of what living means."[19] To be unafraid of life involves a willingness to confront and, if one is an artist, to describe reality in its full tragic complexity. Ondaatje has done this, and his poems, among the most impressive of his generation, are the re-enactments of such confrontations with life and art.

1 " 'The gate in his head,' " in *Rat Jelly* (Toronto: Coach House Press, 1973), p. 62.

2 Compare, Michael Ondaatje, *Leonard Cohen* (Toronto: McClelland and Stewart, 1970), p. 36.

3 R.P. Blackmur, *Form and Value in Modern Poetry* (New York: Anchor, 1957), p. 256.

4 This kind of interrogation is also present in Ondaatje's most recent film, *The Clinton Special*, in which an actor speculates about the quality of Theatre Passe Muraille's interpretation of rural life. The scene was not in the original script of *The Farm Show*.

5 Compare the image of the hands to Margaret Atwood's "the green man": "They did not look / in his green pockets, where he kept / his hands changing their shape" (*The Animals in That Country* [Toronto: Oxford University Press, 1973], p. 13). See also the artist with "the murderer's bloodstained hands" in "Las Manos de Orlac" in Malcolm Lowry's *Under the Volcano*, Chapter One.

6 In "King Kong" the psychological implications are even clearer: "we renew him / capable in the zoo of night" only to murder or sacrifice him in the morning (*RJ*, 44).

7 This idea that the poem is never the whole truth also appears in two of the epigraphs used by Ondaatje in *The Dainty Monsters* and *Rat Jelly*, which warn the reader that the artist may be lying.

8 Billy describes the cobwebs in the barn as follows: "When I walked I avoided the cobwebs who had places to grow to, who had stories to finish. The flies caught in those acrobat nets were the only murder I saw" (17). For a slightly different use of webs and acrobats, see "We're at the graveyard" in *Rat Jelly*, (51).

9 For the line "the gate in his head" see "Day 20" in *One Eye Love* (Toronto: Coach House Press, 1967).

10 Compare this to Cohen's "A scar is what happens when the word is made flesh" (*The Favourite Game* [Toronto: McClelland and Stewart, 1970], p. 8).

11 Interview in *Rune*, No. 2 (Spring 1975), 50.

12 "Engagement," in *Noten zur Literatur III* (Frankfurt am Main: Suhrkamp Verlag, 1965), pp. 125–26.

13 For other rare examples of Ondaatje's use of more traditional images and symbols, see the apple in "Burning Hills" (*RJ*, 58), "the eye of a needle" in "White Dwarfs" (*RJ*, 71).

14 "Letters and Other Worlds," in *Rat Jelly*, pp. 24–26.

15 For a provocative discussion of this aspect of modernism, see Susan Sontag's "The Aesthetics of Silence" and "Bergman's Persona" in *Styles of Radical Will* (New York: Delta, 1970).

16 "Michael Ondaatje: The Mechanization of Death," *Open Letter*, Third Series, No. 1 (Winter 1974–75), 161.

Douglas Barbour
CONTROLLING THE JUNGLE:
A REVIEW OF *THE DAINTY MONSTERS*

This, in my opinion, is the finest first book of poems to appear since Margaret Avison's *Winter Sun*. Michael Ondaatje represents a healthy reaction in modern Canadian poetry. Although a completely contemporary writer, he eschews the "simple," almost barren, style of so many of the poets influenced by the Black Mountain group. He owes much of his originality to his background, I think. The exotic imagery which crowds the pages of this book appears to stem from his childhood memories of Ceylon. His poems are jungle-lush, but, unlike a jungle, they are cultivated and controlled. Their profuseness suggests a full and fertile mind always at work.

Imagery, in itself, is not enough, of course. Michael Ondaatje is also sensitive to poetic form, and he exercises a firm rhythmic control over his language. There is also, in his longer poems, his sense of plot, or story. In the poems of the second part of the book, he demonstrates a fine and subtle understanding of poetic narrative. This does not mean he longwindedly "tells the story." Rather, the story exists behind the poem, always present to focus the specific incident in a precisely imagined context. This suggestion of a story context often occurs in the shorter poems, too. In "The Moving to Griffin," for example, there is a gain in density from the implied context of the poet's life story.

Ondaatje's imagery is obsessively natural: the book is a kind of modern bestiary, with birds, predatory and domestic animals, and the beast, man, always present, always active. Images of birds, especially, occur again and again. Yet in the poem "Song to Alfred Hitchcock and Wilkinson," he does the unexpected, and the poem fairly leaps from the page as a result:

111

Flif flif flif flif very fast
is the noise the birds make
running over us.
A poet would say 'fluttering,'
or
'see-sawing with sun on their wings.'
But all it is
is flif flif flif flif very fast.

Although his poems are filled with images of violence and terror, his
love poems are able to stand against this vision. Life is seldom gentle in
these poems, but the love lyrics salvage and savour those moments of
deep gentleness which cannot last but must be accepted joyfully in their
passing. "The Diverse Causes," "She Carries a 'Fat Gold Watch,'"
"Christmas Poem 1965," "Four Eyes," as well as the poems of love
in the Troy Town section, all present the particular moments of communion with an intensity sufficient to command belief. We accept the
validity of such moments because the poems poignantly create that
validity. "The Diverse Causes" is my favourite:

Three clouds and a tree
reflect themselves on a toaster.
The kitchen window hangs scarred,
shattered by winter hunters.

We are in a cell of civilised magic.
Stravinsky roars at breakfast,
our milk is powdered.

Outside, a May god
moves his paws to alter wind
to scatter shadows of tree and cloud.
The minute birds walk confident
jostling the cold grass.
The world not yet of men.

We clean buckets of their sand
to fetch water in the morning,
reach for winter cobwebs,
sweep up moths who have forgotten to waken.
When the children sleep, angled
behind their bottles, you can hear mice prowl.
I turn a page
careful not to break the rhythms

112

of your sleeping head on my hip,
watch the moving under your eyelid
that turns like fire,
and we have love and the god outside
until ice starts to limp
in brown hidden waterfalls,
or my daughter burns the lake
by reflecting her red shoes in it.

Yet Ondaatje's poetry never dissolves into sentimentality. His sure control, and the precision of his vision won't allow that. The ironies of his animal poems, his use of tone, the mythic vision of the Troy Town poems, the sense of the power in others, of our inability to control or protect others, which comes through in " 'Lovely the Country of Peacocks,' " "The Inheritors," and "Come to the Desert," all preclude sentimentality. He is too tough-minded, too aware of the complexities of life, and his poetry offers no answers or escapes, as sentimentality always does.

"Troy Town," the second part of *The Dainty Monsters*, is concerned with myth and the creation of myth. This is a difficult term; but it should be sufficient to suggest that, in these poems, Ondaatje tells "stories" which engender responses of awe and admiration. The life of these poems is violent, for they deal with the permutations of human violence. He has used the well-known myths of Troy and Lilith for some of these poems, but he has also created new myths out of history, or, in "Peter," probably the finest poem in the collection, out of his own imagination. The poem on Egypt, and the Elizabeth poems, where the fabled queen enters an entirely new mythical life, are fascinating for their sense of the person. These are monologues, and, especially in "Elizabeth," he has achieved a high degree of dramatic realism. I have said that he has a clear imaginative understanding of violence, yet this violence never overwhelms the poet. The poetry is not voluptuous in its violence; it is chiseled and carefully wrought. The old idea of decorum applies perfectly to these poems. This is especially true of "Peter," where the poet deals with varieties of physical and mental violence in an almost virginally pure style and manner. The result is a tremendous gain in imaginative force over most modern treatments of the theme.

This is a beautiful book. It is this in both senses of the word, as a work of poet's craft and as a work of printer's craft.

113

Bert Almon
A BITTER ASPIC: A REVIEW OF *RAT JELLY*

The striking cover of this book promises an ambiguous feast: a detail from a stained glass window found in a nursery school has been reproduced in sumptuous color. It depicts an impish, even leering baker with platter of pies. The title printed by the man's image indicates that Ondaatje wants to shock:

> See the rat in the jelly
> steaming dirty hair
> frozen, bring it out on a glass tray
> split the pie four ways and eat
> I took great care cooking this treat for you

So the title poem begins. Another piece is called "Looking into *The Projector*," and it surely offers a hint about the author's intentions. *The Projector* is the brilliant cartoon-novel published by The Coach House Press, and it contains a series of horrifying images of death and transformation in a mechanized, sadistic culture. Ondaatje's poems offer similar images, and recurrent ones at that, as in the novel by Martin Vaughn-James.

I found the feast disappointing. Repeated images become merely repetitive more easily in poetry than in drawings, or at least they do in *Rat Jelly*. And a reader familiar with Ondaatje's other work will find some images (wounded or dead birds and animals especially) and allusions (the paintings of Henri Rousseau) too familiar. The campish poems about King Kong and the tributes to friends don't carry their

114

own weight either, and the frequent references to various American poets are puzzling rather than illuminating. Ondaatje has obviously tried to put together a book, not just a collection of poems: his division of *Rat Jelly* into sections, each with an epigraph and controlling theme, shows that, but the important poems — the ones exploring suffering and the creative process — are mixed in with light and occasional pieces. There are too many ingredients in the aspic.

I for one resist being shocked, even by a platter of rat pies. I feel suspicious of bloodshed and maimed animals as literary devices. "Heron Rex" is a fine poem marred by this ending:

> These small birds so precise
> frail as morning neon
> they are royalty melted down
> they are the glass core at the heart of kings
> yet 15 year old boys could enter the cage
> and break them in minutes
> as easily as a long fingernail

It's the *could* in these lines that disturbs me: as if real outrages aren't enough, Ondaatje creates hypothetical ones. The mutilation in this book can deaden emotional responses as easily as create them. (I should admit that I don't like Peckinpah pictures.)

There are strong poems in the collection, to be sure. When Ondaatje explores suffering through believable situations (or mythical ones, like "Philoctetes on the island") he is very moving. "Billboards" deals with the complexities of living with a wife who has been married before and has children from that marriage. "Letters and Other Worlds" considers an alcoholic and temperamental father and moves brilliantly from bitter comedy to the pathos of his solitary death. And some of the poems about writing should be mentioned: "Spider Blues" is a *tour de force* — poet as spider — and "Burning Hills" looks at the role of memory in creation. The last poem in the book, "White Dwarfs," asks the hardest questions. The best contemporary artists seem to move to the edge of silence, the edge of whiteness — the minimal work, or even no work at all. Think of Beckett. The silence, Ondaatje suggests, may have two sources: pain that leaves the artist mute, or insight that makes expression superfluous. Awareness of pain may lead the writer to care only for the "perfect white between the

115

words'' while awareness of a transcendent whiteness may turn him into a white dwarf, an imploded star with nothing to say. We should hope that this poet will remain more interested in words than in the perfect whiteness between them.

Stephen Scobie
THE LIES STAY IN: A REVIEW OF *THERE'S A TRICK WITH A KNIFE I'M LEARNING TO DO*

Only Ondaatje, people say, shaking their heads in knowing admiration, only Michael could have found the cover illustration. A woman stands against a wooden board, a target, with knives all round her; the words of the title also cluster around, she is their target too. "There's" thuds in at her right ear; "Knife" at her left shoulder. The knife-thrower has no arms; he uses his feet to hurl his weapons. He wears special socks that leave the toes bare, like fingerless gloves. It is the *left* foot he is using: like Billy the Kid, sinister, the left-handed gun.

The trick is to land the word in exactly the right place — and, since words are weapons, there is danger involved. Ondaatje's poems inhabit a world on the edge, the balanced knife-edge, the "perfect edge / where there is no social fuel," the edge Buddy Bolden falls over, the sharpened edge. The assertion that the poet / knife-thrower is only "learning" to do this trick is not a modest confession (not in the same sense as bp Nichol, for instance, professes his "apprenticeship" to language), but a dash of additional spice: the danger is greater for non-experts. ("Leave me, my dark AMATEUR!") The photograph was not taken in the circus ring, in performance, but out in a field among the caravans, in a practice session. A dress re-hearse-al rag, as Leonard Cohen would sing.

Only Ondaatje, they say, could have found this photograph, or the epigraph, from a magazine article on wine, which now prefaces the selections from *Rat Jelly*:

Deep colour and big, shaggy nose. Rather a jumbly, untidy sort of wine, with fruitiness shooting off one way, firmness another, and body

117

pushing about underneath. It will be as comfortable and comforting as the 1961 Nuits St George when it has pulled its ends in and settled down.

Just recently, Ondaatje sent his friends a magazine article on a large black Labrador which had attempted to make love to a postman. The taste for the bizarre, the delight in eccentricity, is tinged also with a possible cruelty; the edge of mockery at the wine critic's pretention is not entirely kindly, and the edge of the knives is, potentially, a literal metaphor. Like Peter, *l'enfant sauvage*, Ondaatje forms "violent beauty," and there is no room in his poem for Dr. Itard. Peter's tongue is cut out (by a trick with a knife) like the tongues of the Gurkhas' mules ("White Dwarfs"), but what would he wish to *speak* of, anyway? He says what he has to say, pouring out his "loathing" to which the poet of "War Machine" is content to "listen." Itard was not content merely to listen; he had things to speak of, anyway.

Ondaatje's first temptation is silence; the silence of exclusion ("3rd man hung so high and lonely"), the silence of spiders ("working black architects" intent on their "murderous art" — Ingmar Bergman used the spider as a metaphor for God), the silence of animals stopped short of speech or the silence of Dashiell Hammett retreating into its interstices, the silence into which the white dwarf stars "implode...after parading in the sky" (with Bolden blowing his mind in the midst of their parade). "Perhaps / wd like to live mute / all day long / not talk." Perhaps.

Or perhaps not. In "Letters & Other Worlds" (the greatest of Ondaatje's poems, I would argue, the greatest single poem in Canadian literature), a man moves out of silence, out of the frustrations of his jealousy in the face of "articulate emotion," and finds something to say which is not loathing:

> Letters in a clear hand of the most complete empathy
> his heart widening and widening and widening
> to all manner of change in his children and friends

How many people can accept that kind of change? It is in those we love that change is most difficult to accept, more difficult than change in jobs, in governments, in casual acquaintances. The tragedy of the character, and of the poem, is of course that he is unable to extend this

118

empathy the one last stage — to himself:

> while he himself edged
> into the terrible acute hatred
> of his own privacy
> till he balanced and fell

Ondaatje is fascinated, still, by that balance and by that fall. He catches the moments when the "new equilibrium" holds; moments that may only be as long as a camera's click, fixing the image of the turning wheels, "some blur on top... but sharp in the main... men walking are no trick" (with or without a knife). The photograph, for instance, which Victor Coleman sends from Gibson's, of a bird in flight:

> The beautiful formed things caught at the wrong moment
> so they are shapeless, awkward
> moving to the clear.

Always moving "to" the clear, never quite arriving: "not clarity but the sense of shift." Or, if necessary, moving *away* from the clear, falling, like John, into "the beautiful dark orgasm of his mouth." Does Ondaatje luxuriate too much in these images of violence? His father's ultimate falling is "without metaphor," but metaphor is Ondaatje's second temptation, his method of photograph, his way of fixing the equilibrium's precarious balance. His poetry is full of these images of suspended time, process stopped dead-or-alive, the privileged moments surrounded by flux — as in "Late Movies with Skyler," when "the perfect world" lasts as long as a movie (including commercials), after which he knows

> ...the heroes
> after skilled swordplay and moral victories
> leave with absolutely nothing
> to do for the rest of their lives.

Father and (step)son sit late watching movies: father and son, son and father, recur throughout the book about knives. "Letters & Other Worlds" was the first of the major poems about his family which continues through "Light" and the Coach House Manuscript Edition

119

"Claude Glass" into the currently in-progress "Running in the Family." These works confront directly the theme of the search-for-the-father which Billy the Kid displaced onto Pat Garrett, who killed him, and John Chisum, who hired Pat Garrett to kill him. The Oedipal implications are there for anyone to read, if you care for that kind of criticism. The psychological vulnerability of the poems would be almost embarrassing—if it were not for Ondaatje's deviousness ("devious" is one of his favourite words). The father in "Letters & Other Worlds" also "hides" in the room of his letters, just as Ondaatje hides the source of the poem's epigraph (Alfred Jarry, literalizing another image, dying in — without metaphor — the "ether peripheries"). At the end of "Burning Hills," Ondaatje surveys the process of his creation:

> He has written slowly and carefully
> with great love and great coldness.
> When he finishes he will go back
> hunting for the lies that are obvious.

The lies that are not obvious presumably stay in: are they then evidence of the coldness, or of the love?

Douglas Barbour
ALL THAT POETRY SHOULD BE: A REVIEW OF
THERE'S A TRICK WITH A KNIFE I'M LEARNING TO DO

In a game of match the title to the author, no one familiar with contemporary poetry in Canada would have difficulty identifying *There's a Trick with a Knife I'm Learning to Do* as a Michael Ondaatje title. Subtitled ''Poems 1963–1978,'' the new book offers generous selections from *The Dainty Monsters* and *Rat Jelly* plus nineteen new poems in the section ''Pig Glass (1973–78).'' In making this gathering, Ondaatje has made a careful culling of his early poems, especially those in *The Dainty Monsters*, of which he has kept only nineteen; of *Rat Jelly*, on the other hand, he has retained twenty-six.

What he has omitted: a number of animal poems (though I would still like to see the delightful and ironic ''Song to Alfred Hitchcock and Wilkinson''; but no choice can satisfy every reader); many of the historical and mythical poems, like ''Pyramid,'' ''Prometheus, with Wings,'' ''Lilith'' and ''Paris,'' which might be read as too dependent upon a dictionary of mythology. He has kept poems which have what Frank Davey calls ''kinetic mythology,'' a mythic tone emerging out of the perceived events of life rather than imported via old stories. There is the long poem, ''Peter,'' the major piece in *The Dainty Monsters*. Although its structure, the shifts of violence, sexuality, power and art, remind one of old myths and legends, its psychological and emotional narrative is rooted in the perceived world and emerges naturally from the interactions of the characters with their environment and each other.

Other poems point to the directions Ondaatje's poetry has taken in *Rat Jelly* and elsewhere. Rather than domesticate mythology, he mythologizes domesticity in poems which speak to and from the world

121

of family and friends. Events from the ordinary life of the poet are charged with the perceptions of mythic thought thus bringing the power of myth closer to home as in the superb and slightly frightening spring ritual of "The Diverse Causes." As well, he writes about certain Romantic figures, who achieve a kind of iconographic presence in his imagination, like Henri Rousseau, who returns again and again in his work.

Rat Jelly saw a great advance in Ondaatje's poetic, and it's appropriate that more poems from that book appear in *Trick with a Knife*. Domestic mythology is continued and extended in the poems which now head that section. The temporal and genetic connections to past and future, especially through parents and children, enter these poems in more complex ways. As well, there is a series of poems which explore the springs of art and the simultaneous existence of self-destructive impulses with the need to create. Some of his finest poems turn about the figure of the "landscape suicide," the artist who moves to silence, "to the perfect white between the words," and often to the "new equilibrium" which is ultimate silence — death. These figures — his father in "Letters & Other Worlds," Dashiell Hammett in "White Dwarfs" — are heroic in their isolation alone in a dark glory, and they are an obvious temptation, as is Buddy Bolden, the protagonist of Ondaatje's *Coming Through Slaughter*. Yet it's in "White Dwarfs" that the poet confesses his "fear / of no words of / falling without words," so he finally acknowledges but does not choose that white silence. His need is to write, to communicate not just with the others who may read him but with whatever "other" chaos his mind-net pours onto the page.

"A blind lover, dont know / what I love till I write it out," he says, and then:

> And that is all this writing should be then.
> The beautiful formed things caught at the wrong moment,
> so they are shapeless, awkward
> moving to the clear.

Thus, if it's obvious, and many critics have commented on it at length, that one of Ondaatje's major literary obsessions has been those figures who have violently and often self-destructively engaged the chaotic world of the senses, from the mute sculptor Peter through

122

suicidal Heron Rex to the heroes who choose to implode into silence like the dark stars of the poem which honours them, the choice of poem in *Trick with a Knife* reveals another and equally powerful obsession — the need to "deviously [think] out plots / across the character of his friends." This is perhaps best imaged in the delicate yet tough recognition of communion among "Stuart Sally Kim and I / watching still stars" in "We're at the graveyard," a poem I now see as central in Ondaatje's work. Beneath those distant stars, their "clear charts, / the systems" intricate branches, "are the friends / whose minds and bodies / shift like acrobats to each other." That shift with all its implications about community / communication / communion, is the emerging theme of Ondaatje's work, the most important strand in his web of language. And the new poems, with their increased insistence on the necessary complex intimacy with family and friends, show that the earlier poems have been selected with this theme in mind.

The poems of "Pig Glass" range far and wide, travelling the world with the poet, and moving back and forward in time with his seeking mind and heart. Yet such a delicate lyric as "Farre Off" reveals how far Ondaatje has outstripped the kind of historical writing he has left out of "The Dainty Monsters" section. Here the poet, fully here with his dogs in the pasture now, still connects with the past a quick poet wrote; he looks "out into the dark pasture / past where even the moonlight stops" but his "eyes are against the ink of Campion."

But the underlying theme of community appears in the various gently comic poems about his and his friends' ordinary / extraordinary lives. The generosity of spirit that moves through poems like "Walking to Bellrock," "Late Movies with Skyler" and, with difficult pain, "Pure Memory / Chris Dewdney" is large, and it lights up the surrounding landscape with all its figures in a ground. Mind you, part of the excitement in these poems is generated by the tension that develops out of an awareness of the difficult tenuousness of and the hope in the connections they honour. "Stan and I laughing joking going summer crazy / as we lived against each other," he says, that harsh preposition precisely underlining how difficult the connections are. Yet there is real love, right alongside the concomitant fear of losing touch.

These are not the only poems, or poetic concerns, of course. The poems from Ceylon are full of perception, love of the world and occasional rich humour. There is a greater depth of recognition of the com-

123

plexly human in everything we see and remember in these poems than Ondaatje has been able to sustain, at this intensity of vision, for more than a poem's length previously. "Pig Glass" is immensely rich in its almost geological emotional perception of the things which are. And his conclusion, the brilliant "Light," dedicated to his mother, gathers the themes of family history, communion and connection he has been exploring into a rich, dark tapestry as "complex ambiguous grainy" as the photographs which impel the poem. Like bp Nichol, Ondaatje sees in these poems that history as he *knows* it is "his story," a story without clear beginning or end. In the flux of time and friends, he finds all there is and that is both awe-full and joyful, or so I read the mood of the poems.

All of which means that *There's a Trick with a Knife I'm Learning to Do* is a beautiful, major collection of poems. The trick is to cut right to the bone and leave no obvious scar. But make sure the cut remains, raw and necessary as skin. Ondaatje is not just learning the trick; in his best poems he shows he is an accomplished practitioner of the art.

Sam Solecki
COMING THROUGH: A REVIEW OF *SECULAR LOVE*

Although we don't usually think of it this way, poetry like life has its historically significant dates: 1798, the first *Lyrical Ballads*, 1857, *Les Fleurs du Mal*, and 1922, *The Waste Land* are for us not just dates of publication but also demarcation points indicating that after that particular moment our conception of poetry changed and our view of human sensibility subtly altered. In our own time perhaps the most significant year for many was 1959 which saw the appearance of Robert Lowell's *Life Studies*, a sequence of intensely personal poems and prose pieces dealing with Lowell's family background and his own life. Disconcertingly, even shockingly frank, the volume reveals a poet stripped of most of his defences and willingly describing the most intimate details of his life. In a later volume, savagely reviewed by Adrienne Rich, Lowell would even include parts of his estranged wife's letters in his sonnets. If Lowell inaugurated an era of what later came to be called confessional poetry, his book set a daunting standard in style and quality of experience that would be unmatched by most of his imitators. After 1959 anyone writing about the self would do so in the shadow of Lowell's intimidating example.

Because of his emphasis on his emotional and psychological problems — the whole sad history is described in detail in Ian Hamilton's recent biography — confessional came to be defined as synonymous with extreme states of being, and the most authentic poems and poetic careers were seen as those in which poetry and life most closely coincided. James Fenton's "Letter to John Fuller," while mocking Al Alvarez's celebration of this school, notes some of its essential assumptions:

[He] tell[s] you, in the sombrest notes
If poets want to get their oats
The first step is to slit their throats.
    The way to divide
The sheep of poetry from the goats
    Is suicide.
Hardy and Hopkins hacked off their honkers.
Auden took laudanum in Yonkers.
Yeats ate a fatal plate of conkers;
    On Margate sands
Eliot was found stark staring bonkers
    Slashing his hands.

Although Lowell died of a heart attack in the back seat of a taxi, Sylvia Plath, Anne Sexton (both sometime students of his) and John Berryman all committed suicide. Just as Mark Rothko's suicide alters our conception of the Rothko chapel in Houston, completed just before his death, the deaths of the three poets seem, in retrospect, to offer an inevitable climax authenticating the claims of the poems. The breakdowns and suicides prod literary criticism into pathology.

On the basis of Michael Ondaatje's first seven books few readers would claim that he has much in common with Lowell or confessional writing in general. If anything most of his work stands opposed to the constitutive assumptions of that poetry, although *Coming Through Slaughter*, his novel about a jazz cornetist whose obsessive art leads to silence and madness, and the crucial lyrics ''Letter and Other Worlds'' and ''White Dwarfs'' certainly reveal a compulsive fascination with an intensely subjective and directly expressive art. The speaker in most of the lyrics seems to be Ondaatje but he's rarely interested in enacting or describing his darkest and most problematic emotions and situations: the voice is too laconic, the tone too detached and the attitude to the self is ironic, even self-mocking. Often we sense, however, that the artifice and control not only shape and present the material at hand but also hint at repressed or displaced experiences and aspects of the self the writer is unwilling or unable to deal with. Ondaatje's suicidal herons and artists, his fascination with the jungle, the various hints at autobiography in *The Collected Works of Billy the Kid* and *Coming Through Slaughter*—both studies in pathological creativity—all point to personal events underlying the work. The publication in 1982 of the frankly autobiographical if often fictional *Running in the Family* seemed to

126

confirm the impression that Ondaatje's work had, over the past decade, been moving towards a more direct engagement with his intimate experiences and memories. In a manner of speaking *Running in the Family* is Ondaatje's equivalent of the early family oriented sections of *Life Studies*; *Secular Love* is the ruthless and unembarrassed engagement with the self.

The book is made up of four chronologically arranged sequences telling the story of the break-up of a marriage and a way of life, the poet's own near-breakdown and finally, after what one section calls "Rock Bottom," his recovery and return through the love of another woman. The book should be read as a seamless poetic journal rather than as a collection of discrete lyrics. Some of the poems, like the lovingly nuanced and mutedly elegiac "To a Sad Daughter," can be read by themselves yet the volume is so closely organized with so much of the overall emotional and artistic effect depending on repetitions and echoes of sound, image, situation and emotion that the poems often seem more like the chapters of a novel than parts of a collection. (Another equally significant context is provided by Ondaatje's earlier work, and sections of *Secular Love* often seem like rewritings of earlier texts.)

The opening epigraph from Peter Handke's *The Left-Handed Woman* simultaneously warns us about the unexpected stylistic and experiential openness, even rawness of *Secular Love* and offers an implied judgment on Ondaatje's earlier work:

> "Your trouble, I believe, is that you always hold back something of yourself. You're not shameless enough for an actor. In my opinion you should learn how to run properly and scream properly, with your mouth wide open. I've noticed that even when you yawn you're afraid to open your mouth all the way."

In poetry, as in any art, holding back or opening up is obviously a matter of degree as well as of technique; by holding back the clutter of irrelevant detail and by compressing events and characters the writer can often create a greater impression of self-exposure and openness. *Secular Love* shows a writer who has found a style and a form that allow openness without sacrificing the economy and selectivity necessary for art. A crucial aspect of that style is Ondaatje's delicate management of what I call the book's two voices or points of view: the first is that of Ondaatje the character in the story; the second of Ondaatje the poet and creative voyeur who watches his own life, reflects and recreates it as art. This is the slightly guilty voice of the man who observes life even as he lives it, always in the hope of turning "these giant scratches / of pain: into art"; who when he writes that "I fear / how anything can grow from this" knows that in addition to the growing suffering and pain there is also the potential poem. This is the voice that knows that for the poet "Il faut que tu te voies mourir / Pour savoir que tu vis encore" (Paul Eluard). Although at one point we read that "There are those who are in / and there are those who look in" we know that this doesn't apply to Ondaatje—he's both.

The opening section is pervaded by images of merging, drowning, darkness, disappearance and drunkenness. This is the book's dark night of the soul, the son's rewriting in personal terms of the father's breakdown in "Letters and Other Worlds" and *Running in the Family*. At once, it's an apology, an *hommage* and the beginning of another story in which the central character—described here only as "he"—is shown at a party on a farm, surrounded by family and friends, and inexplicably but inexorably drinking himself into oblivion. A disturbing point of departure for the love story to follow, it sketches in a suggestive emotional landscape of unfocussed discontent and undefined anxiety and pain leaving the reader wondering why the central figure feels like an intruder, drinks so heavily and longs for the darkness of the surrounding fields. The answers can be inferred from some of the details available later in the book: a marriage and a family are breaking up.

> In the midst of love for you
> my wife's suffering
> anger in every direction
> and the children wise
> as tough shrubs
> but they are not tough
> —so I fear
> how anything can grow from this

Without self-pity, simplification or sentimentality *Secular Love* follows the course of the one story and one story only of our time. It's a sign of Ondaatje's integrity as an artist (and as a human being) that he registers the impact of the break-up on everyone. The transitional lyric just quoted places the love affair within the full and necessary context reminding us of a suffering other than the speaker's. And even in the final affirmative, celebratory section, "Skin Boat," images and words repeated from earlier poems recall what has been lived through. The gentle, genial "Pacific Letter" celebrates friendship—and by the way shows Ondaatje's ability to deal with the domestic emotions of the middle range—but recalls that "After separation had come to its worst / we met and travelled the Mazinaw with my sons / through all the thirty-six folds of that creature river / into the valley of bright lichen." The beautifully poignant "To My Sad Daughter" (which will bring to tears all fathers with teenage daughters) offers advice about getting through while letting the images of swimming and drowning and "cuts and wounds" recall the earlier darker experiences against which the poem must be read. Telling his daughter that "If you break / break going out not in" Ondaatje takes us back not only to the earlier lyrics but also to "White Dwarfs," a poem of the early 1970s about "imploding" as well as to *Coming Through Slaughter* whose hero "broke into" silence and madness. The book closes, although one aspect of the story is just beginning, with a tender prose piece in which a man and woman walk in and along a shallow creek in a scene recalled by him at night as he lies next to her. Walking he loses his balance, falls in, recovers and surfaces looking for her:

> He stands very still and cold in the shadow of long trees. He has
> gone far enough to look for a bridge and has not found it. Turns
> upriver. He holds onto the cedar root the way he holds her forearm.

The entire section has a quiet inevitability after the perfervid panic of much of the book, a panic recalled in the slip into the cold water. Similarly the merging of "the cedar root" and "her forearm" reminds us why in his day-to-day life he no longer feels that he is drowning, why, in D.H. Lawrence's words, he has come through. Begun in darkness, drowning and panic, the unfinished story ends with light, surfacing and tenderness.

I began with Robert Lowell partly because it seemed to me that one of the creative problems Ondaatje faced in writing *Secular Love*—note the adjective, by the way, semantically allied with profane, phonetically with sacred—was how to stay out of the shadow of confessional poetry as well as how to be "open" without simply committing himself to nothing more than a loosely prosaic poetry dealing with intensely sub-

129

jective extreme states of being. He certainly points in that direction by telling us that "This last year I was sure / I was going to die," or, referring to another poet's suicide, that

> ...one is able now
> in ideal situations
> to plot a stroll
> to new continents
> "doing the Berryman walk"

His problem was how to transform an intensely subjective set of experiences into an artistic whole while avoiding, on the one hand, excessive subjectivity, solipsistic self-dramatization, and sentimentality — "These are *my* feelings and therefore they're important" —or, on the other, losing the full texture of emotional immediacy through a too impersonal and objective artistry. Ondaatje solves the problem, in part, by beginning the book with a sequence narrated in the third person and following it with one shifting among "I," "you," and the implicating "we." Several poems even omit the subject leaving us with the impression of a pure, unmediated if anonymous voice. Similarly by omitting the names of the main characters Ondaatje generalizes the potential significance of the events so that what we read becomes something more than simply a chronological account of a particular set of experiences involving a specific group of people. The sources of the story may be as obviously autobiographical as those of Lawrence's *Look! We Have Come Through!* but the end result is a work of consummate poetry enacting a life and love story transcending the individuals originally involved in it.

It's worth recalling that Bertrand Russell's response to Lawrence's poetic sequence about his love for Frieda was along the lines of, so they've come through but why should we care? The answer is obvious: because Lawrence transformed his love affair with Frieda into art it has become ours. As well, we no longer read it simply for the tale but also in order to linger over the telling, the sheer artistry of the thing. This is also why we *reread* it. The same is true of *Secular Love*, a book rich in human experience, carefully structured and beautifully crafted. Almost every page shows evidence of Ondaatje's brilliant visual imagination and his auditory sensitivity to the musical possibilities of free verse. Consider the following fragments:

130

At certain hours of the night
ducks are nothing but landscape
just voices breaking as they nightmare.
The weasel wears their blood
home like a scarf,
cows drain over the horizon
                and the dark
vegetables hum onward underground
but the mouth
      wants plum.

. . .

We know their type of course, local heroes
who take off their bandanas and leap naked,
night green, seduced
by the whispers of michelin.

. . .

sleeping like the rumour of pearl
in the embrace of oyster.

. . .

a flute
from the throat
of a loon

. . .

and most of all
         this
small bamboo pipe
not quite horizontal
that drips
every ten seconds
to a shallow bowl

A series of small but inimitable gestures that evoke reflective smiles and appreciative nods: "nightmare" used surprisingly as a verb; a casual surrealism recalling Mark Strand, "cows drain over the horizon"; the Getz-like sussuration of "whispers of michelin"; and the almost Oriental sculptural sense of form as something organic developing out of the relationships not only between words ("flute" / "throat" / "loon" or "small bamboo pipe" / "drips" / "seconds" / "shallow bowl") but also between the protracting and pregnant silences of white spaces.

Few do it better.

The Longer Works

* Nora/~~c~~came home to find a man [~~named Webb~~] sitting on her step, ~~smoking~~
~~and breathing into his raincoat.~~ Immaculate and ~~in shoes so black you could~~
~~almost see red in them. He said he wanted to get in touch with Bolden.~~
"He's gone, look for him somewhere else"

"Who was he last seen with"

"~~I don't know~~"
He ~~grabs~~ her by the front of the blouse.

"~~Who~~" "Tell me."

"~~What the hell are you....He play~~ed with someone called Crawley, another cornet
player, 6 months ago. That was about 70 miles north of here, ~~in Baton Rouge~~"

"~~Listen, this is very important or to me what else~~"

          Has covered her against the wood wall, leaning very close to her,
like a lover.

"He won't last ~~Mix~~ long (Nora) by himself, he's going to explode. ~~if he hasn't~~
~~got some continuity. He's left the shop, you, the cricket, everything.~~ He's
~~loose. He needs~~ ~~discipline~~"

"~~Thanks~~"

"~~No you~~ I used to ~~know~~ him before he came here. ~~Now where can I~~
~~find Crawley.~~ I don't have very long,"

          ~~She tells him~~ and Webb ~~smiles and lets her go.~~

"Buddy has gone crazy and I don't know what he's up to."He didnt say anything."

"~~Are you~~ ~~gone~~"

          A long silence then.

"No"

"~~Good.~~"

Sam Solecki
POINT BLANK:
NARRATIVE IN *the man with seven toes*

In view of the acclaim and the attention received by Michael Ondaatje's
The Collected Works of Billy the Kid (1970) and *Coming Through
Slaughter* (1976) it is inevitable that his first book-length work, *the man
with seven toes* (1969) is often overlooked in most discussions either of
his work or of contemporary Canadian writing. This is unfortunate
because this long sequence of poems is a complex work, interesting in
its own right, and a pivotal book in Ondaatje's development. It is with
the man with seven toes that we first see him moving toward the longer
and more experimental forms that will become characteristic in his two
major works. And although *the man with seven toes* does not go as far as
they do in the direction of a temporally discontinuous form, nevertheless, aspects of its style and structure clearly anticipate the later
developments. The shift toward the longer forms that is first seen with
the man with seven toes is of particular importance in Ondaatje's development as a writer because not only are his longer works more experimental than his lyrics but it is in them that we find a style and form fully expressive of his vision. This is not to denigrate his very fine lyrics
but only to emphasize that he seems to need the longer form or structure in order to create a world embodying and expressing his vision.
    The final section in Ondaatje's first book, *The Dainty Monsters*
(1967), showed him to be interested in writing a longer poem but
neither of its two medium-length sequences, "Paris" and "Peter"
captures, in form or content, what I take to be Ondaatje's unique way
of looking at reality which is already there in some of the earlier lyrics in
the collection — "Dragon," "The Republic," "Henri Rousseau and
Friends," and "In Another Fashion." There is a sense in these early

135

lyrics that material and psychological reality is fundamentally random or in a state of flux, and that poetry should communicate this particular quality of reality without, however, succumbing to either formalism or formlessness. These poems explore the borderline between form and formlessness, civilization and nature, the human and the natural, and the conscious reasoning mind and the unconscious world of instinct. They compel the reader to enter into and experience the mode of being associated with the second of the paired terms. But they do so primarily on the level of content by means of contrasted actions, settings or images. In *the man with seven toes*, on the other hand, it is the form as well as the content that pushes the reader into the unfamiliar ground of the work to the point that his reading of the sections of the text becomes roughly analagous to what is happening in the story, the heroine's harrowing journey through a wilderness. Beginning with this book Ondaatje turns to a variant of what Barthes terms a *"scriptible"* [1] (as opposed to a *"lisible"*) text, one that demands the reader's active participation as an interpreter of a reality that is often not only ambiguous but even chaotic.

To achieve this Ondaatje attempts to "make new" both the form and content of his work so that neither will predispose the reader towards a preconceived approach to the text. I mention both form and content because at the same time that Ondaatje is creating a new form that will eventually develop into the radically discontinuous forms of his two later works, his choice of subject in *the man with seven toes* foreshadows as well the kinds of characters and themes to be dealt with in his later work. Where the medium-length narrative poems in his first book, *The Dainty Monsters*, had dealt with figures drawn from classical mythology ("Paris") or who felt as if they belonged in classical myth ("Peter"), *the man with seven toes* is based on the experiences of a semi-legendary English-woman who, like Billy the Kid and Buddy Bolden, existed on the edge of history and about whose experiences there are contradictory accounts. [2] The life story of each of these characters provides Ondaatje with a ready-made but incomplete and ambiguous narrative straddling the border between fact and fiction, history and legend or myth. *The man with seven toes* shows Ondaatje turning towards myths or mythic poems based on materials not usually associated with traditional myths but rather on what we normally refer to as legends. Ondaatje's definition of myth will seem idiosyncratic to anyone nurtured on *Fables of Identity* but there is a consistency in his various references to the subject in his poems, prose works, critical writings and films. For him, a myth is any powerful story with an archetypal or universal significance; but in order for the story to become truly mythic, to have what in the article on *Tay John* he calls "the raw power of myth," it must be represented in such a way that "the original myth [story] is given to us point blank."[3] What he means is that the reader must be exposed to as direct and unmediated a representation or, better, re-enactment of the original event as art will allow; he must become or feel that he has become a participant in it, a figure in the ground of the story.

In *the man with seven toes*, for example, the reader enters the nightmarelike world of an anonymous white woman who spends a period of time living with a group of primitives before being rescued by a white man and taken back to civilization. A brief note at the end of the book indicates that the source of Ondaatje's story lies in the experiences of a Mrs. Fraser who, in 1836, was shipwrecked off the Queensland coast of Australia, captured by aborigines, and finally rescued by a convict named Bracefell whom she betrayed once they reached civilization. Ondaatje told me that this version of the story as summarized by Colin MacInnes and painted by Sidney Nolan in his Mrs. Fraser series (1947–1957) is the only account with which he was familiar at the time of the writing of his poem.[4] In his hands the story becomes a mythic exploration, in the form of related brief and often imagistic poems, of how an unnamed white woman perceives and experiences a primitive and anarchic world totally alien to her civilized assumptions and mode of being. Like Margaret Atwood's Susanna Moodie she is compelled into a confrontation in which she must acknowledge violent and primitive aspects of life within and outside herself which she had previously either not known or ignored. This basic opposition between aspects of self, and self and land from which many of the poem's other antitheses develop is also central to Nolan's version. His first painting shows Mrs. Fraser naked and crawling on all fours with her white body placed against a setting of green jungle and blue sky; her face is covered by lank black hair, and her limbs are slightly distorted, indistinct, already on the point of becoming subtly dehumanized.[5] Both the lack of clothing and the absence of identity remove her from civilization; the effect is rather like the first collage in Atwood's *Journals* where Susanna Moodie seems to be drifting down into the middle of the forest: the human being and the landscape are contiguous but there is no connection between them.[6]

Both Ondaatje and Nolan — and later Patrick White in *A Fringe of Leaves* — use Mrs. Fraser as the basis of a myth. In Nolan's series she becomes an Australian version of Atwood's Susanna Moodie, gradually developing from a situation in which she is alienated from the land to the point where she is one with it, and can be represented as an aboriginal rock painting. In contrast to Nolan, Ondaatje universalizes the meaning of her experiences by creating her in the image of an anonymous white woman. He further creates the potential for her development as an archetypal or mythic figure by moving the story from the Australian historical context in which he found it to an unspecified time and place. The overall effect of these changes is to focus attention on the story's essential content, the effect upon an individual of her confrontation with a totally alien landscape and mode of being.

But this story with a potentially archetypal dimension cannot become mythic, in Ondaatje's sense of the word, unless expressed in a form and style that make the reading of the story as unmediated a confrontation with the events as is possible. To achieve this Ondaatje relies on a form made up of brief self-contained, often cinematic, lyrics each of which explodes upon the reader with a single startling revelation. To read from one to the next as the woman moves from experience to experience is to encounter a series of sensory and emotional shocks until, finally, like the character herself, the reader is numbed into accepting this surreal world as real.[7] Ondaatje has described the book's form as similar to "a kind of necklace in which each bead-poem while being related to the others on the string, was, nevertheless, self-sufficient, independent."[8] The continuity is implied rather than made explicit, and the terse almost imagistic poems are related by means of various kinds of montage (tonal, intellectual etc.) or juxtaposition as well as through the echoing of images from poem to poem. This kind of "bonding" (Hopkins' term) of essentially separate lyrics by means of recurring images is important to Ondaatje particularly as it relates to myth and mythic poems. He has written that "myth is. . . achieved by a very careful use of echoes — of phrases and images. There may be no logical connection when these are placed side by side but the variations are always there setting up parallels."[9] In *the man with seven toes*, for example, the woman is raped both by the natives and by the convict (32); she is "tongued" by the natives (14), Potter's fingers are "chipped tongues" (21); and he bends his "tongue down her throat / drink her throat sweat, like coconut" (35); the natives tear a fox open with their hands (16), Potter "crept up and bit open / the hot vein of a sleeping wolf" (29); the natives have "maps on the soles of their feet"(13), and at the book's end the woman lies on a bed "sensing herself like a map" (41). Ondaatje does not amplify his point to indicate how such echoes and parallels achieve a sense of the mythic but one of their effects is to create a common ground or structure—even the possiblity of an unsuspected metaphysical order—underlying the separate lyrics. Contrasts and comparisons are established between individual characters, events and settings otherwise related only on the basis of a tenuous narrative line. But the structure remains deliberately indefinite and avoids becoming a constricting grid, just as the repeated images themselves stop short of shifting into a symbolic mode of meaning. It is almost as if Ondaatje is playing with the reader, undercutting his conventional notions about structure and symbolism. Most readers, for example, assume that an image, repeated often enough in a variety of contexts, will, at some point, shift in function and meaning from being simply an image to assume the status of a symbol. This is precisely the kind of expectation Ondaatje creates only in order to deny. Disoriented, the reader is compelled to reexamine the nature of his relationship to the text and to move more tentatively through it. This is as true of the individual lyrics as it is of the work as a whole.

A closer reading through the text will illustrate more clearly some of the general points I have been making. The book opens with the following lyric.

The train hummed like a low bird
over the rails, through
desert and pale scrub,
air spun in the carriages.

She moved to the doorless steps
where wind could beat her knees.
When they stopped for water she got off
sat by the rails on the wrist thick stones.

The train shuddered, then wheeled away from her.

She was too tired even to call.
Though, come back, she murmured to herself. (9)

Ondaatje's words describing the structure of Leonard Cohen's *The Favourite Game* also apply here: this is "a potent and enigmatic sketch rather than a full blown detailed narrative." The opening lyric has a haunting and disturbing quality because it is so brief, because so much is left unexplained. As in one of Alex Colville's enigmatic and dream-like paintings there is no explanation of why the train leaves the woman behind nor why she is too tired to call. The situation is disturbing precisely because it occurs without an overall explanatory context to give it some kind of causal perspective. The character and the scene are isolated in space — "desert and pale scrub" — and time. The reader knowing nothing about the scene's past can make no valid conjectures about the future. By itself, and then in relation to the next lyric, this poem establishes how Ondaatje wants *the man with seven toes* to be read.

Each poem in the sequence presents a new scene or a new experience with the effect that the reader follows the woman's path, and often point of view, as she moves from one shocking and inevitably defamiliarizing experience to another. The events of each new poem are literally unexpected because Ondaatje's structuring has increased the number of narrative possibilities that each lyric creates, to the point that the reader simply does not know what to expect from poem to poem. The very form of each lyric works deliberately against a predictable narrative continuity with the effect that each poem stands out separately as a complete scene. Ondaatje has written that myth is "brief, imagistic"[11] and this certainly applies to his own poem. The revelations in *the man with seven toes* come in brief and enigmatic flashes which disappear and are then replaced by new ones; the effect is rather like that of a film in which the director cuts quickly and dynamically from scene to scene allowing the various kinds of montage to create the meaning. The second poem, for example, begins with a dog sitting beside her, the third with her entry into a native clearing. There is no temporal, spatial or syntactical continuity indicated between these opening lyrics.

Entered the clearing and they turned
faces scarred with decoration
feathers, bones, paint from clay
pasted, skewered to their skin.

Fanatically thin,
black ropes of muscle. (11)

A sense of immediacy is created by the elliptical syntax of the opening line. Because the terse poem begins with the verb — "entered" — the reader's attention is focussed on the action itself. The ellipsis of the subject — either "I" or "she" — achieves an abruptness and shocking directness which would have otherwise been lacking. The effect is then reinforced by the brief catalogue of images, one piled upon the other, exotic to both character and reader. The cumulative effect of the rhetoric is to indicate the disorientation of the woman and to achieve that of the reader.

The woman has entered a physical and psychological landscape or wilderness her reaction to which is caught in the violently beautiful imagery and dismembered rhythms of successive lyrics.

Goats   black goats, balls bushed in the centre
cocks rising like birds flying to you   reeling on you
and smiles smiles as they ruffle you open
spill you down, jump and spill over you
white leaping like fountains in your hair
your head and mouth till it dries
and tightens your face like a scar
Then up to cook a fox or whatever, or goats
goats eating goats heaving the bodies
open like purple cunts under ribs, then tear
like to you a knife down their pit, a hand in the warm
the hot the dark boiling belly and rip
open and blood spraying out like dynamite
caught in the children's mouths on the ground
laughing collecting it in their hands
or off to a pan, holding blood like gold
and the men rip flesh tearing, the muscles
nerves green and red still jumping
stringing them out, like you (16)

The syntax, imagery and rhythm — the entire whirling movement of the verse — re-enact her complex response to an experience which prior to leaving the train she could not even have imagined. Her confusion is registered in her simultaneously positive and negative responses to her rape. There is a moving lyricism in the natural vitality of the men's

141

"cocks rising like birds flying to you" and in the description of their ejaculations as "white leaping like fountains in your hair." But the "fountains" suddenly dry on her "face like a scar" and the subsequent similes serve to reinforce the hinted at connection between her violation and the killing and ripping open of an animal. The cuts in the animal are "like purple cunts," the knife pushed into the animal is also the phallus forced into her, and the bleeding animal body is also hers — "like you." This kind of comparison allows her to dramatize her emotions by making them part of a response to an event outside of herself — the killing of "a fox or whatever, or goats." It is almost as if she cannot articulate directly the personal violation that took place; only through her empathic response to the animal's suffering can she describe her own experience. And her recourse to similes, here and in other poems written from her point of view, is an indication of an analogous attempt to appropriate in slightly more familiar images a primal landscape and a set of experiences she finds almost indescribable. A later poem, for example, begins as follows:

> Evening. Sky was a wrecked black boot
> a white world spilling through.
> Noise like electricity in the leaves. (32)

The metaphor ("wrecked black boot") and simile ("like electricity") are imported from the world of civilization in order to render this wilderness slightly more comprehensible, to mediate between its natural language, so to speak, and the character's mode of comprehending and describing the world. But even as these more familiar images achieve the effect of mediating between the two worlds the sense of incongruity caused by their anomalous presence serves, paradoxically, to heighten our awareness of the distance between the two.

The woman's return to the world in which these words are appropriate begins with her rescue by the convict Potter whose striped shirt, in Ondaatje as in Nolan (see the paintings "Escaped Convict," and "In the Cave"), indicates his connection, however tenuous, with civilization.[12] He rescues her from the natives — never referred to as aborigines — but not from the violent existence she had led with them. All the expectations justifiably created by the rescue are immediately thwarted.

Stripe arm caught my dress
the shirt wheeling into me
gouging me, ankles manacles,
cock like an ostrich, mouth
a salamander
thrashing in my throat.
Above us, birds peeing from the branches (32)

Unexpectedly, for both reader and character, the rescue recapitulates
the events of the period of capture. Her rape by the natives is a prelude
to this one, and the imagery indicates that Ondaatje wants the two
scenes compared: the natives had "cocks like birds," Potter's "cock
[is] like an ostrich"; the natives had previously been compared to
"sticklebacks" while Potter's mouth is "a salamander." Potter has
replaced the natives as her keeper but the nightmare quality of her
journey through a physical and psychological chaos has not changed.
Her rape, for example, is simultaneously violent, terrifying and
ridiculous. The "birds peeing from the branches" put it into a grotesque perspective. Our standard shocked response to the event is suddenly qualified by a new and unanticipated context created by the absurd last line. Yet in this poem as in so much of Ondaatje's poetry the
unexpected, the absurd and the surreal gradually become the normal
and the familiar: a dog runs away with a knife stuck in its head (27);
birds drugged on cocaine stagger across the sand (28). As Potter says,
"Sometimes I don't believe what's going on" (27). The woman's attitude to these kinds of experiences is finally one of numbed and passive
acceptance; had they occurred earlier they would have both startled and
horrified her.

So we came from there to there
the sun over our shoulders and no one watching
no witness to our pain our broken mouths and bodies.
Things came at us and hit us.
Things happened and went out like matches. (38)

Because of the reference to "broken mouths" I assume that the speaker
is the woman; it is her mouth that has been pried open by the natives
(14) and by Potter (35). The poem's vagueness—"from there to
there," "Things" — is an effective register of her unemotional attitude
at this point. The rhythmic and tonal flatness of "Things came at us

and hit us / Things happened" is a fine preparation for the poem's unexpected closing simile. In poetry as in architecture, less is often more and the final image— "matches"—is a stunning close to a poem almost devoid of colour and metaphor.[13] The poem's texture creates a simultaneous awareness in the reader of both the essentially shocking nature of what is happening and the paradoxical fact that this no longer surprises the woman.

After her return to civilization, this violently beautiful world seems to pursue her even into the safe Royal Hotel.

> She slept in the heart of the Royal Hotel
> Her burnt arms and thighs
> soaking the cold off the sheets.
> She moved fingers onto the rough skin,
> traced the obvious ribs, the running heart,
> sensing herself like a map, then
> lowering her hands into her body.
>
> In the morning she found pieces of a bird
> chopped and scattered by the fan
> blood sprayed onto the mosquito net,
> its body leaving paths on the walls
> like red snails that drifted down in lumps.
>
> She could imagine the feathers
> while she had slept
> falling around her
> like slow rain. (41)

The narrative itself closes with this ambiguous and densely allusive poem whose almost every image echoes some image or situation occurring earlier. Given the poem's position in the body of the text it is inevitable that we look to it to provide some kind of summarizing judgement upon the story. It does so but only through an ambiguous image or metaphor. The key to interpretation seems to lie in the image of the dead bird and the woman's attitude to it in the final stanza. I assume there is an implicit analogy between the bird's violent death and the woman's horrific and brutal experiences in the wilderness. If this is so then her response to the presence of the slaughtered bird should provide an insight into her attitude to her earlier experiences. Her reaction is either sentimental and romantic or it indicates a full acceptance of the violent natural world into which she had been thrust. I tend towards the second reading because this lyric follows a poem in which the woman's attitude toward the convict, now a memory from her past, is completely positive; and secondly, because the opening stanza seems to point to a physical and psychological awareness and acceptance of the self she has become ("sensing herself like a map, then / lowering her hands into her body"). This new attitude corresponds roughly with Nolan's later paintings of Mrs. Fraser and the land as finally indistinguishable from one another.[14] In Ondaatje, this merging of self and wilderness is reinterpreted as a rediscovery of the instinctual world within the self; the experience of the physical wilderness has led to a reperception, or even an initial awareness, of the natural world within. Here as in D.H. Lawrence's "The Woman Who Rode Away" the physical journey away from civilization is simultaneously a psychological one as well. In fact, it is safe to say that here and in his other work Ondaatje is primarily interested in landscape in so far as it can be used to reveal inner states of being.[15]

The original Mrs. Fraser returned to England, married her ship's master, a Captain Greene, and keeping her marriage a secret, "was able to exhibit herself at 6d a showing in Hyde Park." Ondaatje deals with this return to civilization in a ballad—perhaps sung by his central character—which functions as an epilogue offering another ambiguous summary. (It is worth noting that *the man with seven toes*, like Ondaatje's later book-length works, has more than one ending.)

When we came into Glasgow town
we were a lovely sight to see
My love was all in red velvet
and I myself in cramasie

Three dogs came out from still grey streets
they barked as loud as city noise,
their tails and ears were like torn flags
and after them came girls and boys

The people drank the silver wine
they ate the meals that came in pans
And after eating watched a lady
singing with her throat and hands

Green wild rivers in these people

145

running under ice that's calm,
God bring you all some tender stories
and keep you all from hurt and harm (42)

The original Scots' ballad "Waly, Waly" from which Ondaatje borrows his opening stanza is a song of regret and disillusion in which a woman laments having given herself to her lover:

"But had I wist before I kiss'd
That love had been sae ill to win,
I'd lock my heart in a case of gowd
And pin'd it we'a siller pin."[16]

In "Waly, Waly" the apparent is not the real: a tree seems "trusty" but breaks, a lover seems true but is not. A similar duality exists in Ondaatje's version: the ostensible order and stability of Glasgow town rest upon people in whom "Green wild rivers" run "under ice that's calm." The full force of the contrast between the two images can only be felt, however, if we place them in the context of the whole text; then the ice is seen as relating to consciousness, order, civilization — everything that was left behind when the woman stepped off the train — and the "rivers" represent everything that is unconscious, chaotic and natural — the world she stepped into. The ice does not crack in the ballad but the reader, keeping in mind the action of the book, realizes how tenuous the equilibrium of civilization really is, how at any moment the ice could crack and melt letting through everything implied by the "Green wild rivers." If the book has a theme, or what Ondaatje prefers to call a "moral," it is summarized metaphorically in the interplay of these two images.[17]

But it is also important to note that although the ballad summarizes or comprehends the book's dualities and constitutive tensions it does not resolve them. This deliberate irresolution leaves the sequence with a sense of open-endedness re-inforced by the grammar of the last sentence whose verb ("God keep you"), in the subjunctive mood, points to the future. Like the present tenses in the endings of *The Collected Works of Billy the Kid* ("I smell the smoke still in my shirt") and *Coming Through Slaughter* ("There are no prizes") this gives the book an ending without finality or resolution, an ending struggling against the closure inevitable in every work of art. The reader is left with a sense of the continuity of the story and its implications into present and future time. At the precise moment when the book is being finished and about to be put aside it forces itself into the reader's time. One aspect of the book's form — its various discontinuities — compelled the reader to enter the narrative as a figure in the story's ground, as a kind of character surrogate; another aspect, the lack of closure or resolution, reverses the spatial and temporal situation by having the book extend itself into the reader's world. A slight shift in the verb's mood or tense is the final aspect of a narrative form and a poetic rhetoric attempting to achieve a "point blank" and, from Ondaatje's viewpoint, mythic presentation.

Both *The Collected Works of Billy the Kid* and *Coming Through Slaughter* go further than *the man with seven toes* in bringing the reader into the text, in making his experience of its world as unmediated as possible.[18] But the more ambitious and greater achievement of these later works should not prevent us from acknowledging this minor, though by no means negligible, poem which anticipates them in so many respects.

1 Roland Barthes, *S/Z*, trans. Richard Miller (New York: Hill and Wang, 1975), pp. 5-6.

2 For other accounts of the story see Bill Beatty, *Tales of Old Australia* (Sydney: Ure Smith, 1966); Bill Wannan, *Legendary Australians* (Adelaide: Rigby, 1974); Patrick White, *A Fringe of Leaves* (New York: Viking, 1977).

3 "O'Hagan's Rough-Edged Chronicle," *Canadian Literature*, 61 (Summer, 1974), 24.

4 Ondaatje quotes from MacInnes in a note at the end of the book. See *the man with seven toes* (Toronto: Coach House Press, 1969), p. 45. All future references will be to this edition and will be cited in the body of the essay.

5 Bryan Robertson has described this painting as follows: "This animal-like figure conveys something of the shock and horror of a white, northern European body flung down in the wild bush of a Pacific island, and forced to fend for itself: a body that has not been exposed to the ravages of a strong sun before, straddles horrifically across the land, isolated and lost. Her face is hidden by her hair and this device for anonymity is also employed in all the later paintings of Mrs Fraser." Kenneth Clark, Colin MacInnes and Bryan Robertson, *Sidney Nolan* (London: Thames and Hudson, 1961), p. 74.

6 Margaret Atwood, *The Journals of Susanna Moodie* (Toronto: Oxford University Press, 1970), p. 8.

7 Francis Bacon's comment about his paintings is relevant here: "we all need to be aware of the potential disaster which stalks us at every moment of the day." John Russell, *Francis Bacon* (London: Thames and Hudson, 1971), p. 31. Other points of comparison that could be drawn between Ondaatje and Bacon relate to their interest in the beauty of violence, in their mutual attempts to describe motion, and the sense or colour of menace that pervades their work.

8 "Interview with Michael Ondaatje," *Rune*, 2 (Spring 1975), 51.

9 *Canadian Literature, op cit.*, 25-6.

10 Michael Ondaatje, *Leonard Cohen* (Toronto: McClelland and Stewart, 1970), p. 23.

11 *Canadian Literature, op. cit.*, 25.

12 In White's *A Fringe of Leaves* the convict's name is Jack Chance and his status as a man existing between civilization and wilderness is evident in the fact that he has almost completely forgotten the English language. White replaces the striped shirt with scars, an image that Ondaatje would probably respond to since his own work — "A Time Around Scars," *Coming Through Slaughter* — reveals a fascination with emotional and physical scars. "[She] realized that she was touching the scars she had first noticed on his first appearing at the black's camp, when their apparently motiveless welter distinguished them from the formal incisions in native backs," (p. 290).

13 Ondaatje quotes the following sentence from *Tay John* in his article: "indeed, to tell a story is to leave most of it untold," p. 30.

14 "Woman and Billabong," "Woman in Swamp," "Woman in Mangroves."

15 In *A Fringe of Leaves*, the encounter with the wilderness is simultaneously an encounter with "secret depths with which even she, perhaps, is unacquainted, and which sooner or later must be troubled" (p. 20).

16 See Willa Muir, *Living With Ballads* (London: Hogarth Press, 1965), pp. 224-5. For the earliest treatment of Mrs. Fraser's experiences see the ballad "Wreck of the 'Stirling Castle,'" reprinted in Bill Wannan's *Legendary Australians*, pp. 47-9. As Wannan points out, "This 'Copy of Mournful Verses' was originally published in broadsheet form in 1837, by the printer of broadsides J. Catnach, of Seven Dials, London." The last two stanzas should give sufficient indication of its quality:

> The chief mate too they did despatch,
> By cutting off his head,

And plac'd on one of their canoes
All for a figure head.
Also, a fine young man they bound,
And burnt without a dread,
With a slow fire at his feet at first
So up unto his head.

When you read the tortures I went thro'
'Twill grieve your heart full sore,
But now thank HEAVEN, I am returned
Unto my native shore.
I always shall remember,
And my prayers will ever be,
For the safety of both age and sex,
Who sail on the raging sea.

17 In *Leonard Cohen* Ondaatje writes that the world of *Let Us Compare Mythologies* is one "where the morals are imagistic, as they always are in the context of dreams," p. 14.

18 There are two other particularly important differences between *the man with seven toes* and its more famous successors: the later works are more autobiographical, if obliquely so, and self-reflexive.

M. Travis Lane
DREAM AS HISTORY:
A REVIEW OF *the man with seven toes*

The poet who tackles a sizeable dramatic monologue makes a claim to artistic importance that the writer of short lyrics or unambitious anecdotes does not. Ondaatje's version of the dramatic monologue rarely uses direct speech, characterizing persons by their interior monologues rather than by their communications. The associative, dream-like image for non-verbal states of mind comes less oddly to us, after Joyce, Eliot, and Lowell. We have learned to read a man through his sleep and through his madness. But although Ondaatje avoids dramatized-as-real speech, he also avoids ostensible dream material and the material of the characterized person's associative memory. In *the man with seven toes* we are neither North of Boston nor down under in Earwicker-land. Instead, as with Browning's Childe Roland, we are shown primarily the perceptual present of Ondaatje's characters: what they see and feel to be the real world. And it is their perceptions, more than their reflections, that characterize them.

The perceptive field of *the man with seven toes* is intensely limited. Although a "narrator"-voice is sparingly used, it is uncharacterized, and appears more as something overheard by the chief character than as something perceiving, rather as if the chief character dreamily saw herself in the third person. The ironic or satiric possibilities of the plot are deliberately omitted. The social histories of the poem's two characters are largely omitted, again focussing our attention not on things past or things hoped form, but upon the present, unintellectualized perception. By so doing Ondaatje would have us consider that the parallels between our dreams and our histories are somewhat of our own making — that our history is to some extent the effect of our perceptions, our fears, and our behaviours — that we create the myths and circuses of our lives, that what comes to us in reality is, like our dreams, both beyond our control and created by us.

The Mrs. Fraser whose history suggested Ondaatje's fable was shipwrecked. But Ondaatje's unnamed heroine (for convenience here labeled Mrs. X) deliberately enters her nightmare: fainting with heat she steps off a train into a fever-like desert, too tired to assert herself, or get back onto the train before it starts up again. We meet her already self-abandoned. At one level of suggestion the poem is a history of her illness; overtly the poem is a history of the trouble she endured getting back to civilization; and at a third level, presumably intentional, the poem is her encounter with and her "escape" from her own sexual wilderness, her "shadow" self ("animus," "id," what-have-you).

As a history of a sickness, the poem takes us from Mrs. X's initial feverish swoon, into a period of convulsions, back into a long-drawn-out-fever, and finally, into a wakening release. Shortly after she loses consciousness in the heat of the desert she enters a camp of aborigines where close-packed images of rape, goat-killing, yelling, dancing, drinking of blood (from fresh-slaughtered goats presented as analogous to the freshly raped Mrs. X) are all described through Mrs. X's perceptions as "throbbing," "thrumming," or "banging" within her. Even the food she eats is thought of as alive and as being as throbbingly sexually invasive as the savage's penis (although the food is also "like" her, the living, being-eaten victim). For Mrs. X both swallowing and sexual intercourse involve something alien to her, "alive" in her. On the level of the poem as a record of an illness, these sensations parallel the heightened sense of heart-beat, the throbbing nerves, and the nausea of a fever's delirious height. The savages are, likewise at this level, figures of a delirium, and her voiceless passivity towards them the stupor of sickness. After the delirium of the aborigine camp the long trek cityward is presented still as a passive struggling, a long enduring, "bloodwarm" or hotter sweat, with painful hungers, nauseas and violent, ill-assuaged thirsts, and repeated swoons. The poem ends in images of cool wet, of rain, of rivers under calm ice, and in a dream lullaby of coolness, of sleep, of the city: hotel, cool bed, and civilized peoples.

But Ondaatje insists that the Australia of *the man with seven toes* is as objectively real for his characters as Wessex is for Tess. Mrs. X steps off

151

a real train, and joins real aborigines, who kindly feed her, excessively explore her, and exuberantly rape her. She meets an escaped convict named Potter, still wearing his striped prison shirt, who escorts her along the desert river back to the city. She appears to find the convict as wild, as exotic, as repelling but sexually fascinating as the aborigines. And she is glad to be rid of him. Say the townspeople, on finding the two:

> Were found bathing in a river
> like strange wild animals
> sticking out of the water.
>
> She when seeing us said
> god has saved me.

There is no evidence before this that Mrs. X thinks or speaks of "god." Who saves her and keeps her alive, with considerable difficulty, is Potter (who got, we are given to suppose, some sexual compensation). Indeed Mrs. X doesn't think at all. It is as if the poem is her dream and Potter, the title-hero, the chief figure of her dream. Ondaatje insists that Potter has a name and a pre-poem history (unlike Mrs. X). The insistence underlines the fact that Potter is not real for Mrs. X, and it is in her mind that we begin, endure, and conclude the poem.

the man with seven toes presents not a dream so much as history as a dream, as the creation of Mrs. X's obsessions. For when Mrs. X steps off the train her state of soul is at once made clear and in it, both aborigines and convict are predicted:

> When they stopped for water she got off
> sat by the rails on the wrist thick stones.
>
> The train shuddered, then wheeled away from her.
> She was too tired even to call.
> Though, come back, she murmured to herself.
>
>   *   *   *
>
> She woke and there was a dog
> sitting on her shoulder
> doing nothing, not even looking at her
> but out over the land.

152

She lurched and it sauntered
feet away and licked its penis
as if some red flower in the desert.
She looked away but everything around her was empty.

That this common canine action should so strike her, and that she should feel her identity ignored, is appropriate to what is going to happen to her. She remains without name and almost without speech or ego until the end of the poem where she seems to be recovering a token apprehension of herself through exploring her body with her hands, "sensing herself like a map."

The image of the red sexual flower of the wild, the animal flower, repeats itself literally and figuratively throughout the poem and is a figure for Mrs. X herself, who wears a red dress, has it stripped from her by the aborigines, gets it back, and is first identified by the convict through its redness as a non-aboriginal female. When at the end of the poem she sees a bird chopped redly into pieces by the hotel fan, she relaxes blissfully under the image of this living thing, this red thing, destroyed, as under a soothing rain. The reds and bruised purples of wounds, wounded animals, of sexual parts perceived as wounds, along with the continually analogized liquids of blood, sweat, semen, undrinkable waters, and miscellaneous salty fluids, make of the Australian desert river-side a sexual hell. Even the occasional healthy birds are perceived as peeing in the trees or as making hideous noises; their eyelids are like foreskins, etc. Indeed our poor opinion of the aborigines' reception of Mrs. X must be qualified by the sex-obsessed stupor (and the red dress) in which she approached them, as we are reminded again when poor Potter encounters her:

His eyes stammering
at the sudden colour
of woman on the bank
her red dress tucked into her thighs

Mrs. X is the sick psyche, sick physically as well as spiritually. She is shown being fed, assisted, propped up, carried, sponged, grappled with — as inertly passive as a sleeper, yet as tensely horror-perceiving as the "I" in a bad dream. To her the convict appears from the general wild sexual menace of the tribesmen as a more individualized figure, as a

153

more personal figure (a white man with a name) but made out of the same material as the tribesmen. He, also, is a man of the wilderness: he is tattoed with "wild" drawings, branded with a snake like a sign of the devil, striped-shirted like a fabulous wild animal, like the aborigines a hunter of considerable hunting skill (an uncivilized skill: he kills a wolf with his teeth). Furthermore, as convict, Potter is the bad Will, the thinker of bad-sexual deeds, Mrs. X's bad lover, her primitive desires escaped from jail, and thus at home in the nightmare wilderness. And Potter is he-who-can-cope; he is the thinker of the poem; and this bad and branded male Will is going to take the passive female body back to the city. The primitive Will restores Mrs. X to her city self, the opposite of the sexual wilderness, because she is not complete without him. He is an aspect of her, the male "shadow" of her subconscious.

Ondaatje's poem can thus be taken as representing a loss of the conscious self and a descent into the feared subconscious. The woman's own sexual fears (her bad, wild desires) become analogous to all that is uncivilized, hot, wounding, ugly. As the convict carries her through the nightmare, the wilderness is perceived as predominantly sexual and sick, and both the convict and the woman suffer physically. But Mrs. X is only exhausted, drained, sunburned. The man, already prison-branded and tattooed, loses three of his toes and gets his mouth badly cut (both castration analogies within the poem). Moreover, as the two walk along and through the various stinking, "blood-warm" waters, Potter and the woman are continually re-immersing themselves. When they are finally discovered in the river and Mrs. X cries out "god has saved me," it is as if Potter is, in a sense, washed away. In the last sections of the poem she is cleansed of him. We don't know what happens to him; she doesn't care. Nor does she remember.

The concluding dream-level ballad parallels in city terms the first days of the poem. The red dress, which has recurred throughout (the bad lover achieves a red shirt from biting a wolf to death; the cocaine-stupefied birds that can be caught to be eaten have red vomit — the biter-bitten animal aspect of Mrs. X which is at last redly destroyed, as bird, in the city hotel fan) turns up again in the first line of the lullaby ballad, along with dogs and children, now harmless and asexual, with ceremonial eating (but not blood: "silver wine" and "food in pans") and ceremonial entertainment (but not male aborigines dancing: a lady singing) and a river (but not blood-warm: under "calm ice"). It is a cool dream after long sickness. But it is not a well dream.

It is proper that, though we know Potter has a "real" existence outside of Mrs. X's dream-like perception of him, that we should not know what happens to him. For Mrs. X has sealed the door to her subconscious. To her Potter is the savage, sexual, criminally branded Bad self. If he could cope with the nightmare, he was also part of the nightmare, and she got rid of him: "god has saved me." She has treated her history as if it were a dream. Jung wouldn't call it a happy ending.

A final note. The book itself is odd-shaped. Clearly the handsome, wide pages with their glaring white spaces are meant both to suggest the long sun-lit spaces of desert travel and, also, to slow down the reader's eye pace. A poet must insist that his poetry be read at blood-speed (what is poetry that we should mangle it like a bird in an electric fan?), but to do so by changing the shape of a book to the shape of a child's picture book is doubtful practice. The librarians may have to file *the man with seven toes* sideways, without the title showing — a bibliophile's abomination.

Sheila Watson
MICHAEL ONDAATJE: THE MECHANIZATION OF DEATH

Michael Ondaatje was born in 1943. Two years before that Siegfried
Giedion published *Space, Time and Architecture, the Growth of a New
Tradition*. In this work Giedion concentrated on the renewed interest in
organic form, "the ten fingered grasp of reality" which had been
destroyed when Descartes had unlocked the door to mechanization. All
about him Giedion saw symptoms of change—in the concept of space-
time, in Einstein's early concern with simultaneity, in the use of new
terms like "acoustic space," and in all the arts especially in the "optical
revolution."

Seven years later in 1948 Giedion published his now classic study of
industrial archaeology, *Mechanization Takes Command*. Like Orpheus
and like Lot's wife he was looking backward as he well knew. About
this time someone must have taken the small picture of Ondaatje which
is reproduced on the final page of *The Collected Works of Billy the Kid*.
The reproduction is not distinct enough to reveal whether or not the
cowboy is a "hand" or a "gun." Encapsulated in the lower right hand
segment of a 4" by 7" rectangle, however, it brings *The Collected
Works of Billy the Kid*, by an abrupt boxing, back to the bland 4" square
above the opening statement, "I send you a picture of Billy...."

Outlining his project, Giedion wrote: "We begin with the concept
of Movement which underlies all mechanization. There follows the
Hand, which is to be supplanted; and mechanization as a Phenomenon.
The elimination of the complicated handcraft marks the beginning of
high mechanization. This transition takes place in America during the
second half of the nineteenth century."

It is from America in the last half of the nineteenth century that

156

Ondaatje salvages images for his new work. The place and time are clearly stated: "Christmas at Fort Sumner, 1880." The outcome of events is set down with precision. "These are the killed. / (By me)——. . . (By them)——." It is a list of the dead, some named, some nameless statistics. The list paradoxically includes the name of the sheriff Garrett, who survived to record the experience in print.

The hand is ambiguously present in these "Left Handed Poems." Billy notes the sheriff's hands: "Pat Garrett, ideal assassin. Public figure, the mind of a doctor, his hands hairy, scarred, burned by rope .... Ideal assassin for his mind was unwarped ... An academic murderer" (28). Garrett notes Billy's hand: "I saw the hand, it was virgin white. Later when we talked about it, I explained about how a hand or muscle unused for much work would atrophy, grow small.... From then on I noticed his left hand churning within itself, each finger circling alternately like a train wheel. Curling into balls, pouring like waves across a tablecloth. It was the most hypnotising beautiful thing I ever saw" (43). At one point the sun becomes a pair of hands which turns Billy inside out as he is taken to avoid lynchers along the Carrizozo plains (with their railway city) and along the telegraph lines to Punta de la Glorietta, where the agony begins.

The concept of movement is central to Ondaatje's work. In the credits at the end of the book Ondaatje notes, "The comment about taking photographs around 1870-80 is by the great Western photographer L.A. Huffman and appears in his book *Huffman, Frontier Photographer*." The passage which provides Ondaatje with a kind of epigraph for his work is significant:

I send you a picture of Billy made with the Perry shutter as quick as it can be worked — Pyro and soda developer. I am making daily experiments now and find I am able to take passing horses at a lively trot square across the line of fire — bits of snow in the air — spokes well defined — some blur on top of the wheel but sharp in the main — men walking are no trick — I will send you proofs sometime. I shall show you what can be done from the saddle without ground glass or tripod — please notice when you get the specimens that they were made with the lens wide open and many of the best exposed when my horse was in motion.

Giedion's discussion of mechanization touches down in the same sensitive area. At the beginning of his exploration Giedion concentrates on the invention of the Spymograph by the French physiologist

Marey—that is on the invention of an instrument designed to measure graphically "the form and frequency of the human pulse beat." In his study of what Marey called "the language of the phenomena themselves," Giedion saw the union of the experimental psychologist with the engineer. In the early eighties, twenty years after the invention of the Spymograph, Giedion records, Marey began to use photography to capture the true form of movement as it is described in space. Taking hints from the "astronomical revolver" of his colleague Jannsen and stimulated by the photographic studies of the American Muybridge, whose serial pictures were only tangentially connected with his own interest in capturing successive phases of motion on a single plate, Marey invented the Photo-gun.

Calling attention to the period between 1918-1939, Giedion observed: "What occurs in art at this period gives the most intimate insight regarding how deeply mechanization penetrated man's inner existence." Symptoms of the malady can be seen everywhere in the visual arts. To impress his point Giedion calls to witness Giorgio de Chirico's obsessive dream: " 'I struggle in vain with the man whose eyes are suspicious and very gentle. Each time I grasp him, he frees himself quietly spreading his arms... like those gigantic cranes.' " Giedion's choice of dates is significant. To strengthen his point he ignores ten years of experiment during which some artists at least had attempted to establish a new balance as they were moving swiftly into a new technological age.

On his round of the London galleries in 1949, Wyndham Lewis stopped to look at two exhibitions of de Chirico's paintings and to remark the uneasy destiny of a painter whose preoccupation with the Roman world of the machine-age had first led him into "a high metaphysical region" but had now "betrayed him into platitude" (the languidly prancing horse, the fatigued symbolic charger). During the same months Lewis drew attention, too, to the work of "one of the most original of young painters—Francis Bacon." In the *Listener* (17 November 1949) Lewis wrote: "I must not attempt to describe these amazing pictures, their dissolving ganglia the size of a small fist in which one can always discern the shouting mouth, the wild distended eye. In the *Nude*, in front of not the least ominous of curtains, about to enter, the artist is seen at his best. Bacon is one of the most powerful artists in Europe today and is perfectly in tune with his time."

158

In the early days of the "new tradition" Lewis had been much concerned with the brutalizing of the conceptual forms which organize the perceptual flux and also with the fate of the untidy organic snag which separates men from their machines. That the archetypes of the mechanical age were buried deep in human flesh he was well aware. His insight at the time illustrates his criticism of various aspects of futurism, dada, and surrealism and, too, of the cult of primitivism and the neo-primitivist — especially of the "primitif *voulu*," the elderly child "who acrobatically adapts himself to a different stage of social development" without the shrewd perceptual awareness of the "Naif" — the real thing, as he thought the Douanier Rousseau to be.

Lewis's observations are interesting because in the passages I have alluded to he refers in significant context to two of the painters in whose work Ondaatje is known to be interested and to one of whom, Henri Rousseau, he addresses a poem in his first book of poetry *The Dainty Monsters*.

As I re-read Ondaatje's early poetry after finishing *The Collected Works of Billy the Kid* I recalled a passage from *The Caliph's Design*, a small volume of Lewis's writing about art and about the climate in which the artist had to function immediately after the war of 1914-1918 — the period chosen by Giedion to illustrate the way in which the crude and frequently brutal functioning of the industrial or scientific machine was being interiorized and had begun to cohabit with whatever else had been thrust down into the Freudian unconscious. "The creation of a work of art," Lewis wrote, "is an act of the same description as the evolution of wings on the side of a fish, the feathering of its fins, or the invention of a weapon within the body of a hymenopter to enable it to meet the terrible needs of its life."

Ondaatje's response to these needs is both sensitive and measured. It is also unusually intense. His vision is steady — or at least like Huffman he works from the saddle effectively. His voice is simple and flexible. It has considerable range. Although he is often ironic, unlike Auden whom he quotes for epigraph in his first volume of poems, he rarely shields himself with irony. He is as intelligent as Auden but less afraid of what living means. He suffers less from shock than some poets of the generation which preceded him because he has been attentive to the seismograms which their experience affords him. He does not seem to be unduly preoccupied in any absolute way with his function as a poet

159

because, if I can judge from his poetry, he is aware that all life maintains itself by functional specialization of some kind and as often as not loses itself for the same reason. If one wanted to take the parrot in "Henry Rousseau and Friends" as a symbol of the poet he is reminded that "the parrot is interchangeable" — like the gun parts which Thomas Jefferson saw a mechanic manufacturing in 1792.

Ondaatje's monsters are flesh and like all flesh are grass but they are also machines. They fly with the precision of watches and arch their feet like compasses. Heavy with flesh they gyrate. Axed in the shoulder and neck they wheel and waltz "in the French style" to their knees. In man and beast the movement is the same. The tails of the old dragons whose "flesh drags in folds" keep "the beat of a waltz."

As for the parrot it has been used as a symbol by Lawrence in a context which is close to the area of Ondaatje's concern. But Lawrence's parrot with all its "strange penetrating antediluvian malevolence" is not Ondaatje's parrot I think. If I had to match parrots with Ondaatje's I would choose Félicité's "pauvre Loulou," the parrot in Flaubert's tale *Un Coeur simple.*

> A l'église elle contemplait toujours le Saint-Esprit, et observa qu'il avait quelque chose du perroquet. Sa resemblance lui parut encore plus manifeste sur une image d'Epinal, représentant le baptême de Notre-Seigneur. Avec ses ailes de pourpre et son corps d'émeraude, c'était vraiment le portrait de Loulou. L'ayant acheté, elle le suspendit à place du comte d'Artois, — de sort que, du même coup d'oeil, elle les voyait ensemble. Ils s'associèrent dans sa pensée, le perroquet se trouvant sanctifié par ce rapport avec le Saint-Esprit qui devenait plus vivant à ses yeux et intelligible. Le Père pour s'anoncer, n'avait pu choisir une colombe, puisque ces bêtes-la n'ont pas de voix, mais plutôt un des ancêtres de Loulou.

In *the man with seven toes*, his second book, Ondaatje continues the exploration which he begins in his first. The world which he explores is a primitive world invaded by primitive machines. He begins with a train in a desolate part of the Australian continent and ends with a domesticated outpost of Victoria's empire — the Royal Hotel. In this world the absent minded train hums like a low flying bird and stops for water like any beast; birds stagger doped with cocaine sucked from the bark of trees; the lady and the convict suck half-flesh out of two pale green eggs; swamp-flesh with teeth as sharp as "ideal knives" severs toes from the convict's feet which have been strengthened with wolf's blood and have outwitted bird-disguised men so primitive that their maps are "encoded in the soles of their feet." The final image, the death of a bird in its own clumsy cliché, is a literal irony used with delicate skill. The French, as Sterne said, manage these affairs better. In France the sticks of a folding fan are called "brins," the two outer guards "panaches" and the mount "feuille."

In *The Collected Works of Billy the Kid* Ondaatje takes up the theme again and turns this time from a version of mechanism which is rooted in the bourgeois dream of Hausmann's Paris — the Central Slaughterhouse of La Villette, that curious symbiosis of handcraft with centralization, as Giedion calls it. Ondaatje moves west, however across the ocean, beyond New England, to the shaved legs of Miss Angela Dickinson of Tucson, beyond the Union Stockyards of Chicago, beyond Cincinnati, beyond McCoy's new shipping sheds in the abandoned settlement of Abilene, Kansas, to Texas, to John Chisum's cattle drives, to the Lincoln County War, to "surplus production and artificial dissipation," to the lengthening shadow of what Giedion calls "the mechanization of death" — to death in its "biological nakedness" — to "the sudden, incalculable destruction of organic creatures."

Ondaatje's Billy muses:

> well some morals are physical
> must be clear and open
> like diagram of watch or star
> one must eliminate much
> that is one turns when the bullet leaves you
> walk off see none of the thrashing
> the very eyes welling up like bad drains
> believing then the moral of newspapers or gun
> where bodies are mindless as paper flowers you dont feed
> or give to drink
> that is why I can watch the stomach of clocks
> shift their wheels and pins into each other
> and emerge living, for hours (11)

Kipling watched the slaughter of organic creatures in Chicago with a certain stoicism. After all Queen Victoria had fired the first shot from a Whitworth rifle at the initial meeting of the National Rifle Association at Wimbledon in 1860 and had struck the bull's eye. In 1906, in America, Upton Sinclair took a hard look at Chicago and wrote *The Jungle*.

More recently Kurt Vonnegut's Billy Pilgrim, captured, carried off in a box-car, and sheltered by chance in Schlachthof-fünf, is seen, back in his own country, speaking before a capacity audience in a ball park covered with a geodesic dome. "The flag of the country is behind him. It is a Hereford bull on a field of green." In the preface to his play *Happy Birthday Wanda June* Vonnegut recalls that his brother looking at quail which his father had shot, remarked, "my gosh — that's like smashing a fine Swiss watch." The play itself, originally called *Penelope*, Vonnegut says, and conceived fifteen years before it was produced, had taken shape in his mind "when Ernest Hemingway was still alive and seemingly well. So [he] felt free to imagine a modern Odysseus who was a lot like that part of Hemingway which [he] detested — the slayer of nearly extinct animals which meant no harm." If at first Vonnegut was moved by too easy compassion, by the time he wrote *Slaughterhouse Five* he had found a more comprehensive archetype.

Mailer, too, wrote with the truth in his nostrils when he focussed his eyes on the Chicago Ampitheatre in 1968.

Ondaatje works on the periphery. Since his phrase at one point recalls Upton Sinclair he is no doubt aware of the difficulty of his task. For Sinclair the urgency was not the passing of a pure food act anymore than the question now is legally and democratically controlled pollution and re-cycling or the humanitarian distribution of those instruments which, in the Kid's now mythic world, were called "equalizers." His legend, Ondaatje says of the Kid, is "a jungle sleep."

Ondaatje digs where the brute fact of Mailer's Chicago is parodied in the heroics of frontier legend which is even now being thumbed through again and rephotographed by students of south-western history or by amateur historians like Robert Mullin, retired General Manager of a Marketing Division of Gulf Oil Corporation, as Monograph #17 (South Western Studies, University of Texas at El Paso, 1967) shows. So on the ground where the tale of the "immortal outlaw" is still being married to the myth of "the ordinary kind of fellow," the friendly and light-hearted Bill, "the sort of boy the frontier development would produce," Ondaatje finds cause to recall the story of Livingstone's incestuous spaniels and with a Tocquevillian clarity to focus through the open V back-sight of Miss Angela D's shaved legs past the mechanical hog-scrapers, past the acid casualties of the pelting and pickling rooms, past the *liarges* and *bergeries* of La Villette, to the fatted French noblemen who bred bassetts because their "hounds" were too fast for them when they went "hunting."

Vonnegut, with serial insistence, orchestrates his material with the use of the phrase, "So it goes." Like Ondaatje, who recalls the transformation point of industrial mechanism, the point at which the genius of the mechanical engineer is married to the genius of the biologist, the chemist and the electrical engineer, Vonnegut focuses attention on the pornographic picture of the woman and the horse, the work of Daguerre's pupil André Le Fevre.

Mailer in *Miami and the Siege of Chicago* settles for outrage, toughmindedness and an appeal *ad hominem.* "The smell of entrails and the agonized blood electrified by all the outer neons of ultimate fear" drifts away from the scene of the convention "North to Evanston to remind the polite that *inter faeces et urinam* we are born" as Crazy Jane reminded her tidy-minded bishop.

Ondaatje's Billy has his own thoughts:

> You know hunters
> are the gentlest
> anywhere in the world
>
> they halt caterpillars
> from path dangers
> lift a drowning moth from a bowl
> remarkable in peace
>
> in the same way assassins
> come to chaos neutral (47)

Then later:

> In Mexico the flowers
> like brain the blood drained out
> packed with all the liquor perfume
> sweat like lilac urine smell
> getting to me from across a room
>
> if you cut the stalk
> your face near it
> you feel the puff of air escape
> the flower gets small smells sane
> deteriorates in a hand (56)

163

Ondaatje's method is paratactic and explosive. He does not speak of the slaughterhouse. However, the centre of which the trains, the telegraph, and the refrigerated cars are extensions makes itself felt in phrase after phrase, as it does, for instance, when Billy fires into the "slow wheel" of the drunken rats in the deserted barn, or where Billy remembers

> the dark grey yards where trains are fitted
> and the clean speed of machines
> that make machines, their
> red golden pouring which when cooled
> mists out to rust or grey.
>
> The beautiful machines pivoting on themselves
> sealing and fusing to others
> and men throwing levers like coins at them
> And there is there the same stress as with stars,
> the one altered move that will make them maniac. (41)

From the source material which he uses, Walter Noble Burns' *The Saga of Billy the Kid*, Ondaatje lifts a passage which occurs early in Burns' narrative account (48) to place at the centre of his own work. The sequence begins:

> A motive? some reasoning we can give to explain all this violence. Was there a source for all this? yup — (54)

Then the passage from Burns follows. In the passage Burns describes how Tunstall, a central figure in the cattle war, is shot, then how the shooting is turned into an "orgy."

> They killed Tunstall's horse, stretched Tunstall's body beside the dead animal, face to the sky, arms folded across his breast, feet together. Under the man's head they placed his hat and under the horse's head his coat carefully folded by way of pillows. So murdered man and dead horse suggested they had crawled into bed and gone to sleep together....
>
> Lucky for Billy the Kid and Brewer that they had gone hunting wild turkeys...

In his work Ondaatje expresses no moral outrage. He dwells on paradox in the dangerous cognitive region which lies between reportage and myth — or again, somewhere in the expanse which separates Bunuel's *Le Chien Andalou* from the sardonic and neutral romanticism of Howard Hawkes.

In an article in *The Listener* (29 August 1946) "Canadian Nature and its Painters" Lewis who had recently returned from Canada to England wrote:

> The Canadian consciousness must always, to a peculiar degree, be implicated with nature, seeing that Canada is first and foremost an agricultural and raw material nation, and, still more important, is everywhere on the frontiers of the wilderness.
>
> The development of the cultural life of Canada will necessarily be conditioned — or so it seems to me — by these facts, however much today anti-regionalism there may seek to ignore them. On the other hand its situation on the North American continent also deeply involves it in the Machine Age. The neighbourhood of Chicago and of Detroit is a formidable fact.

Ondaatje mentions Canada twice, once early in the work:

> Two years ago Charlie Bowdre and I criss-crossed the Canadian border. Ten miles north of it ten miles south. Our horses stepped from country to country, across low rivers, through different colours of tree green. The two of us, our criss-cross like a whip in slow motion, the ridge of action rising and falling, getting narrower in radius till it ended and we drifted down to Mexico and old heat. That there is nothing of depth, of significant accuracy, of wealth in the image, I know. It is there for a beginning. (20)

The other reference is in the long quoted passage headed "The Texas Star March 1881 The Kid Tells All Exclusive Jail Interview:"

> I: What about pastimes? Did you have many when you were free? Did you like books, music, dancing?
>
> B: Dancing I like, I'm a pretty good dancer. Fond of music too. There's a Canadian group, a sort of orchestra, that is the best. Great. Heard them often when I was up there trying to get hold of a man who went by the name of Captain P----.* Never found him. But that group will be remembered a long time. (85)

165

Dennis Lee
SAVAGE FIELDS:
THE COLLECTED WORKS OF BILLY THE KID

Part One: Six Moments

The Collected Works of Billy the Kid, Michael Ondaatje's third book, is a strange object. Some of its 68 sections are lyric poems. But others, in prose, are virtually short stories. And then there are ballads, photographs, tall tales, an invented newspaper story, dialogue from a comic book, excerpts from authentic memoirs. The book juxtaposes poetry, fiction and documents in a form Ondaatje seems to have invented, deploying a variety of genres and orchestrating a wide range of voices. Rather than making it choppy or disjointed, however, this polyphony introduces an exuberant flow into the book's movement, which carries a reader with ease through the discontinuities of the plot.

The events are based on the life of William Bonney (1859–81), the notorious Billy the Kid. They also deal with Billy's sidekicks, like Charlie Bowdre and Tom O'Folliard; his older friends, John and Sallie Chisum; his girlfriend Angela Dickinson; and his mortal enemy, Pat Garrett. But while the dates and locations are accurate, and while Ondaatje doesn't entirely ignore the gunslinging that made Bonney famous, the book draws very little of its strength from the domain of historical fact. Ondaatje has completely invented many incidents (those with the Chisums, for instance), and he has assigned Billy meditations on nature and violence which are not even conjectural biography.

The ongoing legend of Billy the Kid was obviously the catalyst for the book Ondaatje wrote. But if that book illuminates the life of the historical William Bonney, it does so almost by accident.

The subject of *Billy the Kid* is the strife of world and earth. The book recreates a concrete model of the savage field.

Rather than "nature" and "civilisation" we will speak of "*world*" and "*earth*." New wine in new bottles. The point of the change is to indicate that each term is more than a sub-heading within some larger cosmological category. "World" is to be understood as a basic and irreducible ensemble which envelops the planet we live on; so is "earth."

It would be normal to clarify the terms by listing some typical members of each domain. But for reasons which will emerge later, that is not a helpful approach. It is better to try, at the outset, to indicate what makes world "world" and what makes earth "earth."

"World" includes "civilisation," but it is more than civilisations as it has traditionally been understood. World is the ensemble of beings which are either conscious, or manipulated by consciousness for its own purposes. And world's main purpose is to dominate the earth. It does this by reducing earth to modes of existence which it can control: first and foremost, to the status of being neutral or value-free.

"Earth" includes "nature," but it is more than nature as it has traditionally been understood. Earth appears to world as the ensemble of beings which are some or all of: material, alive, and powered by an unself-consciousness instinct. Earth sets itself against world by tantalizing or humiliating world; it accomplishes this by the fact of existing, which obliges world to recognize that it too is earth — material, alive, and powered by instinct.

Billy the Kid depicts the strife by freezing it, again and again, in one or another of six "moments." These moments played no conscious part in the writing or editing; they are critical constructs, devised after the fact. But virtually every episode assimilates itself to one or another of these paradigms of strife. Learning to hear *Billy the Kid* on its own wave-length is a matter of recognizing them as they recur, and seeing how they slide into, collide with, and pass through one another to create the texture of lived time in a planet at civil war.

There are three major moments, which I identify as *earth assault, world assault,* and *earth-in-world.* There are also three minor moments which occur less frequently, as grace-notes within the process: *stasis, union,* and the *skeletal moment.*

1. Earth Assault

In the moment of earth assault, a human consciousness is pummelled and nearly demolished by instinctual energy. Billy is caught in this moment, perpetually battered by the onslaught of earth. Other men in the book are beset in the same way, though to a lesser extent. Poem after poem is a straight-forward account of the experience; a few examples will suffice.

Sometimes the attack is literal in origin.[2]

> ... this chicken paddles out to him
> and as he was falling hops on his neck
> digs the beak into his throat
> straightens legs and heaves
> a red and blue vein out
>
> Meanwhile he fell
> and the chicken walked away
>
> still tugging at the vein
> till it was 12 yards long ... (15)

> On the fifth day the sun turned into a pair of hands
> and began to pull out the hairs in my head. Twist
> pluck twist pluck .... The sun took a towel and wiped
> the dried dribble off, like red powder on the towel
> now. Then with very thin careful fingers it began to
> unfold my head drawing back each layer of skin and
> letting it flap over my ears. (76)

While earth's assault is often literal, it can also take place internally, at the level of perception.

> To be near flowers in the rain
> all that pollen stink buds
> bloated split
> leaves their juices
> bursting the white drop of spend
> out into the air at you
> the smell of things dying flamboyant
> smell stuffing up your nose
> and up like wet cotton in the brain
> can hardly breathe nothing
> nothing thick sugar death   (55)

2. World Assault

The complementary moment is world assault, in which men torment and slaughter the creatures of instinct. Many of the narrative sections depict this moment: Billy's massacre of the crazed rats (18) and the sick cat Ferns (44-45); Livingstone's sadistic experiments on the dogs (60-62); Garrett's reception of the stuffed birds (88). And there are numerous shorter examples.

> catching flies with my left hand
> bringing the fist to my ear
> hearing the scream grey buzz
> as their legs cramp their
> heads with no air
> so eyes split and release   (58)

> Crossed a crooked river
> loving in my head
> ambled dry on stubble
> shot a crooked bird

> Held it in my fingers
> the eyes were small and far
> it yelled out like a trumpet
> destroyed it of its fear   (14)

World assault depends on men living out a particular image of themselves, and adopting a particular ideology. Ondaatje depicts man as the animal which mechanizes itself — which becomes a killing machine. Gun, machine, and mind: in *Billy the Kid* these are the weapons of the world.

The basic move is to identify with one's gun. At one point Pat asks Billy why he refuses to use his left hand for anything but shooting, when it might atrophy as a result.

> He said he did finger exercises subconsciously, on the
> average 12 hours a day. And it was true. From then on
> I noticed his left hand churning within itself, each
> finger circling alternately like a train wheel. Curling
> into balls, pouring like waves across a tablecloth.   (43)

Fingers are becoming train wheels. The naturally organic is being con-

169

verted to a machine; Billy is defining himself as an instrument of murder, a citizen of the world.

He reflects on the ideology of self-mechanization in a rather elliptical passage:

> one must eliminate much
> that is one turns when the bullet leaves you
> walk off see none of the thrashing
> the very eyes welling up like bad drains
> believing then the moral of newspapers or gun
> where bodies are mindless as paper flowers you dont feed
> or give to drink
> that is why I can watch the stomach of clocks
> shift their wheels and pins into each other
> and emerge living, for hours   (11)

Billy kills by adopting "the moral of newspapers or gun" — the moral vision which consciousness-controlled planet needs in order to function. In that ideology (which Ondaatje is depicting, not endorsing), world and earth are totally separate domains. World exists in order to control earth, usually by violence. And earth is neutral, value-free, like a bunch of "paper flowers." It can't suffer while it is brutalized, in any way that matters, because it lacks consciousness; it is "mindless." And the only reality to be taken seriously is consciousness itself, the medium of the world. Because Billy embraces that ideology, he can "walk off" nonchalantly as the bodies he has shot writhe and die. (Men's own instinctual being is clearly a casualty in this vision of things. Billy has to exile the human body to the domain of neutral earth in order to persuade himself that its suffering is alien, essentially unreal.)

This horrific moral vision is the basic ideology of the world. And Billy needs that ideology just as much as he needs his gun. It is a complete denial of one's creaturehood, of course — but that is the point. "One must eliminate much . . . like diagram of watch or star." What Billy eliminates, or longs to eliminate, is all sense of citizenship in earth.

Mechanizing oneself and oversimplifying one's vision of planet makes it possible to go through with the project of total mastery to which the world is dedicated. And the great icons of civil contemplation are given at once :

> I can watch the stomach of clocks
> shift their wheels and pins into each other
> and emerge living, for hours.

It is this vision of a mechanical perfection, wholly detached from the reality of bodies that suffer as they die, which sustains world's desperate project of conquest and self-sufficiency. The ideal result would be to remake earth completely in world's self-image, as a machine.

To this airless delight in the precision of diagram or machine, however, there is later added a fascination with their hairspring balance on the very edge of breakdown.

> The beautiful machines pivoting on themselves
> sealing and fusing to others
> and men throwing levers like coins at them.
> And there is there the same stress as with stars,
> the one altered move that will make them maniac. (41)

These principles of mechanical stress apply to machines. But they apply equally to men who make themselves into machines. When Tom O'Folliard's rifle explodes and maims him (50), he merely experiences a more graphic version of the fate awaiting all men who mechanize themselves; that is, (in *Billy the Kid*), all men. The project of world may succeed, Billy knows intuitively, but it will self-destruct at the same time.

The substance of the book is precisely this interplay between lethally-alive earth and lethally-machined world. And the process of the book, poem by poem, is the record of their collisions: earth assault, world assault, metamorphosis into new versions of the same struggle. There is no other subject, because it is this process which informs everything that lives. The book moves around it; there is nowhere else for it to go.

3. Earth-In-World

World needs to believe that it has nothing in common with earth. And *Billy the Kid* shows world hypnotizing itself with that belief. But the book's own vision of the two domains is very different; it shows them coinciding completely, each person and thing a member of both domains at once.

It is easy to see that earth is everywhere drafted into world. More startling is the complementary moment, in which a member of world is forced to accept the instinctual basis of his being. This is the moment of "earth-in-world" (which might equally be termed the moment of "world-as-earth"). It necessitates the cosmological model of a world and an earth coinciding like two fields of force in a single space, rather than standing over against each other like two armies on a battlefield.

The recognition of instinctual energy at the core of world keeps muscling into Billy's consciousness when his guard is down. In an account of his hallucinations, for instance, he mentions how "Sometimes a normal forehead in front of me leaked brain gasses" (10) — a suspiciously unmechanical emanation from the bastion of pure mind. And when he sits killing flies, he hears their frantic dying in the same place: "angry weather in my head, too" (58). By the same token, the exercises with his gun do not simply turn his fingers into "a train wheel." They go on "pouring like waves across a tablecloth" (43), retaining the organic basis he is trying to deny.

But if Billy cannot wholly suppress his membership in earth, at least he can regulate it to an inferior status in his own makeup, not to be taken seriously. This internal division — which is not a personal quirk, but a manifestation of world's whole schizophrenia — accounts for an odd detail in the scene where he is outside at the Chisums' retching. "The machinery in me that organizes my throwing up" begins to function; "Put my fingers into the mushrooms of my throat and up it comes again and flies out like a pack of miniature canaries" (70). Billy finds the familiar separation into organic and mechanical — into "mushrooms" and "canaries," on the one hand, and "machinery" on the other — inside himself; it is the organic, of course, which must be expelled. And this experience of involuntary willed dualism illuminates the startling remark that the wind is aiming the smell off dead animals across the desert "at me and my body" (70).

But as Billy dies, he is unable to suppress the knowledge of what he is. His ultimate vision is of:

> oranges reeling across the room AND I KNOW I KNOW
> it is my brain coming out like red grass
> this breaking where red things wade (95)

Though he has tried to deny his earth-citizenship, he must finally recognize that his own brain is "oranges," "red grass," and wading "red things."

The most horrific moment of earth-in-world occurs in the long section describing Billy's sunstroke (76-78). As he rides back to face prison and execution Billy undergoes an hallucinatory rape by the sun, which penetrates him through the top of his head. Every inch of its downward passage sears an elemental lesson through him: he is a living body that can suffer. A small portion of this riveting, extremely painful episode runs as follows:

> He took a thin cold hand and sank it into my head
> down past the roof of my mouth and washed his
> fingers in my tongue. Down the long cool hand went
> scratching the freckles and warts in my throat
> breaking through veins like pieces of long glass
> tubing, touched my heart with his wrist, down he
> went the liquid yellow from my busted brain finally
> vanishing as it passed through soft warm stomach like
> a luscious blood wet oasis . . .   (76-77)

From one perspective, this is the climactic section of the book. The earth which Billy has been assaulting recoils and shows him, on his own nerve-ends, that he himself *is a body*, a creature of earth — with a "soft warm stomach like a luscious blood wet oasis," and all the rest of his body catalogued by pain.

Yet Billy is not changed a whit. So far as we see, he learns nothing from the experience. For the very existence of world—which is the medium of his being human — is posited on the denial of earth and the exalting of consciousness. That positing is engrained right in him, like a stubborn reflex. And for Billy to accept himself as part of earth would mean single-handedly reversing the life-stance of contemporary world — its whole way of being human, of worlding.

He can't do it. Unlike the protagonists of Ondaatje's later work, he can't even try. The only way to survive, in the face of his all-but-overwhelming sense of affinity with the creatures of the earth, has been to convert himself into a living trigger finger, which obeys its own reason for being at all times and never reflects. He must kill earth dead, again and again, even if what he kills is himself.

173

Being fucked by the sun does not put an end to strife; it becomes merely another case of earth assault. Billy goes on fighting on both sides, but most vehemently against earth.

4. Stasis

While these three moments define the structure of planet in *Billy the Kid*, there are three secondary moments which also recur. The first is one in which an observer, usually Billy, falls into a kind of lucid trance in his perception of both world and earth.

This is the moment of stasis. It is a period of loaded neutrality, an uneasy truce of aggressors, and needs only a slight shift in its internal stresses for earth to begin savaging the perceiver, or for him to explode in fury against earth. But as long as it lasts there is a brief quiescence, and a finely-honed apprehension of visual detail; often the laws of perspective are re-arranged. To cite three of many examples:

> Strange that how I feel people
> not close to me
> as if their dress were against my shoulder
> and as they bend down
> the strange smell of their breath
> moving across my face
> or my eyes
> magnifying the bones across a room
> shifting in a wrist   (39)
>
> . . .
>
> she is crossing the sun
> sits on her leg here
> sweeping off the peels
>
> traces the thin bones on me
> turns toppling slow back to the pillow
> Bonney Bonney
>
> I am very still
> I take in all the angles of the room   (21)
>
> . . .
>
> I am on the edge of the cold dark
> watching the white landscape in its frame
> a world that's so precise

174

every nail and cobweb
has magnified itself to my presence (74)

5. Union

The second minor moment also finds world and earth at temporary peace. But unlike the moment of stasis, the moment of union reconciles them deeply, rather than merely allowing them to coexist without fighting.

One instance of union occurs in memory. A younger Billy — perhaps at seventeen or so — takes refuge in a barn to sweat out a fever. He experiences a ''calm week,'' a remarkable parole from strife during which the microcosm of earth in the barn receives him and allows him. His mind tunes out, his body tunes in.

> I began to block my mind of all thought. Just sensed
> the room and learnt what my body could do .... There
> were animals who did not move out and accepted me
> as a larger breed. (17)

During this interlude the organic domain is gentle, and purposeful with its own necessities. Billy accepts himself as an animal among animals and goes his way unharmed.

But the union doesn't last. Rats in the neighbouring barn begin to eat fermented grain and go berserk (17). Faced with the sickening familiarity of earth assault, Billy reacts the only way he knows how: he fires again and again into the midst of the mad animals. At once the strife is raging again. The sequence is paradigmatic, and functions in the book as a kind of first fall.

It is striking that union is possible only when world accepts assimilation by earth. Billy puts his mind aside in the barn and enters his body; the lover doffs his hat as he enters his lady, and becomes a whale (68); the writer enters the sun-drugged animals (72). There is nowhere the image of a union in which each member can be itself while being completed by the other. Which makes it understandable that world always recoils and takes up its weapons again.

175

6. The Skeletal Moment

The sixth paradigmatic moment is the skeletal. It comes when the onslaught of earth strips away a man's vein and tissue, and reduces him to pure bone and metal.

Once Billy watches the moment of earth assault slide over into the skeletal before his eyes:

> . . .
> the waves of ants on him
> millions a moving vest up his neck
> over his head down his back
> leaving a bright skull white smirking
> to drop to ankles
> ribs blossoming out like springs . . . (40)

The inventory of Livingstone's remains (62), after the tortured dogs have taken their revenge, yields the same skeletal / metallic list: bones, a regurgitated watch, and his left wrist.

And Billy's posthumous fate is handled in interesting terms:

> Imagine if you dug him up and brought him out.
> You'd see very little. There'd be the *buck teeth*. Perhaps
> Garrett's *bullet* no longer in thick wet flesh would roll
> in the *skull* like a *marble*. From the head there'd be a
> trail of *vertebrae* like a row of *pearl buttons* off a rich coat
> . . . . And a pair of *handcuffs* holding ridiculously the fine
> *ankle bones*. (Even though dead they buried him in *leg
> irons*.) There would be the *silver* from the toe of each
> boot.
>
> His legend a jungle sleep (97, my emphases)

As a dead man, Billy exists in the skeletal moment, all metal and bone. As a legend, he has entered into "jungle sleep" — a perfect but anti-climatic union with earth.

The skeletal moment is the moment of death. But this casts a sinister light on world's fascination with "the stomach of clocks" (11) and the "beautiful machines pivoting on themselves" (41). Those mechanical

176

icons seemed to promise power over the organic domain without, and separation of the ego from the organic domain within; they were emblems of the whole triumphant campaign of world against earth. But in fact the great machines were continuous — in imagery and in fact — with the metal and skeleton that world will be reduced to at last. Infatuation with the power that decimates earth reveals itself, finally, as infatuation with death.

7. The Cosmology of "Billy the Kid"

Billy the Kid makes most sense as a picture of civilisation and instinct at war. The warfare of the two domains is so all-pervasive that it is reasonable to generalize the two to "world" and "earth." And as the recurring moment of earth-in-world makes clear, one must understand their conflict as a struggle between the whole of planet construed as instinctual force and the whole of planet construed as the empire of consciousness, driving to mastery. The subject of *Billy the Kid* is the savage field of that strife; the book tacitly enacts a cosmology.

Ondaatje's account of the savage field can be summarized (in a form which bypasses all its rich detail) as follows. Most of the time, earth assaults world and world assaults earth. World's assault depends on glorifying mechanical technique, in machines, guns, and the ruthless mind, and denying the reality of instinctual experience. Yet every thing that is belongs entirely to both domains; hence a man keeps discovering his oneness with the creatures of earth even as he slaughters them.

Beyond the odd company truce, however, there is no let-up in the strife. There are moments when members of world achieve an uneasy stasis vis-a-vis earth; and there are rarer moments when they accept their membership in earth and enter temporary union with it. But each living member of world is eventually stripped down to a dead skeleton, which turns out to be a close cousin to world's great icons of technological mastery.

That, in outline, is the cosmology of *The Collected Works of Billy the Kid*.

177

Part Two: Other Perspectives

One way of using the model of savage fields is to see how it illuminates the book from other perspectives.

1. Inflections of Strife

If all things do occur in strife, it should be impossible to depict anything faithfully without recreating the way strife modulates the inflections of its existence, however lightly. We cannot examine the whole book in these terms here, though that is the way to read it. But consider an episode which is instructive from this perspective, because it is not conspicuously "about" the strife of world and earth at all.

One night when Billy is visiting the Chisums, John takes him out to see their animals and birds (36-37). The two men stand by the cages in the darkness, then start back towards the house. Nothing else happens. The vignette is compelling enough, but it seems to have nothing to do with the plot (Garrett's search for Billy), nor with the strife of world and earth.

But that is too hasty, for what Billy encounters is unmistakably raw instinct, imprisoned. There is a mixture of fascination, trepidation, and fellow-feeling in his response to the beasts, and he peers in at them in a kind of edgy standoff.

> We came to the low brooding whirr of noise, night
> sleep of animals. They were stunning things in the
> dark. Just shapes that shifted. You could peer into a
> cage and see nothing till a rattle of claws hit the grid
> an inch from your face and their churning feathers
> seemed to hiss, and a yellow pearl of an eye cracked
> with veins glowed through the criss crossed fence.

It is a moment of uneasy stasis in the savage field: a member of world viewing members of earth in captivity. Billy is alert to the menace they confront him with, as a citizen of the mastering domain. Yet since he also belongs to earth, he is enthralled with their simmering energy. He

178

perceives it as a blind distribution of force, ready to erupt into flesh or sound at any point.

The power of this muted confrontation derives from the double meaning which "caged instinct" has for Billy. And Ondaatje recreates the subtle tensions of the moment with finesse. There is no editorializing, however; the incident is charged directly, though lightly, with the resonance of strife.

Ondaatje arrests the scene in a deeper moment of stasis as the men return to the house.

> Half way back to the house, the building we moved
> towards seemed to be stuffed with something yellow
> and wet. The night, the dark air, made it all mad.
> That fifteen yards away there were bright birds in
> cages and here John Chisum and me walked, strange
> bodies. Around us total blackness, nothing out there
> but a desert for seventy miles or more, and to the left,
> a few yards away, a house stuffed with yellow wet
> light where within the frame of a window we saw a
> woman move carrying fire in a glass funnel and con-
> tainer towards the window, towards the edge of the
> dark where we stood.

Billy now stands poised among intoxicating, menacing energies, and the sheer risk of existing in their midst spooks and exhilarates him. The vignette gives a kind of fingertip probing of planet as he inhabits it.

The scene is "all mad" for him — charged with a bizarre power which might seem out of all proportion to its familiarity and calm. If we observe the dynamics of the savage field coursing through him, however, his reaction is not surprising.

First, his body has gone "strange," though this should be no surprise. It is the most immediate reminder of his taboo participation in earth; when he gets skittish, the first thing to go is his sense of being at home in his body. And the blind energy in the birds, the night and the desert bear in on him as equally "mad." But that too is predictable, since those alien / intimate forces are old earth antagonists, and he cannot admit their kinship either.

What is surprising is that the house does not reach out to him as a civil bulwark; it too inhabits the madness. Nor does it appear in world's usual guise, as some variant of gun or metallic machine. Instead

179

it is "stuffed" with a distinctly organic presence: with "something yellow and wet. . . yellow wet light." The house is there to withstand earth, yet for some reason it too has become charged with the subversive instinctual process.

It is another moment of earth-in-world. For it is "a woman's" lamp (Sallie's) which lights the house from within. And for men, women are overwhelmingly creatures of earth. Once again, earth has risen up rampant inside the constructs of world. In itself, of course, such a perception of threat in Sallie is paranoid. But as a subliminal perception of Billy's whole life-situation in planet, it is perfectly accurate. Every civil foothold *is* wet, bright, drenched with organic kinship.

Once the old paradigm of earth-in-world begins to surface — lightly though its presence is felt — Billy brings up short, his sense of delicious menace triggered again. Anything and everything can reawaken it, even on this relaxed weekend with friends. For the savage field comprises everything that is, and there is no escape.

There is no large statement being made about the strife of world and earth in this vignette. It simply shows Billy revved up and spooked in the field — in a state of heightened awareness, racing, half-contained energy, and mild paranoia which can scarcely locate an object. That is a normal state in which to move through the savage field, and depicting it, in its setting, is the point of the episode.

Moving from our first, casual perception of the incident to one which includes strife as the context does not mean cancelling out whatever we perceived first. It means absorbing its full resonance, as we see how world and earth inflect this particular moment by their warfare.

And when we reach this way of reading *Billy the Kid*, sections which had seemed to be merely local colour turn out to be mined from below, charged with the desperate energies of the savage field. On and on it goes, each poem recording further episodes in the strife, new onslaughts, fresh temporary balances of power between the warring domains.

2. Form

The form of *Billy the Kid* is affected by its cosmological intuition.

The formal coherence of details, which are so various that it is hard to see what holds them together, is provided by the six moments into which they keep configuring themselves. Despite the bewildering multiplicity of Ondaatje's planet, there are a limited number of combinations into which world and earth actually enter. Those paradigmatic combinations are the six moments we have discussed. The individual participants keep changing, and any particular thing may play opposing roles in consecutive moments. What does not change, however, is the recurrent conjunction of world and earth *in* those moments.

As Ondaatje traces the way a flood of volatile details combine and recombine in these moments, they come to function as a basic syntax of strife, and hence as novel formal categories within the book. Strife is inflected differently, it *means* with a different colour and texture, at every moment. But the moments in which it articulates itself rhyme. World assault, for example, may echo with itself five times in the course of ten pages: in a lyric, an anecdote, a quoted fragment from the period, a ballad, a yarn.

And *Billy the Kid* is a poem of strife. Its orchestration of moments and its subtle, large-scale echoes and rhythms can be felt across scores of pages in the slide and tumble of its details. A reader is likely to recognize this only subliminally at first. But it is the deft orchestration of moments which makes the book feel coherent and firmly ordered, long before there is any perceptible reason why such a potpourri *should* be coherent.

It is an admirable strategy. For it allows each thing the freedom on the page to respond as it does in the savage field — now as earth, now as world, now as both; yet it also articulates a shapely order in the flux through the recurrent paradigms, so that things do not degenerate into a pointless mishmash. The six moments constitute a coherent structural language of strife, caught in the very flexing of its changes.

Anyone who reads *Billy the Kid* probably orients himself, at first, by the narrative sections which are dotted through the book. There are seven of these, comprising perhaps a tenth of the total length; they begin with Garrett's attempt to flush Billy out of Fort Sumner, proceed through the chase, capture and escape, and end with Billy's death. The presence of this linear story raises an interesting formal point, since the

181

book as a whole does not take the form of a sequence which leads to its own completion.

In principle, it is an accident that the particular zone of strife which *Billy the Kid* depicts does happen to include an action with a beginning, middle and end. As Ondaatje presents it, the savage field distills itself now into lyric perceptions, now into yarns, now into vaudeville turns, now into narratable events. The main action of the book — the real "plot" — is occurring just as conclusively in a lyric poem, like the one where Billy is catching flies, as in the narrative sections where Garrett pursues Billy. Instead of the lyric and other forms being appendages to a "central narrative," then (as they would be in an aristotelian work), all sections of the book — narrative, lyric, ballad, and the rest — are direct manifestations of the central action: the strife of world and earth.

Nevertheless, Ondaatje has no objection to complete actions, provided they are not taken as normative in their tidy completeness. And the presence of the linear story of the chase, drifting up piecemeal in the midst of the book's non-linear structure, creates a secondary formal logic in the book which *is* sequential. This produces a peculiar aesthetic pleasure, and modern structural canons trace out their differing necessities simultaneously.

3. Seeing the Present

All this talk of six moments, even of world and earth, could easily distract from the text. It must be stressed that they are critical constructs, useful but after the fact. Ondaatje was not writing from a schema; he was presumably trying to find real words for a horse, an outlaw, a woman — to recreate their ways of being themselves as adequately as he could. Before all else, he is a literal writer. And the perception of recurrent configurations of strife was apparently intuitive, snagged with no conceptual bait by virtue of telling the truth about things in the planet we live in.

His refusal to theorize is absolute.

> A motive? Some reasoning we can give to explain all
> this violence. Was there a source for all this? yup —   (54)

Ondaatje interrupts his own account of the savage field, at one point, with this mock-earnest question. But his answer is jokey and riddling; he quotes as "explanation" an excerpt from a pulp version of Billy's exploits, published in 1926. It begins:

> "Hill leaped from his horse and, sticking a rifle to the back of Tunstall's head, blew out his brains. Half drunk with whiskey and mad with the taste of blood, the savages turned the murder of the defenceless man into an orgy . . . "

The lip-smacking prose of the unnamed author does contribute its own unwitting comment to the picture of strife. Like the newspaper interview (81-84) and the comic-book episode (98-102), it indicates how the real energy that is in heroes — however problematic their heroism — gets cheapened in a world that cannot face real energy. But as an answer to the question, Why has the planet gone so amok?, the passage responds only by making a conspicuous point of not responding.

Billy the Kid does not explain why the savage field exists; it doesn't even ask why, in a serious way. It simply assumes, with a magisterial finality which seems beyond special pleading, that this is what our planet is like now. The only task it sets itself is to create images of that planet in action.

Other works of the savage field, including Ondaatje's later books, assume a planet which looks and acts essentially like that of *Billy the Kid*. But they go on to rehearse an elemental human action within it: coming of age, being saved or damned, dying. *The Collected Works of Billy the Kid* is almost unique in this literature, however, in that it pays very little attention to foreground action of such a kind. It expends virtually all its imaginative energy on the utterly simple and demanding task of mapping savage fields.

Billy the Kid has no explanation for the violence of the savage field. But it is possible to ask about the same thing in a different way.

Why have Ondaatje and other writers, in the seventh and eighth decades of this century, started writing books which imagine the order of what-is in a different way from their predecessors? It is not a matter of their imputing more violence to men than did, say, the Jacobean dramatists. They don't. It is rather a matter of their taking the violence between planet-as-controlled-by-consciousness and planet-as-powered-by-instinct to be the first fact about contemporary existence. Why should that cosmology have cropped up at this point in history?

The answer, I believe, is that these are visionary writers: they are able to discern the lineaments of the present.

As we hurtle further and further into the technological era, everything is changed — from the physical condition of the planet we call "earth" to the subtlest recesses of family space or of private feeling. It is hard to assimilate that fact, beyond the large musings of doomsday rhetoric. But the planet we inhabit, with all the finely-interstressed ecology of matter, life and consciousness which developed over millennia, has been made into a different thing by the advent of men's ability to master it technologically, and by the world-stance which produced that ability. It is a new entity, and must be imagined and understood as such. For the changes brought about by technology are not simply a series of discrete alterations within a permanent structure. Eventually, under their cumulative impact, the planet comes to be structured in a way it has not been before.

With the full emergence of technology in the last decades (however far back its motivating spirit goes), the strife of world and earth may have supplanted other structures and become the basis of order on the planet. The cosmology of savage fields may be a catastrophic necessity now for the first time, because it may accurately imagine the structure which has become primary only in recent years. If that is so, Ondaatje and his colleagues are doing nothing different from artists before them; they are telling the way things are. It is just that the way things are has changed.

1 All references are to Michael Ondaatje's *The Collected Works of Billy the Kid*, (Toronto: House of Anansi, 1970), and are included in the body of the essay.

Stephen Scobie
TWO AUTHORS IN SEARCH OF A CHARACTER:
bp NICHOL AND MICHAEL ONDAATJE

It was surely coincidence enough that two of Canada's finest young poets should both, in one year, produce books on the notably non-Canadian legend of Billy the Kid, without the further coincidence that both should win Governor-General's Awards. Of course, bp Nichol's award was for four books, of which *The True Eventual Story of Billy the Kid* is the shortest, and perhaps the slightest; this point has had to be made in response to the controversy over giving such an award to "fifteen paragraphs of bad pornography." If Nichol's book is "bad pornography," that is only because it is good art; and although it is, at least superficially, a very much slighter book than Michael Ondaatje's *The Collected Works of Billy the Kid*, it is not wholly absurd to examine them in the same light. The reasons why these authors should choose this subject — rather than some roughly equivalent Canadian figure, such as Louis Riel, or even Paul Rose — are to a great degree personal. It is quite possible that bp wrote his book just for fun, because Michael was writing his.[1] More relevantly, Ondaatje's book is a natural outgrowth from his love of Hollywood (and Italian) Westerns: among his favourite films are Sergio Leone's mythic *Once Upon a Time in the West*, and Arthur Penn's contribution to the legend of Billy the Kid, *The Left Handed Gun*. (Ondaatje's book is subtitled "Left Handed Poems.") But in addition to these personal reasons, the figure of Billy the Kid is particularly relevant to certain central concerns in the work of these poets, and, especially in Ondaatje's case, their treatment of him becomes a major contribution to the development of their work. The purpose of this article, then, is to examine the two books and their widely different approaches to the legend of Billy the Kid, and to see

185

how these approaches illuminate the characteristic concerns and obsessions of the two poets.

It should perhaps be stressed at the outset that this kind of approach is in a way a distortion of Nichol's book. *The True Eventual Story of Billy the Kid* is primarily a joke, a clever and light-hearted skit, as opposed to the intense seriousness of Ondaatje's approach. Nichol's jokes are, however, on potentially serious subjects. To work out all the thematic implications which his fifteen paragraphs barely suggest may seem like building mountains out of molehills; and, though I believe the foundations are there for such an enterprise, the elaboration should not obscure the fact that the most characteristic virtues of Nichol's book are its wit, its economy, and its refusal to take itself too seriously.

Nichol's title stands in a long tradition of books claiming to tell the "truth" about Billy: *The True Life of Billy the Kid* by Don Jenardo (1881); *The Authentic Life of Billy, the Kid* by Pat Garrett (ghost-written by Ash Upson) (1882); *Billy the Kid, the True Story of a Western "Bad Man"* by Emerson Hough (1901); *The Saga of Billy the Kid* by Walter Noble Burns (1926); *The Real Billy the Kid* by Miguel Otero (1936); *The Authentic Death of Hendry Jones* by Charles Neider (1956); *The True Story of Billy the Kid* by William Lee Hamlin (1959) etc. The point about all these "true" and "authentic" biographies is that very few of them are. The historical facts about Billy have been buried under a vast accretion of legend.

The legend itself has changed and developed over the years. For the first twenty years or so after Billy's death, writers strove to outdo each other in creating ever more extravagant pictures of his villainy; he became a devil incarnate, a paragon of evil. Then, about the beginning of this century, the trend reversed; Billy became sentimentalised into a poor misunderstood kid, excuses and justifications were found for his killings, he was transformed into a folk-hero of the Robin Hood variety. In 1930 the first of Hollywood's film versions of Billy the Kid starred the former All-American football star, Johnny Mack Brown; thirty years later, Penn's film starred Paul Newman.

The major work in this posthumous "rehabilitation" of Billy's reputation is Walter Noble Burns' *The Saga of Billy the Kid*, which Ondaatje acknowledges as his major source. Burns' book is of highly questionable historical accuracy, and is filled with writing in the style of the following:

186

Fate set a stage. Out of nowhere into the drama stepped this unknown boy. Opposite him played Death. It was a drama of Death and the Boy. Death dogged his trail relentlessly. It was for ever clutching at him with skeleton hands. It lay in ambush for him. It edged him to the gallows' stairs. By bullets, conflagration, stratagems, every lethal trick, it sought to compass his destruction. But the boy was not to be trapped. He escaped by apparent miracles; he was saved as if by necromancy. He laughed at Death. Death was a joke. He waved Death a jaunty good-bye and was off to new adventures. But again the inexorable circle closed. Now life seemed sweet. It beckoned to love and happiness. A golden vista opened before him. He set his foot upon the sunlit road. Perhaps for a moment the boy dreamed this drama was destined to a happy ending. But no. Fate prompted from the wings. The moment of climax was at hand. The boy had his hour. It was Death's turn. And so the curtain.

Although Ondaatje's literary abilities are far above Burns', several of the legendary accretions which Burns perpetuated show up again in Ondaatje's book. For instance, Ondaatje follows Burns in setting the shooting of Tom O'Folliard by Pat Garrett on Christmas night. This was one of many emotional touches added by Burns to reflect against Garrett's character (for, as Billy changed from villain to hero, Garrett necessarily swung in the opposite direction) and to develop the theme of Billy's betrayal. In actual fact, the shooting took place on December 18th. Further, Ondaatje's account of Azariah F. Wild's participation in this event is pure invention; both Burns and Garrett himself mention Wild only once in passing, and not in connection with this incident.

This kind of consideration is important, of course, only to the very limited extent to which Ondaatje's book is concerned with giving an accurate historical view of the Kid. Clearly this is not his intention, though some passages (such as the death of Charlie Bowdre) do appear to be quite accurate, and the general tone of many of the descriptions, the wealth of detail and the intensity of the images' realization, must appear very convincing to the unwary reader. Like many writers, Ondaatje alters the facts of Billy's death (as, hilariously, does Nichol); one of the standard tricks of writers sentimentalizing Billy was to pretend that someone else (in one version, his own father!) had been shot by mistake and that Billy, complete with Mexican sweetheart, rode off into the sunset. Penn's film has Billy committing virtual suicide by pretending to go for his gun when he is in fact unarmed; after Garrett's shot, Billy staggers forward holding out his empty hand to the killer. But Ondaatje's and Nichol's alterations and manipulations of

187

historical fact are not due, as is the case with many previous writers of "true" and "authentic" histories, to ignorance or to the desire to "justify" Billy; rather they fit in with the most recent developments of the legend of Billy the Kid, which move away from the simple pendulum of what Kent Ladd Steckmesser calls "The Satanic Billy" and "The Saintly Billy" towards much more complex uses of the total *idea* of Billy the Kid, fact and fiction, as a mythological character. This examination of the mythology of Billy the Kid is apparent in such works as Samuel R. Delany's splendid SF novel *The Einstein Intersection*, in which he appears as "Bonny William" or "Kid Death," and Michael McClure's play *The Beard*, in which, somewhere in eternity, he conducts a brilliant, repetitive, and obscene dialogue with Jean Harlow.

This, incidentally, may be one reason why both Ondaatje and Nichol treated a "non-Canadian" subject: few Canadian outlaw-heroes have been as widely and as thoroughly mythologized as Billy the Kid, though the process is perhaps taking place with Riel. Anyway, "non-Canadian" is a red herring: mythology may be national in origin, but the significance of a figure as completely metamorphosed as Billy the Kid is totally international.

To return, then, to Nichol's title: "this" he assures us "is the true eventual story of billy the kid." The first page of Nichol's book is a demonstration of the absolute relativity of any definition of "truth" in a case like this.

> It is not the story as he told it for he did not tell it to me. he told it to others who wrote it down, but not correctly. there is no true eventual story but this one. had he told it to me i would have written a different one. i could not write the true one had he told it to me.

Compare this with Pat Garrett's "Authentic Life," which opens with the claim that "I have listened, at camp-fires, on the trail, on the prairies and at many different plazas, to his disconnected relations of events of his early and more recent life." Garrett continues to list a number of people who knew Billy and whom he has personally interviewed or written to; he can therefore "safely guarantee that the reader will find in my little book a true and concise relation of the principal interesting events therein, without exaggeration or exusation." The whole is intended "to correct the thousand false statements which have appeared in the public newspapers and in yellow-covered, cheap novels." Burns at one point disingenuously admits:

> The foregoing tales may be regarded, as you please, as the apocryphal cantos of the saga of Billy the Kid. They are not thoroughly authenticated, though possibly they are, in the main, true. Most of them are perhaps too ugly to have been inventions. If you are skeptical, your doubt may be tempered by the fact that they have at least always gone with the legend and have such authority as long-established currency may confer.

Nichol's paragraph may be read as a commentary on these and all similar claims. The "true" and "eventual" story cannot be told by any eye-witness; the more "reliable" their claims are, the less they are to be trusted. If Billy himself had told the story to Nichol, "i would have written a different one." The paragraph is a dismissal of any possibility of objective truth in reporting; it insists that any observer changes what he sees as soon as he attempts to express it. Language does not report reality: it creates reality. From this, two conclusions might emerge: first, that even if Billy himself were to tell his own story, he could not tell it truly; and second, that the only "true" story is the one which rejects any attempt at historicity and aims instead at the "truth" of a work of art; "eventually all other stories will appear untrue beside this one." Of course there is a tongue-in-cheek element here: Nichol is fully enjoying his outrageous claim that his fifteen-paragraph joke is going to replace all other versions of the story, including, presumably, that being written by his friend Michael Ondaatje. But beneath the joke is the deadly seriousness of the artist who can dismiss everything outside his own creation, claiming it alone as an absolute. And these views of language and art are surely at the very centre of Nichol's aesthetic, his proclamation of "the language revolution." What matters, then, is not so much the factual record—how many men Billy actually killed or in what year he was actually born—as the legendary image that he lived 21 years and killed 21 men. (For what it's worth, it appears more probable that he lived about 24 and killed about 7.) The "eventual" story of Billy the Kid is beyond history.

The "historical" view is even more explicitly rejected in Nichol's second chapter. The first paragraph reads:

189

> history says that billy the kid was a coward. the true eventual story is
> that billy the kid is dead or he'd probably shoot history in the balls.
> history always stands back calling people cowards or failures.

It should be remembered that the mythical image of Billy as outlaw-hero is a Romantic idea, as the figure of the Outsider is, from Goethe's Werther on, the central Romantic image; and that Nichol himself (as Ondaatje acknowledged in a recent interview) is a Romantic. This condemnation of history — as an impersonal process which coldly "stands back" from its subjects and thus judges rather than sympathizes — is also a Romantic view. History may even be seen as the "official" view of an Establishment which has to reject all rebels and outlaws as "cowards or failures." It is only at a safe distance in time that a figure like Louis Riel can be "officially" viewed as a hero. The task of the rebel, then, is not to stand back, but to get in there and "shoot history in the balls." But Nichol's Billy, being dead, can't do this. In fact, as becomes clearer, Nichol's Billy is the ultimate loser. What, then, is beyond history? It is legend, or myth. This is the level at which Ondaatje's book operates, but not Nichol's: and this is one of the fundamental differences between them. For Nichol's legend is as much a liar as history:

> legend says that billy the kid was a hero who liked to screw. the true
> eventual story is that were billy the kid alive he'd probably take legend
> out for a drink, match off in the bathroom, then blow him full of holes,
> legend always has a bigger dick than history and history has a bigger dick
> than billy had.

This view sees legend as more potent (literally as well as metaphorically) than history, but equally dangerous. And the danger lies precisely in its power, its stability, its vividness, its energy — all the qualities, in fact, of Ondaatje's book. But Nichol's Billy is at the bottom of the power structure, he always has the shortest dick. His status is that of the ultimate loser, and he is always ephemeral:

> rumour has it that billy the kid never died. rumour is billy the kid. he
> never gets anywhere, being too short-lived.

This underlies the difference in length between the two books. It is

190

not simply that Nichol's is a small joke tossed off in fifteen paragraphs: the shortness, the casualness of the book are intrinsic to its view of Billy. The difference between Ondaatje's 100 pages and Nichol's 5 is the difference between legend and rumour. Ondaatje's book *fixes* a certain view of the Kid into an intense, fully realized image; but for Nichol, the "eventual" truth is beyond even this, and his image of Billy is insubstantial, flickering, changing, dying. Ondaatje creates a myth; Nichol tells a joke.

Ondaatje's mythmaking is a careful process, built up by various means and he indicates in several ways the degree to which he is presenting a legendary or poetic image of the Kid. There is, for instance, the concern with photographs. The book opens with an account of photography at the time of Billy's life, indicating the difficulty (which is also Ondaatje's) of taking a sharp image of a moving object. Huffman, the photographer, claims to have succeeded: "spokes well defined — some blur on top of wheel but sharp in the main." In the same way, Ondaatje has fixed an image of Nichol's evanescent rumour. The very fine cover, by Roger Silvester, uses an image by the early experimental photographer Muybridge, who made studies of the motions of people and animals through multiple exposures: again, there are possible analogies to Ondaatje's methods. But what the photograph shows is not always accurate: Paulita Maxwell claims that a photograph of Billy doesn't do him justice — surely an ironic phrase. Indeed, it was the reversed image of one famous photograph of Billy which led to the mistaken idea that he was left-handed. All contemporary authorities, including Garrett, remember Billy as right-handed; but his left-handedness fits in better with the legendary image of the outsider. Burns mentions Billy's being left-handed, but doesn't make anything of it; Ondaatje gives to Garrett a brilliantly sinister account of watching Billy subsconsciously doing finger-exercises with his left hand. As already remarked, Ondaatje's subtitle, "Left Handed Poems" derives from Penn's film *The Left Handed Gun.*

The film image is a further way in which Ondaatje transforms the historical Billy into a legendary image. The sub-title casts the image of Penn's film across the whole book, and also recalls Penn's later master-piece, *Bonnie and Clyde,* in which the outlaw figures are subjected to a mythologizing process within the film itself. (As when, on their first meeting, Clyde asks Bonnie, "Are you a movie star?") Penn also is

191

fascinated by photography: in both *The Left Handed Gun* and *Bonnie and Clyde* important scenes are devoted to the outlaws getting their pictures taken, and the image recurs in all Penn's films. Ondaatje uses comedy in much the same way as Penn: grotesque images of violence become almost simultaneously comic and horrible. Compare the poem about Gregory's death and the chicken with the scene in *The Left Handed Gun* where Billy's shotgun blast lifts Ollinger right out of his boots and leaves them standing, empty, on the street; a little girl starts laughing at the empty boots, until her mother's horrified slap stops her. In these scenes the humour works to intensify the image of violence; Ondaatje even succeeds in introducing a note of humour at the absolute climax of his story, as Garrett is about to shoot Billy. A similar combination of violence and humour may be found in other of Ondaatje's favourite films, such as the Italian Westerns of Sergio Leone, or John Boorman's *Point Blank. Point Blank* also uses a fragmented time-scheme, with the same repeated, slow-motion, dreamlike exposures of violence as in Ondaatje's book. Further, *Point Blank's* female lead is Angie Dickinson, and who should appear as Billy's sweetheart but "Miss Angela Dickinson of Tucson" — a name entirely of Ondaatje's own invention, not present in Burns nor in any "authentic" biography? The historical reality of the Old West and its Hollywood myth representation meet each other in the brief story Ondaatje inserts of Frank James tearing tickets at a Los Angeles movie theatre. Finally, closely akin to the movie image is the comic-book legend which forms Billy's apotheosis. (Ondaatje's own film on bp Nichol, *Sons of Captain Poetry*, celebrates Nichol's fascination with old comics.) This is the final transformation of Billy in pop culture into the upright clean-living hero, as in a delightfully absurd film, which I saw several years ago and which Ondaatje told me he had also seen, *Billy the Kid vs. Dracula.*

But although Ondaatje's image of Billy the Kid may be influenced by the images of comic-books and the movies, these references are merely the context in which Ondaatje sets his own central image of Billy; and, as with Nichol, it is the book's title which points to the nature of that image.

Immediately after the quotation from Huffman, Ondaatje gives a list of "the killed." To Billy he ascribes 20 victims (curiously, for the usual legendary number is 21), most of whom, including the "blacksmith when I was twelve, with a knife,'' are totally unsubstantiated historically. Then he gives Garrett's victims, ending

... and Pat Garrett
sliced off my head.
Blood a necklace on me all my life.

The strange, violent beauty of the image, together with the use of the first person, point towards the concept behind the title *The Collected Works of Billy the Kid*. Ondaatje's legendary context for Billy is poetry; the transformation will be carried out mainly through the poetic image; the book will present Billy himself as an artist. Of course, "work" is ambiguous: it can also refer to Billy's actions, the killings. But Ondaatje is clearly working within the Romantic tradition of the artist as outsider, just as Samuel R. Delany in his novels is obsessed with the identity of the artist and the outlaw. Nichol's Billy "was not fast with words so he became fast with a gun,'' but for Ondaatje Billy's status as outlaw is intimately connected with the nature of his perception. He is placed outside society not only by what he does, but by the very way in which he sees the world:

The others, I know, did not see the wounds appearing in the sky, in the air. Sometimes a normal forehead in front of me leaked brain gasses. Once a nose clogged right before me, a lock of skin formed over the nostrils, and the shocked face had to start breathing through the mouth, but then the mustache bound itself in the lower teeth and he began to gasp loud the hah! hah! going strong — churned onto the floor, collapsed out, seeming in the end to be breathing out of his eye — tiny needle jets of air reaching into the throat. I told no one. If Angela D. had been with me then, not even her; not Sallie, John, Charlie, or Pat. In the end the only thing that never changed, never became deformed, were animals. (10)

Of course, Billy's poetic personality is not entirely distinct from Michael Ondaatje's. The concern with animals — apparent throughout the book — is familiar to any reader of Ondaatje's poetry. What results from the title "*The Collected Works of Billy the Kid* by Michael Ondaatje" is in fact a composite figure: Billy the Kid, outlaw as artist, and Michael Ondaatje, artist as outlaw, meeting in one persona, which is part history, part legend, part aesthetic image, part creator of images. It is in terms of this complex persona that the book approaches its material.

That material may be seen as a narrative with two main strands: the conflict between Billy and Pat Garrett, culminating in the manhunt and the deaths of Tom O'Folliard, Charlie Bowdre, and Billy himself; and the opposite of conflict, the scenes of peace and companionship, centering on Miss Angela D and the Chisum ranch. Underlying these two narrative strands is the central theme of violence, as it erupts in both outlaw and artist.

But fully as important as what *is* in the book is what is missed out. Ondaatje has exercised great selectivity in this presentation of Billy, and what he deliberately omits or suppresses from his sources is of great interest. One thing that should be noted about the narrative structure outlined above is that it ignores, almost completely, what is for all the biographers, however "true" or "authentic", the most important event of Billy's life: the Lincoln County War. (Burns devotes over half of his book to it.) Ondaatje's one reference to it is in connection with the question of motivation:

> A motive? some reasoning we can give to explain all this violence. Was there a source for all this? yup —

There follows Burns' account of Tunstall's murder, which he says Billy witnessed "from a distant hillside" having luckily been off "hunting wild turkeys." (In fact, it appears more probable that Billy was with Tunstall, and ran away.) Most apologists for Billy make this the central point of their exposition: Billy's career begins as an understandable search for vengeance on the murderers of his idealistic and honest friend. "Others fought for hire," Burns claims; "Billy the Kid's inspiration was the loyalty of friendship." (Again, in fact it is certain that Tunstall was neither idealistic nor honest, and highly doubtful that he was especially friendly with Billy.) But the casual tone of Ondaatje's "yup" suggests that he does not take this idea too seriously, and there is no further mention of this stage of Billy's career. It is possible that this passage is introduced only to make fun of simplistic psychological "explanations" of the sources of Billy's violence. Ondaatje has more serious things to say on that subject.

Similarly, Nichol introduces an "explanation" of Billy's violence as a joke, but a joke with more serious implications. The central conceit of

194

Nichol's book is the reversal of "Kid" to "Dick". Indeed, reversal of the normal image is Nichol's central tactic. So Nichol presents the extended joke that all Billy's activities were due to his having a small penis. At one level, this a light-hearted version of the too easily oversimplified theory that guns are used as compensation by males with fears of sexual inadequacy. Nichol recognizes that this can be used too simplistically, and also makes fun of psychological determinist attitudes by revealing that "the sherrif had a short dick too, which was why he was sherrif & not out robbing banks. these things affect people differently." But behind these jokes is serious awareness, present also in Ondaatje's book, of the tremendous force of the connection between violence and sexuality, and the centrality of these two aspects in contemporary American life. Make love not war — if you can. And it is surely no accident that Nichol twice points out that Billy's short dick is "short for richard." Richard, that is, as in Nixon. The Lincoln County War has been represented as a clash between the "good guys," Tunstall and McSween, idealistic supporters of the small farmers, and the "bad guys," the oppressive monopoly of Murphy, Dolan, and Riley; in fact, it appears to have been a fairly cynical gang war for economic control of the territory, in which neither side shows to advantage. Most of the victims in the "war" were shot in the back or from ambush. Parallels to the Vietnam war may be drawn at each reader's personal political discretion; but it does seem clear that Nichol is fully conscious of political applications, in his use of "richard," and again, later, in his cynical comment on one of Nixon's favourite slogans:

> billy ran around shooting his mouth off, & the dicks off everybody else, & the sherrif stood on the sidelines cheering. this is how law & order came to the old west.

Nichol's jokes on Billy's motivation also touch lightly on a subject which is absolutely central to his own poetry: the power of language, the almost magical efficacy of words.

> could they have called him instead billy the man or bloody bonney? would he have bothered having a faster gun? who can tell.

Again, the joke can be taken absolutely seriously. Names make you what

195

you are; you become what you are called. The historical Billy went through several changes of name. He started life as William H. Bonney; when his father died, his mother reverted to her maiden name and he became Henry McCarty; she remarried, he became Henry Antrim; when he first began to run foul of the law he acquired the name The Kid; by his own choice he reverted to William H. Bonney; but to history and legend he is only Billy the Kid. The naming is all-important: it fixes the image, it creates the personality. In Nichol's study of Billy's motivation, that non-committal "who can tell" is the most loaded phrase of all.

Having rejected any "historical" explanation in terms of the Lincoln County War, and omitting also such legendary accretions as Billy's youthful murder of a loafer who had insulted his mother, Ondaatje presents Billy's violence in terms of the poetic image of energy: the energy necessary to both outlaw and artist. The central text for this is the poem on page 41:

> I have seen pictures of great stars,
> drawings which show them straining to the centre
> that would explode their white
> if temperature and the speed they moved at
> shifted one degree.
>
> Or in the East have seen
> the dark grey yards where trains are fitted
> and the clean speed of machines
> that make machines, their
> red golden pouring which when cooled
> mists out to rust or grey.
>
> The beautiful machines pivoting on themselves
> sealing and fusing to others
> and men throwing levers like coins at them.
> And there is there the same stress as with stars,
> the one altered move that will make them maniac.

Energy tightly controlled by form is one definition of a work of art; and in art the "one altered move" will result in the dissipation of energy, a bad poem. Or, when the energy of the work of art is directly expressive of violence, and when it is transmitted in a context where such artistic controls as irony are severely compromised, then the "one altered move" can be physically destructive beyond the aesthetic bounds, as in

196

the case of the murder by the Hell's Angels during the Rolling Stones concert at Altamont. Ondaatje's book depicts the shattering of the precarious control over the energy of Billy's violence, and the violence he evokes in those around him; the events then drive inexorably towards his death. There is a close relationship here to the previously mentioned two strands of narrative: the scenes of control are (mainly, but not exclusively) associated with the Chisums and Angela D ; the "one altered move" is (mainly, but not exclusively) Pat Garrett. And, despite Billy's statement that "the only thing that never changed, never became deformed, were animals," both the harmony and the maniac destruction are most clearly seen in the animal references.

The first of Ondaatje's images of harmony, of what might be called the "pastoral interludes" in the book, comes in the description of Billy's weeklong stay in a deserted barn. Here, attracted by "the colour and the light," he stays to get rid of a fever. "It became a calm week" in which Billy and the animals are able to live together in harmony.

> There were animals who did not move out and accepted me as a larger breed. I ate the old grain with them, drank from a constant puddle about twenty yards away from the barn. I saw no human and heard no human voice, learned to squat the best way when shitting, used leaves for wiping, never ate flesh or touched another animal's flesh, never entered his boundary. We were all aware and allowed each other. The fly who sat on my arm, after his inquiry, just went away, ate his disease and kept it in him. When I walked I avoided the cobwebs, who had places to grow to, who had stories to finish. The flies caught in those acrobat nets were the only murder I saw.

But if this image of harmony is presented in terms of animals, it is also in terms of animals that the "one altered move" breaks in and destroys this scene: rats eat grain fermented by rain and become maniac, killing a chipmunk, eating each other, until Billy, with "the noise breaking out the seal of silence in my ears," exhausts his bullet supply in shooting them. At the end "no other animal of any kind remained in that room," except the human with his gun. This brief scene is a paradigm for what is to come later, at the Chisum ranch. If a writer's intentions can be most clearly seen in the places where he most drastically alters his source material, then Ondaatje's metamorphosis of the Chisums must be the very centre of his work. The impression that Ondaatje's book gives is that the Chisum ranch is a fairly small place, out in the desert miles from anywhere, inhabited only by Sallie and John, who is seen as a gentle, peace-loving man with little interest or influence in the world beyond his ranch. In fact, John Chisum was one of the largest and most influential landowners and cattlemen in the territory; and Burns describes the ranch thus:

> Chisum abandoned Bosque Grande as his headquarters in 1873, and moving down the Pecos forty miles, established South Spring Ranch, which remained his home to the end of his life. Where the South Spring River gushes from the earth in a never-failing giant spring of crystal water, he built a home fit for a cattle-king and made it one of the show places of the Southwest. Cottonwood trees brought from Las Vegas by mule pack-train he planted about his dwelling and in two winding rows that formed a noble avenue a quarter of a mile long leading from road to residence. He sowed eight hundred acres to alfafa. He brought fruit trees from Arkansas and set out a vast acreage in orchards of apple, pear, peach, and plum. He imported roses from Texas to make a hedge about the house, and scarlet tanagers and bob-white quail from Tennessee — birds unknown to New Mexico — and set them at liberty in the oasis of beauty he had created.
>
> Here, with royal hand, Chisum dispensed frontier hospitality. His great, rambling, one-storey adobe house, with verandas at front and rear, stood on the highway between Texas and New Mexico, and the stranger was as free as the invited guest to bed and board for as long as he wanted to stay, and no money or questions asked. Every day at breakfast, dinner, and supper, the table in the dining hall was set for twenty-six guests, twelve on each side and one at each end, and hardly a meal was served in ten years at which every chair was not occupied.

Ondaatje has not merely "edited, rephrased, and slightly reworked the originals"; he has made a complete, vivid, and detailed creation in absolute opposition to his original.

Ondaatje's suppression of the Lincoln County War also involves his omitting the facts that Chisum was the chief (though silent) force behind the Tunstall-McSween faction, and that after the war there was considerable conflict between Chisum and Billy, who claimed that Chisum owed him money for his part in the fighting. Burns quotes Sallie Chisum as attempting to discount this conflict, but there are persistent stories of Billy rustling Chisum's cattle, and, in some more imaginative versions, killing Chisum's cowboys. In a letter to Governor Lew Wallace, December 12th, 1880, Billy blamed accusations against him on "the impression put out by Chisum and his tools."

Steckmesser speculates that Joe Grant, one of Billy's victims, "may well have been hired by Chisum or another cattleman to remove the troublesome Kid." Even Burns, who downplays the whole conflict, admits that Chisum was responsible, along with other local cattle barons, for hiring Pat Garrett to get rid of Billy, and that their motives for this were primarily commercial. All this is totally changed or omitted in Ondaatje's version. It may also be noted that Garrett's own account never mentions his meeting Billy at the Chisum ranch, either for the first or any other time. (Garrett is, of course, understandably reticent about his early friendship with Billy.)

The image presented in Ondaatje's book is, then, largely his own invention; and the pains he has taken to alter his source material indicate the importance he attaches to it. The Chisum ranch is the "still centre" of Billy's world. It is a place of peace, of affection, of comradeship. None of the apologists for Billy as a poor misunderstood child driven against his will to violence have ever provided him with such a beautiful and fully realized context for his "true nature": but Ondaatje succeeds in doing this without in the least sentimentalizing Billy.

The first presentation occurs in Billy's mind as he and Angela D ride towards the house "Forty miles ahead of us." As they approach, Billy remembers in a wealth of loving details the small, everyday details of the life of John and Sallie Chisum: the remains of breakfast, their wordless "dialogue of noise," the shutters which made the house "silent and dark blue with sunless quiet," and Sallie herself in her bare feet,

> like a ghost across the room moving in white dresses, her hair knotted as always at the neck and continuing down until it splayed and withered like eternal smoke half way between the shoulder blades and the base of cobble spine.
> Yes. In white long dresses in the dark house, the large bones somehow taking on the quietness of the house. Yes I remember. (33)

These ethereal images of peace and beauty are reinforced by the solid human friendship, the recollections of long evenings on the porch when "we have talked slowly through nights expecting the long silences and we have taken our time thinking the replies." Even throwing up after a long night's drinking becomes a kind of act of community; and it is significant that Garrett is specifically excluded from it, just as he falls

199

asleep during the conversation on the porch. Again, this is a detail specifically altered from Burns' book, where Sallie Chisum describes Garrett as often being "the life of the company that used to sit on the porch of an evening."

Angela D fits into this world: Billy brings her to it. (Garrett arrives on his own, by accident, and is "deaf" when he arrives.) The most graphic of the sexual scenes between Billy and Angela D takes place at the Chisum ranch, and Billy wakes there to the vision of "Beautiful ladies in white rooms in the morning" (71).

But, as in the pastoral tradition, *et in Arcadia ego*, elements of disruption are present even in this perfectly achieved harmony, balance, control of energy. Indeed, the indications of the "one altered move" are introduced, typically, at the very centre of the harmony, Sallie Chisum's love of animals. The first description of the Chisum ranch ends with an account of Sallie's strange collection of pet animals: "the tame, the half born, the wild, the wounded." John Chisum takes Billy out to the cages in darkness: "You could peer into a cage and see nothing till a rattle of claws hit the grid an inch from your face and their churning feathers seemed to hiss" (36). There is the bizarre image of the one-eyed owls, the intense realization of the animals' presence and awareness, which "continued like that all night while we slept." Despite the love which Sallie obviously bears for these animals, the atmosphere of the scene is sinister, filled with impending violence. Billy feels himself to be standing on "the edge of the dark" and concludes "The night, the dark air, made it all mad." The madness and violence break out immediately in a poem in which mad rats fight in Billy's head, horses foam white with madness, and a deadly barracuda floats in his brain.

Another extended episode at the Chisum ranch is John's horrifying story of the man who systematically breeds a group of dogs into madness until they turn on him and rip him to pieces. The story is shatteringly out of place in the calm and beautiful atmosphere of the ranch; Sallie comments, to her dog, "Aint that a nasty story Henry, aint it? Aint it nasty" (62). Henry, like Ondaatje's own dog, is a bassett; Henry is also what the H. stands for in William H. Bonney.

Garrett's presence at the Chisums' is another signal of disruption, and it is Garrett who narrates the story of Billy killing Sallie's snake-bitten cat. The imagery is closely tied together: it is this event which, according to Garrett, terrifies Angela D; the account of Angela's shot arm immediately precedes the narrative of the night of slow talking and drinking from which Garrett is so pointedly excluded; and the beauty of the morning after is brought to an end when Billy sees that "On the nail above the bed the black holster and gun is coiled like a snake." Another careful juxtaposition is that between Billy's shooting the cat and the first flashforward to the final shooting; and this flashforward begins:

> Down the street was a dog. Some mut spaniel, black and white. One dog, Garrett and two friends, stud looking, came down the street to the house, to me. (46)

As a final touch to this continual association of animals and violence, Ondaatje tells us, right at the end of the book, just before the climactic description of Billy's death, that Garrett also liked animals: but not live ones, like Sallie Chisum. Pat Garrett stuffed dead birds.

But Garrett is an essential part of Billy's legend. Many reasons can be given for the longevity of that legend — Billy's youth; the attractiveness, admitted even by his enemies, of his personality; the possibility of seeing him as fighting on the "right" side of the Lincoln County War; the fact that most of his victims in one sense or another deserved what they got; the exotic Mexican background — but one of the strongest motifs is that of Betrayal. Kent Ladd Steckmesser says of this point:

> The theme of 'betrayal' has been carefully pointed up by Bonney's biographers and has gripped the folk imagination. Time and again we are told that the Kid would have settled down and become a law-abiding citizen if only the man hunters had given him half a chance. But Governor Wallace 'double-crossed' the Kid by reneging on a promise of an amnesty. Garrett was a Judas who tracked down his friend for a few silver dollars. The story unfolds like a classical Greek drama, with the tragic hero moving inexorably toward death by treachery.

Just as Robin Hood had his Sheriff of Nottingham and Jesse James had Robert Ford, Billy the Kid had Pat Garrett. As has already been remarked, their fates are linked in legend as in life. So long as Billy was regarded as an extravagantly evil villain, Garrett was a hero, saviour of law and order, etc.; but as the view of Billy changes, Garrett becomes

201

the betrayer, the manhunter, the assassin. (In 1908, Garrett was himself assassinated, in circumstances which have never been fully explained.) This is, essentially, the approach which Ondaatje takes; but Nichol, characteristically, takes the whole idea and stands it on its head.

Nichol's version of Pat Garrett is "the sherrif" (sic), and

> the true eventual story is billy & the sherrif were friends. if they had been more aware they would have been lovers. they were not more aware.

Nichol's sherrif does not betray Billy: Billy is betrayed by history, by legend, by god, and ultimately by himself, but not by the sherrif. Indeed, the sherrif occupies in Nichol's book much the place that Angela D occupies in Ondaatje's. Nichol takes the idea of the symbiosis which binds together hero and villain, hunter and hunted, assassin and victim, and turns it into an identity of interests directed against the outside world. The sherrif shares Billy's predicament, but, as already noted, "these things affect people differently." The sherrif simply "stood on the sidelines cheering." This can of course be read as a cynical comment on the collusion between lawmen and criminals; but it seems more important as Nichol's only expression of community, of a harmonious relationship between two people. The two outsiders, losers of society, join together; their friendship is beautiful, the fact that they "were not more aware" is tragic, the farewell they take of each other is touching in its simplicity. Again, Nichol's surface tone is one of light-hearted joking, but the words he puts down can be taken perfectly seriously. And the sherrif does not destroy Billy: Billy in the end destroys himself, as his own violence catches up with him in a furiously self-destructive joke:

> the true eventual story is that billy the kid shot it out with himself. there was no-one faster. he snuck up on himself & shot himself from behind the grocery store.

Nichol's Billy is in fact a more violent character than Ondaatje's: but he is not betrayed. Whatever God, history, or legend say, rumour and the sherrif remain true to him. They deny the impositions of history and legend, presenting instead, clearly and strongly, a reversed image. The subtitle "Left Handed Poems" could well be applied more accurately to Nichol's book than to Ondaatje's. In the reversed photo

202

image, William H. Bonney becomes The Left Handed Gun; and Pat Garrett, strangely but not without beauty, becomes a sherrif not quite aware enough to be a lover.

Ondaatje's view of Garrett is more conventional; and here it should be noted that Ondaatje's highly selective presentation of Billy's history involves a very strong bias against Garrett. As already noted, Ondaatje omits any account of Billy's early activities such as his murders in the Lincoln County War, and presents him mainly in two contexts: the peace and beauty of the Chisum ranch, and the final chase and manhunt. In other words, Billy is seen almost entirely as victim. There are three extended accounts of killings in the book — those of Tom O'Folliard, Charlie Bowdre, and Billy himself — and in every case the killer is Garrett. We never get any similar account of a killing by Billy. Even in the strange and bizarre account of the killing of Gregory (whoever he is supposed to be), Ondaatje is careful to have Billy say that:

I'd shot him well and careful
made it explode under his heart
so it wouldn t last long

In other words, Billy is a humane murderer; the gruesome images which follow can be blamed on the chicken, not Billy. There is a detailed narrative of the chase and of the tortures Billy suffers in captivity, but only the sketchiest idea is given of Billy's escape from jail, and his murder of Bell and Ollinger. Ondaatje concentrates instead on the depiction of Ollinger as a sadistic villain: a device, largely invented by Burns, which has no historical basis whatever. In short, Ondaatje stacks his deck. If the reader reacts in horror or disgust from the violence in the book, he is reacting mainly *against* Garrett. Although Ondaatje's Billy is far from a blameless character, there is a definite implication that the violence exists around him rather than in him; Nichol's farcical conclusion gives a far greater sense of a character destroyed from within by his own violence. The interconnectedness of Garrett and Billy works inexorably: if Nichol makes Garrett a friend, then the violence has to shift back to Billy, while the more Ondaatje presents Pat Garrett as the assassin, the man-hunter, the more he whitewashes his Billy.

Garrett is presented as "that rare thing — a sane assassin."

203

Ondaatje's account of his early life gives a plausible background of psychological motivation for Garrett's suppression of emotion; but it stresses that even before Juanita's death Garrett was capable of efforts of will such as his learning French and learning to drink. Garrett "comes to chaos neutral": but his neutrality cuts him off from any contact with humanity, so that his violence becomes cold and inhuman. Twice we have the picture of his victims (Tom O'Folliard and Charlie Bowdre) staggering towards him in death; in each case he stands unmoved, waiting for them to die. Even his reaction to Billy's death is reported in a totally unemotional manner. Garrett, more than any other single factor in the book, *is* that "one altered move" that makes everything around him "maniac." The word itself is echoed in the description of Billy's arm breaking through the window after the shooting:

> Guitterrez goes to hold the arm but it is manic, breaks
> her second finger. His veins that controlled triggers —
> now tearing all they touch.

Nichol's Billy destroys himself; but Ondaatje's is destroyed by something outside himself, something that itself remains calm and indestructible: and therefore, all the more terrifying. Garrett's character thus presents an interesting paradox: he is himself an embodiment of order, control; yet in contact with Billy he becomes the "altered move" which produces chaos.

Or is it chaos? It is violence, certainly, and death; but there is a kind of direction to it. Within the terms of the legend, it is an inexorable progress, and what it ends in is not Billy's death but Billy's apotheosis into legend: the creation, that is, of an aesthetic image. If Billy is one image of the artist, then surely Pat Garrett, even if his material is dead bodies, like his birds, is another? *The Collected Works of Billy the Kid* is, after all, a tightly controlled book: Ondaatje is a careful artist, and the images of violence are never allowed to get out of hand in the book. The book is not chaos, the book is not manic. It is an attempt to comprehend the legend of Billy the Kid, to see him as one of the exemplary figures of modern consciousness, outlaw as artist, artist as outlaw. He is involved with violence, but the violence results from the conflict between himself and his society, it is a product of his symbiotic relationship with Pat Garrett. Ondaatje's final image of Billy sees him waking

204

up after a bad night: the smell of smoke, the stain of violence, is still with him — but only in his shirt, which can be changed. We turn the page and find a photograph of a small boy smiling in a cowboy outfit: Billy's costume of violence turned into an image, a toy. That small boy is Michael Ondaatje, poet.

Ondaatje's Billy does not have the substantiality of history; his history is changed and fashioned into something else: legend, the aesthetic image in all its depth and detail, its vividness and force. Nichol's Billy is, in its way, a much more radical image of the outsider's consciousness, for it rejects any notion of substance whatever. His Billy is rumour, and essentially short-lived, like the smoke which Ondaatje's Billy sees on his ceiling, ready to blow away whenever a window is opened. His energy dissipates itself, sneaks up behind and shoots itself. Yet Nichol's is also a carefully crafted and constructed book. The surface seems superficial and whimsical, yet the words will always yield a serious meaning if you give them a chance. Perhaps rumour is that way too. The truth lies only in what the words can say, and what they say is never fixed. It is a process, an event, a becoming; the truth is always eventual.

Such as, for example, the "truth" that on July 14th, 1881, in Pete Maxwell's dark bedroom, Pat Garrett shot Billy the Kid just above the heart, and the next day, "neatly and properly dressed" (according to Garrett), he was buried in the military cemetary at Old Fort Sumner, in the state of New Mexico.

1 In a letter to the author, bp Nichol states, 'my version of Billy predates michaels
I told michael in 68 when he let slip at a party at his house that he was working on a
billy the kid poem that id written it & he refused to read it coz he didnt want to
be influenced by it in 69 we swapped manuscripts.' Incidentally, Nichol also notes
that the total amount he and Ondaatje received as Governor-General's Awards —
$5000 — is the same as the original reward offered for Billy the Kid.

NOTE:

The primary texts are:
Nichol, bp. *The True Eventual Story of Billy the Kid.* Toronto: Weed/Flower Press, 1970.
Ondaatje, Michael. *The Collected Works of Billy the Kid.* Toronto: Anansi, 1970.

For a great deal of my information about Billy the Kid in both history and legend, I am deeply indebted to:
Steckmesser, Kent Ladd. *The Western Hero in History and Legend.* University of Oklahoma Press, 1965.

I have also consulted the book which Ondaatje acknowledges as his main source:
Burns, Walter Noble. *The Saga of Billy the Kid.* New York: Doubleday & Company, 1926.

Finally, I have made reference to:
Garrett, Pat F. *The Authentic Life of Billy the Kid.* With an Introduction by J.C. Dykes. University of Oklahoma Press, 1954.

Postscript (1984)

In the twelve years that have passed since this article was published, I have continued to read and teach *The Collected Works of Billy the Kid*, and my view of it has necessarily changed, at least in some details, though not fundamentally. Rather than attempting a full-scale revision of the essay for this collection (and believing that, as the first published article on the book, the 1972 text should be left intact), I have decided to add this brief postscript by way of updating.

When I wrote the article, my major source for information about Billy's life and legend was a book by Kent Ladd Steckmesser called *The Western Hero In Myth And Legend.* Since then, a much fuller and more accurate acount has appeared, using recent historical research on the facts of the Kid's life and discussing his many manifestations in art and literature (up to and including Ondaatje) in the century since his death. This is Stephen Tatum's *Inventing Billy the Kid: Visions of the Outlaw in America, 1881–1981* (Albuquerque: University of New Mexico Press, 1982), and it is now the essential volume for all students of Billy.

Tatum's information would, for instance, modify my list of Billy's historical names.

A few minor corrections to my essay. I speculate on the possibility that "bp wrote his book just for fun, because Michael was writing his"; in fact, both books were conceived and written independently, neither author seeing the other's MS until both were completed. My discussion of the implications of Robert Silvester's cover has been somewhat blunted by subsequent editions of the book, which now use the back cover for laudatory comments, whereas in the original edition the back cover image was a reversed negative of the front. I say that all references to Chisum's role as a cattle baron who was party to the hiring of Garrett were "totally changed or omitted in Ondaatje's version"; I had overlooked the stray reference, surely vestigial from another text, to "cattle politicians like Chisum" (*CW*, 7). If I were rewriting the essay now, I would greatly expand the paragraph which deals with the sequence of images around the gun and the holster "coiled like a snake" above the bed, especially in relation to the repeated visual image which illustrates the point and links it to Garrett (*CW*, 45, 91). But these are minor points.

The major point I wish to make in this postscript deals with what I perceive to be a major trend in recent criticism of *The Collected Works of Billy the Kid*, specifically in Dennis Lee's *Savage Fields* (Toronto: Anansi, 1977), Perry M. Nodelman's "The Collected Photographs of Billy the Kid," *Canadian Literature*, 87 (Winter, 1980), and Judith Owens' "'I Send You a Picture': Ondaatje's Portrait of Billy the Kid," *Studies in Canadian Literature*, VIII, 1, (1983). I would describe this trend as "anti-Billy," in the sense that it sees Ondaatje's book as deeply critical and even hostile to its protagonist. My own essay, with its slightly idealised view of "a composite figure: Billy the Kid, outlaw as artist, and Michael Ondaatje, artist as outlaw," may be too "pro-Billy," but I still believe it is a more satisfactory reading than those proposed by the critics I have mentioned.

My view attempts to maintain a balance (a project which I think is typical of Ondaatje) between the two aspects of artist and outlaw. Lee, in contrast, sees Billy almost entirely as an outlaw, as "an instrument of murder" who kills "casually, absent-mindedly, out of the periphery of his vision" (Lee, 19, 39). I have already offered a detailed refutation of Lee's reading in my review of *Savage Fields*, "A Scheme is not a

Vision" (*Canadian Literature*, 78 (Autumn, 1978)), where I argued that part of Lee's problem was his difficulties with fitting the concept of the artist into his cosmology of "savage fields."

Nodelman and Owens advance more subtle forms of the argument, but despite many excellent points in both their essays, I believe that it is still essentially the same argument as Lee's, and that it fails for the same reasons. Nodelman and Owens *do* see Billy as an artist, the controlling consciousness of the book: in fact, their thesis is that he exerts, or attempts to exert, *too much* control. Nodelman sees Billy as using both photographs and guns to keep his emotional distance from a world of change which he distrusts and fears; the result is that "the poems and sections in prose are as devoid of emotion as the actual photographs Ondaatje chose to include" (Nodelman, 69). Owens similarly argues that Billy is obsessed with order and with a fear of mortality, and that he shapes his own "works" in an attempt "to assume control over his world, to order the world to his liking" (Owens, 126).

In response, I would say first of all that I find it impossible to accept Nodelman's description of the book in general, or of Billy in particular, as "devoid of emotion." On the contrary, it strikes me as an extraordinarily emotional book, and Billy's consciousness presents his world with almost unbearable intensity, whether it is the horror of Charlie Bowdre's death, or the sensuous savouring of making love with Angie (*CW*, 14, 21). I do not see how anyone could describe either of these poems as distanced or unemotional (but see Owens for an ingenious counter-reading). Nodelman claims that "all the smells of living offend Billy, particularly those of other people. He dislikes 'the strange smell of their breath / moving across my face'" (Nodelman, 73, quoting *CW*, 39). But if you look at that poem, there is nothing in it to support Nodelman's word "dislikes": what Billy finds "strange," but not at all displeasing, is his own ability to "feel people / not close to me," that is, to bridge instinctively the very distance which Nodelman claims he is trying to set up.

Nodelman also points to Billy's dislike of the smell of flowers (*CW*, 55-56), but fails to note that what Billy is reacting to here is the smell of *dying* flowers. Nodelman quotes the line about the cut flower which "gets small smells sane," and comments "For Billy, death smells good. The only true sanity comes with the elimination of a painfully changing thing that smells disturbingly of life" (Nodelman, 74). But this ignores the fact that the word "sane" does not carry in this book its usual positive connotations, since it is overwhelmingly associated with Pat Garrett, the "sane assassin" (*CW*, 29). Billy not unreasonably associates this kind of "only true sanity" with his *enemy*, his *opposite*. Indeed, all three of these critics, Lee, Nodelman, and Owens, neglect or simply ignore Pat Garrett. He is made redundant in their schemes, for they have put Billy in his place. But for Ondaatje, Garrett is a major structural pole of the book; to pass over the differences between Billy and Garrett is seriously to distort the book that Ondaatje actually wrote.

The crucial poem in this discussion is the one about the "newsman's brain" (*CW*, 11), in which Billy describes the world-view that can "eliminate much" and turn away from killings, "walk off see none of the thrashing." Lee says that Billy "embraces that ideology" and "kills by adopting [it]" (Lee, 19). Nodelman also sees Billy as accepting this world-view (Nodelman, 75), while Owens says that he "advocates" it and "constructs an argument" to support it (Owens, 120). But all three of them miss, disastrously, the force of the initial "if": "*if* I had a newsman's brain I'd say" — but Billy does *not* have such a brain, and the immediately following poems (indeed, the whole book) demonstrate his total inability to adopt this ethos. The person who *does* adopt it is Garrett, and Billy is fascinated by him, "drawn to opposites" like Buddy Bolden (*Coming Through Slaughter*, 96). The whole point of the "newsman's brain" poem is to demonstrate Billy's acute apprehension (in both senses of the word) of an ideology which fascinates him only because it is his opposite, his enemy, that which will ultimately kill him. To say that he "embraces" or "advocates" it is, I believe, totally to misread both this poem and Billy's whole character.

I do not wish to deny that Billy is in many ways a neurotic character, or that he fights desperately losing battles to control the chaos and violence in and around him. But I think that the issue of control, especially aesthetic control, is more complex than Nodelman and Owens make it appear. At the risk of oversimplifying their essays, I would say that both of them seem to imply that "distance" and "control" are inherently negative or life-denying forces. By ignoring or downplaying Garrett, they have to shift all these negative connotations onto Billy, but they thus miss the possibility that the book presents, in the contrast between Billy and Garrett, different *kinds* of control and distancing from the emotions. Garrett, with his never-used mastery of French and his fondness for stuffed birds, is certainly life-denying and mechanistic. Billy's notion of control may use the imagery of "beautiful machines" (CW, 41), but paradoxically, and despite Nodelman (75) and Owens (133-134), it is *not* mechanistic. Rather, it involves a dynamic notion of balance, or equilibrium, which is much closer to Ondaatje's own idea of artistic control, as shown in his other works. (See my comments on this idea in "His Legend a Jungle Sleep.") Billy, I would argue, is Michael Ondaatje's type of artist, and a more successful one, even, than Buddy Bolden. Of course there are moments when he loses control, when he is overwhelmed by chaos, disgust, fear of mortality, all the "loathing" Ondaatje himself speaks of in "War Machine." And one might well argue that Ondaatje is always attracted to characters whose "equilibrium" is precarious precisely because he knows that their balance will not hold. But that balance is not in itself a negative or life-denying force: it has to be defended against the "one altered move" (CW, 41) that threatens to disrupt it, especially when that move, in the guise of Pat Garrett (or Webb, or Robichaux) is a perversion of the idea of control itself. Billy makes that defence, to the end and beyond; and that is why I still feel compelled to defend *him* against critical views which, like the photograph Paulita Maxwell comments on (CW, 19), do him less than justice.

July, 1984

Dennis Cooley
"I AM HERE ON THE EDGE":
MODERN HERO / POSTMODERN POETICS IN
THE COLLECTED WORKS OF BILLY THE KID

1. Doorway

Michael Ondaatje has always been fascinated by unorthodox poetics and characters, notably Billy the Kid in *The Collected Works of Billy the Kid*, the Australian convict in *the man with seven toes*, and Buddy Bolden in *Coming Through Slaughter*. The two concerns have always gone hand in hand for Ondaatje. He's equally drawn to strange figures pressing the limits of society and writing that explores the formal boundaries of art. His two chief protagonists, Billy and Buddy, both raise some radical questions about the worlds they know and make. Throughout *Billy the Kid* and *Slaughter* (especially in their climaxes) their tortured art orgasmically explodes "out there" — in the hot, open spaces beyond the provisional edges where they constantly find themselves.[1]
    Ondaatje's Billy, sitting inside a room alongside a doorway, tells us at one point "I am on the edge of the cold dark," then says "I am here on the edge of sun / that would ignite me":

>   This nightmare by this 7 foot high doorway
>   waiting for friends to come
>   mine or theirs
>   I am 4 feet inside the room
>   in the brown cold dark
>   the doorway's slide of sun
>   three inches from my shoes
>   I am on the edge of the cold dark
>   watching the white landscape in its frame
>   a world that's so precise
>   every nail and cobweb
>   has magnified itself to my presence

211

Waiting
nothing breaks my vision
but flies in their black path
like inverted stars,
or the shock sweep of a bird
that's grown too hot
and moves into the cool for an hour

If I hold up my finger
I blot out the horizon
if I hold up my thumb
I'd ignore a man who comes
on a three mile trip to here
The dog near me breathes out
his lungs make a pattern of sound
when he shakes
his ears go off like whips
he is outside the door
mind clean, the heat
floating his brain in fantasy

I am here on the edge of sun
that would ignite me
looking out into pitch white
sky and grass overdeveloped to meaninglessness
waiting for enemies' friends or mine [2]

We find Billy, typically, staring warily at the edge, constantly on edge. In every way an out-law, he tries, at times distends and transgresses, boundaries. More often, he fears to cross the lines, hopes to defend his hard-held borders against all trespassers. Billy's marginal situation is here represented by the doorway he sits watching, in a position he assumes throughout much of the book. That doorway provides him with a frame for the white landscape burning outside, a rigid framework which sharply defines that outer space. Its straight vertical and horizontal lines hold that world in place, as Billy himself wants and needs to contain it. But even as Billy fits his frame upon that world, he sits dangerously close to it, occupying a narrow 4-foot strip between the enclosed spaces he barely controls and the wide-open nightmare territory which boils just outside the door. Billy's exquisite sense of vulnerability is heightened even more by his perception that "the doorway's slide of sun / [is] three inches from my shoes."

The most immediate threat to Billy is physical — his chronic and justifiable fear that Pat Garrett's gang will get him. A more basic and more interesting terror rises out of his reaction to the sun. As we overhear in Billy's meditation, it is the sun, not his enemies, that would push him over the edge, "ignite" him. The sun constantly scrapes and slams against the dark inner fortifications Billy prefers to occupy (including the shelter he finds in the many intensely private *interior* monologues where he digs in against outside intrusions). So we read about "arcs of sun... digging into the floor" (34), the "huge" sun that "came in and pushed out the walls... hitting and swirling" in his room (69), and "the bent oblong of sun / [that] hoists itself across the room" (21), the sun's shifting pressure being recorded as oblique lines that transgress, or as irregular lines that arch and curve. Billy's resistance depends on predictable straight lines (verticals or horizontals) that try to straighten up an unruly world.

The menacing violence that Billy finds in the blazing heat and light constantly threatens to erupt within him and to blow him up. As he so fearfully knows, things can be "melted [out of shape] by getting close to fire" (51). So he goes berserk when he takes the lid off a hot biscuit tin, releasing a frantic rat:

> bang it went was hot
> under my eye
> was hot small bang did it
> almost a pop
> I didnt hear till I was red
> had a rat fyt in my head (38)

When the lid comes off Billy loses his composure, as the pell-mell jerky rhythms, repetitions, confusions, and broken syntax indicate. The stroke Billy later suffers, when Pat Garrett lugs him unshaded across the desert, shows even more graphically the insanity he develops in light of the sun's violent assaults, which he ordinarily associates with Garrett. That sun is so savage that Billy compares it to "a fleshy hawk" (26) and observes its formidable power in his phrase "on the edge of sun" (75), where the absence of an article (we read simply "sun," not "a" or "the" sun) nearly transforms the sun into a verb by creating a sense of its direct felt force. He always becomes disoriented when phenomena shed their inertness, shake off their solidity, begin to "melt." Ultimately those connections between urgent heat and light bring us to Billy's violent death when the room where he is shot fills with packets of little suns and his perceptions fragment into a series of "lovely perfect sun balls / breaking at each other click / click click click" (95).

One of Billy's lovers, Angela D, pulls him into the galvanic frenzy he experiences in that bright world, until he takes his ultimate revenge upon her in a macabre vaudevillian song (64). Terrified that "Her throat is a kitchen / red food and old heat," and remembering that in their wild sexual encounters she nearly paralyzes him, he tries to get back at Angie with his doggerel. His horror of being broken or engulfed by Angela D is only faintly masked in his jingling verses and grotesque humour. Billy's assumption of a false innocence in these verses, culminating in his baby talk ("Her toes take your ribs / her fingers your mind / her turns a gorilla / to swallow you blind") only heightens our recognition of his childish and impotent rage. Finally, when he's disintegrating in death, Billy pictures "oranges reeling across the room" (95), an image that picks up a previous episode between himself and Angie. In that meeting she closes in on him from the door and sweeps the bright orange peels off the bed (21). At the same time she lets loose the sun in his room when she "jams" up the sackcloth on the window. The "slide of sun" which she admits, like her own intrusions on his retreats, threatens to ignite Billy.

In contrast, Sallie Chisum, Billy's other (though less obvious) lover, shuts out the searing heat and light when he, like hundreds of other broken animals, comes trailing in from the desert, seeking refuge at her ranch. Opaque. Sallie and her husband, John, empty the lamps each morning "to avoid fire." More dramatically, Sallie

> had John build shutters for every door and window, every hole in the wall. So that at eleven in the morning all she did was close and lock them all until the house was silent and dark blue with sunless quiet. (33)

When Billy comes to recuperate at this "little world in itself" (30) after burning his legs, Sallie shuts out the day, creating a cool dark room for him where he's safe from the sun's abrasions. Heat discharging into her room. The peacefulness and slowing of time conveyed by the long, easy rhythms of the "Chisum" prose counterbalances the taut, nervous speed of Billy's poems when he's under stress. (It's interesting to note the similarities between the quiet Chisum ranch and the other shelter Billy finds in a barn, where he also tries to rid himself of the heat, in this case a fever burning inside him.) Though Sallie also is erotic (and possibly in her own way even an unwitting jailer), she acts as a maternal figure who nurses a defenceless Billy back to health, whereas Angie initiates him into a frenzied world where he goes to pieces. They are both at the edge with him, but each of them offers different responses to it. Sallie protects Billy's precarious boundaries and maintains his sanity, Angie violates them and brings with her the sun's undoing.

2. Photographer

In visual terms, Sallie helps Billy to hold the lines he so badly wants in life. She strengthens the frames he tries to set on everything, so Billy can be reassured "the sun drops in perfect verticals" (72). Those upright lines embody Billy's attempts to fight off the massive long low horizontal sky which threatens to swallow and crush him. Sallie's cool dim shelter seems to ensure that the awesome sky fire won't get in. Ondaatje's terms for that protection are distinctly visual. Sallie's closed shutters and black room provide Billy with what amounts to a photographer's darkroom or, better: a camera whose shutter can be closed down to eliminate light.

The notion may at first seem strained, but when we remember Ondaatje's fascination with film and photography, it seems more likely.[3] Once we read through Billy the Kid with this hunch in mind we find much evidence to confirm it. As a matter of fact, Perry M. Nodelman, in his article "The Collected Photographs of Billy the Kid," has elaborated on the extensive and central role of "Billy's photographic objectivity" in Ondaatje's book.[4]

Photographic terms frequently emerge in Billy's mind as he sits tensely "on the edge of sun." We certainly can see his acute anxiety in the anaphoric structure of the poem I quoted earlier — the turns and returns on key expressions about his position: "I am," "If I," "watching," "looking," "waiting." On the lookout. We can also see Billy's edginess in his insistent noting of size and distance: there is "this 7 foot high doorway," "I am 4 feet inside the room," the sun is "three inches from my shoes," a man might come "on a three mile trip to here." He's trying to figure things out, to size up life, to seize it in the stability of known quantities. The importance Billy places on exact and frequent measurements marks his attempts to survey and to take hold of that room, to mark it off (doubly framed) as safely known and securely occupied, to take analgesic measures against life. But the quantitative manoeuvres are almost insignificant alongside the vast forces leaning against him, as we notice from the small and declining space he holds onto: it shrinks from a 7 foot doorway to a 4 foot buffer zone and then to a mere 3 inches of shade.

Billy is so concerned about being caught by surprise that, like a photographer (or a director), he calculates actual lines of sight, meant to obliterate the appearance of certain images he'd rather not see:

> If I hold up my finger
> I blot out the horizon
> if I hold up my thumb
> I'd ignore a man who comes
> on a three mile trip to here (74)[5]

Billy also notices details with such intensity that they become startingly exaggerated in size:

> a world that's so precise
> every nail and cobweb
> has magnified itself to my presence

To concentrate — to center himself in this world: ego-centric. These responses are remarkable, not only because they show extraordinary acuity in Billy's sense, but also for the photographer's eye they bring to focus.[6] First the nails and cobwebs "magnified. . . to my presence," as if Billy were a special close-up lens enlarging the details because of his agitated state. In those perceptions he is extracting objects from their usual positions and viewing the edited pieces in an expanded way, so that they take on a strange hugeness, should they appear, small with the long look he's taking through the door, blocking and blacking them out.

The whole poem climbs out of an overwhelming visual sense (though we also find some strong tactile and auditory images, which

216

occur in other Billy poems). Billy's photographic stance shows elsewhere in the "doorway" poem when, fearing exposure, he is "watching the white landscape in its frame" nightmarishly jump forward, when he notices "flies in their black path / like inverted stars," and when he is "looking out into pitch white / sky and grass overdeveloped to meaninglessness," the cool, serene and receding greens eaten out of the image (74). What Billy notices here no unaided human eye could possibly see. Only a camera lens can admit the simultaneous perception of field and ground, particularly when the foreground is heavily shaded and the background brilliantly lit, as they are here. So we read in *Coming Through Slaughter*, that under sunlight "There can be *either* the narrow dark focus of the eye *or* the crazy chaos of white."[7] Billy's human eye, adjusted to the interior dimness, couldn't sense the slugs of sunlight banging against him, but in this poem he characteristically does, using his camera eye to take on the impression. In *On Photography*, Susan Sontag mentions that early photography was called heliography, literally "sun-writing," the sort of inscribing that Billy constantly undergoes.[8]

I'm not suggesting that Ondaatje has made a mistake in ascribing this perspective to his protagonist. Ondaatje knows exactly what he's doing. He's deliberately working with references to a camera view to show Billy's anxious and unremitting attempts to manage life and to extricate himself from it. That's why Billy speculates (longingly, I think) about blotting out the horizon and ignoring a man behind his controlled sight lines. That's also why he would prefer to find that "nothing breaks my vision" (74), and why, on the very next page, he says his every move "is planned by my eye" (75). Billy desperately wants, more than anything, by his unblinking gaze, to freeze action in a series of still photographs, or a series of shots approaching still photographs. In Billy's perhaps envious accusations about how "you" (we as the readers, I guess) might escape in "blackout" (72) there may be an expression of his own last-ditch tactics to fend off discomfitting, complex images by withdrawing into photographic darkrooms and negatives. In this book, then, photos do not figure as unmediated access to reality; rather, they serve as tactical interceptions of it.

That decided wish to hide within stills, empty screens (or, on occasion, diagrams) shows up early in the book:

217

so if I had a newsman's brain I'd say
well some morals are physical
must be clear and open
like diagram of watch or star
one must eliminate much
that is one turns when the bullet leaves you
walk off see none of the thrashing
the very eyes welling up like bad drains
believing then the moral of newspapers or gun
where bodies are mindless as paper flowers you dont feed
or give to drink
that is why I can watch the stomach of clocks
shift their wheels and pins into each other
and emerge living, for hours (11)

There's no doubt that Billy tries verbal strategies to ward off appalling realities he'd rather not face: it's not "I" but "one" or "you" who does these things, not "I" who shoots the bullet but the "bullet [that] leaves you."

It's also worth reminding ourselves about Billy's most obvious dodge — side-stepping behind black humour, a common defence in the twentieth century against a monstrous and brutal world. Though only partly successful, Billy's retreats into grim humour provide a spur-of-the-moment defence when he's caught off guard. Shocked, he watches Charlie Bowdre dying in terrible agony; his words of horror come only after a long numb silence (which is registered by a wide visual gap in the text):

Jesus I never knew that did you
the nerves shot out
the liver running around there
like a headless hen jerking
brown all over the yard
seen that too at my aunt's
never eaten hen since then (12)

The flippancy is not a sign of callousness. It shows Billy's struggle to mask what he's seen, just as the absence of a grammatical subject in the penultimate line reveals his transparent attempt to remove himself from the frightening knowledge of his friend's death. Similar devices work in the section where he describes Gregory's death. Billy describes how

218

he is leaving Gregory on the street

> when this chicken paddles out to him
> and as he was falling hops on his neck
> digs the beak into his throat
> straightens legs and heaves
> a red and blue vein out
>
> Meanwhile he fell
> and the chicken walked away
>
> still tugging at the vein
> till it was 12 yards long
> as if it held that body like a kite
> Gregory's last words being
>
> get away from me yer stupid chicken (15)

The demonstrative pronouns and definite articles create a distancing, impersonalizing, and comical effect ("this chicken," "the beak," "that body"), but so does the ridiculous exaggeration and distortion of normal movement ("chicken paddles out"), and so does the impossible simile with its outrageous hints of innocence, however faint, in the comparison of the body to a kite. The passive voice with which Billy begins this monologue ("After shooting Gregory / this is what happened") does much the same thing in minimizing his own responsibility and awareness. These devices form what is meant to be a verbal narcotic: "these things just happened, rather comically, and they don't have much of anything to do with me."

More immediate to my argument: the newsman's mind and the newspaper photo Billy mentions earlier represent the obliviousness he so badly wants. When Billy's thrashing victims are caught in a journalist's snap-shots they become reduced to "mindless flowers" on the dull flat page of newsprint, shaved clean of their real-life depth and agony, which is inescapably expressed in the jerking eyes of their actual bodies — eyes that won't stand still, stricken lives that in their furnace heat flail and jump past him. Overrun by those scenes, Billy would like to turn life into a series of safe stills; he'd "eliminate much," "turn his back on" the excruciating suffering. So, when Angela D comes into his room, lets in the heavy sun, and closes in on Billy with the electricity crackling inside her, he reacts with a physical catatonia rendered in

219

appropriately photographic words: "I am very still / I take in all the angles of the room" (21).

Above all, in his frame of mind Billy doesn't want to see things changed or de-formed because when that happens his eyes start "burning from the pain of change" (68). His ceremonies of control are meant to ensure that the future will be a predictable copy of the past. Intact. His utter terror at seeing gasping people "collapsed" in their dying (10) therefore leads him immediately into attempted denial: first of all in his abrupt statement "I told no one" (10). That numb sentence brings to an emphatic halt the rush of words that describe his vivid memory of numerous deaths:

> Sometimes a normal forehead in front of me leaked brain gasses. Once a nose clogged right before me, a lock of skin formed over the nostrils, and the shocked face had to start breathing through mouth, but then the mustache bound itself in the lower teeth and he began to gasp loud the hah! hah! going strong — churned onto the floor, collapsed out, seeming in the end to be breathing out of his eye — tiny needle jets of air reaching into the throat. I told no one. (10)

Billy then moves on in the following poem to the newsman's brain and his own love of unchanging machinery, as if he were trying to put off the frightening images swarming around him. Barely hanging on, deeply conservative.

His love of machines figures strikingly in his admiring description of railway yards, the train's couplings and levers removing the intricacies of organic life in their reassuringly abstracted shapes, their singularly pure forms. Perfectly repetitive, invariably there. As always. In all ways the same. Mechanisms to rob people of their animal properties, animals of their animation. So Billy can distill life, still his fears:

> I have seen pictures of great stars,
> drawings which show them straining to the centre
> that would explode their white
> if temperature and the speed they moved at
> shifted one degree.
>
> Or in the East have seen
> the dark grey yards where trains are fitted
> and the clean speed of machines
> that make machines, their
> red golden pouring which when cooled
> mists out to rust or grey.

The beautiful machines pivoting on themselves
sealing and fusing to others
and men throwing levers like coins at them.
And there is there the same stress as with stars,
the one altered move that will make them maniac. (41)

In the train world, all the separate parts are "fitted," speed is "clean,"
and "The beautiful machines [are] pivoting on themselves / sealing and
fusing to others." Billy finds some composure in these thoughts,
hoping that this integrated and immobilized world, at least, will not
break up, will guarantee his immunity. Bodies may be collapsing,[9] but
trains are "fusing." Yet, he can't count on even this possibility. Like
the stars that would explode if "shifted one degree" (in space as well as
in temperature), even the trains are not exempt from "the one altered
move that will make them maniac."

Here, too, in this poem about stars and trains, we find more
references to photography. In Billy's unusually lyrical words, the
molten ore (reminiscent of the angry red weather and the red "rat fyt"
that boil over in his brain) "mists out to rust or grey." Out of the
aggressive orange and reds, into a clockwork grey. By itself this line
couldn't begin to carry my argument but, seen as part of a whole range
of related words, it can be viewed as an oblique reference to the muted
sepia prints common in Billy's day; and common in the grays, dark
blues, faint browns, silvers, and whites constantly blooming in Sallie
Chisum's cool quiet dark room, with its granular textures and
soothing colours suggestive of pictures taken under low light with a
fast film and the lens (like Huffman's) wide open. Undoubtedly Billy
would find peace in transforming the hot reds into quiet darker shades
that are less volatile. To put the case in photographic terms, we might
consider him as turning colour into absence of colour (as in black and
white photography), colour into only the semblance of its colour (as in
monochromatic prints), or glaring colour into softened colour (as in
sepia prints). It may be worth remembering what Ondaatje surely
knows — that photography in Billy's time had developed no great
capacity for accommodating colour.

Billy thinks of his visual extractions as some form of near-magical
possession to control powers outside of himself that keep threatening to
get out of hand. He is almost primitive in his hope of appropriating, if
not actually propitiating, those powers. In doing so, he is only insisting

221

on a stance which, according to Susan Sontag, we bring to photography in the twentieth century:

> Our irrepressible feeling that the photographic process is something magical has a genuine basis. No one takes an easel painting to be in any sense co-substantial with its subject; it only represents or refers. But a photograph is not only like its subject, an homage to the subject. It is *part of, an extension of that subject; and a potent means of acquiring it, of gaining control over it.* (my emphasis)[10]

Billy's photographic excisions are not cherished in any sentimental way, but they may serve him as talismans.[11]

Finally, Billy shows little capacity for denial of any kind. Wanting to black out, to become as negative as possible, he desperately struggles to get the world into alignment and to keep it there. But he can't. Even Sallie Chisum keeps getting out of focus, as she does in Billy's delirious view of her:

> Sallie approaching from the far end of the room like some ghost. I didn't know who it was.... Me screaming stop stop STOP THERE you're going to *fall* on me! My picture now sliding so she with her tray and her lamp jerked up to the ceiling and floated down calm again and continued forward crushing me against the wall only I didnt feel anything yet. (34)

The intractability of life runs throughout *Billy the Kid* in consistently visual terms.[12]

3. Cinema

More to the point, Billy's double focusing comes right out of cinema, or as we more tellingly say, the movies. In Ondaatje's book cinema provides a fitting version of a mobile world that cannot be isolated and edited into stills, that resists Billy's steps to solidify motion, to turn events into nouns. In an essay called "Rhetoric of the Image," Roland Barthes argues that "the distinction between film and photograph is not a simple difference of degree but a radical opposition. Film can no longer be seen as animated photographs: the *having-been-there* [of the photograph] gives way before a *being-there* of the thing [in film]." The photograph eludes history by presenting "the always

222

stupefying evidence of *this is how it was*, giving us, by a precious miracle, a reality from which we are sheltered."[13] Photographs exist in space, movies in time — the dimension which Billy has tried to escape and into which he ultimately is catapulted. We return to *Billy the Kid*, then, to remember the rat "reeling" off a panic-stricken Billy and the oranges "reeling" across the room as the redness breaks up Billy in death. When the "real" world goes "reeling" past and comes "reeling" in the photographic eye loses its freeze on life. Billy's stills never offer much of a hold; at best they provide a temporary and tenuous stay. In his flat takes Billy wants to deny what is out there but can't because that wheeling, often brutal, existence powers in upon him. Its predominance is facilitated by Billy's susceptibility — here on the edge "with the range for everything" (72), trying to preserve an impossible position. So grim and so savage is that world that Billy's feeble response proves to be inadequate. It is also far too simple an answer to a complex, shifting world, no more than a cliche — the French term for a trite expression *and* a photographic negative.

It is therefore necessary to qualify my earlier statement about Billy's photographic posture. In a number of his interior monologues he actually assumes the position of a *movie* camera, but he uses it in the hope of avoiding the images erupting around him.[14] So he swivels away from Angela's frantic sexuality to take in the angles of the room, in effect panning the corners of the room as a movie camera would, though in the shooting he hopes to displace Angela's galvanic presence with the safe stability of geometric shapes. By the same token, as he sits near the doorway in the poem we earlier considered, he is not exactly shooting photos.

It would be more accurate to say that metaphorically he runs film footage behind his lens, filming a landscape devoid of images but constantly on the verge of filling up with them, its very emptiness drawing our attention to imminent presences lurking just off camera. In the "doorway" poem the vast horizon looms above Billy, ready to suck something or someone into its emptiness. Billy looks for some intrusion, sensing that something is there, mysterious and powerful, just off screen, and about to press into the vacuum. Billy, in a weak position below the frame, is most afraid of what he can't see — what is out of sight but not out of mind. The minimal movement in the scene guarantees that the slightest flicker in it will become explosively magnified. So does the almost interminable waiting built into the prolonged description. The scene can be taken in within a split second by the eye, but the language Billy uses to set it down inexorably emphasizes time, heightening the sense of anxiety to an almost unbearable degree: "what will happen next?" "will it never end?" The absence of motion in relatively empty and starkly geometric screens creates an eerie effect that approaches the nature of photographic prints.

Billy has always wanted to arrest objects on a two-dimensional plane in order to remove depth of field and motion, alarming dimensions which both exist in time. Outside of time or motion there would be no suffering or experience of suffering. In movies time catches up with Billy; he must pass through it. It is this persistent cinematic pressure, including its depth or range, that finally defeats Billy's strategy of visual reduction.

As soon as the images pass through rapid change in time — that is, whenever they become cinematic — Billy's already weak position collapses and he's forced to face the turbulence. In the following piece, where we get a critical parallel to reversed film footage (the sequence of lines exactly reverses itself between the two stanzas), we discover how badly shaken Billy becomes when the outside world impinges upon his provisional immunity:

> His stomach was warm
> remembered this when I put my hand into
> a pot of luke warm tea to wash it out
> dragging out the stomach to get the bullet
> he wanted to see when taking tea
> with Sallie Chisum in Paris Texas
>
> With Sallie Chisum in Paris Texas
> he wanted to see when taking tea
> dragging out the stomach to get the bullet
> a pot of luke warm tea to wash it out
> remembered this when I put my hand into
> his stomach was warm (27)

The chiasmic passage shows how possessed Billy has become by his memory of digging out the bullet. The inversion further heightens the sense of trauma when it returns the poem to its point of origin, reminding us in stark finality that "his stomach was warm." Coming in the

224

closing and framing line, these words gain special emphasis and turn our consideration to the source of Billy's horror — his direct, visceral realization of death, and the degree to which heat can set him off. At the same time, the sequence of lines in the second stanza totally undermines the more normal syntax and rational discourse of the first. The broken lines derive from a growing confusion and fear that breaks out in Billy's mind after he has lost his customary visual distance and made the primitive tactile association in the first place, an appalling discovery made all the more startling by Ondaatje's juxtaposition of the brutal act in the past with the domestic innocence of removing a bag from a teapot.

The most obvious and sustained equivalents of cinematic action in the book occur in the broken sequence that depicts Garrett closing in on Billy. Those chunks read like director's scripts or descriptions of movie scenes.[15] Take this section which presents the verbal equivalent of a slow-motion rerun of a movie clip; the sharp visual conceptions and the anomalous note on the camera's position reveal how cinematically the scenes are rendered; the exaggerated slowness of Garrett's approach and the almost intolerable duration of the repeated "footage" register Billy's oppressive sense of threat in an overpowering force:

> Down the street was a dog. Some mut spaniel, black and white. One dog, Garrett and two friends, stud looking, came down the street to the house, to me.
>
> Again.
>
> Down the street was a dog. Some mut spaniel, black and white. One dog, Garrett and two friends came down the street to the house, to me.
>
> Garrett takes off his hat and leaves it outside the door. The others laugh. Garrett smiles, pokes his gun towards the door. The others melt and surround.
> All this I would have seen if I was on the roof looking. (46)

The surprising last line shows us that, though we thought otherwise, we have not been inside Billy's head for all of this clip. The startling revelation (how can Billy know what he doesn't know, be privileged with two visions?) is there as part of Ondaatje's brand of postmodernism, just as that same aesthetics allows him to introduce his own contemporaries, bp Nichol and The Four Horsemen, into a fabricated 1881 interview later in the book (84). But there are other internal reasons for overturning our expectations: as the cinematic world moves in on Billy's world of still photography or stable movie shots, he begins to lose control. As a matter of fact, Billy is able to shoot his still or empty film only when he withdraws into his silent interior monologues, where he himself can lop off time, depth, and sound that come to him in the shifting images and buzzing sound track of the movie playing around him. In the narrative and dramatic sections of the poem, including the tight film scripts — all taking place in time — Billy is never in charge. Those events occur outside of Billy and total-ly beyond his control. As the book goes on, the film scripts increase in frequency and intensity and they crowd Billy more out of the picture. In the "roof-top" scene Billy records the action as if he were in a high camera tilted down onto the action and slowly panning with it. The camera's superior position, detached above the men, faintly suggests that Billy faces unavoidable forces, while, by slowly and suspensefully following the action, it creates a sense that we are on the verge of discovery. As the overseeing camera leads us, ominously, heavily, to Billy who's helplessly riveted to the spot, we realize he's closer than ever to a violent death. Once, when he had some control in his life, he operated like a low stationary camera recording a relatively static world. Now the world has become animated and impinging, and the camera, no longer quite his, begins to rise and tilt and pivot after him.

The clips virtually take over the book as we move closer to Billy's death, though Billy still figures marginally in most of the scenes until the end: he is the central consciousness in the take of Garrett lying in wait for him on Maxwell's bed (90); he submerges into the third-person while an unidentified character sets up a long script (92–3); then he reemerges briefly as a silent but implied viewer in the third-person account of his death (94). The steady erosion of Billy's verbal and visual control in the dramatic scenes indicates his approaching death, which comes, as it must, in a fragmentary world. Only in Billy's dying does his interior monologue, the place for his still photos, return, but only to record Billy's lost hold on a life broken away from him and filmed in a movie camera. The first scene about Billy finding Pat Garrett in Max-well's bed begins with the directions of a movie script: "Sound up" (90). An intensely amplified sound then dominates the poem, including

226

"the burning hum of flies," a frequent symbol of Billy's high tension — and reminiscent of the caged birds' "brooding whirr of noise" and "steady hum" at the Chisums (36, 37); and of Billy's own barely controlled humming as he rides under heat:

MMMMMMMM mm thinking
moving across the world on horses
body split at the edge of their necks
neck sweat eating at my jeans (11)

Now, as the cinematic world takes over Billy responds with his *ear* (before, always, it has been his *eye*), hearing each straw blade "loud in its clear flick against another," the heat "crack at the glass" (90), Garrett's serpentine breathing "hisssssssss sssssssss," the loud sound track overriding the silence of Billy's distinctly visual stance. The eye, with the distance it keeps, succumbing to the ear, to the greater nearness it demands — sounds shoving the outside dangerously close to him. Sounds that break in upon his interior meditations, countering Billy's spatialization of time in his silent capsules. Impelled to speech — "saying stop jeesus jesus jesus JESUS" (73). The responsibility and the danger of it: acknowledging other, entering time. To be of and in the world, where his nerves brush it. Once afraid to utter a sound, Billy now "outers" himself, puts himself out in the open where he is vulnerable. Driven out of his lyric intervals, he now hears and articulates at the joints, joins (at great risk) the outside world.

Then, further signs of impinging, Billy is thrown into narrative. Until now he has hidden, consistently, in lyric. He has sought lacunae in the story, sought to enlarge them. But his attempts to shrug off the rain of time no longer work. He is forced out of inner silence into sound, into narrative. Pried out of his privileged position. There's the long narrative section (92–3) summarizing his final minutes. It opens with an emphatically visual account of the action. The passage reads much like a director's script, especially in its insistent phrase "well and buckets centre."

Then, in the last scene before Billy's own final monologue, we get six to eight different camera shots in rapid-fire succession, not one of them controlled by Billy:

OUTSIDE
    the outline of houses

227

Garrett running from a door
— all seen sliding round
the screen of a horse's eye

NOW dead centre in the square is Garrett with Poe
— hands in back pockets — argues, nodding his head
and then ALL TURNING as the naked arm, the arm from
the body, breaks through the window. The window —
what remains between the splits — reflecting all the
moving too.

Guitterrez goes to hold the arm but it is manic, breaks
her second finger. His veins that controlled triggers —
now tearing all they touch. (94)

As Pat Garrett takes over the visual space, he in Billy's pun stands
"dead centre" in it. Just before that point, we get a running Garrett as
he is seen "sliding round / the screen of a horse's eye." The eye acts as a
fish-eye lens, which grossly exaggerates the lines at the edge of the
image. Those bulges would imply that Billy is losing his eye-hold and
that Garrett is forcing his way into Billy's territory, defined as usual by
the verticals of his doors and windows. Now, the extreme wide-angle
lens grotesquely warps the images where, in Billy's peripheral vision,
they were at the best of times unresolved or dissolving. Finally, the very
short lens speeds up movement toward the camera because of its focal
length. The shots show how fully Garrett is now dominating Billy,
particularly when we remember that earlier, when Billy controlled the
camera, he evidently was seeing through a telephoto lens, which
minimizes forward movement because of its greater depth of field.

By the time we get to Billy's death, then, the use of the camera has
changed radically. In the long "doorway" scene, where Billy enjoys as
much security as he ever finds, there is a fixed camera, controlled by
Billy, in a long-drawn scan over a large and empty space, and using a
long focal length. That shooting registers Billy's attempts to inform
and protect himself. Now, as his world disintegrates, we get many
shots that step up the tempo. And we get cameras, some of them moving, all of them recording movement, all of them shooting at close
range, and all out of Billy's hands. Once Billy's lines distend and his
frames break apart, he crashes out through the window, at once
trapped by the tightly framed image of himself in the window, and
driven out of his fortified position, finally out of his mind.

As he lies dying (95), the camera returns momentarily into his hands and we see, looking up from his position of the floor, "Garrett's jaw and stomach" filling the screen.[16] The extreme low tilt shot dramatizes Billy's impotence. When the images click and lurch past, we get the verbal equivalent of a spinning, hand-held camera shot. In its jerky turning, Billy's subjective camera records the frantic instability and vulnerability he feels now that he's blown out of his fragile sanctuary.

In the confused release that accompanies his death Billy goes through his earlier prophetic dream about his own death where Pat Garrett figured as a "blurred" star (73), an image that indicates a loss of the clear focus that in Billy's past has incisively defined the world as photograph or empty screen. Billy's negations have always been precisely shot, rather than softly focused, as we might have suspected they would be, because he wants to keep his eye on things, preferring vigilance to blindness. He is in such a nervous state and is so preoccupied with what he might find that he can't avoid seeing with a razor clarity.

In the end Billy becomes unbalanced, goes over the edge, and as his arm breaks through the window it twitches in a "manic" way (94). Radically decentered. He has taken the crucial step, "the one altered move" that would make things "maniac" (41). Eccentric. Like Tom O'Folliard (7) and Charlie Bowdre (22) before him, Billy dies violently at the very edge of the frames — that dangerous, terrifying interface where Garrett cold-bloodedly kills them. Billy fails spectacularly in his bid as door man, but there's a fine irony about the door man in *Billy the Kid*. In one short, seemingly irrelevant passage we discover Frank James, who has ended up guarding the door to a Los Angeles movie theatre:

> After the amnesty he was given, Frank had many jobs. When Jim's grandfather met him, he was the doorman at the Fresco Theatre.
> GET YOUR TICKET TORN UP BY FRANK JAMES the poster said, and people came for that rather than the film. Frank would say, 'Thanks for coming, go on in.'
> . . . He was by then an alcoholic. (24)

Frank James's pathetic alcoholism and his reduction from the status of a true Western hero to a movie pimp guarding the wrong doors hints at the future Billy would have faced if he had held the door.[17]

229

4. Coda

Finally, we can schematize a set of distinctions running through the book. These polarities represent the distance Bill is forced to travel by the time the book ends.

space (static)	time (dynamic)
eye	ear
noun	verb
private (inner)	public (outer)
lyric (meditation)	narrative (action)
photo	cinema
centered	decentered
cool	hot
dark	bright

Although by my reading Garrett enjoys no heroic stature, he does operate in the very world Billy needs to face. That Garrett moves through that world largely undisturbed by appalling human suffering is, of course, no credit to him.

5. Moderns

In the end Garrett kills Billy, not because Garrett is more venturesome or any more flexible. On the contrary, the law man, Garrett, "gets" Billy because he is far more successful than Billy ever could be at denying life through resorts to engineered responses. Though Billy must fight to subdue his frenzy, Garrett's imposition is so total that he becomes the consummate murderer in the book. He casually shoots his old friends, then without a twinge watches them die in graphic agony. An "academic murderer" with "the mind of a doctor," he organizes schedules, develops "the ability to kill someone on the street walk back and finish a joke," and fears flowers because "they grew so slowly that he couldn't tell what they planned to do" (28). Garrett brings the same analytical, clinical mind to his hobby of taxidermy, surgically preparing dead specimens "with a rubber glove in his right hand" (88). In every respect, as killer and collector, he acts as a right-handed, right-minded man of death, in no way bringing the kind of jangled nerves that the ir-

230

rational, left-handed Billy does to their world of ruthless violence. Garrett complains, in modernist fashion, about the seductive qualities of Billy's imagination, "which was usually pointless and never in control" (43). In the end, his "precise but forced" (90) response to existence takes on the sinister overtones of a snake lying in wait for Billy, as he earlier (64-71) broke up the idyllic life at the Chisum ranch with his serpentine presence:

> And then that breathing, not Maxwell's but *the other's*. The breathing precise but forced into quiet but regular streams. Think of the dark air going up through the nose, down to the stomach rolling around on itself, and then up and out like a fountain spilling through his teeth hisssssssssssssssssssssssss (90)

Garrett is, above all, the hero of narrative. Billy, who has sought to survive inside lyric monologue, proves no match for Garrett once he's bounced into the story line. Supremely triumphant on the paradigmatic axis, Billy is no match, finally, for Garrett on the syntagmatic axis where time happens. There Garrett operates unreflectingly, unaffected by time, having no need to resist it: Garrett as pure story, exterior life. A man with no inner existence, without lyric, he knows motion without emotion. The perfect hero of adventure stories — always moving but never moved. As Billy's interior monologues begin to collapse, the once scattered and forestalled narrative moves into place, enlarges its role. Garrett, the law man and the story man, lays claim to the book, on Billy and on the reader. We are thrown out of Billy's mind (he out of his mind) into exterior action and into the larger structures that Garrett imposes. Garrett's story. Billy's death. [18]

Livingstone, another bizarre character, operates in much the same terms. He breeds a freak strain out of "originally beautiful" spaniels, brings the same "perverse logic" to the defilement of life: "Their eyes bulged like marbles; some were blind, their eyes had split" (61). Fencing up the dogs, he turns them into sterile monsters — the ultimate desecration of nature, shaped by a mind which, fearing and loathing unsettled organic processes, quite deliberately and systematically seeks to dominate, even to eradicate it. In John Chisum's words, Livingstone "seemed a pretty sane guy" but "had been mad apparently" (60). Because, like Garrett, he acts "clinically and scientifically" (61), Livingstone ironically reminds us of a famous doctor with the same

231

name. The two eminently rational "doctors" in the book both are monstrous killers, in contrast to the maternal Sallie Chisum who nurses Billy and other broken creatures back to life.[19]

In important ways Livingstone and Garrett only succeed in doing what Billy always wants to do: they anaesthetize themselves to life. Perfect though extreme modernists, they manage to subvert and convert life, in some overarching version of meaning, to the point of destroying it. They are so prepared to maintain large structures that their eminent sanity proves to be insane in any sense that matters. As we read in the hysterical language (probably, though not necessarily, Billy's) that finishes the long passage about Garrett's manoeuvres through life, he is "a sane assassin sane assassin sane assassin sane assassin sane assassin sane" (29). When the words run together in rapid fusion, the ends of the nouns begin to couple with the beginnings of the adjectives so that a new word, "in sane," begins to emerge between them.

Garrett *is* disturbing in his utter insensitivity to life. In still more general terms Garrett is too rigid. As a result, he fails artistically as well as morally. *The Collected Works of Billy the Kid* invites us to see that the world is postmodern — fluid, unpredictable, and ultimately uncontrollable (Livingstone is eaten by his twisted creations) or wrongly controlled (Garrett gains power by becoming the greatest human casualty in the entire book). The book also presents Garrett and Livingstone to us as unforgettable examples of excessively modernist responses to life — the belief that the world is chaotic and that we'd better impose some order, some superstructure, upon it. Billy gets caught between those two positions, wanting more than anything to be a modernist, but finally not being able to because Ondaatje's world reveals itself to be essentially postmodern. When Billy opts for the snapshot or the empty or static shot, he tries to assume a modernist posture in a postmodern world which, in the basic language of the text, asserts itself in cinematic forms. Would-be modernist, he wants to act as a still camera eye in a postmodern world that is chimerical — always out of control.

Still, it would be wrong to argue that the camera shot is *necessarily* an assault on life or a rejection of it. L.A. Huffman, the Western photographer whose words we read as *Billy the Kid* opens, talks about how he has used his camera:

> I send you a picture of Billy made with the Perry shutter *as quick as it can be worked*. . . . I am making daily experiments now and find I am able to take passing horses at a lively trot square across the line of fire — bits of snow in the air — spokes *well defined* — *some blur* on top of wheel but *sharp in the main* — men walking are no trick — I will send you proofs sometime. I shall show you what can be done from the saddle without ground glass or tripod — please notice when you get the specimens that they were made *with the lens wide open* and many of the best exposed when my horse was *in motion*. (5, my emphases)

Despite the scattered words of detachment or aggression in Huffman's account ("the line of fire," "making. . . experiments," "proofs," and "specimens") — words that in this context Ondaatje may have found amusing, if not innocent — Huffman brings the essential Ondaatje virtues to his art: a shutter that he sets "quick as it can be worked" and a lens that he runs "wide open"; it's at least as important that he takes photographs of moving subjects and that he does so when he is himself "in motion." Open, quick, mobile — that's the kind of postmodern sensibility you bring to life and to art. Identifying with Huffman and his promise to send us a picture of Billy, Ondaatje leaves the frame above Huffman's statement empty (perhaps because a picture could not do him justice, would in its very specificity fix him too definitely in a shape), then sends us a parody of Billy's picture at the end of the book, a tiny copy of himself as a seven-year-old dressed in a cowboy costume. Huffman brings the right methods, then. He also comes through with the best results: "bits of snow in the air — spokes well defined — some blur on top of wheel but sharp in the main."

6. Postmodern World

We get a glimpse of a world in motion where nothing is settled, where things only approach clarity.

This passage in *Billy the Kid* immediately brings to mind that central Ondaatje poem "'The gate in his head'" (*RJ*, 62), which, as Sam Solecki has suggested, stands at the centre of Ondaatje's poetics.[20] In that poem, which comes out of the same period as *Billy the Kid*, Ondaatje writes of wanting "not clarity but the sense of shift / a few lines, the tracks of thought," not foreplanning but discovery. Victor Coleman, for whom the poem is written and after whom it is titled, has sent his friend, Michael Ondaatje, a letter

> with a blurred photograph of a gull.
> Caught vision. The stunning white bird
> an unclear stir.
>
> And that is all this writing should be then.
> The beautiful formed things caught at the wrong moment
> so they are shapeless, awkward
> moving to the clear. (*RJ*, 62)

Art in the blurred glimpse, the artist scanning the shifting world for flashes of beauty, traces of life, surrendering to "the immaculate moment [that] is now" (*RJ*, 55).[21] So that the rational mind succumbs to the body's knowledge, just as Billy on one rare occasion lapses out of intransigence into one of those unwilled uncapturable moments:

> and my fingers touch
> this soft blue paper notebook
> control a pencil that shifts up and sideways
> mapping my thinking going its own way
> like light wet glasses drifting on polished wood. (72)

In Solecki's words, "the ultimate poem for Ondaatje is the one which transforms reality into poetry without 'crucifying' it."[22]

The modernist, Wallace Stevens, won't give things enough room when he appears in another Ondaatje poem, "his head making his hand / move where he wanted / and he saw his hand was saying / the mind is never finished, no, never" (*RJ*, 21). In yet another Ondaatje poem Stevens offers his own "fences" to life's "chaos" and would clean up and shave the hairiness of life in his "murderer's" pose (*RJ*, 61).[23] In "Spider Blues" a spider symbolizes the modernist artist: here the "finicky" spider with its "classic" control "thinks a path" before it crosses it (*RJ*, 63), "murderous" in its art, and defied only by fly, which says in proper (playful) postmodern fashion

> no I choose who I die with
> you spider poets are all the same
> you in your close vanity of making,
> you minor drag, your saliva stars always
> soaking up the liquid from our atmosphere.

And the spider in his loathing
crucifies his victims in his spit
making them the art he cannot be. (*RJ*, 64)[24]

The fly figures throughout *Billy the Kid* as a sign of the life buzzing
everywhere around Billy:

nothing breaks my [fixed] vision
but flies in their black path
like inverted stars (74)

catching flies with my left hand
bringing the fist to my ear
hearing the scream grey buzz
as their legs cramp their
heads with no air
so eyes split and release

open fingers
the air and sun hit them like pollen
sun flood drying them red
catching flies
angry weather in my head, too (58)

Sound up. Loud and vibrating in the room. My ears picking up all the
burning hum of flies letting go across the room. (90)

Rat that fights and fits in Billy's head, that finally becomes Billy's head
— "smaller than a rat" (104) when he dies. Rat that Ondaatje, "thinking of you," dishes up in his own poem "Rat Jelly" — full of all the
disgusting and stinking hair that the modernist Stevens would shave
from his pure poems. Rat that in true postmodern fashion will not
clean up its act, will not sweep the slate clean of all the shit and junk; rat
with his "dirt thought we want as guest / travelling mad within the
poem," unquestionably, eminently, in "A bad taste" (*RJ*, 42-3).
"Rat fyt" in the postmodern Ondaatje brain. The dirty rat that won't
fit politely into the controlled poem, with its improvements on life, its
impositions of single-minded orders on a presumed chaos. The modern
poem with its agoraphobic withdrawal from life, its authors wanting
severance and certainty in art — cut out and cut off from open-ended
living. An art that Ondaatje detests, hating the notions of manipulating
his material or his audience, preferring to let us in and out as we enter

235

his world. In Billy's words we get the invitation: "Find the beginning, the slight silver key to unlock it, to dig it out. Here then is a maze to begin, be in" (20). How's that for starters?

1 Frank Davey and Stephen Scobie have pointed out that Ondaatje's Billy the Kid is in some special way an artist. See Davey's excellent essay on Ondaatje in *From There to Here: A Guide to English-Canadian Literature Since 1960*, (Erin, Ont.: Press Porcepic, 1974), pp. 222-7. Scobie's essay "Two Authors in Search of a Character: bp Nichol and Michael Ondaatje" appeared in *Canadian Literature*, No. 54 (Autumn 1972), 37-55.

2 *The Collected Works of Billy the Kid: Left Handed Poems* (Toronto: Anansi, 1970), p. 74. From now on all references to the book will appear within the essay and will be indicated simply by page number.

3 "The first time I went to a movie I knew my vision of paradise would be a cosmic-movie-theatre," he has confessed in an interview in *Manna:A Review of Contemporary Poetry*, No. 1 (March 1972), p. 22. That love immediately connects with his writing of *Billy the Kid*. Ondaatje says in the crucial 1975 interview with Sam Solecki, "With *Billy the Kid* I was trying to make the film I couldn't afford to shoot, in the form of a book." "An Interview with Michael Ondaatje," *Rune*, No. 2 (Spring 1975), p. 46.

4 *Canadian Literature*, No. 87 (Winter 1980), p. 70. Though I agree with most of the examples in Nodelman's paper (I use several of them myself), and with his assertion that "Billy views things photographically himself to avoid emotional involvement with them" (p. 70) in a world that keeps moving (p. 73), I don't agree with him on three points. Nodelman argues that Billy actually "'fixes'" life in his own emotionally "dead" perceptions, and that he does so out of "disgust" for things that move and change (p. 76). I argue that Billy is extremely sensitive, that he only tries to fix life but is unsuccessful in his attempts, and that he feels terror, not revulsion, at what he confronts.

5 This image is hardly new with Ondaatje. John G. Cawelti in Jack Nachbar, ed., *Focus on the Western* (Engelwood Cliffs, New Jersey: Prentice Hall, 1974) p. 59, describes "the scene, beloved of Western directors, in which a rider appears like an infinitely small dot at the far end of a great empty horizon and then rides toward us across the intervening space."

6 Billy's visual skills are so finely tuned that he shows an exceptional awareness of eyes, often others', often animals', and often damaged. Here is an incomplete list of such references: "the eyes grew all over his body" (12), "eyes will / move in head like a rat" (38), "a yellow pearl of an eye cracked with veins glowed" (36), "a frozen bird's eye" (26), "the screen of a horse's eye" (94), "planned by my eye" (75), "eyes split and release" (58), "the [bird's] eyes were small and far" (14), "the very eyes welling up like bad drains" (11), dogs' "eyes bulged like marbles; some were blind, their eyes had split" (61).

7 (Toronto: Anansi, 1976), p. 68; my emphasis.

8 (New York: Farrar, Straus and Giroux, 1977), p. 160. Louis D. Giannetti points out that surrealist filmmaker Jean Cocteau insisted the film-poet wrote with the "ink of light." *Understanding Movies*, 2nd ed. (Englewood Cliffs, N.J.: Prentice-Hall, 1976), p. 395. I am indebted to Giannetti for part of my argument on cinematic techniques later in this paper. I have also to a lesser extent used David Bordwell and Kristen Thompson, *Film Art: An Introduction* (Reading, Mass.: Addison-Wesley, 1979), and Ross Huss and Norman Silverstein, *The Film Experience: Elements of Motion Picture Art* (New York: Delta, 1968).

9 Billy shows a constant awareness of broken bodies. He sees his friends mutilated before his eyes, each of them blown up or blown to pieces by Pat Garrett — their jaws shot off or their guts burst open. When their bodies leak and collapse, a stunned Billy seeks comfort in the thought that *some* stability may exist in death: "In the end the only thing that never changed, never became deformed, were animals" (10).

10 *On Photography*, pp. 155-6.

11 Michel Foucault has written a fascinating study on the powers of surveillance: *Discipline & Punish: The Birth of the Prison*, trans. Alan Sheridan (New York: Random, 1979). Foucault's account offers startling parallels to Billy's geometries of control.

12 Ironically, my argument about photography doesn't take account of the actual photographs in *The Collected Works of Billy the Kid* — twelve altogether, if you count the "absent" photographs (on pages 5 and 19). Most of them convey an age long gone — log houses, cavalry officers, people in gingham, a floosy, those sorts of thing. What's especially interesting is the total absence of caption and photograph together. In the case of the "absent" photos we do get extended descriptions. The actual photos sit alone. Uncaptioned. For good reason. Captions would too surely capture the photographs (the words — caption, capture — come from the same root: to seize, take). They would insist on overly determined readings. Ondaatje wants an uncertainty, openness in the text that will allow the pieces to float inside the text, unweighted by subtitles that would invest them with fixed meaning (appalling thought in this "writerly" text).

Unanchored, they are free to attach themselves where they may. More accurately: where *we* may. We are left/required to make our own connections, knowing they can be only ours. Indeterminate.

13 *Image-Music-Text*, selected and translated by Stephen Heath (London: Fontana/Collins, 1977), pp. 44, 45.

14 There is a fine line between a static movie screen and a still photograph, as Ondaatje's own remark in the Solecki interview shows. Ondaatje explains how he got into a quarrel with the camera man working on one of his films: "he kept saying that the camera should be zooming or the film would be very dull." But Ondaatje wanted that sense throughout the film that each shot would almost be a static photograph." *Rune*, p. 42.

15 Davey and Blott have discussed these qualities.

16 Rudolf Arnheim's observation about the relative size of tolerable images in a field is applicable here: "In order to be comfortably visible the relevant position of a visual field must be large enough to be sufficiently discernible in its detail [Billy watching over empty space] and small enough to fit into the field [Pat Garrett looming at the window when Billy dies]." *Visual Thinking* (Berkeley: U of California, 1969), p. 26.

17 For a different reading of *Billy the Kid* see Lynette Hunter, "Form and Energy in the Poetry of Michael Ondaatje," *Journal of Canadian Poetry*, 2, No. 1 (Winter 1978), 47–70.

18 Judith Owens has written a brilliant piece on narrative in the book, showing how it registers Billy's efforts and how it affects our page-by-page reading: " 'I Send You a Picture': Ondaatje's Portrait of Billy the Kid," *Studies in Canadian Literature* 8, No. 1 (1983), 117–39. Owens argues Billy needs and welcomes narrative, but that he needs to trace out his *own* narrative.

19 Though Livingstone cold-bloodedly destroys the dogs, they ultimately resist by eating him. I take it that life cannot be totally denied and that it will assert itself, in horrible reprisals if necessary.

20 "Nets and Chaos: The Poetry of Michael Ondaatje," *Studies in Canadian Literature*, 2, No. 1 (Winter 1977), 36–48. I am indebted to this piece, though I don't put as much stock as Solecki does in Ondaatje's control.

21 In *On Photography*, p. 121, Sontag describes a remarkably similar view of photography in "Robert Frank's waiting for the moment of revealing disequilibrium, to catch reality off-guard, in what he calls the 'in-between moments.' "

22 "Nets and Chaos," p. 44.

23 Sam Solecki reads this poem very differently, finding Stevens much more attractive than I do. See his "Making and Destroying: Michael Ondaatje's *Coming Through Slaughter* and Extremist Art," *Essays on Canadian Writing*, No. 12 (Fall 1978), p. 31.

24 In the Solecki interview Ondaatje criticizes the spider mentality behind "the CBC kind of documentary which knows what it's going to say before the actual filming begins" (p. 41). Ondaatje claims "I really don't plan anything and this is what makes me very frightened while writing" (p. 53) "on the border where... craft meets the accidental and the unconscious, as close as possible to the unconscious" (p. 49). In this same interview Ondaatje makes it clear that he revises and edits a lot, but that the first takes of his poems come unpremeditated.

David Donnell
NOTES ON
THE COLLECTED WORKS OF BILLY THE KID

There was a lot of interest in Billy the Kid around the end of the 60s. Michael McClure wrote some poems about Billy that seem to pick up from McClure's motorcycle period more than they do from what was happening in the south-west in the 1880s. McClure also wrote a famous play called *The Beard*. There's an early Jack Spicer poem about Billy from part-way through the San Francisco period which may have nudged bp Nichol in Toronto. Nichol wrote a terrific short poem called *The True Eventual Story of Billy the Kid*. I think Spicer was thinking about youth and destiny. bp was thinking about the human ego. There have been several films.

Ondaatje's book isn't called *The Collected Works of Billy The Kid* because it draws on previous works, but because it does something the previous works don't do, namely, it historiographs, places the Kid, quotes people who knew him or may have known him, juxtaposes fact and fiction with a biographical override at the center. Ondaatje's life of Billy begins with a quote from the great western photographer L.A. Huffman:

> I send you a picture of Billy made with the Perry shutter as quick as it can be worked — Pyro and soda developer. I am making daily experiments now and find I am able to take passing horses at a lively trot square across the line of fire — bits of snow in the air — spokes well defined — some blur on top of wheel but sharp in the main — men walking are no trick — I will send you proofs sometime.

Huffman was interested in the dynamic of western images and the development of a new explorative artistic method. The quotation suggests the direction, although not the violence, that is about to spread the frame of the camera.

Simple things like fire or caged owls or a frying pan or a long white dress, paraffin, alcohol, urine, a plate of bacon on a table, a cup and saucer, a pump, are given a quiet filmic clarity in contrast to the actual shootings. Common British / European objects acquire an undeniable Frontier quality in the south-western landscape. Ondaatje is writing on two levels at once, landscape and center; the south-western landscape has a quiet documentary film quality; Billy is always at the center, brooding, but not trying to get out, not trapped exactly, but quietly and perceptively doomed. There is a cyclical quality, to my reading at least, somewhat like the structure of the recent Burroughs novel, *The Place of Dead Roads*, in which Kim Carsons is shot, not quite at the beginning, re-emerges, and is then killed at the end of the book. Billy has a sense of his own death at the beginning of this quiet landscape and is then killed at the end.

Billy is almost always presented in a defensive situation. Miss Angela Dickinson straddles him in the washroom, he watches Garrett gun down his friend Charlie Bowdre, they have to surrender, it snows. Billy's voice takes a variety of forms, as in his memory of Sallie Chisum telling the story of the devoured English bassett breeder. The story of Garrett's stuffed birds sounds like the photographer speaking and becomes an almost human side to Garrett's tin badge. Badlands, Charlie Bowdre's wedding, Billy's triumphant jailbreak (dealt with in more detail in the Audie Murphy version), trampling Ollinger with his horse. The sense of flat elegy in the final song about William Bonney dead makes the comic book material Ondaatje quotes at the end do its job. Billy is a control person who is never in control. Ondaatje pushes it, how much ketchup can the Kid take? for the purpose of purging. Death is amazing and almost visual. Sometimes death is funny. Death and violence aren't the same thing or are they? Death may or may not be significant. Billy is actually in Garrett's rifle sights by the middle of the first page.

The fact that Bonney's own murders (6) are hardly recorded in the book allows the deep persona to register the events around him with the uninterrupted quality of a camera. Billy's reactions to scenes like Charlie Bowdre's death show Billy as a compassionate friend. But this is partly because we never see Billy shooting the five Indians from "behind a rock." When Garrett shoots the Kid from the safety of Pete

Maxwell's dark bedroom at the end of the book (which is how it happened) then the schema is almost perfect. Consider Billy's context:

> 300 of the dead in Boot Hill died violently
> 200 by guns, over 50 by knives
> some were pushed under trains — a popular
> and overlooked form of murder in the west. (9)

Ollinger, the deputy Billy kills with a shotgun when he breaks out of jail, used to walk up to people, shake hands, and then shoot them in the chest while he was saying hello.

Ondaatje is very much on top of the possibility that his chosen outlaw may in real life have been little more than a Hell's Angels sidekick. Even Garrett has more of a moral cause. But the most compelling images in the book aren't descriptions of Billy committing acts of violence, we never really see the famous "fast gun" in action, so much as Billy's perceptions of events which have his death written into them with strokes as large as the Texas stars:

> When I caught Charlie Bowdre dying
> tossed 3 feet by bang bullets giggling
> at me face tossed in a gaggle
> he pissing into his trouser legs in pain
> face changing like fast sunshine o my god
> o my god billy I'm pissing watch
> your hands
>   while the eyes grew all over his body (12)

Billy is caught between recklessness and paranoia and Ondaatje steers his apprehensions into a continual existentialist and surrealist shock of recognition.

This unfolding of Billy's season in hell is socially diverse, it takes in narrative accounts of Billy's friends, typical western living rooms, parrot cages, newspaper items, guns. But the center of the book is Billy's mind: blood, dogs, the nature of the brain, darkness, hot sun, dust (fields never get mentioned), the dreaming stars (cattle never get mentioned, there are no trains), vomit, perfume, the flowers of the brain. The photographer has a very strong sense of sight and smell — urine, vomit, organs of the body, continual images of the world going out of focus.

"Sad Billy's out / floating barracuda in the brain" could easily be a

242

comment on Billy's position in the book, floating in the foreground and jerking like a barracuda with a hook in its mouth. Billy is ambivalent about his attachment to the scene. He thinks about the cold dreaming stars a lot. Ondaatje's handling of Billy's involuntary state is part of the genius of the book although I think it comes close to contradicting the biography. The "beautiful machines" that pivot on themselves "sealing and fusing to others" is both a negative and a positive image. Billy isn't nihilistic precisely because he's more reflective than violent, and his sense of violence is inseparably part of his apprehension of the world (Garrett, for example) as better organized than himself. But the restrained violence is constantly ambivalent, i.e. Billy's base line is his quick draw: "Last night was dreamed into a bartender / with an axe I drove into glasses of gin lifted up to be tasted."

The central focus of the book is explicit violence to the human body, especially the face, head, brain and stomach, as observed, fended off, not fended off, surrendered to, by the surprised and ultimately vulnerable brain: Billy's spiralling temporal red and yellow flowers of personal consciousness. There are more deliriums, tension, vomiting, diarrhea and flaky red-mud western migraine headaches than there are actual gunfights at OK corral. No cattle and no lynchings or crowd scenes. Audie Murphy's green leather windbreaker never appears. Billy is young and half in love with "easeful death." But half isn't purposeful. This Billy is tense, allatime tense: I'm not sure if the real Billy was or not. Ondaatje's Billy likes action but is afraid of being shot. Who isn't?

Casually-dressed thoughtful gentleman Billy isn't a coward about being shot in the face with a .44, but he has premonitions of his own death while he watches Bowdre and O'Folliard go down. Ondaatje shows him casually sitting with his left hand on his right knee; eating or reaching for a drink always with the right hand, but casual, easy, in contrast to the disturbed sea in his mind. Garrett sees him as a bird of prey who doesn't shoot first, therefore deluded. "From then on I noticed his left hand churning within itself, each finger circling alternately like a train wheel. Curling into balls, pouring like waves across a tablecloth. It was the most hypnotising beautiful thing I ever saw." This is the closest Garrett ever comes to love, closer than the stuffed birds or his own shootings. It is also the closest Billy ever comes to accomplishment, apart from his stamina, his polite speech and tequila humor, and Ondaatje's considerable capacity for describing physical

243

wounding.

Wounding and sun and threatening night. Ondaatje excels at applying filmic clarity, postmodern pyro and soda developer, the chicken image, Billy sliding under the belly of the horse, the caged owls at night, to states of violent ambivalence. This *in situ* life of Bonney is more a book of purgation, than it is a glorification or an appropriate elegy. The women who remember the funny way Billy used to smile, a "half" smile, ". . . buck teeth you at the paper would call it," when he was belting back the southwestern whiskey, add a note of sadness to Billy's demise, but his sad likely outlaw death is tagged at the very beginning. The image Billy has of Charlie Bowdre shortly before Charlie is killed, "one night in the open I turned to say goodnight to Charlie who was about ten yards away and there was the moon balanced perfect on his nose" (79). That's got some elegy to it, the different elements of elegy are part of the ambivalence, but the center of the book, the gunfights, destructive sun, accidents, rifles that blow apart, Garrett's vomiting and Billy's vomiting (". . . the wind carrying it like a yellow ribbon a good foot to my right. . . like a pack of miniature canaries. A flock" [70]) are purgative and more a vomiting of Billy's violent contradictions than an elegy, despite the politeness, the discretions of the plotting, and the line which summarizes Billy's death across the creek from innocence: "His veins that controlled triggers — now tearing all they touch" (94).

The last two voices in the book could be Pete Maxwell's, "Poor young William's dead / with blood planets in his head / with a fish stare, with a giggle / like he said" (104), and L.A. Huffman's after the events are over and the meticulous photographer has photographed everything there is to photograph, the surly heads & shoulders of typical western outlaws who didn't really intend to become outlaws, or at least they didn't intend to get killed, in a period which came and went faster than you could whisper Civil War or Robert E. Lee:

> It is now early morning, was a bad night. The hotel room seems large. The morning sun has concentrated all the cigarette smoke so one can see it hanging in pillars or sliding along the roof like amoeba. In the bathroom, I wash the loose nicotine out of my mouth. I smell the smoke still in my shirt." (105)

These are the voices at the end of this multi-aspect work which put the

244

quick-draw hot-dog to bed. The "proofs" from Huffman have been negatives, prints, studio pieces, portraits, action shots and narrative dossiers. The men haven't been "walking men" very much (as Huffman describes in his opening quote). The conditions of the sensing body in this Ondaatje work are generally male; and the positions of the male body are standing, sitting, lying down, knocked down, screaming, riding, leanover puking, squinting (if this can be called a position), dragged between the legs of a horse, lying face down chained to a jail bed, asleep, poised, hunched, drunk, and knocked down blood splash maimed shoulder by bang bullets dead.

Billy's stamina and discretion probably save his possibly worthless skin as many times as his much-publicized quick draw. They save him the first time Garrett brings him in rolling from the horse's back to its cool belly like a "soft shell-less egg wrapped in thin white silk" (78) splashing him against the dust "blind and white" while the chain holds him, after the cabin shoot-out that does in Charlie Bowdre. Likewise when he breaks out of jail over the dead bodies of Bell and Ollinger. But they don't save him the final night at Maxwell's ranch when he walks all spontaneity and accident, (life is contingent, says Jean Luc Godard) into Pete's dark bedroom framed by the moon with Garrett unexpectedly there in the middle of waking up Maxwell.

He should have had his guns out at that first hint of trouble, but the Kid was more spontaneous than most historians have given him credit for being:

> And then that breathing, not Maxwell's but *the other's*. The breathing precise but forced into quiet but regular streams. Think of the dark air going up through the nose, down to the stomach rolling around on itself, and then up and out like a fountain spilling through his teeth hissssssssssssssssssss

Billy's death is both inevitable and unexpected. Garrett's rifle leaves a powder burn on Pete Maxwell's cheek that stays "with him all his life" (93). You can go back to the beginning and see that it was all cyclical: it was tagged but Bonney was always watching his hands. The missing gun-fights and the decision not to account for Billy's murders are made worthwhile. Ondaatje's book isn't about ethics so much as it's about death and the nature of history.

245

Sam Solecki
MAKING AND DESTROYING:
COMING THROUGH SLAUGHTER AND EXTREMIST ART

You are using your own skin for wallpaper, and nothing can
save you.
— Gottfried Benn[1]

Madness. Suicide. Murder.
Is there no way out but these?
— Adrienne Rich[2]

In an early section of Michael Ondaatje's *The Collected Works of Billy the
Kid*, Billy tells the reader to look for "the slight silver key to unlock"
the meaning of his story. In *Coming Through Slaughter* "the slight silver
key" to the "maze" of Ondaatje's novel[3] is in the description of
Bellocq, the photographer of Storyville's whores, some of whose
photographs have knife slashes across the bodies (55) of the posers. The
presence of the slashes indicates, according to Ondaatje, that in Bellocq
"the making and destroying [came] from the same source, same lust,
same surgery his brain was capable of." When Bellocq later commits
suicide we realize that the "destroying" did not refer solely to his
slashing of the pictures but also to the potential for self-destruction in
Bellocq himself. The remark directs our attention to a particular kind of
art or creativity in which making and destroying, particularly self-
destroying, are integrally related. It is an art that almost inevitably calls
to mind names such as Celan, Borowski, Pavese, Plath, Sexton, and
Berryman. Mental illness and/or suicide are the obvious connection between these writers, Bellocq, and Bellocq's friend the cornetist Buddy
Bolden; but these are only inevitable for a particular kind of artist, the

246

one who, in Gottfried Benn's metaphor makes "wallpaper" out of his own "skin," who creates, in other words, an aesthetic artifact directly, recklessly, even violently out of his own experiences. While the ordinary artist (and I don't intend that pejoratively) also recreates his own life in art, the artist I am concerned with literally flays himself psychologically as he returns obsessively to rending emotions and experiences to provide himself with a subject matter. The difference between the two, the normal and the extremist,[4] begins as one of degree but leads ultimately to almost one of kind as the extremist writer is compelled towards an art radical in form or content, often both, that distinguishes him from his non-extremist contemporaries. Inevitably it also happens that the modern audience anticipates, even demands, that this kind of writer take greater and greater risks with his own sanity in order to produce work closer to what the audience regards as the psychological and emotional ultimate in human experience. The most characteristic work in this tradition — Lowell's *Life Studies,* Plath's *Ariel,* Sexton's *The Death Notebooks* — is produced on what Alfred Alvarez has aptly termed "the friable edge"[5] of existence where the continuance and value of life are repeatedly confronted with chaos, madness and suicide, and art with its negation, silence. The rhetoric of suffering becomes the mark of sincerity in the work itself; and, in popular mythology, the madness or suicide of the artist authenticates the *oeuvre.*

To my mind, one of the finest examples of this kind of art, and a work that seems to constitute a summary and criticism of it, is Michael Ondaatje's recent novel *Coming Through Slaughter,* a compelling study of the compulsively destructive nature of the creative impulse. Given our knowledge of contemporary cultural history it is almost impossible not to see the suicidal cornetist Buddy Bolden as representing not just Ondaatje but also a particular kind of modern artist; he becomes, as we read the novel, the artist as exemplary sufferer, exemplary not only because, as Susan Sontag argues, "it is the author naked which the modern audience demands,"[6] but also because we inevitably discern the shadowy presences of Plath and others looming behind him. This startling effect depends not on allusions to other writers but on nothing more than the publication of the novel at this particular time; because *Coming Through Slaughter* appeared in 1976, Bolden, in reality the symbolic precursor, became, anachronistically, the exemplary embodiment

247

of a tone, an attitude, a trend in twentieth century art. By a sort of fictive *trompe d'oeil* he is simultaneously at the beginning and end of the
modern era; as historical character he exists before the First World
War; as hero of a novel he arrives on the scene in 1976 as the avatar of a
contemporary Canadian writer. Ondaatje's choice of a musician rather
than a writer for the central character in a novel about the end of art is
particularly felicitous. The act of creation when expressed through or
embodied in a cornetist is a physical act that presents the reader's
imagination with a concrete image that can be easily, because sensuous-
ly, grasped. In contrast, there is nothing less dramatic or exciting that
watching a film or reading a book about a writer or a composer composing: the end product, either *Hamlet* or Schoenberg's *Moses and
Aaron*, may be a work of genius but the manner in which the work was
produced is rarely of sufficient interest to become the subject of its own
artwork. The use of a cornetist also allows Ondaatje to avoid another
one of the pitfalls of writing about a writer, whether fictive or semi-
legendary: the need to reproduce examples of his work. The English
novelist, Susan Hill, faces this problem in *The Bird of Night*, her novel
about the suicidal poet Francis Croft. She tells the reader that Croft is
one of the major voices of the century but she cannot provide examples
of his work because that would entail the almost impossible act of
writing original poetry of the highest calibre. Any other would have an
ironic effect. In contrast, Ondaatje's choice of Bolden, a semi-legendary
cornetist who seems never to have been recorded, has obvious advan-
tages. And finally, the use of a cornetist makes the images of a fall into
silence particularly forceful; given that the novel is about both a musician (Bolden) and a writer (Ondaatje and others) the silence — an ending without finality — is simultaneously literal and figurative.
Bolden's madness is a literal collapse into silence, it is an emptying of
acoustic space in so far as his cornet will never sound again; but for a
writer, silence is figurative because in an age of print he never creates
noise or sound. Writing is a silent, private act. By turning to Bolden as
his exemplary artist Ondaatje has found a means of externalizing and
dramatizing this privacy and also of making the figurative literal.
Ondaatje's novel, I suggest, needs to be examined within the contexts
implied above. It represents, in effect, a summary of Ondaatje's work
to the present, and it probably marks an end of a phase of his career; furthermore, we need to interpret the novel's central character, the cor-

248

netist Buddy Bolden, as a representative figure through whom Ondaatje is examining critically both the complex nature of his own creativity and three problematic notions central to modern art: the relationship between self-destructiveness and creativity, the influence of the audience upon the artist, and, by implication, the concept of the avant-garde.

Aspects of Bolden are already evident in Ondaatje's earlier work. The subject of suicide, for example, appears as early as the lyric "Birds for Janet — The Heron" in *The Dainty Monsters* (1967). The dangerous topic is treated impersonally and objectively within the tautly controlled form and through the spare diction of an animal poem written for the poet's sister.

> We found the path
> of a heron's suicide
> tracks left empty
> walking to the centre of the lake [7]

The mention of suicide in the poem's final lines personifies the heron but it leaves the reader anticipating a closing revelation — about the cause of the suicide — that never comes. Or at least it doesn't come until three books later in *Rat Jelly* (1973) when Ondaatje picks up the image and theme in "Heron Rex" where the heron, once again suicidal, is a surrogate for all suicides.

> There are ways of going
> physically mad, physically
> mad when you perfect the mind
> where you sacrifice yourself for the race
> when you are the representative when you allow
> yourself to be paraded in cages
> celebrity a razor in the body [8]

The ambiguity of the repeated "you" (it could mean "you" or "one") indicates, I think, a movement away from the total objective anonymity of "Birds for Janet — The Heron" toward a partial avowal that the heron is a mask for the speaker. Neither of the two poems is a complete success because in both Ondaatje wants to say more that he has said. His heron has an indeterminate status between being an image — heron as heron — and a symbol — heron as something more — which

249

while it ensures the success of the poems on a surreal or oneiric level prevents the fuller expression of the meaning implicit in them.

Ondaatje's poetry as a whole can be seen as a gradual development away from the impersonality of *The Dainty Monsters* and *the man with seven toes* (1969) towards a more directly subjective, though still controlled, dispassionate and dramatic, examination of his own case, his life as a man and as an artist. Since the publication of *The Collected Works of Billy the Kid* (1970) which began with the non-picture of Billy and ended with a photograph of the young Michael Ondaatje, he has turned increasingly and more and more directly to his own life for his subject matter; and the aspect of his life that has most fascinated him is the fundamentally ambiguous nature of his own creativity; the important lyrics in *Rat Jelly* and the novel *Coming Through Slaughter* show clear evidence of this concern. "Taking," "Burning Hills," "King Kong meets Wallace Stevens," " 'The gate in his head,' " "Spider Blues," and "White Dwarfs" are all, in general, about the problematic relationship between the nets of poetry and the anarchy of experience. They deal with the poet's attempt to catch

> The beautiful formed things . . . at the wrong moment
> so they are shapeless, awkward
> moving to the clear. (" 'The gate in his head'," (62))

or

> . . . to pour the exact arc
> of steel still soft and crazy
> before it hits the page. ("Taking" (55))

or

> to swivel to new regions
> where the raw of feelings exist. ("Spider Blues," (64))

These complex lyrics in the final section of the book constitute Ondaatje's poetic; they present a "theory" of art which recognizes (1) the difficulty of creating a poetic language and form supple enough to be expressive of life's anarchic energy and randomness, and (2) the psychological risks the writer takes both in trying to assimilate reality and in dredging up from his memory or subconscious impulses, events and characters that he proposes to use in his art. As will be seen in the

250

discussion of *Coming Through Slaughter* the two ideas are often integrally related in Ondaatje's work, and the kind of separation made here between them is purely one of critical convenience.

The idea that the writer takes risks by creating is powerfully and tragically present in Ondaatje's fine elegy for his father, "Letters & Other Worlds," which deals with the father who could only write his beautifully tender letters after having become

> the man who once a week
> disappeared into his room with bottles
> and stayed there until he was drunk
> and until he was sober. (26)

The father is a writer whose creativity originates in his self-destruction, and it is only by taking risks that he achieves "Letters in a clear hand / . . . without metaphor." The letters, like Ondaatje's poem, are written out of intense pain, suffering and remorse but in both one senses peace and control: the poem and the letters flow into one another as father and son write with what another poem calls the "clarity of architects" about "the raw of feelings" which in letter and poem appear ordered and controlled. The very fact that the father's writing is emphasized by being placed at the poem's end cannot but remind us of that other painful act of expiatory writing, the creation of the elegy. And as we become aware of the intense suffering underlying the father's achieved clarity, surely we also inevitably begin to sense, even though it is never made explicit, the personal agony that the creation of the poem must have involved for the poet.

The diction here, and in the lyrics I have referred to, includes such emotion-charged words as chaos, murder, bellow, nightmares, raw, kill, crucify, mad, and suicide but the poems remain controlled, understated ("I admire the spider, his control classic")[9] and impersonally personal as Ondaatje treats a more and more hazardous subject matter. It's worth noting that this is also the diction of Anne Sexton but a reader would never confuse the deliberately frenzied and hysterical tone and nervous rhythms of a poem like her "Wanting to Die" with the control and detachment exemplified in Ondaatje's work. Ondaatje is probing and clarifying a similar geography of inner experience; he too is writing about dying and wanting to die, but he doesn't enact or recreate sensations and events with the kind of direct, subjective

251

immediacy, from within as it were, that is the distinctive characteristic of Sexton's verse and that constitutes both her strength and her weakness. His manner, in contrast, is elliptical, indirect, cool; he objectifies, dramatizes, keeping the emotionally-charged subject matter distant from himself, only occasionally and off-handedly acknowledging its importance to him. As a result, there is a tension in almost every line of the major lyrics between the restrained and restraining style and the startling content. The reading act itself becomes hazardous as the reader progresses tentatively from line to line expecting, and both wanting and not wanting, the control to break. In "Letters & Other Worlds," for example, Ondaatje sustains his detached tone to the end while simultaneously managing by means of a series of insistent yet simple repetitions to make the reader aware of the difficulty of his restraint.

This tension between control and chaos is also evident in the comically yet frighteningly surrealistic lyric "King Kong meets Wallace Stevens" in which he uses Stevens and Kong as masks for himself and only lifts the disguise in one artfully ingenuous parenthesis.

> Take two photographs —
> Wallace Stevens and King Kong
> (Is it significant that I eat bananas as I write this?)
>
> Stevens is portly, benign, a white brush cut
> striped tie. Businessman but
> for the dark thick hands, the naked brain
> the thought in him (61)

The parenthetical question has a casual quality and a playful tone but its import is serious; the "bananas" are the link between Stevens-Kong and Ondaatje; even more they are our first suggestion of the presence of Kong and all he represents — anarchy, violence, destructive and creative energy — not only in Stevens but also in Stevens' admirer, Michael Ondaatje. The hint of self-mockery is completely appropriate if we remember that the parenthetical question is helping to establish an implied, almost hubristic, identification between Wallace Stevens, one of the century's most important voices, and Michael Ondaatje. In effect, the poem implies that one of the reasons for that ambivalent admiration is Stevens' ability to subdue and transmute (perhaps, on occasion, by killing) the internal and external flux of life (Kong) into poetry. Ondaatje's own lyric is a similar kind of triumph but it is also more; like the other lyrics about poetry in *Rat Jelly* it also enacts the difficulties involved in that "intolerable wrestle" not only with "words and meanings"[10] but also with varieties of experience. The particular kind of creativity taking place in these poems is often interpreted by Ondaatje as a form of destruction, a mode of violence, an inevitable suffering. Thus in "King Kong meets Wallace Stevens," for example, we end with "the bellow of locked blood" and "the murderer's shadow"; the former refers to Kong within Stevens, the latter to Stevens himself. The implication of the poem's final metaphor is that Stevens, because he is a poet, subdues or even murders an aspect of himself during the act of creation. If we have kept the parenthetical question in mind while reading through the poem we realize that the final metaphor also refers to Michael Ondaatje.[11]

Suicide and murder (in the form of a crucifixion) are also at the centre of Ondaatje's last lyric in *Rat Jelly*, the haunting "White Dwarfs" which I suspect we now read as a finale to one movement in his work and as a prelude to another, *Coming Through Slaughter*. "White Dwarfs" is probably Ondaatje's most complex lyric; the poem has a questioning reflective tone that deliberately disguises the terrifying theme at the core. It is a lyric that objectifies the poet's simultaneous longing for and fear of the end of life and art, an end that he envisions as the prelude to the attaining of some transcendent mode of being.

> There is my fear
> of no words   of
> falling without words
> over and over   of
> mouthing the silence
> Why do I love most
> among my heroes those
> who sail to that perfect edge
> where there is no social fuel (70)

The fascination with suicide, first shown in the heron poems, and the exploration of hidden aspects of himself ("Letters & Other Worlds") coalesce here in a poem pointing beyond art and social being to a consciously chosen negation of art and life, a kind of suicide. The implication throughout the poem is that only in silence, even the silence of death, does one find an authentic, because ultimate and irreducible, self.

253

Different motives underlie the various disappearances described in the poem but in one case, that of the writer Dashiell Hammett, it is suggested that his "success" or celebrity as a writer compelled him to move beyond "social fuel" into silence and anonymity in order to retain a sense of integrity. When in the next stanza we confront the stark and lonely image of "those burned out stars / who implode into silence / after parading in the sky" we realize that we have shifted almost imperceptibly into the mental geography of *Coming Through Slaughter*.[12] The three concerns I have been discussing — the relationship between art and reality, art and the artist's own life, art and suicide — merge into the story of the jazz cornetist Buddy Bolden "whose music was immediately on top of his own life"[13] and who eventually imploded "into silence / after parading."

But *Coming Through Slaughter*, even granting that it is fiction and not autobiography or even confessional poetry, is the story of Michael Ondaatje; it is the work in which he most explicitly declares that a fictional character created by him is really a self-portrait. Bolden's *métier*, or craft, may be jazz but there are enough parallels between Ondaatje's writing and Bolden's playing to make a comparison inevitable. And as if the implicit parallels weren't enough Ondaatje enters the novel in the final section to declare his sense of affinity with Bolden's life. Gone are the playful, wary and ambiguous hints of the lyrics, and the inconclusively suggestive photograph at the end of *Billy the Kid*; instead, in what is one of the most startling scenes in contemporary fiction, we read the author's admission that his character, Buddy Bolden, is in some crucial aspects his mirror image.

... When he went mad he was the same age as I am now.

The photograph moves and becomes a mirror. When I read he stood in front of mirrors and attacked himself, there was the shock of memory. For I had done that. Stood, and with a razorblade cut into cheeks and forehead, shaved hair. Defiling people we did not wish to be.

The thin sheaf of information. Why did my senses stop at you? There was the sentence, 'Buddy Bolden who became a legend when he went berserk in a parade ... ' What was there in that, before I knew your nation your colour your age, that made me push my arm forward and ... clutch myself? There was the climax of the parade and then you removed yourself from the 20th century game of fame, the rest of your life a desert of facts. Cut them open and spread them out like garbage. (133-34)

254

Here the distance between character and author collapses as Bolden becomes the mirror image of Ondaatje.

Ondaatje must have found Bolden's a particularly interesting case history because in it, unlike in the lives of Mrs. Fraser (*the man with seven toes*) and Billy the Kid, he was reading about the life of an artist. Furthermore, it was an artist about whom there existed only a "thin sheaf of information" so that again as with Mrs. Fraser and Billy, Ondaatje could expand and polish facts "to suit the truth of fiction."[14] Each life story provided him with a ready made though thinly sketched and ambiguous story closer to legend than history. It is also worth noting that in all three works he has chosen figures from the pre-contemporary era (though he has been moving gradually closer to the present) all of whom lived in places and societies radically different from his own. This is not because he is an artist like Visconti who is fascinated by the outward trappings of a period; rather the choice provides him with an immediate temporal and spatial distance from the real subject of his work, himself and the nature of his creativity. While the entire thrust of his vision is intensely psychological the frame or context for that interior probing is ostensibly historical; I write "ostensibly" because his characters tend to be disconcertingly contemporary in their language and manners. This deliberate merging of past and present, while preserving an ostensible historical distance, is his means of freeing his vision from time and history in order to ground it more definitely in psychology and myth.

The meagreness of "the thin sheaf of information" is also an assurance of an incomplete story, one whose full meaning is finally indeterminate, ambiguous, as, in fact, are the sources of Ondaatje's two other full length works. *Coming Through Slaughter* expands upon this sheaf without, if I can put it this way, making determinate and falsifying the fundamental ambiguities of the original story of the creative artist whose creativity destroyed him. Chronological organization is avoided, as in the discontinuous *Billy the Kid*, presumably because chronology compels a particular kind of reading act that assumes *a priori* temporal notions of cause and effect. Here as in the lyrics in *Rat Jelly* he is concerned with not falsifying life's randomness by imposing an implicit or explicit historicity upon it. Writing about a musician who "did nothing but leap into the mass of changes" (15) Ondaatje has done so in a complex form that expresses both the anarchy ("'mass of changes'") and ambiguity (stories about Bolden are like "spokes on a rimless wheel" [63]) of the musician's life. He has placed the reader within the mental and physical geography of Buddy Bolden, and has left it up to him to discern the truth or truths about the cornetist. By the novel's end the thin sheaf has been suggestively expanded but its ambiguous quality has been retained.

Frank Lewis's account of Bolden is probably the best place to begin an interpretation of the cornetist's career since of the several judgments made on Bolden by various people it is closest to what I sense the overall judgment of the text to be as well.

> But there was a discipline, it was just that we didn't understand. We thought he was formless, but I think now he was tormented by order, what was outside it. He tore apart the plot — see his music was immediately on top of his own life. Echoing. As if, when he was playing he was lost and hunting for the right accidental notes. . . . He would be describing something 27 ways. There was pain and gentleness everything jammed into each number. (37)

Bolden's music is completely spontaneous, anarchic and transient; yet as Lewis perceptively indicates there is a kind of self-discipline in Bolden's compulsion to find "what was outside order." But to play beyond order Bolden must create in so powerful and self-expressive a way ("immediately on top of his own life") that his existence as a private being is continually being called into question as he empties himself into a music that can never stand still or repeat itself: "The music was coarse and rough, immediate, dated in half an hour, was about bodies in the river, knives, lovepains, cockiness" (43). To keep on succeeding as a musician Bolden must remain always sensitive to the pressure of the moment, he must be the loudest cornet player in New Orleans, and he must be predictably unpredictable. He is a one man avant-garde who must stay ahead not only of what others have done and are doing but even ahead of what he himself has recently done. To surrender himself to this kind of creativity, a complete immersion in the immediate, the momentary, means extinguishing any possibility of achieving and possessing a stable, private self. The instability of his life is perfectly imaged in the block of "ice [that] changed shape all day before your eyes" in the window of Joseph's shaving parlour. It is this

256

very quality, the constant sense of shift, that both makes possible his extreme art and prevents him from having a stable identity. To continue as a successful cornetist he cannot alter his mode of being, to do so would mean the end of the kind of music that is uniquely his. It is for this reason that "he was almost completely governed by fears of certainty" (15) because certainty or predictability is inimical to his kind of creativity.

> But his own mind was helpless against every moment's headline. He did nothing but leap into the mass of changes and explore them and all the tiny facets so that eventually he was almost completely governed by fears of certainty. He distrusted it in anyone but Nora for there it went to the spine, and yet he attacked it again and again in her, cruelly, hating it, the sure lanes of the probable. Breaking chairs and windows glass doors in fury at her certain answers.
>
> Once they were sitting at the kitchen table opposite each other. To his right and to her left was a window. Furious at something he drew his right hand across his body and lashed out. Half way there at full speed he realised it was a window he would be hitting and braked. For a fraction of a second his open palm touched the glass, beginning simultaneously to draw back. The window starred and crumpled slowly two floors down. His hand miraculously uncut. It had acted exactly like a whip violating the target and still free, retreating from the outline of a star. She was delighted by the performance. Surprised he examined his fingers. (15-16)

Yet as the narrator later points out, after even these minimal certainties are shattered by Nora's suspected infidelity with Tom Pickett, Bolden both "loathed and needed" (78) "the certainties" that she brought into his life. She alone provided his chaotic existence with a focus, a centre that would always be there, unchanging, no matter how random the remainder of his life was. Even as a whore she "had managed to save delicate rules and ceremonies for herself" (15). As much as Bolden may loathe these because they are inherently inimical to his art, he needs them in her because they provide the only continuity in his life; only with Nora does he have a private identity. But even in the relationship with her, as the last sentence of the above quotation makes clear, there is always the potential of violence on Bolden's part. The slow-motion image of the window shattering in "the outline of a star" summarizes the relationship between beauty and violence in Bolden, but it also does more. Since the violence occurs in a scene with Nora — and is repeated in slightly different form with Robin — it indicates the extent to which

257

certainty and anarchy, love and violence co-exist in Bolden's world, the thin line at all times between them.

What Ondaatje seems to be implying is that Bolden, even before meeting Bellocq the photographer, is already a doomed figure, a man whose violent life and art will inevitably lead to self-destruction. The drinking, whoring and fighting are interrelated aspects of a personality that finds compulsive expression in an increasingly extreme music. As Martin Williams points out, one of the traditional explanations of Bolden's breakdown emphasizes that he over-extended himself in his playing, that "his mind deteriorated because he overblew the cornet."[15]

Bolden's music is contrasted to John Robichaux's whom Bolden hears on the radio while staying at Webb's cabin.

> John Robichaux! Playing his waltzes. And I hate to admit it but I enjoyed listening to the clear forms. Every note part of the large curve, so carefully patterned that for the first time I appreciated the possibilities of a mind moving ahead of the instruments in time and waiting with pleasure for them to catch up. I had never been aware of that mechanistic pleasure, that trust.
>
> Did you ever meet Robichaux? I never did. I loathed everything he stood for. He dominated his audiences. He put his emotions into patterns which a listening crowd had to follow. (93)

There is an explicit contrast here between the artist who creates by conscious choice and is in control of what he is doing (Robichaux), and one who is driven compulsively and instinctively to practise an art which seems to dominate him. Where Robichaux is able to "put his emotions into patterns," Bolden's patterns are determined by the emotions. If Robichaux can be said to be a musician who dominates his art and his audiences, Bolden, in contrast, is dominated by both. Bolden's *need* to play is evident throughout the novel in scenes such as the one in which while making love with Robin Brewitt he presses his fingers into "the flesh on her back as though he were plunging them into a cornet. . . . He had been improving on Cakewalking Babies" (59).

Scenes such as this one indicate that his two year escape from his career and fame was always only partial since he could never really escape from his compulsion to play. Furthermore, due to the influence of Bellocq, the Buddy Bolden who escapes "the giraffes of fame" and "the 20th century game of fame" is self-conscious and introspective in a way he has never been before. Of the various images associated with Bellocq in the text — window, blackness, white — the one most insistently repeated is "brain"; it's an image that only occurs in scenes involving Bolden *after* he has met Bellocq. In the author's note Ondaatje refers to the "private and fictional magnets" that "drew him and Bolden together" (158), and in the body of the text itself he describes their friendship as follows:

> The connection between Bellocq and Buddy was strange. Buddy was a social dog, talked always to three or four people at once, a racer. He had no deceit but he roamed through conversations as if they were the countryside not listening carefully just picking up moments. And what was strong in Bellocq was the slow convolution of that brain. He was self-sufficient, complete as a perpetual motion machine. What could Buddy have to do with him? (56)

At this point in the novel, "the slow convolution" of "brain" is strong in Bellocq and non-existent in Bolden. But a few pages later the narrator suggests how Bellocq's mode of thinking became Bolden's during their "small almost unnecessary friendship."

> [Bellocq] had pushed his imagination into Buddy's brain, had passed it awkwardly across the table and entertained him, had seen him take it in return for the company, not knowing the conversations were becoming steel in his only friend. They had talked for hours moving gradually off the edge of the social world. As Bellocq lived at the edge in any case he was at ease there and as Buddy did not he moved on past him like a naïve explorer looking for footholds. Bellocq did not expect that. Or he could have easily explained the ironies. The mystic privacy one can be so proud of has no alphabet of noise or meaning to the people outside. (64)

Bolden's new mode of thinking / feeling supersedes one in which what distinguished him was his ability to function and respond instinctively without recourse to Bellocq's kind of deliberate self-consciousness. For instance, when Bolden describes Happy Galloway's guitar playing he emphasizes both that "every note [was] new and raw and chance. Never repeated," and that Galloway's "brain had lost control of his fingers" (95).[16] As the reader realizes immediately, this is also a description of Bolden's own music and technique which become impossible or, at least, radically altered when his brain begins to control the fingers and mouth. The shift in mode, "the one altered move" (*Billy the Kid*,

259

41), the intrusion of consciousness into a pre-conscious movement produces a different kind of music. Bolden's ability to continue as a musician whose "music was immediately on top of his own life" depended on a technique independent of "brain."

Bolden's debilitating introspection becomes apparent in his constant references to his brain. He mentions that "my brain has walked away and is watching me" (100), "my brain suicided" (119), and the narrator speaks of

> Bolden's hand going up into the air
> in agony.
> His brain driving it up into the
> path of the circling fan. (136)

The kind of unified and limited sensibility evident in Bolden in the early part of the novel is here replaced by an image of a self divided against itself. The obsession with the brain, expressed through the repeated neurological images, signals a radical alteration in Bolden's character in the direction of Bellocq's. Where he had previously been unconsciously spontaneous, on his return he self-consciously and relentlessly prods himself into playing an anarchic and elemental music until he breaks. If nothing else his suicide from music provides him with an existence freed from the private and public compulsions that previously governed him. I call Bolden's fall, or rather rush, into madness a suicide because he himself refers to "suicided brain" and to Webb's notion that "all suicides all acts of privacy are romantic" (101). Also, the text tends to treat his madness as synonymous with suicide. In addition to the random references to suicide there are also the compelling oneiric scenes in which Bolden dreams of what is in essence a "focal suicide" [17] involving the destruction of his hand, "the dream of the wheel over his hand" (40), which would liberate him from the compulsion to play.

I have so far emphasized one cause of Bolden's suicide, the inexplicable nature of his particular kind of genius in which creativity depends to a great extent upon the artist's ability to give expression to the chaos within and outside the self. As I wrote earlier Bolden's mode of being and creating involves a complete "submission to chance" (Charles Simic's term),[18] and his music seems to be an expression of whatever particular atmosphere he played in (37). But Ondaatje also suggests that in addition to Bolden's compulsive genius another factor prodded him to push himself as he did: the audience. (Martin Williams points out that for the real Bolden "There was *no* success except in pleasing his audience."[19]) When the detective Webb watches Bolden play he imagines the vampire-like audience "crowding round to suck that joy" (36). Later on, while wandering through the district of the mattress-whores, Bolden thinks of himself as the audience's whore, as someone paid for. Like the whores, now diseased and aged, he also once took pleasure and pride in what he did without realizing that the seeds of an eventual self-destruction — for him madness, for them disease — were already in that pleasure. Also like a whore he is someone who fulfills certain expectations; for instance, that he will play louder and louder, and behave more and more unpredictably. In a paradoxical sense his very unpredictability becomes a label, a predictable certainty because of the ever-present pressure of the audience which demands and expects a certain kind of music and behaviour from him. Whether they know it or not his listeners are urging him on to a music which involves the risk of suicide. One senses the same situation in Sylvia Plath's "Lady Lazarus" where the speaker begins by announcing casually

> I have done it again.
> One year in every ten
> I manage it —

The intimation here is that suicide is somehow in her very nature but as the poem develops we are startled to realize that she is playing to an audience expecting this violent artistry from her.

> It's easy enough to do it in a cell.
> It's easy enough to do it and stay put.
> It's the theatrical
>
> Comeback in broad day
> To the same place, the same face, the same brute
> Amused shout
>
> 'A miracle!'
> That knocks me out.

The scene of the suicide attempt includes "The peanut-crunching crowd" that "Shoves in to see / The big strip tease."

261

It's a poem as much about rebirth as about suicide as the speaker attempts to kill one self, or a number of past selves, in order to free a new self from the burden of her past. The poem offers three causes underlying her attempts at suicide: something innate and inexplicable within the character of the speaker; her ambivalent relationship with the implied father; and, finally, the thrilling sensation she feels in perceiving the crowd's fascination with her attempts at self-destruction.[20] Her involvement with the audience differs from Bolden's but for each the crowd is a constitutive part of the motive for returning to a dangerous performance. For each, "celebrity" becomes "a razor in the body" ("Heron Rex") because it is achieved by means of a performance that depends on risking self-destruction. The artist is, to a certain extent, under the influence of an audience that expects this kind of performance from him. In contrast to Plath and Bolden stands John Robichaux who "dominated his audiences" and just as Plath or Berryman could not have written the poems of, say John Hollander, so Bolden cannot play the music of Robichaux or assume his attitude toward the audience: Robichaux is playing Hollander's *A Crackling of Thorns*, Bolden Lowell's *Life Studies*.

The only possible lasting release for Bolden from art and audience lies in madness or suicide. This is probably the single most disturbing notion in the novel. We gradually come to realize that in Bolden's case only two alternatives, both leading to the same result, were possible: to "overblow" the trumpet accidentally or deliberately. With or without Bellocq's influence Bolden would have destroyed himself just as some of the men whom he calls his "fathers" or "teachers" (95) had done. Bellocq simply hastened the process by making Bolden self-conscious of the inherent contradiction in his situation: he must go on playing yet his playing will eventually destroy him.

The release comes in the novel's stunning climactic scene, a parade in which Bolden makes his first public appearance after his two year absence. The audience urging him on is sensually and dramatically focalized in a lithe young dancer who, beginning by moving in time to Bolden's squawks, ends by controlling him and compelling him to play faster and more violently to keep up with her movements.

God this is what I wanted to play for, if no one else I always guessed there would be this, this mirror somewhere, she closer to me now and her eyes over mine tough and young and come from god knows where. Never seen her before but testing me taunting me to make it past her, old hero, old ego tested against one as cold and pure as himself, this tall bitch breasts jumping loose under the light shirt she wears that's wet from energy and me fixing them with the aimed horn tracing up to the throat. Half dead, can't take more, hardly hit the squawks anymore but when I do my body flicks at them as if I'm the dancer till the music is out there .... this is what I wanted, always, loss of privacy in the playing, leaving the stage, the rectangle of band on the street, this hearer who can throw me in the direction and the speed she wishes like an angry shadow. (130)

His last thought as he collapses is ''What I wanted'' and it sums up, without contradiction, the two contrasting desires in Bolden: to play an ultimate music in which the self is totally negated, and, contrastingly, to find release from this anxiety-ridden compulsion to play. This release, unlike the two year escape, is permanent because within it the tensions generated by the contradictory desires for privacy and fame, certainty and uncertainty, order and anarchy, character and personality, have been finally resolved by the silence of ''Dementia Praecox. Paranoid Type'' (132). Like the various figures in ''White Dwarfs'' Bolden has gone beyond ''social fuel'' to a mode of being (normal in the lyric, psychotic in the novel) that excludes self-expression and art.[21] For the first time since meeting Bellocq, Bolden achieves a wholeness of being, an equanimity and peace. It is for this reason that the novel's final movement is simultaneously savage and mellow; Bolden lives in an asylum where rapes and beatings are everyday occurrences but his attitude to them is ''sublime'' and tranquil. The irony of the situation is obvious and tragic: in madness he has found the peace he never possessed or could possess when sane. Alvarez makes a similar point about Artaud, an artist who asserted that he chose or would choose madness and suicide ''not to destroy myself but to put myself back together again. Suicide will be for me only one means of violently reconquering myself.... By suicide, I reintroduce my design in nature, I shall for the first time give things the shape of my will.''[22] For Artaud as for Bolden, suicide / madness was the only way to reconstitute the self, to recreate one's self independently of outside influences. Silence, in both cases, has no transcendent significance, it does not signify more than language: it is simply a release from the compulsion to create, from a too-demanding art. Yet by its very attractiveness and desirability it constitutes an implicit judgment on that art. The silence of schizophrenia into which Bolden plunges, like one of Audubon's birds diving into the depths, becomes paradoxically the only mode of being within which his continuing survival is possible. This is contingent upon Bolden having moved beyond art. Thus this silence, unlike the silence discussed by Susan Sontag or Norman O. Brown[23] or even Artaud, signifies the end of a particular kind of creativity and a particular kind of art. I suggest furthermore that it is not farfetched to see *Coming Through Slaughter* as announcing the ultimate bankruptcy of extremist art. What Ondaatje seems to be saying is that even silence is preferable to the internal and external. demands of such a mode of creativity. The novel places the reader of Celan, Berryman, and Plath in the position, unfortunately only hypothetical, of having to decide whether the art, undoubtedly great as it is, is worth the price paid in human suffering to achieve it.

I want to end by re-examining something discussed earlier in the essay, Ondaatje's relationship to Bolden. I wrote that through Bolden Ondaatje was examining some of his own central assumptions about art. But Ondaatje's identification, implicit and explicit, with Bolden should not prevent us from realizing the radical difference between the two: Ondaatje is using Bolden to enact and to examine warily and objectively issues which when lived existentially — as in Bolden's life — could destroy an artist. The issues are raised within a text whose language and form are controlled by a cool sensibility that can imagine and recreate convincingly Bolden's anguish, that can even temporarily submit itself to it, without ever making a complete assimilation with that mode of being. In the novel, as in "White Dwarfs," Ondaatje remains fascinated by a life that rejects language and art but, contrastingly, his primary commitment is to an *artistic* examination — through poem or novel — of that fascination. If Bolden's final commitment is to chaos, madness and silence, Ondaatje's is to a controlled art that tries to understand Bolden's case — his own case — to make its contradictions intelligible without succumbing to them. He moves back and forth between Bolden's world and his own — or between two aspects of himself — between silence and art, anarchy and order, artistically rendering the psychic tensions inherent in the often lacerating interplay between the extremes.

He chooses deliberately, and wisely I think, not to attempt what would have been an inevitably reductive psychological explanation of

264

why Bolden is the kind of artist he is; Bolden's psychology — the psychology of a particular kind of self-destructive genius — is part of the novel's given, and everything is predicated upon it. Ondaatje examines Bolden's life between two points: from the day Webb "watched his nervous friend walk jauntily out of the crowd into the path of a parade and begin to play" (36) to the day that he played himself into madness during another parade (131). Various aspects of Bolden's life can be explained, for instance some of the pressures that drove him to suicide, but the constitutive aspects of his character, what it was that compelled him to create in his unique way and thus made him susceptible to these pressures, these are beyond explanation. Similarly we cannot explain why Ondaatje is able to write about the very problems that drove Bolden mad. We can refer to the artist's "manic defences" as Alvarez does,[24] or to the artist's "histrionic simulation" of madness (Anthony Storr[25]) but neither term or argument explains why in one case — Hughes's *Gaudete* or Ondaatje's novel — the writer remains in control of his material, while in another — Bolden's music — the material overwhelms him. The distinction here is not between a greater and a lesser artist or art but between two personalities both dealing with "the roots of emotions, the obscurest springs of... personality"[26] one of which is able "to manipulate these experiences with an informed and intelligent mind"[27] (Plath's words) and maintain sanity, while the other lapses into madness or suicide. In a manner of speaking the two individuals of *Coming Through Slaughter* are Ondaatje and Bolden or, as I put it above, two aspects of Ondaatje himself.

In writing about Bolden Ondaatje seems to have placed to rest an urgent idea or impulse that if acted upon could have only meant the end of his own art.[28] As it is, out of the encounter with the impulse towards chaos and silence he has produced an impressive group of lyrics and one of the finest novels of recent years. As in Beckett's trilogy, the questioning of the validity and value of speech and art has resulted in an art that, paradoxically, affirms the very things questioned. Furthermore his personal experience as expressed through the story of a jazz cornetist,[29] expands, by novel's end, into a convincing statement about a central aspect of modern writing and about that related group of dead and living writers also concerned with the issues central to Ondaatje's novel.

1 Gottfried Benn, *Primal Vision*, (New York: New Directions, 1960), p. 206.

2 "The Phenomenology of Anger," in *Adrienne Rich's Poetry*, (New York: Norton, 1975), p. 69.

3 *The Collected Works of Billy the Kid* (Toronto: House of Anansi Press, 1970), p. 20. *Coming Through Slaughter*, (Toronto: House of Anansi Press, 1976). All future references will be to this edition of *Coming Through Slaughter* and will be included in the body of the essay.

4 The term is Alfred Alvarez's. See *The Savage God*, (Penguin, 1975), p. 278. See also *Beyond All This Fiddle*, (New York: Random House, 1973). For a more recent discussion of extremist work see Irvin Ehrenpreis, "At the Poles of Poetry," *The New York Review of Books*, Vol. XXV, No. 13, August 17, 1978, 48.

5 *The Savage God*, p. 278.

6 *Against Interpretation*, (New York: Farrar, Straus and Giroux, 1966), p. 42.

7 *The Dainty Monsters*, (Toronto: Coach House Press, 1967), p. 12.

8 *Rat Jelly*, (Toronto: Coach House Press, 1973), p. 53.

9 In "Spider Blues" (*Rat Jelly*, p. 63) as in *The Collected Works of Billy the Kid* and *Coming Through Slaughter* the spider represents the artist, his control as well as his ruthlessness.

10 T.S. Eliot, *Four Quartets*, (London: Faber and Faber, 1963), p. 26.

11 The relationship between violence and creativity is also evident in the early poem, "Peter," which deals with a young boy who channels his suffering and desire for revenge into a macabre art.

12 See *Books in Canada*, Vol. 6, No. 6, June-July 1977, pp. 7-10, for Ondaatje's statement that "the problems Bolden has are the problems any artist has at some time. It's almost like the parable of any 20th-century artist." What I have referred to as Bolden's "mental geography" is also that of Hammett, Ondaatje and, as Ondaatje recognizes though he overstates the point, many other modern writers.

13 See the interview with Anne Sexton in *American Poets in 1976*, edited by William Heyen, (Indianapolis: Bobbs-Merrill, 1976), for an indication of how apt a description this is of her work.

14 The full end note reads as follows: "While I have used real names and characters and historical situations I have also used more personal pieces of friends and fathers. There have been some date changes, some characters brought together, and some facts have been expanded or polished to suit the truth of fiction."

15 *Jazz Masters of New Orleans*, (New York: The Macmillan Co., 1967), p. 167.

16 Earlier in the novel Bolden, watching Robin Brewitt cutting carrots realizes that "if she thinks what she is doing she will lose control. He knows that the only way to catch a fly for instance is to move the hand without the brain telling it to move fast, interfering" (p. 31). This image of catching the fly without the brain interfering also occurs in *Billy the Kid*, p. 58, and in one of Ondaatje's favourite westerns, Sergio Leone's *Once Upon a Time in the West.*

17 See Karl Menninger, *Man Against Himself*, (New York: Vintage Books, 1965), p. 200. Bolden's biting of his "nails chewed down and indistinguishable from the callouses of his fingers" (p. 49) is another example of this kind of focal self-destruction which directs our attention to his sub-conscious desire to destroy that aspect of himself (his ability to play) which creates his tensions.

18 "Elementary Cosmogony" in *Return to a Place Lit by a Glass of Milk*, (New York: George Braziller, 1974), p. 31.

19 Williams, *op. cit.*, p. 11.

20 Antonin Artaud, in the essay "Van Gogh, the Man Suicided by Society" (1947), turns the noun suicide into a transitive verb in order to emphasize that the artist-suicide is the victim of a murder perpetrated by his audience. Antonin Artaud, *Selected Writings*, (New York: Farrar, Straus and Giroux, 1976), p. 487.

21 There is a line in Adrienne Rich's "From an Old House in America" that sums up Bolden's case perfectly; she refers to "the final autistic statement / of the self-destroyer." *Adrienne Rich's Poetry*, p. 78. Sexton's "Ninth Psalm" in *The Death Notebooks* also seems to have been written in response to an experience of the same kind: "For I am placing fist over fist on rock and plunging into the altitude of words. The silence of words" (p. 112).

22 Alvarez, *The Savage God*, p. 153.

23 See Susan Sontag, "The Aesthetics of Silence" in *Styles of Radical Will*, (New York: Delta, 1973). Also Norman O. Brown, *Love's Body*, (New York: Vintage, 1966); especially relevant is section XVI, "Nothing."

24 "Sylvia Plath" in *Beyond All This Fiddle*, p. 56.

25 *The Dynamics of Creation*, (Penguin, 1977), p. 260.

26 *Beyond All This Fiddle*, p. 69.

27 The words are Sylvia Plath's from a BBC broadcast; they are quoted by Alvarez in *Beyond All This Fiddle*, p. 52.

28 Robert Lowell's comment on the writing and aftermath of *Life Studies* is germane here: "When I finished *Life Studies*, I was left hanging on a question mark. I am still hanging there. I don't know whether it is a death rope or a lifeline." *New York Times Book Review*, Oct. 4, 1964, 34.

Constance Rooke
DOG IN A GREY ROOM:
THE HAPPY ENDING OF
COMING THROUGH SLAUGHTER

I know that many readers have found *Coming Through Slaughter*, and especially its conclusion, extraordinarily bleak. I do not. The more I read the book, the more convinced I am that *Slaughter* has a happy ending. And I think you have to do that: really enter the book, travel in a visceral way through the images, to see the affirmation that lies on the other side of *Slaughter*. If you stay on this side, the story is undeniably grim. But if you can go far enough with Ondaatje, follow through the immensely complex and proliferating images, his yearnings, as Ondaatje followed Bolden's, then a *bouleversement* will occur for you as well. It is the motive force of the book, why it was written at all, and why I love it.

I take Buddy Bolden to be the hero of the novel, indeed an exemplary case of the artist as hero. Sam Solecki, in a footnote to his essay "Making and Destroying: Michael Ondaatje's *Coming Through Slaughter* and Extremist Art," quotes Ondaatje as having said that " 'the problems Bolden has are the problems any artist has at some time,' " and then says that Ondaatje "overstates the point."[1] Solecki argues that there are two kinds of artist, the "ordinary" or "normal" artist and the "extremist." The difference, he says, "begins as one of degree but leads ultimately to almost one of kind."[2] Stephen Scobie, in "*Coming Through Slaughter:* Fictional Magnets and Spider's Webbs," also regards the novel as a portrait of the artist — "or more precisely a certain kind of artist."[3] Both critics are therefore concerned with splitting off the self-destructive Buddy Bolden from Ondaatje as articulate survivor. And both read *Coming Through Slaughter* as, in Solecki's words, "announcing the bankruptcy of extremist art."[4]

268

I would not deny the usefulness of Solecki's distinction between two kinds of artists, but I think that it can lead to a mistaken emphasis in the interpretation of *Coming Through Slaughter*. It seems to me wrong to divorce author and character at the end, to suggest that one (Ondaatje, like Conrad's Marlowe in *Heart of Darkness*) is saved by caution and the other (Bolden, like Kurtz) is doomed by excess. Imaginatively — and again I would claim that this is the *reason* for the book — Ondaatje goes with Bolden all the way. If in actuality he does not, that is beside the point. If at the end we sense a part of him moving away, that is only because the book is over now. Bolden the extremist knows what Ondaatje knows: that the need to break through "certainties," to find new ways of thinking and seeing and being, is the very essence of creativity. Extremist art is that which in its style and subject matter takes that "breaking through" somehow more literally than the normal artist may do. And particularly because such a visceral or extreme response to the imperative of breaking through may find expression in the artist's life as well as in his work, there will always be a natural attraction to and fear of the extremist.

Take marriage now, as a synecdoche for life: the task there is not, I think, to make a seemly, stable artifact. You don't want to figure out a reasonably good way of being, and then stick to that. Any more than you would want to write *The Rape of the Lock* over again, or a verbatim repeat of your own last novel. Or if you do, you're not an artist. It may be argued that artists in particular are tempted by domestic certainty — to balance the risk-taking of their art, to get their work *done*. But surely the best thing is to keep both life and art on the move. And that is partly the explanation of the peculiar attraction we may feel to those extremist artists who live out the extremes, as well as write about them. In some way it *is* a validation of their art. Both Solecki and Ondaatje are concerned with the grotesquerie of the audience which cries out for blood, "the peanut-crunching crowd" of Sylvia Plath's "Lady Lazarus" that "Shoves in to see/ The big strip tease." But there is also an honourable motive for our fascination with the extreme, and from the perspective of that motive the suffering extremist is observed not as scapegoat but as hero. I say this because I believe it's only accident, or only history, that makes us associate extremism with madness, stereotypically "wild" living, suicide and the like: I think other forms of extremism are there for the making, in life as in art. However literally the usual modes of extremism are lived out, they are still primarily metaphors for breaking through. As such, they have an evolutionary thrust. And "self-destruction" is a loaded term, hiding — it may be — the chance of growth.

I do not intend this argument as a hymn to the wife-battering genius. Nor do I think I'm romanticizing the suicide or lunatic. Margarethe von Trotta's film *Marianne and Juliane* may help to make my point. In that film, however profoundly we may deplore the actions of the sister who becomes a terrorist, we come to understand that she is motivated at least in part by something purely admirable: she has *looked*, harder than most of us have, at the intolerable misery, the inadequacy of the given world. She strikes out at that. And we make a bad mistake if we concern ourselves only with psychoanalysis or politics, the question of why and how she went wrong. Lessons of moderation are not the only lessons to be learned. Only by understanding the point at which she is right, that extremity of vision, will we discover the right response to what she sees. Solecki uses as an epigraph for his essay two lines from Adrienne Rich: "Madness. Suicide. Murder. / Is there no way out but these?" The answer must eventually be yes. In the meantime, such extremism may land the artist in a still more wretched part of hell; or it may yield him peace through nothingness, a mere cessation of life's pain and contradictions. But there is also a chance of imaginative transcendence, entry into a state of being which is prophetic of our goal on *this* side of Slaughter. This last, I think, is what happens to Buddy Bolden.

The position elaborated in this essay may seem to place me in opposition to Stephen Scobie and Sam Solecki, whose essays on *Coming Through Slaughter* I admire. In fact, my own essay will assume much of the ground covered by Scobie and Solecki. I shall be filling in their map — looking at images and thinking about characters partly in ways they have not, arriving at a different place with their help. In terms of theme, I shall be concerned with issues of love and power, with egoism and the transcendence of ego, with old questions about the self and the other, the one and the many. Among the image patterns I shall examine, high roads and by-ways on Michael Ondaatje's own map, are the following: landscape, rooms and wallpaper, clouds, veins, the polarity of black and white, the colour blue, dogs, the mattress whores, and the dolphin sonographs. *Coming Through Slaughter* is intensely poetic; its logic—its argument if you like—is that of poetry. But it is also a novel, whose characters (and their deployment) must not recede from view; and so I have chosen to place Bolden's journey in the foreground, to deal with the images as they arise, rather than to pursue each pattern separately. For reasons of economy, and with great reluctance, I shall have to ignore to a considerable degree Ondaatje's brilliant juxtapositions, the temporal dislocations and orchestration of voices in his text, and will move through Bolden's journey in chronological order.

As the title may suggest, the most pervasive kind of imagery in *Coming Through Slaughter* is spatial: the idea of a landscape (the life journey) through which Bolden moves, the parade (of display to others) which he enters and exits, and the rooms (the psychic space) in which he lives alone and with others. Of his first life phase we know nothing, for "Bolden had never spoken of his past....Landscape suicide." At fifteen he meets Webb, telling nothing, and at seventeen they take an apartment together: we enter his landscape at that point.

They live in a neutral, "brown painted apartment" (42) where they "gradually paste their characters [like wallpaper] onto each other." They spend a week alone "building up the apartment in Pontchartrain," establishing their relationship, the space they occupy together. Their activities are parallel: Webb's play with the magnets and Bolden's with the cornet. Each of these activities is a performance, and each involves opposing forces in the air—"the precision of the forces" that Webb must explain to Bolden. At first, Webb is the dominant partner, "Webb who was the public figure, Bolden the side-kick." When they emerge from that week in the room, however, their relationship seems equal, their friendship "a public act of repartee" as they bounce "jokes off each other in female company" (35), performing for women they trade back and forth, their taste in whom, "diverse at first, became embarrassingly similar" (42). This is the language of exchange, and it connects with Buddy's later account of the usual pattern of relationship between the sexes: "the slow true intimacy, disintegration after they exchanged personalities and mannerisms, the growing tired of each other's speed" (88).

Now they begin to move apart. More precisely, Bolden moves ahead: "It was Bolden who had jumped up, who had swallowed everything Webb was" (36). Buddy's persona is launched upon the world with his "very famous entrance" (38) into the New Orleans parade. And

271

Bolden's success as an artist is torment to Webb, because it is proof of his superior magnetism; it is torment also because Webb has been "swallowed" by Bolden and cannot let him go. But this does not mean that Webb is powerless. If Bolden has "swallowed" Webb, he has also internalized him. The Bolden who "jumped up" did so at the internal behest of Webb, responding automatically to his magnets — the pull of audience.

Webb's behaviour throughout the novel needs to be understood in these terms. Like Buddy, he is "drawn to opposites . . . . In terror we lean in the direction that is most unlike us. Running past your own character into pain" (96). As audience, Webb is attracted to Buddy the artist; as detective, to Buddy of the criminal silence, the mysterious "landscape suicide." He draws him out of nothingness, until he "jumps up" as Bolden's photographic image will do in Bellocq's darkroom, again at the insistence of Webb. Only by returning the Bolden who contains him to the artist's path can Webb convince himself of his own continuing existence. Recalling their shared space in the apartment, he attempts (rather like Ondaatje) to enter imaginatively into Bolden's body and brain and so to track him down. Ultimately he fails. Bolden's return to the parade turns out to be the act which propels him successfully into another space, beyond Webb's reach or power of explanation. Bolden "breaks through" the window and lands in a room in which there is no further need to shatter the glass. Webb, to whom Buddy had said "You come too. Put your hand through this window" (91), cannot follow. Attempting to escape the room in which he learns of that other room in the asylum where Bolden lives on, Webb's "unknown flesh" (the Bolden in him that he cannot know) tries to "break through the wall" and crashes over the "hands and glasses" that Bolden breaks to achieve his goal. But Webb-the-spider's brain, "puffed . . . up with poison" (150) by the news of Bolden's incarceration, cannot work itself free of the asylum room; his body too fails to expel the poison. He cannot vomit (cannot express the feeling that pours through Bolden's horn in the parade), and so Webb ends a ruined and imprisoned man. His sweat, as Bella Cornish observes, has "driven itself onto the wall" (151). (Ondaatje fares better: without explanation, he can enter Bolden's last room and know it for something different from the horror that is all Webb sees.)

Leaving Webb and the Pontchartrain apartment Bolden goes to New

272

Orleans. "His life at this time had a fine and precise balance to it, with a careful allotment of hours. A barber, publisher of *The Cricket*, a cornet player, good husband and father, and an infamous man about town" (13). These activities — "labels" (106) he derisively calls them on his later return to this terrain — balance one another to comprise Bolden's persona and to fill out his day. Still Bolden's complex persona does not satisfy him, for it does not include *enough*; he is "tormented by order, what was outside it" (37). It is for this reason that diverse stories about Bolden "were like spokes on a rimless wheel ending in air" (63): Bolden's hunger for more kept the rim at bay.

Each role in turn involves its own balance, a principle of exchange and of risk. As a barber, he ministers to "the vanity of others," and the work seems a kind of "slavery" (48); at the same time he is a skilled performer and occupies a central position, as the others come to him. "Offering visions of new styles" (12), he lures them toward something perceived as dangerous: "Men hate to see themselves change. . . . This is the power I live in. I manipulate their looks" (48). Thus Bolden's razor supplies to others the chance of beauty or of disfigurement (the two possible conclusions of the novel). And all of this occurs within a room, the perimeter of which reinforces this issue of the instability of personality or image. To reflect and multiply the image there are mirrors, including the one Pickett breaks when he is disfigured by Buddy; "against the window" through which Pickett and Bolden will later crash there is "ice [that] changed shape all day before your eyes"; on the wall against which Bolden's figure is defined there is "the wallpaper of Louisiana birds," recalling the paranoid and self-destructive birds drawn by Audubon; and, finally, on the ceiling is another image of that rimless wheel, the fan "turning like a giant knife" (47) that hovers over all the book.

As publisher of *The Cricket*, Bolden practices the art of exchange by taking in the multitudinous, chaotic life of the street and expelling it "unedited" (13). In the barber shop he copes with "thick facts" (24) in the same way that he breathes in the "hair flecks" he must then "blow. . . cough. . . and spit out" (47) again. The news comes to him from customers and from " 'spiders' " (13) who are extensions of Bolden-the-spider, as Bolden himself is an extension of Webb. Relationship nearly always works this way in *Coming Through Slaughter*, the other becoming somehow identified with the self as "exchanged per-

273

sonalities" (88). *The Cricket* is Bolden's diary "and everybody else's." Its "intricacy" is a history of exchange, involving "details of the children and the ladies changing hands like coins or a cigarette travelling at mouth level around the room." This picture comes to Buddy, however, only when he can look back at *The Cricket* and realize that its structure (significantly male-dominated) does not make the inclusive "sense" he had supposed it did: "that was the crazyness I left. Cricket noises and Cricket music for that is what we are when watched by people bigger than us" (113-114). The self is larger when its ego is less.

With its "excessive references to death," *The Cricket* is also informed by a principle of risk. It is important to see that the half dozen examples cited are all of one kind: as in the case of "referees slashed to death by fighting cocks," the deaths result from what one does (profession or deed). "The possibilities [of chaos, extinction] were terrifying to Bolden and he hunted out examples obsessively as if building a wall. A boy with a fear of heights climbing slowly up a tree." Buddy's actions, that is, take him always closer to the edge. The deaths of others, lived out imaginatively by Bolden, are prophetic of his own collapse: the *Cricket* stories, the "dreams of his children dying," and the death of his wife's mother, which is "saved by its fictional quality and nothing else" (24). The "wall" of print or dream or "fictional quality" cannot hold forever; the self must ultimately cross over to the other's fate. The "dreams of his children dying" are Buddy's dreams, his responsibility (as glimpsed in the previously cited passage about "children... changing hands like coins"); and so in one dream the news of his child's death leads Buddy to pick up "the wood handled knife with the serrated edge and [push] it again and again into his left wrist" (29). The death of Nora's mother (who tells Bolden about the self-destructive birds) similarly connects with Bolden's own end. According to Webb, she is strangled in her car by her pet python as Isadora Duncan was by her own scarf; she is killed, that is, by what she does and by a linear, turning thing (snake or scarf, like the spoke of a rimless wheel) that connects her with the other. Also, her body disappears, and Bolden is suspected of her murder; but he is innocent of that, just as I believe he is innocent of his own. Past Audubon's country, they simply disappear from view.

It is as a musician that Bolden practises exchange and risk most vividly. "Unconcerned with the crack of the lip... he was obsessed with

274

the magic of air, those smells that turned neuter as they revolved in his lung then spat out in the chosen key." Although Bolden's music is drawn from "those smells" within a room, and though he sees it as "animals fighting in the room," his music also seems to reach for a purer space: "his mouth would drag a net of air in and dress it in notes and make it last and last, yearning to leave it up there in the sky like air transformed into cloud. He could see the air, could tell where it was freshest in a room by the colour" (14). The cloud cycle is parallel to the circulation of air; the cloud itself suggests that point where the cycle achieves tangible, but still evanescent form. This helps to explain Bolden's preference for music that shows "all the possibilities in the middle of the story." He could "dive into the stories found in the barbershop" (43), as into a river, and come up with cloud. The cycle begins with the audience or with Bolden *as* audience: "the perfect audience" reacting "excessively to the stories his clients in the chair told him, throwing himself into the situation" (42). Bolden's famed loudness is necessary to balance the weight of all he takes in, but it is also a function of his extremism or excess, his yearning for more than a room contains: " 'the patrons in the front rows of the theatre always got up after the first number and moved back' " (44).

"Bolden broke the path" precisely because he wanted to keep the pattern of his music open — "As if, when he was playing, he was lost and hunting for the right accidental notes" (37). Again, the landscape metaphor suggests Bolden's wish not to be subject to an order imposed by himself or others. To find where he wants to go, Bolden must eschew conventional "wisdom" — the orderliness of music like Robichaux's, of putting "emotions into patterns which a listening crowd had to follow." He avoids it because "it is not real" (93). Instead, he plays "a music that had so little wisdom you wanted to clean nearly every note he passed, passed it seemed along the way as if travelling in a car, passed before he had even approached it and saw it clearly." Bolden is driven by the wish to include it all — "pain and gentleness and everything jammed into each number" (37) — and by the need to keep all of these strands flying so that one day he might arrive at a place of "real" order, "real" wisdom. Vision and peace at last.

Bolden is also a family man and "famous fucker" (106). The relationship with his children begins his day (as they are at the start of theirs) and is enacted on "washed, empty streets" as Bolden walks them to school

275

— "giv[ing] himself completely to them during the walk, no barriers." Again, he practices exchange, tells them "all he knew at the moment... in turn learn[ing] the new street songs from them" (13). The relationship with Nora, however, is troubled by the past. She brings to their union a history of the street, her time as a whore and the original hope — "the roads she imagined she could take as a child" (54) — that Bellocq tries to capture in his photographs of the whores. In Nora's case, this is imaged in slightly tarnished form by her lovely street child's fantasy of the sandman who is late because he "just stopped to get a drink" (15). Nora's life now takes place primarily in a room. There she lives with Buddy, "good husband and... infamous man about town" (13), and there she waits for him (as for the sandman) to drag "his bone home" (17).

"She had played Bolden's games, knew his extra sex. When they were alone together it was still a crowded room" (110). This association of the Nora-Bolden relationship with a "crowded room" is enforced by Webb's visit in pursuit of Bolden, and the elaborate attention paid to the apartment at that point. Now that it is empty of Bolden, Nora gestures toward "its old wallpaper and few chairs like a tired showman." Webb hovers at her doorstep before Nora's arrival and again as he leaves, walking backward down the steps: "Nora closing the door more, narrow, just to the width of her face" (21). Webb's insistence, his need to get into Bolden's psychic space, is also revealed in his mimicry of Bolden's role in that room: "He has covered her against the window, leaning very close to her, like a lover" (20).

An important image of the period before the collapse of Bolden's equilibrium comes in the scene where an angry Bolden strikes out at the window of their marriage, and brakes just in time. The window is "starred" (recalling the fan) and "his hand miraculously uncut." Nora's ability to contain the chaos of their crowded room, so long as he will contain it, is clear: "She was delighted by the performance" (16). She seems in fact a very good mate for Bolden. "She had never been a shadow" (110) and even as a whore was able "to save delicate rules and ceremonies for herself." She is like him and not like him: "her body a system of emotions and triggers he got lost in." Nora is right for him equally because of that "system" and because he cannot explain it: "He was lost in the details, he could find no exact focus towards her. And so he drew her power over himself" (15).

Although his love for Nora develops from this perception of a complexity (form and chaos) that is compatible with his own and with his music, Bolden begins to focus on just the "certainties" of Nora. Because he loves her, certainty there "went to the spine" (15); because of his own mounting chaos, and greater need for that "spine," Bolden assigns to her "the certainties he loathed and needed" (78). Her power narrows to those "certain answers" (16) and "short cuts to his arguments [that] at times cleared away the chaos he embraced" (110). It narrows still further to the certainty that Bolden begins to equate with sexual fidelity—her fidelity. Both this sexual inequity and his reduction of her are painful to Nora; she knows "what he owed her and hadn't given her" (121). But the relationship holds until Bolden decides she has been unfaithful with Pickett. Then it seems the spine is broken, then certainty is "liquid at the root" (78), then Bolden goes crashing through the window.

Part One of the novel ends with Buddy at Robin's doorstep. It does not include any discussion of Bellocq or Pickett, the two figures who provide some explanation of how Bolden happened to leave one woman's room for the other. Part Two takes Buddy through his time with Robin and Jaelin, through the discovery by Webb and interval at Webb's cabin, and ends at the point of Bolden's strange return to the New Orleans parade. Part Two, the outer voice of which is Buddy's "explanation" of himself to Webb, is also concerned with Webb's visits to those two figures missing from Part One—first Bellocq, and then Pickett. This order is significant, I think, for it is essentially what happens with Bellocq that drives Buddy to the fight with Pickett. Nora's infidelity, if real, is not the primary cause of Bolden's departure. And Nora recognizes this. Accounting later for her hatred of Bellocq, she tells Buddy: "Look at you. Look at what he did to you" (127).

As Scobie has shown, Bellocq is Webb's opposite—"the friend who scorned all the giraffes of fame" (91). His relationship to Bolden seems to begin at reversed poles, with Bolden as public figure "the patronizing one" (64). Bellocq learns, however, that it is he who patronizes and instructs Bolden—as Webb did initially. In the end, Bolden eludes and surpasses both of his mentors; both strive to enter his space, both feel guilt over what they have done to Bolden, and both fail to achieve his success in coming through Slaughter. So Webb and Bellocq are parallel figures as well. In his role as Webb's opposite, Bellocq urges Bolden

277

"to step back into [his] body as if into a black room. . . . Unable then to be watched by others. . . blind to everything but the owned pain in [him]self" (91). In Bellocq's darkroom there is a chance for Buddy to develop the self which he is in danger of losing to the audience. He must retreat into this "black room" of self in part because his ego (as distinct from the self) has grown unruly in the light of all the adulation he has received. Thus, Bellocq appeals to Bolden as the "first person I met who had absolutely no interest in my music. That sounds vain don't it!" (59). And Bolden has reason to worry about his vanity. But he also needs to retreat into Bellocq's darkroom for the sake of his music, which has not yet achieved the transcendence of the last parade (a perfect blend of self and other). Thus, when Bolden says to Bellocq, "You don't think much of this music do you," his answer is "Not yet" (91).

The Bellocq-Bolden relationship is a study in black and white. Bellocq is primarily associated with "the narrow dark focus of the eye" (the self) as against Buddy and "the crazy chaos of white" (68). He offers the self imaged by a "black shape" arising out of the "pregnant white paper" (52) when Webb comes in search of Buddy. But like Bolden's, the photographer's art requires black *and* white. And Bellocq learns more about the value of white from Bolden. Whiteness signifies chaos, anonymity, and the other — all that is outside the black specificity of self. In the botched photo of his own death, Bellocq finds himself "surrounded by whiteness" as if "a cloud has stuffed itself into his room" (67). That cloud suggests to me the presence of Bolden; it is linked to the whiteness into which Bolden has "already half-receded" in the photo given to Webb. And Bellocq is half-glad that Bolden has eluded them, that he has "reversed the process and gone back into white" (53). So Bellocq is torn between black and white, the self he is and the other he yearns for. In Bellocq's photos, this misery comes out grey: the "light grey" (123) of the whorehouse wallpaper and the "grey light which must have been the yellow shining off" (117) the walls of the opium dens. But in Bolden's final room, a scene only apparently of misery, grey becomes the colour of a perfect blend.

The opposition of black and white is only one metaphor for the difference between Bellocq and Bolden. Whereas Bolden is "a social dog" who roams "through conversations as if they were the countryside not listening carefully just picking up moments," Bellocq in his lonely

278

room is "self-sufficient, complete as a perpetual motion machine." Bolden's spontaneity and lack of focus are balanced by the "slow convolution" of Bellocq's "brain" (56). Because it is the "interfering" (31) brain Buddy watches for as Robin cuts carrots that drives Bolden's hand through the fan at last, the reader (like Nora) may blame the influence of Bellocq for Bolden's end. I do not only because I consider that end triumphant. Bellocq's end, however, is tragic because he cannot include the other in his construction of the self. Bellocq's failure in this regard is scarcely his fault. Lacking utterly Bolden's power to attract, Bellocq in his photographs of the whores does his best to recognize the value and beauty of others — but they will have nothing to do with him, so that he can only "romance them later with a knife" (55).

Bellocq's difference from Bolden yields at many points to likeness. Even the knife Bellocq uses in his effort "to enter the photographs" recalls the knives associated with Bolden. Within the scarred photographs is a willed reciprocity, a principle of exchange, that recalls Bolden's art — as the "genuine scars" on the bodies of the whores and the gouges made by Bellocq "reflect each other." For Bolden as for Bellocq, "the making and destroying [come] from the same source, same lust, same surgery his brain was capable of" (55). For both, that source is the lure of the other; it is the will to include or incorporate the other in the construction of the self. When that effort of inclusion fails, the self lashes out — and particular others will be hurt. Increasingly disgusted, the self at last turns its destruction inward. Bolden finds at that moment an all-inclusive other, as Bellocq does not, and so can destroy one version of the self to make another.

But there are other points of likeness. Each man insists upon the essential kindness of the other. Both are artists, and although neither considers himself professional, both carry their professions "with [them] always, like a wife" — Bolden "his mouthpiece even in exile" (57) and Bellocq the camera gear that also seems a part of his own body. In the subject matter of Bellocq's work, the whores, of course, and the "sections of boats" that he photographed "to help ship designers" (56), there is further evidence of his link to Bolden; he serves "to help" Bolden design a journey (often imaged as a river journey) that Bolden with his fear of water could not have taken without the aid of his crippled friend.

279

What Bolden loved in Bellocq, he says, "were the possibilities in his silence" (91). He despises the clamour of his own art, the inflated ego—posing as self, posing as generous to the other—that is only "stealing chickens, nailing things to the wall." Always taking, he finds that "reputation made the room narrower and narrower, till you were... full of your own echoes, till you were drinking in only your own recycled air" (86). This is the "furnished room" he occupies and contrasts with Bellocq as "a window looking out" (59). He sees in Bellocq's "silence" a chance to construct the self which might truly regard the other. Bellocq, however, fears that his talk and silence have done Bolden a disservice, "tempt[ing] Buddy on. Buddy who was once enviably public." In the suicide room he risks going over the edge himself because it was their talk that moved Bolden "gradually off the edge of the social world." While Bellocq was at ease there—"he lived on the edge in any case"—Bolden was not, and to Bellocq's surprise, "he moved past him like a naive explorer looking for footholds." And so Bellocq regrets also his silence: "he could so easily have explained the ironies," his bitter knowledge that "the mystic privacy one can be so proud of has no alphabet of noise or meaning to the people outside" (64). The real irony, however, is that unknown to Bellocq his naive friend has found other "possibilities" in the silence: "the mystic privacy" Bolden finds at last is different from Bellocq's embittered pride in its successful inclusion of the other, and so it does not matter that it has no "meaning to the people outside."

Bellocq's death scene is a mocking self-portrait. As a hydrocephalic, Bellocq knows that "his blood and water circulation" doom him to an early death; that fact serves as another link to Bolden, who also has difficulty with a build-up of pressure in his brain, but cures himself and lives on. Both Bellocq's "circulation and walk" are impaired, and each is a metaphor for the other—leading him to stage his first and last performance in a room which is also an image of his brain. "He did not walk that much... never shot landscapes, mostly portraits" (57). The final portrait, revealing the influence of Bolden, features a man alone surrounded by a circular (fan-like) "balcony" of empty chairs. His audience is ghostly, brought in to observe the psychodrama of an utterly solitary man. Calmly, Bellocq sets fire to the wallpaper (his self-image or brain's rim) and "formally" breathes in the smoke. Although he must know that he has embarked upon a suicide, part of Bellocq expects this extreme act to provoke the "other" for whom he performs into a miraculous feat of rescue. Or perhaps the force of his irony is such that Bellocq expects to triumph in this way over his need of the other. In either case, he is surprised when the design breaks down. Vomiting out smoke, he goes crashing through the chairs and hopes still to find the wall intact—the wall of "certainty" (of others miraculously there or definitely gone) that would either "catch or hide him." But the wall itself is gone. At this last moment, Bellocq seems to choose life—but without the other there is no life, no opposite and balancing force "to clasp him into a certainty." And so Bellocq "falls, dissolving out of his pose" (67).

Bellocq's influence provokes the assault upon Pickett first in the sense that it brings Bolden to the point where he too must release an intolerable pressure. More particularly, Bolden attacks Pickett because he is suffering from the ego's last ditch conflict with the emergent self's distaste for the way Bolden has been dealing with the other. Details of the fight itself—the broken mirrors, the weapons that join Bolden and Pickett as if they were the same creature, the broken window through which Pickett crashes and Bolden "come[s]... too" (74)—all suggest that Bolden's rampage is essentially directed against himself. Bolden and the voice of Ondaatje, cutting their own faces, are later described as "defiling people they did not wish to be" (133), bringing the "enemy to the surface of the skin" (134). Now Pickett the handsome pimp, who mirrors obscenely Buddy's own strutting ego, is a displaced version of that enemy within. The attack on Pickett's beauty might also be regarded as vengeance for Bellocq, an attempt to deprive this alter-ego of the physical advantage they both possess. Pickett, when he becomes the Fly King in an opium den, is reduced from the lofty stature of pimp to the condition of the mattress whores, photographed and wept over by Bellocq. Like them, and like Bolden when he reaches that state, Pickett no longer protests. His face is cut as the whores are cut in Bellocq's photos. The scars are "roads on his face" (71), a landscape of suffering that has brought him to one of the grey rooms photographed by Bellocq.

Bolden does not quite know what he is doing in the assault on Pickett. "What the hell is wrong with me?" (73), he asks. He is, of course, crazed by the belief that Nora has been unfaithful; the failure of that one "certainty" upsets his whole precarious balance. But beneath

281

his sexual jealousy is a horror at his lust for possession and power, as Bolden nearly sees: "You know... in spite of everything that happens, we still think a helluva lot of ourselves!" That recognition causes Bolden in a fit of self-loathing to bite his wrist and feel "his vein tingling at the near chance it had of almost going free" (79). It is not yet time, however, for Buddy's release. The wish to escape ego continues to clash with crazy expressions of ego in the paranoid behaviour that Bolden exhibits after the fight with Pickett and before his disappearance.

Bolden goes to Shell Beach by boat, a mode of travel that signals both a radical departure and a parallel to his asylum journey; this is the second, as that will be the last, of his landscape suicides. In Shell Beach he meets the Brewitts, who will give him refuge. But as his band boards the train for their return to New Orleans, Buddy is "frozen," incapable of bearing his pain or of choosing between past and future; and then he wakes "to see the train disappearing away from his body like a vein." It is time to go to the Brewitts — "the silent ones. Post music. After ambition." But he is "scared of everybody" (39) and cannot present to them or anyone the self he now loathes. For two days he wanders in a landscape full of whores and music, a "spider perfect[ing] in silence" all that he hears, absorbing the noises and smells of his old life. "He took it in and locked it." This is Bolden's preparation for the time he will spend in Robin's room, when his music stops. As prey and predator, he absorbs the "luscious poison... until he couldn't be entered anymore. A fat full king. The hawk its locked claws full of salmon going under greedy with it for the final time" (40-41). Bolden is trying blindly to lower himself, sinking "through the pavement into the music," resting on its "grid" (41) like a fly (or Fly King) against the web; still he shares in the power of spider, king, and hawk. At last Bolden arrives at Robin's doorstep, "shaking" and pleading for "help," wearing a coat he wants to burn because "it stank so much" (45).

Bolden's entry into a kind of waterscape with the Brewitts is confirmed by his immersion in their bath tub. There his "armour of dirt" explodes, and he rises out of the water feeling "everything drain off him" (58) like a dissolved skin. He can now enter Robin's "white room" (86). Bolden has fled from Bellocq's darkroom, "diving through a wave" (67) as his friend did, because he cannot yet reconcile the black and the white. His movement now toward whiteness is a retreat from the "owned pain" (91) that was too much for him to bear. Unable to find a true order in that world, he wants to recover the "fear of certainties." His sojourn here is nevertheless proof of Bellocq's ascendancy over Webb, for he will live silent, "anonymous and alone in a white room with no history and no parading" (86).

In another sense, Bolden's stay in the white room is an attempt to replay his New Orleans story and to redress its wrongs. His attraction to Robin Brewitt makes sense for Bolden at this time because there is also a Jaelin Brewitt, so that when Bolden uses "his cornet as jewelry" he can make "music for the three of them" (33). His relationship with the Brewitts will give Bolden a chance to explore the possibility of a love that is not possessive, from which ego may retire. This is the meaning of the "Wolf-Ryat star," named for two men who found the star (Robin); it is a "new star" (65), an effort to achieve in the triangular relationship a love that is not ego-bound. Its critical importance for Bolden's quest is revealed in the image of the star that recalls the "starred" (16) window of his marriage to Nora. He hopes this time to live in peace, and counts on reflecting Jaelin's kindness instead of Pickett's ego. Thus, when he and Robin make love for the first time Bolden seems to request the triangle: "I wouldn't feel different if I was [Jaelin]" (58).

Love with Robin takes place in a room, but "it could have been a sky not a ceiling above him" (59). Expressing that sense of freedom, and framing his time with Robin, is this line: "Passing wet chicory that lies in the field like the sky" (60, 85). Because chicory is blue it reflects the sky, as Bolden and Robin reflect one another. This line indicates as well that Bolden's time in the peaceful white room is a prelude to his grey room on the far side of Slaughter, as the chicory field is passed on the way to that last asylum. In the white room, as in the grey, Bolden is "King of Corners"; he can "make something unknown in the shape of this room" (86). When they first lock themselves into the room — "the snap of the lock is the last word [they] speak" — there are other "bodies in the air" (61); but as Bolden presses Robin into the corners, and as their bodies practise the art of exchange, the room is suddenly "empty of other histories." In the making of "something unknown," they are like "animals meeting an unknown breed." They can take "a step past the territory" (62) of all that was known before.

Still the relationship does not achieve what Buddy needs.

"Everybody's love in the air" does not keep Jaelin from being shut out or Bolden's ego shut down. "As dogs wait for their masters to go to sleep" (92), so Jaelin waits each night to assume Bolden's former position—aiming his music at the lovers in their bed. The question of power arises again, and with it the conflict of black and white. Bolden quarrels with Robin, throwing the whiteness of milk in her "lost beautiful brown face" (68) — as if to charge her with the failure of all she had seemed to promise. But this is Bolden's construction, his fantasy. When he asks only whiteness of Robin, and blames her for the intrusion of "dark . . . complications" (69), he repeats the error that he made with Nora. He shuts out a part of her reality. The displacement of his own guilt also reminds us of his time with Nora. He believes now in a choice: "There can be either the narrow dark focus of the eye or the crazy chaos of white, . . . wishing to burn them out till they are stones" (68). But he is wrong. He must still bring them together. And he is wrong to imply that Robin has introduced the darkness to their waterscape: he sees it too. He is only "wishing" for blindness, trying not to see that he does necessarily inflict pain through his affair with Robin. To escape their quarrel, Robin and Buddy go swimming. Diving like loons, they find in the water both darkness and a "dull star of white water." Because the "evil dark . . . creatures" of ego and sexual possession are present now, the Wolf-Ryat star is fading. Still it draws him. And when Robin says, "I'm Jaelin's wife and I'm in love with you, there's nothing simple," Buddy's reply that "it should be" (69) can mean *both* that Robin must choose between them and that there should be no necessity of choice.

Thus, even before Webb arrives to ply his magnets, there is a renewed disturbance in the room. Webb finds Bolden in the bath that frames his time with Robin. Veering away from Webb's insistent "noise," reacting as well to the news of Bellocq's suicide, Buddy attempts like Audubon's water turkey to drown himself. His "eyes staring up aching" (83) recall both his aversion to "eyes clogged with people" (when Robin's "white" house became treacherously "dark") and his attraction to "the crazy chaos of white, that is the eyes wide, wishing to burn them out till they are stones" (68). Since Bolden is still not ready to unify the black and the white, since whiteness now would mean the end of his quest, he is obliged to come up for air. Webb is seen as the trainer of Buddy the "social dog" (56), who "set out to breed

284

[him] into something better" and did. But he went too far, becoming "like those breeders of bull terriers in the Storyville pits" who train their dogs to keep on killing even as they are cut "in half" (89) themselves. In this image and in the other which has Webb-the-trainer compelling him toward "the worthless taste of worthless rabbit" (84), it is clear that Bolden deplores not only his own suicidal bifurcation and the worthlessness of the prize, but also the killer instinct that is being awakened in him once more. Also, he is in agony over what this means to the "unknown breed" (62) of his love with Robin — so that as he is about to tell her of Webb's victory, Bolden is "like a huge, wild animal going round and round the bathroom" (84).

Bolden's last sexual encounter with Robin suggests this vicious pull of audience, as in the white room once empty of parading they "give each other a performance, the wound of ice" (87). Now that Webb has "placed [his] past and future on this table like a road," Nora's "landscape" out of time is "alien" to Bolden. There is history again in the white room, and "barrier glass" (86) between them. Time is the tragedy that has them "already travelling on the morning bus" (87) — a fatality in relationship that Bolden contemplates when he is really on the bus, imagining the whole doomed course of an affair with the woman who sits beside him. What he wants, Bolden decides, is "cruel, pure relationship" (88). The syntax is ambiguous, but I think "cruel" is not primarily a co-ordinate adjective; that is, Bolden wants "pure relationship" and knows that this departure from troublesome particularity is "cruel" both to Robin and Nora and to himself. Thus, his hand goes "crashing" down on Robin's empty "half of the bed" when he sees her "blue cloud light in the room" (87). "Blue" marks the point at which the visible and invisible meet, as the gas when Bolden lit Nora's stove "popped up blue, something invisible finding a form" (124). But now it goes the other way: "she's gone" (87). Bolden too, when he has achieved his "real" (93) form, will retreat into invisibility.

Honeymoon cabin, training ground, darkroom — Webb's cabin at Lake Ponchartrain is the place where Bolden does the painful brainwork on love, music and selfhood that is needed to bring his life together. Always torn between solitude and the need for people (hating whatever "I am doing and want[ing] the other"), he feels now cut "in half" by Webb — for ironically his trainer has "point[ed]" (89) him in the direction of blackness urged by Bellocq. In this prolonged and nearly absolute solitude, Buddy cannot seek the other in his customary ways. As the self develops, therefore, so does the intensity of Bolden's desire for the other.

His one companion is a black dog. Bolden's progress with Robin toward an "unknown breed" (62) advances now to "a major breakthrough in the spread of hound civilization" — as Bolden scratches earth over the dog's piss, "return[ing] the compliment" paid first by the dog, showing that he knows the dog's "system" (90). Each performs with and for the other in perfect equality; and the dog "not used to softness" becomes an avatar of woman, as Bolden is "snuggled against his warmth" (98). Bolden is weaning himself from the need for particular others, moving with the dog toward "pure relationship" (88): at last he will *become* the dog.

His desire for the other, though acute, is now generalized; "I am alone. I desire every woman I remember." Robin "has become anonymous as cloud," blurring "into Nora and everybody else" (100); and then "even her cloud" is gone, as the "lake and sky [that] will be light blue" (102) suggest both the integration of her "blue cloud light" (87) and the "wet chicory that lies in the field like the sky" (60). The light of the other is also imaged by the cabin Buddy sees across the lake: "Everyone I know lives there and when the light is on it means they are there" (98). This abstraction is comforting; it frees him from both fear and hope of others arriving at the dark cabin of the self. When Crawley does arrive with the "girl fan" (a figure of audience and woman in one), Bolden is tormented by the desire "to start a fight," to thrust his "horn in her skirt" (101). This is the violence he fears, the dance of ego, the "passion [that] could twist around and choose someone else just like that" (99). Still he is torn between the particular and the general; and "terrified now of their lost love," the "soft private sentiment" for Nora and his children that he "forgot to explode," Bolden pushes his tongue into the mouth of his friend's girl, whose name he "cannot even remember" (102).

In thinking about his music, Bolden retains the ideal of open form: music that "swallowed moods and kept three or four going at the same time which was what I wanted" (95), music played for an audience that could "come in where they pleased and leave when they please" (94). But there is also a new strength of self in his music, coming from the

286

"owned pain," the "blackness" he tells Webb "there is a need to come home" (91) with, to wed at last with the other. Buddy does not mean to fail. All his "fathers" in music, "those who put their bodies over barbed wire" (95), have failed in one way or another—each becoming "a remnant, a ladder for others" (102). Bolden will not. And so he returns to New Orleans "thinking along a stone path" (102), "knowing it is just stone" (101), but firm in his purpose. Bolden's return to the parade is very different from his first entry, following the time with Webb in the Pontchartrain apartment. This time his talk with Webb has been imaginary; this time it is all in his own head—he knows he is going into "nightmare" (106) and has hardened himself against the fear as well as the lure of particularity. What he intends is a kind of suicide, an exit from the known world. "All suicides all acts of privacy are romantic," Webb says, and Bolden acknowledges that he "may be right" (101). Still it is Bolden's only chance of success. He must face and resolve once and for all "the dream of the wheel over his hand" (40). All he needs for that now are self-discipline and then "the right audience" (89).

Bolden is experiencing the pain of separation from the known world, the hardness and coldness that will achieve it, as on the bus he rubs his "brain against the cold window" (106). He passes the test of Cornish and Nora, whom he regards as "statues of personality," no longer occupying the "landscape" of time in which passion destroys. Bolden has repudiated his possessive love, and the gentle Cornish seems another version of Jaelin whom this time he will not displace. "Hunger[ing] to be as still as them," Bolden is locking the last of his passion in— "boiled down in love and anger into dynamo that cannot move except on itself" (112). The hardness remains even in his ghostly intimacy with Nora: "The diamond had to love the earth it passed along the way, every speck and angle of the other's history, for the diamond had been earth too" (111). And he is able to sit back "with just his face laughing at the jokes," surviving "the people in the house watching him," because essentially he "wasn't even in the room" (120). Bolden is pointed relentlessly toward a new psychic space.

On the second evening of his return, Buddy goes "parading" (118) in the domain of the diseased mattress whores. Because of his "fast rich walk" they fear he is a pimp, come to break their ankles so they cannot return to Storyville. Bolden's old horror at the pimp in himself (the ex-

287

ploiter of others) and his identification with the whores — "my brain tonight has a mattress strapped to its back" — come together, as other opposites will do in his imminent release. Bolden compares himself to the mattress whores, "their bodies murdered and my brain suicided," to acknowledge that the stick-wielding pimp is in his own case internaized. There are two kinds of mattress whores, between whom Bolden is poised: the "gypsy feet" with broken ankles, who are "immune from the swinging stick" (119), and those who still have something to fear, who retreat into the white mist, "the shallows of the river where the pimps with good shoes won't follow" (118). The second type suggests Bolden retreating into his waterscape from Webb, sick at the prostitution of his art. The gypsy foot whores suggest Bolden as he will be in the asylum, when the "swinging stick" has delivered him from any further pain. That connection is strengthened when Bolden declines a fellow inmate's suggestion first of escape and then (when Lord comes back limping) of the sharpened glass with which, to protest their lot, the other inmates cut the tendons of their ankles. Bolden is a "gypsy" in his prison and has no need of protest or escape. Now he sees that "there is no horror in the way they run their lives," and knows that these "grey angels" (119) are pointing the way, "sentries" (118) on his own path.

At last comes the parade, with Bolden's "note like a bird flying out of the shit" (129). Recalling Crawley with his "tail of shit" (30) and the gypsy foot whores with their "driblets of manure" (119), Bolden's transcendent music is founded on shit, on suffering and deprivation, unlike the music of a "technician — which went gliding down river and missed all the shit on the bottom" (95-96). Here the fan or star, representing the opposed influences that have tormented Buddy's life, comes after one last and glorious "spinning" to a stop. Buddy's passion is released in the "parade of ego," as "like a spaniel strutting" (129) he plays to attract the right "bitch," the perfect audience "testing me taunting me to make it past her, old hero, old ego tested against one as cold and pure as himself." As "Robin, Nora, Crawley's girl's tongue" (130) she is the all-inclusive other, offering pure relationship; and she has a male companion, "a beautiful dancer too" (129), so that the triangular relationship is echoed in this final spinning of the star. Self and other merge as Bolden becomes "the dancer" and she throws him "in the direction and the speed she wishes like an angry shadow";

Bolden has what he "wanted, always, loss of privacy in the playing" (130). His "last long squawk" simultaneously "spear[s] her" and goes "like a javelin" through Buddy's brain. "The blood that is real" brings "fresh energy in its suitcase," the vein bursting free so that Bolden has finally "what [he] wanted" (131). A *bouleversement* has occurred, he has entered another space.

Bolden's successful wedding of self and other in his last parade is forecast in the dolphin sonographs that are pictured (in black, white, and grey) and described in the novel's epigraph. The left-hand sonograph shows a squawk, "common emotional expressions that have many frequencies or pitches, which are vocalized simultaneously": this represents the other. The right-hand sonograph shows the "signature whistle," a "pure" sound that identifies a particular dolphin and its location: this represents the self. "The middle sonograph shows a dolphin making two kinds of signals simultaneously," as Bolden does in the parade with his squawks and the pure notes that he trained himself to play in Webb's cabin. As "no one knows how a dolphin makes both" sounds simultaneously, so Bolden's achievement takes him beyond our understanding to an unknown world—where we would need "a machine more sensitive than the human ear" to hear the music playing in his head.

To get to the asylum, which he refers to as "a pound" (139), Bolden passes "*through* the country that Audubon drew" and "*through* Sun-shine . . . and Slaughter" (italics mine). Slaughter and Sunshine — like pain and joy, self and other, the one and the many, ego and the loss of ego — have come together in the "river" (131) of the parade. On the other side of Sunshine and Slaughter, beyond the changing landscape of water and cloud and ice, what looks like an eternal repetition of Slaughter is for Bolden a sun-blessed, heavenly new life. The Mississippi River is "a friend travelling with him, like an audience watching Huck Finn going by train to hell" (155), but the audience is wrong. The reference to Huck Finn suggests (to me at least) the "territory ahead" that Huck sought and Bolden has found—in what looks to the audience like hell, but is really a mysterious heaven. Because the water has been gone *through*, Ondaatje can say that Bolden is buried not in Holtz Cemetery where "the high water table conveniently takes the flesh away in six months" (134), but in First Street where dogs are buried. He has evolved, that is, to an unknown breed; he has become like Bellocq's dog, whom Bolden had watched closely enough to see that although "all day it would seem to be doing nothing . . . it would be *busy*" (59). The significance of Bolden's activity in that territory ahead cannot be rationally understood. "As you try to explain me I will spit you, yellow, out of my mouth" (140), Bolden says — recalling the dog in the cabin who "moves his body into perfect manoeuvering position [as Bolden has done] so he can get his tongue between the yellow [leaves] and reach the invisible water" (90).

The room in which he lives is entirely satisfactory. Bolden can fulfill in this new psychic space the potential of the white room, making "something unknown in the shape of this room" (86). Throughout the novel corners have been a principal locale of sexual activity, because in sex we approach the boundary of the self to press ourselves against the other (whom we "corner" if the approach is aggressive). That need is no longer relevant to Bolden. The reference to corners in the asylum — "there is the corner and there is the corner. . ." (146) — seems ominous, for there we know he will be raped again and again by the "ladies in blue pajamas" (148); but Buddy thinks that "everybody who touches [him] must be beautiful" (135), and he doesn't mind. The attendants in blue pajamas, like the "blue necklace" of his handcuffs, have been imaginatively transformed. Bolden in his "white dress" and the "breastless woman in blue" (139) are beyond gender conflict, and violence is unreal.

Best of all, he has friendship. At night he is alone; but in the day the sun (the light of the other) comes to his room, and Bolden is "blessed by the visit of his friend." The "yellow" of explanation yields to the "warm yellow" of his friend's hand "magically" and "simultaneously" (148) joined to Bolden's hand in tender understanding. Time is no longer destructive, as Buddy measures the sun's progress through his room with a system of strings — a contrast to the frenzy of Webb's magnets which nevertheless reveals Bolden's continuing engagement with the other. The "last movement" into the fan that "happens forever and ever in his memory" (136) suggests not eternal agony, but a transcendence which (beyond explanation) repeats harmoniously the play of opposites — as in "the travelling spokes of light" Buddy can bathe his face *and* dry it. Regarding "work as his duty to the sun"

(148), Bolden unites stillness and motion; he "goes around touching things" (149), the "unimportant objects" (86) that are now the reliable furnishings of his psychic space. And in the world outside the room, his friend has "bleached everything" (133) so that we cannot pin Buddy down.

Back in New Orleans, his friends regard Bolden's fate with horror. They think of the asylum as hell, though their speech is studded with exclamations— "heaven" (149) and *"jesus"* (145) — that should reveal to us the ultimate success of Bolden's effort to play "the devil's music and hymns at the same time" (134). "Lord" uses "his silence as an oracle" (141), knowing that "salvation" has been performed on the "throat" (139) of this man who knew the devil and the shit; but in New Orleans they ask, "What good is all that [suffering] if we can't learn or know?" (145). They will only know if they "come too." They want to learn from his *failure*, making him "a remnant, a ladder for others" (102); and Buddy eludes them. He escapes the fate of Freddie Amacker, for instance, who is happy to be a "remnant" for "a really good [white, dreadful] singer like Perry Como." Amacker's song, furthermore, gives a precise summary of the world that revealed its full horror to Buddy Bolden: "The name of the song is 'All the boys got to love me, that's all' " (154), and it recounts the tale of a man who kills his girl out of jealousy. Neither his compulsion of the audience's love nor the sexual violence of the song bothers Amacker in the least. We know then that Bolden is well out of his game.

The last paragraph of the novel is for many readers a portrait of misery, signalling enclosure, terror, failure — in short, the bankruptcy of extremist art. But it is the right ending, as Bolden has forewarned us: "The right ending is an open door you can't see too far out of. It can mean exactly the opposite of what you are thinking" (94). For me, "the grey walls that darken into corner" and the "window with teeth in it" no longer threaten; there seems no need to look out the window for "clouds and other things," as everything is there in the grey room already. "There are no prizes" (156), Ondaatje concludes. And I can understand how one might read that as a statement of defeat. But say that "You come too. Put your hand through this window" (91), and I think that you would find a place in which the whole, pernicious issue of "prizes" and the contentious ego has simply gone away. The black knight doesn't win, and neither does the white. Another way of saying that is that the dog in a grey room *does*. I should close with an admission that the right ending — ''There are no prizes'' — can mean ''exactly the opposite'' of what I'm thinking too. It is the risk an extremist critic has to take.

1 *Essays on Canadian Writing*, No. 12 (Fall 1978), 25.

2 *Ibid.*, 26.

3 *Essays on Canadian Writing*, No. 12 (Fall 1978) 6.

4 *Op. cit.*, 44.

R.P. Bilan
THE POET NOVELIST

With *Coming Through Slaughter* Michael Ondaatje joins the ranks of contemporary poets, most notably Leonard Cohen and Margaret Atwood, who have turned successfully to prose fiction. For Ondaatje the change is not very drastic, as in his earlier book *The Collected Works of Billy the Kid* he was already well on his way to fiction. Whereas his long "poem" deals with a violent outlaw who has the imagination of an artist, his novel focuses on an artist who must attempt to control his own violence and inner chaos. Ondaatje again takes as his subject an historical figure about whom there is as much legend as fact — in this case Buddy Bolden, "the best and the loudest and most loved jazzman of his time." Through Bolden, Ondaatje examines the fate of the artist who explores his art to the limit, through madness into silence.

Making use of a cinematic narrative technique, abruptly cutting from one brief scene to the next, Ondaatje forces us slowly to piece together our understanding of Bolden's life. Bolden, we learn, is a man distrustful of all order: "He did nothing but leap into the mass of changes and explore them." In his music, which "was coarse and rough, immediate, dated in half an hour," he attempts to capture the very flux of experience. It becomes apparent, however, that Bolden's orderless "leap into the mass of changes" is leading him into his own inner "chaos," and he flees from New Orleans to escape the increasing disorder in his life. Further, Bolden leaves in order to escape being trapped by the patterns of his music and by his fame that "made the room narrower and narrower." Bolden had always been a "public" musician giving direct expression to the world around him, but he befriends a crippled photographer named Bellocq, who stands apart from the ordinary social world and tempts Bolden on into the world of "mystic privacy," inexpressible in his music, where, like "an explorer looking for footholds" he retreats into "black empty spaces."

Bolden, however, eventually returns to New Orleans, and as he plays in a parade he attempts to overcome this opposition between what is inner (private) and what is outer. While he plays a girl begins to dance alongside. She is a perfect mirror of his music, and, as she reflects him, he responds to her and his music is totally identified with her dance: "this is what I wanted, always, loss of privacy in the playing, leaving the stage." This tension or balance, however, is impossible to maintain, and in one of the most brilliant pieces of writing in the book, Ondaatje's prose renders the strain on Bolden, the frenzied, frantic movement of his mind, as it races towards breakdown: "god can't stop god can't stop it can't stop the air the red force coming up can't remove it from my mouth, no intake gasp, so deep blooming it up god I can't choke it the music still pouring in a roughness I've never hit, watch it *listen* it *listen* it, can't see I CAN'T SEE." Having achieved what he wanted, a transcendence of privacy, an ultimate communication with his audience, Bolden's mind "on the pinnacle of something collapsed"; he spent the last twenty-four years of his life in an insane asylum in total silence.

Ondaatje's ability to continually present the immediacy of experience with such striking effect gives this novel its considerable emotional impact and makes his telling of Bolden's story a truly impressive achievement. What Emily Dickinson said about good poetry — "If I feel physically as if the top of my head were taken off, I know that is poetry" — can be said about this novel. Some of the emotional effects are achieved by abrupt cuts into highly charged, often violent, scenes, and certainly the moments when we suddenly enter into Buddy's consciousness, or see his responses, are among the most powerful in the book. And with Ondaatje's poetic ability to present scenes and visual images that are sharply and distinctly *seen*, the novel repeatedly achieves this marked intensity.

Ondaatje's handling of the narrative aspect of the novel, however, is not entirely successful. The novel opens slowly and the film technique of abrupt cuts makes the early part seem somewhat disjointed. But the main difficulty arises in the latter part, where Ondaatje takes the story past the point of Bolden's collapse. In presenting the series of hospital documents, interviews, and the report from the guard who took Bolden from Baton Rouge through Slaughter to the asylum, the novel becomes anticlimactic. This muted ending is perhaps deliberate on Ondaatje's part — an attempt to make us experience the "desert of facts" that constitutes the latter part of Bolden's life — but, if so, it seems self-defeating; we gain no further understanding of Bolden, he remains an enigmatic figure, and the let-down is simply disappointing.

The most striking aspect of this last part is Ondaatje's appearance within his own novel. Just after Bolden collapses in the parade Ondaatje intrudes and observes: "When he went mad he was the same age as I am now." And this self-identification is suggested again by the ambiguous final words of the novel — ambiguous because it is not clear whether they are spoken by Bolden or by Ondaatje himself: "I sit with this room. With the grey walls that darken into corner. . . . Thirty-one years old. There are no prizes." But Ondaatje, I take it, does not intend us to press the analogy too hard; he, after all, has transformed his concerns into art. Ondaatje clearly admires Bolden as a type of the hero he points to in his poem "White Dwarfs," one of "those burned out stars / who implode into silence / after parading in the sky / after such choreography what would they wish to speak of anyway." I am, however, a little puzzled by the fact that Ondaatje seems to approve of Bolden's withdrawal into silence at the same time that he writes his own novel. Nonetheless, while Buddy Bolden may have retreated into silence, Michael Ondaatje, by writing Coming Through Slaughter, has made his strongest bid for a prominent place in what he calls the "20th century game of fame."

Jon Kertzer
THE BLURRED PHOTO:
A REVIEW OF *COMING THROUGH SLAUGHTER*

Why do I love most
among my heroes those
who sail to that perfect edge
                              ("White Dwarfs")

To his acknowledgments at the end of *Coming Through Slaughter*,
Michael Ondaatje adds this final note: "While I have used real names
and characters and historical situations I have also used more personal
pieces of friends and fathers. There have been some date changes, some
characters brought together, and some facts have been expanded or
polished to suit the truth of fiction." He indicates here the intricate
mingling of fact, fiction, and personal reference through which he
records and invents the life of another of his heroes who sail to that
perfect edge: Charles "Buddy" Bolden, a part-time barber and jazz
musician in turn-of-the-century New Orleans. Ondaatje uses
documents, quotations, and interviews combined with his own songs,
poems, and narrative all in the service of the truth of fiction. By blending history and fantasy, he explores the inner life of his subject much as,
in an earlier work, he recorded and invented the inner life of Billy the
Kid. In fact, *The Collected Works of Billy the Kid* also concludes by
acknowledging a source that embodies fictional truth: "The comic
book legend is real." The legend of Buddy Bolden is blended even more
richly when Ondaatje projects himself into the book. In one section, he
describes his first curiosity and sympathy for Bolden who, at the age of
31 (Ondaatje's own age), went berserk while playing in a parade and
then spent the rest of his life in a mental hospital. In this way, Ondaatje

296

weaves himself not only into the history, but also into the fantasy of his poetic-novelistic-biography. He makes his own problems as an artist confronting intriguing but intractable material — a "desert of facts" which he must organize, interpret, and bring to a life — a part of the artistry. He draws a parallel between himself and Bolden that emphasizes how all Bolden's frantic struggles with love, music, and madness are part of the same self-perpetuating imaginative conflict. *Coming Through Slaughter* is a disjointed, though carefully crafted, portrait of the artist; but it is a picture of a particularly volatile artistic temperament.

Art is often seen as an organizing process: the reduction of chaos to order. This is true for John Robichaux, another jazz musician whom Bolden scorns for playing waltzes which "put his emotions into patterns" that never vary and so give only a "mechanistic pleasure." But Bolden's own art — and his life, which is an image of his art — is less orderly. His music is spontaneous, violent, erratic, charged with an emotion it can hardly control. He explores chaos without reducing it to manageable forms. He "did nothing but leap into the mass of changes and explore them.... Every note new and raw and chance. Never repeated." He combines the Lord's hymns and the Devil's blues in the same piece.

> We thought he was formless, but I think now he was tormented by order, what was outside it. He tore apart the plot — see his music was immediately on top of his own life. Echoing.... You were both changing direction with every sentence, sometimes in the middle, using each other as a springboard through the dark. You were moving so fast it was unimportant to finish and clear everything. He would be describing something in 27 ways. (*CTS*, 37)

He is tormented by order. He fears "certainty" in which everything is "complete and exact and final," a condition he associates with death which, in turn, fascinates, repels, and torments him. Instead, he moves outside of order in both music and life. He embraces the vitality of chaos, the quick of life, but he lives so fast and hard that it kills him. He is a wild drinker and lover; he plays the loudest cornet in jazz; he is subject to destructive fits of rage; he dreams continually of pain and mutilation; he is suicidal. He finds that to live passionately is to prepare one's death, that art feeds on madness until it is destroyed by it, that art is an

297

act of communion that isolates the artist, that the energy of creation is also destructive: "The making and destroying coming from the same source, same lust, same surgery his brain was capable of" (CTS, 55).

Bolden's art and madness are set in perspective by two contrasting figures. Webb resembles Pat Garrett in Billy the Kid. He is a detective who patiently tracks down Bolden after he has run off in panic. Webb is calculating, cool and rational, while Bolden is associated with the body, especially the hand and fingers — image of the deft barber and cornetist, of the man of instinct, feeling, and anger, image of the madman. His ultimate nightmare is of having hands cut off at the wrists: "suicide of the hands." Webb is also the old friend who proves an enemy when he tempts Bolden to return to a well-ordered life which he cannot stand. In contrast, tempting Bolden to disorder is Bellocq, a crippled photographer and artist in his own field. He provides us with the only surviving picture of Bolden, a blurred clue to his identity, while his sordid, defaced pictures of New Orleans whores turn into mirrors in which Bolden finds and then loses himself. He too is a man of the body, living in the pain of his deformity. He too is suicidal. He tempts Bolden away from music, fame, and gregariousness to a silent "mystic privacy," to "black empty spaces," and to "mole comfort, mole deceit."

> Him watching me waste myself and wanting me to step back into my body as if into a black room and stumble against whatever was there. Unable then to be watched by others. More and more I said he was wrong and more and more I spent whole evenings with him. (CTS, 91)

Ondaatje follows this retreat into madness, into the corner of a dark room in the Louisana State Hospital, and then, after Bolden's death in 1931, on through the town of Slaughter to the Holtz Cemetery in New Orleans.

Theme and style will be familiar to readers of Ondaatje's work. His poetry is distinguished by its conversational tone, its juxtaposition of the coarse and the lyrical, its playfully grotesque imagery (rat jelly, dainty monsters), and its paradoxical union of sex, pain, art, madness, and death. In short, we are given spasms of the true romantic agony. Ondaatje is drawn to heroic victims, such as "Heron Rex":

There are ways of going
physically mad, physically
mad when you perfect the mind
where you sacrifice yourself for the race
when you are the representative when you allow
yourself to be paraded in the cages
celebrity a razor in the body (*RJ*, 52)

It is not far from herons in the zoo to Bolden, with his fame, his razor, his parades, and his cell. Such suffering requires a centre of perception, an experiencing ego, and consequently much of the poetry is autobiographical or anecdotal. In extended works, the spasmodic insights, which are essentially imagistic and momentary, are reconciled with the narrative impulse by creating a poetic, fictive memoir, such as we have here, in *Billy the Kid*, and in *the man with seven toes*. The result, to borrow the subtitle of Lewis Carroll's *Hunting of the Snark*, is an agony in eight (or eighty) fits. The agony is picaresque and atavistic. The heroic victims make their way across primitive landscapes: the Australian bush, the American wild west, the slums of New Orleans. Here, through a series of encounters and disasters, they are pushed to mental and physical extremes; they "sail to that perfect edge" of experience. Because they live and die with such intensity, they become heroic, perfect, yet typical, figures.

This technique is flexible and eclectic. Almost anything — photographs, blank spaces, dolphin voices, song titles, acknowledgments or literature — can contribute to the total effect, providing it falls within the larger narrative (Bolden's life) or thematic (the agony of that life) pattern. These are shock tactics: images which first strike us as disjointed and disturbing gradually take their place in a mosaic the total design of which is the argument of the book. Ondaatje works his way, fit by fit, around the vicious circle of Bolden's sensibility. He presents a series of illuminating fragments which, while never entirely chaotic, are an apt expression of Bolden's temperament. They are organized, however, by continual reference and cross-reference, by repetition and analogy, by recurring images which grow in density and meaning, and by time-shifts which eventually fall into place within the whole chronology.

Buddy Bolden is a worthy addition to Ondaatje's growing list of heroes, and *Coming Through Slaughter* both deserves and rewards close reading. Because there are so many similarities, it is tempting to compare it with earlier works. Personally, I prefer *Billy the Kid*. I find its images stronger and more startling, its argument more compelling. A symptom of weakness in *Coming Through Slaughter* is its preface, consisting of three sonographs, with commentary, of a dolphin's squawks, whistles, and clicks. This is puzzling, as it was certainly intended to be, but not really intriguing. Although we do eventually realize how this fragment fits into the entire mosaic of the book, it is only after some forcing on Ondaatje's part and some impatience on ours, and by then the effect is lost. Other sections also seem too remote or too contrived, understated or over-dramatic. As a result, Bolden himself remains curiously remote, despite all the attention he receives, and never emerges clearly from the "desert of facts," real or fictional, which comprises his life. Granted, we are not supposed to see him clearly — the photo is blurred — but we are supposed to sense and sympathize with the contradictions that torment him, even though these contradictions cannot be resolved. We must appreciate his torment, his agony, even though the man himself remains a mystery. We learn less about Billy, yet care about him more; and not even a single photo survives of him.

Linda Hutcheon
RUNNING IN THE FAMILY:
THE POSTMODERNIST CHALLENGE

It has rapidly become a cliché of what we seem determined to call post-modernism that textual self-reflexivity has led to a general breakdown of the conventional boundaries between the arts.[1] But it is also clear that other boundaries are being challenged, including those between genres, and, in fact, those between art and reality. Magritte's paintings perhaps stand as the visual model of this kind of challenge. His various paintings called "La Condition Humaine" present paintings within paintings, unframed pictures within window frames whose represented landscapes overlap perfectly those of the "reality" outside the windows. This slippage between image and referent (all within a painting, we must recall) provides what Robert Hughes has called the source of modernist disquiet.[2] In postmodernist fiction, the same art / life slippage occurs within the same self-reflexive framework, but in *fiction* this marks a new move outward beyond the novel's earlier need to assert its supreme autonomy as art.[3] Life can now be let in.

Michael Ondaatje has been described[4] as a writer who is fascinated with borders, including those between literature and reality. Certainly, he is not alone in this fascination: the recent works of Robert Kroetsch, Margaret Atwood, Clark Blaise, Jack Hodgins, Rudy Wiebe, and Timothy Findley attest to the attraction of these borders as sites of novelistic investigation. But Ondaatje has combined *his* challenge to the boundaries of art in general with a defiance of the limits of conventional literary genres. *The Collected Works of Billy the Kid* is a series of poems, with a narrative structure, based on a real historical personage. *Coming Through Slaughter* is a fictionalized biography of the real Buddy Bolden, told in fragments that force the reader to enact the processes of aesthetic

301

ordering and imagining that constitute the narrator's own fictionalizing. *Running in the Family* is, perhaps, the culmination of Ondaatje's challenges to boundaries, at least thus far: its fragmented collection of memories, research, poems, and photographs works to reconstruct a more immediate and personal history — the writer's own. But to write of anyone's history is to order, to give form to disparate facts; in short, to fictionalize. Ondaatje's self-consciousness about this process is part of the very subject of this postmodernist work.

Of all the Canadian poets who have turned to fiction in the last few decades (Cohen, Atwood, Kogawa, Musgrave, and so on) Ondaatje is the one who is most aware of generic borders, and of how they can be transgressed. (A number of both his poetic and prose works have even been transformed into dramatic productions.) Other writers have played about with the borders between the novel and the short story (Alice Munro, Ray Smith) and even poetry and fictional prose (Derk Wynand, Leonard Cohen), but Ondaatje takes such play one step further: beyond the boundaries of what we conventionally accept as *literary* genres and into history and biography.

The writing of history has itself come under considerable scrutiny in the past few years and its links to fictional narrative have been the main focus of attention. Hayden White has argued that historiography is a poetic construct.[5] To write history is to narrate, to reconstruct by means of selection and interpretation. History is made by its writer, even if events seem to speak for themselves. As Fredric Jameson has claimed, narrativization is a form of human comprehension, a way to impose meaning and form on the chaos of historical event.[6] Given this new self-consciousness about history, it is perhaps not surprising that when novelists choose to write of actual, real people — Findley's Duke and Duchess of Windsor, Wiebe's Big Bear and Riel — they should do so equally self-consciously. Like historians, they must use "emplotting" strategies of exclusion, emphasis, and subordination of the elements of a story, and they must also deal with "a veritable chaos of events *already constituted.*"[7] But they have another set of conventions to confront as well: those of fiction. What we end up with is a new, curiously paradoxical form that we might call "historio*graphic metafic*tion" rather than historical fiction.[8]

This, however, is not the only context into which Ondaatje's challenge to generic conventions should be placed. In the critical wake of post-structuralism's stress on textuality, all genre distinctions have been subverted: poetry, fiction, biography, even history—all are texts and must be read as such, that is, with suspicion. What Edward Said calls the "world"[9] is made (some would say, reduced) by such a theory to the site of mutually de-constructing textual forces. Ondaatje's self-aware thematizing of the textuality of the past—when it comes to you through books, records, and even memories—places *Running in the Family* into the post-structuralist as well as postmodernist context. And what is common to both is the shared importance of the role of the reader or interpreter. The boundary between textualized life and textual art is bridged, not only by fictionalizing historians, but by their readers. It is also the reader, ultimately, who defines genre.

Jonathan Culler has argued against the definition of genre as a set of taxonomic categories in which we put works that happen to share certain pre-defined features, and in favour of one that makes the reader central. Genre becomes "a set of expectations, a set of instructions about the type of coherence one is to look for and the ways in which sequences are to be read."[10] Literature which does not fit into genre, therefore, becomes that which resists recuperation and challenges the reader. But the best example of such literature for Culler is one which rejects both representation and human intentionality (the Derridean and *Tel Quel* text) in a way that Ondaatje's works never do, for they are both historical and performative. In other words, they indeed do seek to represent a reality outside literature, and one of the connections between life and art is the performing narrator, whose act of searching and ordering forms part of the narrative itself.

The transgression of generic boundaries may well be a post-structuralist, anti-totalizing gesture,[11] but it has also been responsible for an important critical refocussing on the process of production in art. In our anti-Romantic formalism, we had come to find texts easier to deal with than authors, and reception safer to talk about than production.[12] But postmodernist texts have reintroduced production in their stress on performance: "Signs of the artist's or poet's presence are demanded in the published work....The personal presence is an instance... localization, of a growing concern with particular and local definitions."[13] One of the motives behind such localization is the desire to situate even the most self-reflexive of postmodernist performances in history.[14] As we read of the narrator's search for both the content and

303

form of what we know as *Running in the Family*, we not only *watch* the historiographic and fictionalizing impulses at work, but we also participate in them. As in *The Collected Works of Billy the Kid* and *Coming Through Slaughter*, in this bio- or historiographical *meta*fiction, we experience that postmodernist performance in the act of reading the fragmented text.

It is probably the later work of Roland Barthes[15] that has made the fragment one of the major postmodernist forms.[16] The economy of the fragmented text is such that the reader is implicated directly in the challenge to the boundaries both between genres and between life and art. As Barthes wrote: "Is it not the property of the real to be unmasterable? And is it not the property of the system to master it? How can one proceed, faced with the real, if one refuses mastery?"[17] Barthes' own reply was to dismiss the apparatus of generic system and let in "dissemination," the free play of open language. This is not Ondaatje's response, though he too turns to the fragment in his transgression of the limits of literary genres.

From the more traditional poetic narrative form of *The Collected Works of Billy the Kid*, Ondaatje moved to the equally poetic narrative of *Coming Through Slaughter*, but the use of prose unavoidably introduced the conventions of the novel, conventions which were subsequently challenged by both the historical nature of the subject and the fragmented form of the work. Again Barthes offers one possible explanation: "When one places fragments in succession, is no organization possible? Yes, the fragment is like the musical idea of a song cycle: each piece is self-sufficient, but is never more than the interstice of its neighbours."[18] If *Billy the Kid* is more overtly a poetic song-cycle, *Coming Through Slaughter* (the story of a jazz musician, whose unwritten, unrecorded music lives on only in Ondaatje's printed fragments) is appropriately structured in this musical way. *Running in the Family* carries even further the fragmented presentation of what Barthes elsewhere calls "biographèmes"[19] or units of biography and history. Here it is even more clearly the *reader*, participating in the act of organizing the past, who constitutes the focus of this book.

The reader, like Ondaatje as narrator, becomes the first-level link between life and art and the most direct challenge to the border between them. The author's choice of presentation by fragments is a hermeneutic strategy that suggests a very postmodernist parallel be-

304

tween the acts of reception and production of the text. For example, the section labelled "April 11, 1932" begins with "I remember the wedding...."[20] (of Ondaatje's parents). But the reader's expectations are immediately disappointed, since the wedding remains a textual gap, never to be described. The subsequent section, entitled "Honeymoon," again leads the reader to expect an account at least of what followed the couple's wedding, but once again, we get only a lacuna (37-8). What we are offered instead is a listing of things going on at the time, in Ceylon and elsewhere. These are not randomly selected, however. The couple may not appear, but things that impinged on them do: from the price of beer to the ideal of feminine beauty at the time. It is only much later in the text that the lacuna is partially filled. The section is called "Photograph" and in it we are told, by the narrator, about "the photograph I have been waiting for all my life. My father and mother together. May 1932. They are on their honeymoon" (161). We too have been waiting, if not all our lives, at least for 135 pages of fragments, for this look at the couple. But Ondaatje is not finished playing with his reader's expectations. After describing the photo in detail, only then, on the next page, does he actually reproduce it. By then, of course, it is redundant: words can be as real as photographic reproductions.[21]

The status of language in relation to the representation of reality is an important issue in this book as a whole, as we shall see later. But it is of particular interest at this point because of its implications for the process of reading, as well as writing. When we read a novel, we assume, because of the conventions of the genre, that the referents of the text's language are fictive, rather than real,[22] however much they may be made to resemble the real. The case is somewhat more complex in what we have called historiographic metafiction, because the fictionality of the referents is repeatedly stressed by the text's self-reflexivity, while their historical nature is also constantly being implied: Chris Scott's Giordano Bruno (in *Antichthon*) both is and is not the real historical Giordano Bruno. In writing of both Billy the Kid and Buddy Bolden in the self-consciously metafictional way in which he did, Ondaatje too chose this middle ground of reference, creating what we might call a historiographic referent. Unlike the historical or real referent, this one is created in the text's writing (hence historio*graphic*). The referent here is a dialogic entity, in Bakhtin's sense of the word,[23] partaking of two ontological realities. In *Running in the Family*, Ondaatje adds one further element to this linguistic tension between art and life by making the history a personal one, subject to his own fictionalizing memory as well as that of others.

History, like narrative, becomes, therefore, a process, not a product. It is a lived experience for both reader and writer. Ondaatje literally inserted himself into Billy's textual world in the final photograph of himself as a child in a cowboy outfit; he entered Bolden's New Orleans to interview those who had known the musician and to photograph the places he had inhabited. Here the process of recording and narrating history became part of the text itself. In the most recent work, Ondaatje is not only the recorder, collector, organizer, and narrator of the past, but also the subject of it, both as an Ondaatje whose tale will be told and as the writer who will tell it. Only the initial prefatory section uses the third-person point of view for the narrator; from then on the "I" of the text is a constant presence, the one who is "running." We are always being made aware of his physical presence as he writes: "The air reaches me unevenly with its gusts against my arms, face, and this paper" (24). He reads and copies information about his family from stone inscriptions, church ledgers, old news clippings. As he soon realizes: "I witnessed everything" (70). And so too do we, through him. This is a typical postmodernist challenge to the formalist occulting of the process of literary production.[24] Performance is very much a part of the content of this book.

To write the history of one's own family is to enter the realm of autobiography as well as biography. But in all forms of narrating the past, the realization of the essential subjectivity of the enterprise has recently supplanted any positivist faith in objective representation: the idea of the invention of reality through language, or even of the creation of the self through language, no longer upsets historians and (auto)biographers. And, of course, it has never really upset novelists, even those most attuned to naturalistic representation. Canadian writers have often teased the life / art borders of self-consciously autobiographical fiction: David Young's *Incognito* and most of the work of Audrey Thomas come to mind, for both use photographs in much the same way that Ondaatje's texts do: as supplements and as lures. But Ondaatje has perhaps been the most consistent and thorough in his interrogation of both the inner and the outer boundaries of art.

306

Michel Foucault has claimed that: "The frontiers of a book are never clear-cut: beyond the title, the first lines, and the last full stop, beyond its internal configuration and its autonomous form, it is caught up in a system of references to other books, other texts, other sentences: it is a node within a network."[25] The network of *Running in the Family* includes intertexts of all kinds, both literary and historical. One section, for example, is entitled "Historical Relations" (39). It is a fragment about Ondaatje's family past, so we construe the title to mean the relations or relatives of his own history. It is only later in the book that we discover than *An Historical Relation* is the name of a memoir by Robert Knox, a man who was held captive in Ceylon for twenty years, and that it constitutes one of Ondaatje's major sources of historical information about the land and its traditions. The pun on historical relations as connections within history (which Ondaatje is constantly trying to make) and as relatives from the past underlines the inevitability of the conjunction of the chaos of historical facts and the ordering process of the one who writes history. Some of the intertexts are personal memories of Ondaatje and his family, memories which he spends his time "trying to swell . . . with the order of dates and asides, interlocking them all." In this way, we are told, "history is organized" (26).

The writing of history also involves a hermeneutic process, for it must be preceded by the reading or interpreting of the facts, be they the dates in the church ledger or the complex personal interactions of the people involved. The latter turn out to be the most difficult: "I still cannot break the code" (53). Ondaatje comes to realize that: "Truth disappears with history and gossip tells us in the end nothing of personal relationships" (53). Although he questions his own motives in invading the privacy of the past in this way, he admits that he still wants to know that "lost history," because it too is part of the reality of his past. After offering us a number of people's memories of his father, the narrator concludes: "There is so much to know and we can only guess. Guess around him. To know him from these stray actions I am told about by those who loved him" (200). Therefore his own book will forever remain "incomplete" as a history: "In the end all your children move among the scattered acts and memories with no more clues" (201). If the self can be created in words, it can also be evaded. Language has power, but it is not supreme: the past can escape articulation. It is the ultimate intertext whose significance is both intensely desired and constantly deferred.

The Foucaldian network of texts of *Running in the Family*, however, also includes more manageable intertexts, and one of them is certainly that most influential of postmodernist novels, Gabriel García Márquez's *One Hundred Years of Solitude*. A book which opens with references to ice, a dream, and time cannot help but recall the famous opening of that novel: "Many years later, as he faced the firing squad, Colonel Aureliano Buendia was to remember that distant afternoon when his father took him to discover ice."[26] Throughout Ondaatje's text, the syntax will recall this opening: "Years later, when Lalla was almost a grandmother, she was standing in the rain...." (42). In both books, the writer is from the world he writes of (and creates) and yet outside it, both present and absent in the writing. These two generational tales—of the Buendias and the Ondaatjes—share too a similar setting. Ceylon, conveniently, has a city called Colombo, but even without it, Ondaatje's island bears many resemblances to García Márquez's Columbian Macondo: the extreme of heat, drought, and flood; the exuberant vegetation; the incessant insect activity; the almost mythically exaggerated inhabitants—all culminating in Lalla's "magic ride" to her death on the flood. Ceylon itself is described as an almost mythic place which, throughout its history, has "seduced all of Europe." Its name was constantly being altered to fit the language of the latest invader, just as its shape on maps (based on sightings of the island) grew "from mythic shapes into eventual accuracy" (63). Not surprisingly, the people of this land have developed their own set of myths—both national (the thalagaya tongue as key to verbal brilliance) and familial (the grey cobra as the shade of Mervyn Ondaatje).

Just as Macondo was torn apart by internal dissension, but also had to deal with imperialistic foreigners, Ceylon too has been split by insurrection, but more importantly, it too has spent most of its history coping with the foreign "Karapothas"—the beetles that crawl over the land but see nothing (78). The political dimension of both works is tied to the aesthetic. In *Running in the Family*, a Ceylonese poet is cited: "to our remote / villages the painters came, and our white-washed / mud-huts were splattered with gunfire" (86). Ondaatje answers the poem with a poem, not about painters from outside, but about the people of the land itself: the "toddy tapper" whose beverage Ondaatje had spent his mornings drinking, literally making it into a part of himself. He is not one of the destructive foreigners; he is no alien.

One Hundred Years of Solitude is a novel that has all the narrative energy of the oral traditions of South American storytelling, but we are not allowed to forget that it is as a written text that we experience it: the novel ends when Aureliano Babilonia completes his reading of Melquiades' parchments. Our reading ceases with his. All this oral-seeming tale had been foretold, we learn, and foretold in writing. One of the ways in which Ondaatje deals with this same duality of the oral gossip and tales to be transformed into written history is to turn to poetry, the most oral of written literary forms. The first poem in the book is self-consciously about orality: its epigraph is a quotation about the Sinhalese being the least musical people in the world, with no sense of pitch, line or rhythm (76). What follows is a poem about a voice without music, a poem with a very fine sense of pitch, line, and rhythm. It is one of those poems that deny their own denying subject, like Coleridge's "Dejection: An Ode" and Cohen's entire collection, *The Energy of Slaves*.

This is not the only way in which Ondaatje's text is self-reflexive or postmodernist, of course. The two epigraphs of the book point to the other major metafictional foci: writing and language. We have already seen that Ondaatje is very present in the text as physical writer of it. As a boy, he had only associated the act of writing with the punitive writing out of lines in school: "The only freedom writing brought was as the author of rude expressions on walls and desks" (84). He points to the writing on the walls of prison camps as further testimony of this transgressive kind of freedom through writing. But other examples he gives — of ancient graffiti poems — are subsequently made into images in his own poem (92-4), thereby implying, perhaps, that poetry in general partakes of this same freedom, that all writing forms this ideological connection between art and life.

This self-consciousness about the act of writing (on the first page, we read: "Half a page — and the morning is already ancient" [17]) is matched by an equal concern for language, as we have already seen. After an epigraph that suggests that language conditions perception, the narrator tells us why he wants to write the history of the people of his familial past: "I wanted to touch them into words" (22). In order to do so, he has to journey to the island whose own history is one of invasions by many nations, all claiming "everything with the power of their sword or bible or language" (64). He has to realize that the Dutch

309

spelling of his own name is just a "parody of the ruling language" (64), but that, despite this, it is his name, a name he shares with many others. Kneeling in the church by the gravestone of an ancestor, he reflects that to "see your name chiseled in large letters . . . in some strange way removes vanity, eliminates the personal. It makes your own story a lyric" (65-6). The physicality of language, its concrete letters, is a recurring motif in the text. As a boy in school, he had learned to love the curls and curves of the Sinhalese alphabet. Like a Stephen Dedalus entranced with form, the five-year-old Ondaatje related the shapes of letters to those of the small bones of the human body: "How to write. The self-portrait of language" (83).[27]

We have also seen, however, that the act of reading is as important to this book as that of writing. Ondaatje lays claim to two different family traditions of reading: "my father swallowed the heart of books and kept that knowledge and emotion to himself. My mother read her favourite poems out loud, would make us read plays together and acted herself" (168). From the former, he inherited his sense of secrecy; from the latter, his sense of the dramatic. But Ceylon and the Ondaatje past seem to demand more of his mother's "recording by exaggeration," more of her mythologizing impulse—even in an historical narrative. Again we see the impact of both García Márquez and postmodernist performance.

In Ondaatje's life, it had been his mother who had offered a model of the way in which the boundaries of life and art could be crossed: "Whatever plays my mother acted in publicly were not a patch on the real-life drama she directed and starred in during her married life" (171). But for the reader, another model is provided. A section like "Dialogues," with its different voices and different stories, is a microcosmic version of the structure of the entire text: the fragments of the past that Ondaatje works to put together are mirrored in the fragments he offers his reader. His use of the inclusive first-person plural in the section following "Dialogues" underlines his desire to implicate the reader in his own hermeneutic process of interpreting and ordering the fragments of experience: "During certain hours, at certain years in our lives, we see ourselves as remnants from the earlier generations that were destroyed. So our job becomes to keep peace with enemy camps, eliminate the chaos at the end of Jacobean tragedies, and with 'the mercy of distance' write the histories" (179). The production and reception of the text are both acts of ordering: just as we are shaped by our past, so the past is shaped by us, as we "eliminate the chaos."

As the book draws to a close, these various postmodernist concerns for language, writing, memory, fact, and fiction all come together in the author's attempt to come to terms with his father. After expressing his worry about the power of language ("Words such as *love, passion, duty*, are so continually used they grow to have no meaning—except as coins or weapons" [179]), he then addresses his father directly: "I am now part of an adult's ceremony, but I want to say I am writing this book about you at a time when I am least sure about such words" (180). "Give the word," he begs. What the reader then gets is a bizarre mythic story which Ondaatje claims not to be able to deal with. But what follows that is even more important: the narrative perspective changes from Ondaatje the writer to that of his father. The first-person narration shifts to third-person, except for one telling sequence in which "he" reaches for a whiskey bottle and the "I" drinks from it (188). This identification of the two men had been prefigured on the previous page through the father's offering a ride to the scented cinnamon peeler, a scene that had inspired, or had been inspired by, a poem that his son wrote and that we read over ninety pages earlier (95). In the third-person narrative about his father, though, Ondaatje imagines him trying to deal with his separation from his wife and children. He follows him home and watches him look for a book he was reading. He finds it in the bathroom, being attacked by ants who are carrying the "intimate print" away one sheet at a time. At that moment, the ants—like the reader of Ondaatje's book—had reached page 189. Directly linking the "white rectangle" of the disappearing page with the bathroom mirror whose "company" his father feared, Ondaatje cements the identification with a recall of those earlier questioned words: love, passion, duty. Here the father watches the ants move the page away: "Duty, he thought. But that was just a fragment gazed at by the bottom of his eye" (189). He surrenders the page to the ants, as we surrender it to the narrative and pass on.

At the end, Ondaatje returns to the actual act of writing with which he opened the text, but this time he makes clear that, as a process, it is part of the larger processes of nature: "At midnight this hand is the only thing moving. As discreetly and carefully as whatever animals in the garden fold brown leaves into their mouths, visit the drain for water, or scale the broken glass that crowns the walls. Watch the hand move. Waiting for it to say something, to stumble casually on perception, the shape of an unknown thing'' (190). Along with the text's producer, we watch that hand move as it tries to write of that which will finally make sense of the past. Ondaatje is forced to conclude, however, that his father will remain ''one of those books we long to read whose pages remain uncut'' (200). Since the only books with uncut pages mentioned in the entire book are novels, this may well be an affirmation of the final fictional status of any attempt to capture history. And the author's acknowledgements at the end of the book reinforce this view. After thanking all the people who helped him garner the facts for the work, he adds: ''While all these names may give an air of authenticity, I must confess that the book is not a history but a portrait or 'gesture'. And if those listed above disapprove of the fictional air I apologize and can only say that in Sri Lanka a well-told lie is worth a thousand facts'' (206).

To write self-reflexively of history as process in progress, instead of as completed product, is to break down the finality of formal narrative closure. Such a self-conscious opening up of the borders of both history and narrative is a postmodernist restating of the traditional (and perhaps obligatory) mimetic connection between art and life. Like the historiographic metafictions of writers like John Fowles, Umberto Eco, Salman Rushdie, or, closer to home, Timothy Findley, Rudy Wiebe, and Chris Scott, Ondaatje's *Running in the Family* challenges boundaries, not just between genres, but between what has been called the basic and misleading assumption of much modern criticism: ''that fiction is an antonym of reality.''[28]

1 See the introduction to Part IV, ''Patterns and Consequences of Self-Reflective Art'' in *The Discontinuous Universe*, eds. Sallie Sears and G.W. Lord (New York: Basic Books, 1972), pp. viii-ix.

2 *The Shock of the New* (London: BBC, 1980), p. 247.

3 After Mallarmé, according to Michel Foucault, literature ''breaks with the whole definition of genres as forms adapted to an order of representation, and becomes merely a manifestation of a language which has no other law than that of affirming

—in opposition to all other forms of discourse—its own precipitous existence; and so there is nothing for it to do but to curve back in a perpetual return upon itself, as if its discourse could have no other content than the expression of its own form; it addresses itself to itself as a writing subjectivity, or seeks to re-apprehend the essence of all literature in the movement that brought it into being." See *The Order of Things* (London: Tavistock, 1970), p. 300.

4 By Sam Solecki, entry on Ondaatje in *The Oxford Companion to Canadian Literature* (Toronto: Oxford University Press, 1983), p. 620.

5 *Metahistory* (Baltimore: The Johns Hopkins University Press, 1973), p. ix: history is "a verbal structure in the form of a narrative prose discourse."

6 *The Political Unconscious* (Ithaca: Cornell University Press, 1981). See too Hayden White, "The Narrativization of Real Events," *Critical Inquiry*, 7 (Summer 1981), 793-98.

7 *Metahistory*, p. 6n, his italics.

8 See Linda Hutcheon, "Canadian Historiographic Metafiction," forthcoming in *Essays on Canadian Writing*.

9 *The World, the Text, and the Critic* (Cambridge: Harvard University Press, 1983).

10 "Towards a Theory of Non-Genre Literature" in *Surfiction*, ed. Raymond Federman, 2nd ed. (Chicago: Swallow Press, 1981), p. 255.

11 Ihab Hassan, "Postmodernism: A Vanishing Horizon," paper to the Modern Language Association, New York, December 30, 1983.

12 For one explanation of this process, see Timothy J. Reiss, *The Discourse of Modernism* (Ithaca: Cornell University Press, 1982), and a related review article: Linda Hutcheon, "A Poetics of Postmodernism?" *Diacritics*, 13, 4 (Winter 1983).

13 Jerome Rothenberg, "New Models, New Visions: Some Notes Toward a Poetics of Performance," in *Performance in Postmodern Culture*, eds. Michel Benamou and Charles Carmello (Milwaukee: Center for Twentieth Century Studies, 1977), p. 14.

14 This aesthetic practice would disprove Herbert Blau's accusation that postmodernism represses history, that it is "disinherited, apolitical, vain." See his "Letting Be Be Finale of Seem: The Future of an Illusion," in *Performance in Postmodern Culture*, p. 66.

15 For example, *Le Plaisir du texte, Roland Barthes par Roland Barthes, Fragments d'un discours amoureux*.

16 See Reda Bensmaia, "From Fragment to Detail: Roland Barthes," *Enclitic*, 5, 1

(1981), 66-97. Barthes himself called the fragmental text the matrix of all genre. See "Colloque international sur le genre," *Glyph*, 7 (1980), 235.

17 *Roland Barthes by Roland Barthes*, trans. Richard Howard (New York: Hill and Wang, 1977), p. 122.

18 *Ibid.*, p. 94.

19 *Sade/Fourier/Loyola* (Paris: Seuil, 1971), p. 14.

20 *Running in the Family* (Toronto: McClelland and Steward, 1982), p. 36. All further references will be to this edition and page numbers will appear in parentheses in the text.

21 Another way in which Ondaatje plays with the reader's perception of photographs is to show the picture first, with no context, and then to discuss it. In one case, a nearly blind woman describes the photo with the eyes of memory, and the author writes that the picture "has moved tangible, palpable, into her brain, the way memory invades the present in those who are old" (p. 112). Since we too have actually seen the photograph, it is also tangible and palpable for us.

22 This distinction is that of Georges Lavis, "'Le Texte littéraire, le référent, le réel, le vrai," *Cahiers d'analyse textualle*, 13 (1971), 7-22.

23 See Mikhail Bakhtin, *The Dialogic Imagination*, ed. Michael Holquist, trans. Caryl Emerson and Michael Holquist (Austin and London: University of Texas Press, 1981).

24 This is an occulting ruefully acknowledged by Frank Kermode in *The Genesis of Secrecy* (Cambridge: Harvard University Press, 1979), p. 45: "Even now, when so many theories of interpretation dispense in one way or another with the author, or allow him only a part analogous to that of the dummy hand at bridge, the position is not much altered; the narrative inhabits its proper dark, in which the interpreter traces its lineaments as best he can."

25 *The Archaeology of Knowledge*, trans. Sheridan Smith (New York: Harper and Row, 1976), p. 23.

26 *One Hundred Years of Solitude*, trans. Gregory Rabassa (1970; New York: Avon, 1971), p. 11.

27 This alphabet image reappears a number of times: in the black boar's "wet alphabet of tusk" that could bring death (p. 142) and in the change in his mother's handwriting, as if she "forced herself to cope with a new dark unknown alphabet" (p. 150).

28 *The Act of Reading* (Baltimore: The Johns Hopkins University Press, 1978), p. 53.

Ernest MacIntyre
OUTSIDE OF TIME:
RUNNING IN THE FAMILY

From our vantage point in time we see today that life was quite harshly real for most subject races of the British Empire: the Kandyan peasantry of the Ceylon hill country were dispossessed of their land to make way for tea; the South Indian poor were uprooted from their homelands and transported to the Ceylon hills to labour on the tea; and Leonard Woolf's Sinhalese girls of the arid dry zone became old hags before the age of forty. But as one glances historically upwards along the native economic scale one sees comfortable unreality creeping into the lives of the upper classes of the subject peoples. These were the Sinhalese and Tamil gentlemen who went to Oxford and Cambridge to come back and sit comfortably on their rubber estates or in the Ceylon Civil Service, and who heartily approved the caning and slapping of their offspring if they accidentally spoke the native languages in the corridors of the schools. But even these Sinhalese and Tamil gentlemen were destined to return to ''a kind of reality,'' and have ''a tryst with destiny'' as Nehru comfortably put it. The empire would recede and they would surface to the neo-colonial situation of the struggle against their own countrymen which would explode, in its first phase, in the tragic youth uprising of April 1971.

But there was another community in colonial Ceylon, the Burghers, the local descendants of the previous Dutch Empire who were to enjoy an entire mortality of heightened unreality, a surreality, because they wouldn't be provided with even a humbug of ''a tryst with destiny'' at midnight in 1947 when Ceylon was given the legality of Independence so that the former colonial gentlemen of the majority races, the Sinhalese and Tamils, could carry on regardless, with their race, caste, and politics.

Michael Ondaatje is a Ceylonese "midnight's child" of 1943, born to the Burghers who had no such tryst with a political destiny. The vast majority of the Burghers opted for the reality of Melbourne when in 1956 Bandaranaike replaced English with Sinhalese as the official language of Ceylon. But most of Ondaatje's family were not among these. He was born to a small wealthy inner circle which had become far too used to their Ceylon fantasy to make that very real journey from Tullamarine Airport to the suburbs of Melbourne. This small set of Burghers which had gradually intermarried with the natives providing themselves with a subtle range of colours from Southern Italian olive to near British puffy pink white, would have been quite silly to have given up their rich surreality in this lush tropical setting. Young Ondaatje was plucked away, just in time, by a divorced mother and so was never destined to become the managing director of George Stewart and Co. or Aitken Spence Ltd. or even a famous lawyer, a rich planter, a brilliant surgeon or a colonel in the Ceylon Light-Infantry. For this we must be thankful to his mother. The "midnight's child" left when he was just eleven years old to end up in Canada as one of its best poets and an internationally published writer.

Twenty five years later, he returns to "touch . . . with words" the lives and era of this tiny minority of his Burgher forebears. And he touches their lives in such a way that I at least cannot escape the feeling that the whole explanation of the fantastic way in which they lived, loved and died lies in their perforce happy suspension outside the deception held by their wealthy Sinhalese and Tamil counterparts — that there was a job to be done in shaping the future of a whole nation. With the departure of the British to whom they could never reach out socially, and with the arrival of the native gentlemen whom they could never join massively in political history, these lordly Burghers threw their creative energies into fantastic individual biographies. It is significant that the one time they imagined they were having a tryst with political destiny, in the company of their Sinhalese and Tamil social friends, it had all the features of a fantastic prank concocted at a colonial club with equal portions of professional drinking and amateur political soldiering. Those who react to Michael Ondaatje's *Running in the Family* as fantastic and exaggerated should only bother to go into the details of how these people careered madly into a midnight "manoeuvre" to topple and replace the government of Mrs. Sivimavo Bandaranaike in 1961. Then they will see that the attempted coup of 1961 has been running in the family from as far back as the decades of the 20s, 30s and 40s as Mervyn Ondaatje (the author's father) soaked in gin but thinly clothed in the uniform of the Ceylon Light Infantry runs riot in the Colombo Trinco train, loaded revolver and all, as he senses an imminent Japanese invasion. No one believes him but at the height of his delirium the triumph of poetic truth is his: in that magical transformation which only a great drinker can know, all the pots of buffalo curd in the train become the bombs of the Japanese!

The whole work is invested with this magical transformation of the germ of a fact into some of the finest scenes of the imagination, not soaked in the gin of the father but in the poetry of the son. Those scenes from the book that come alive in fantastic, unreal, poetic imagination convey, to me at least, the real fact of the lives of these people, the spirit in which they *should* have lived, if they had extended their situation to its logical conclusion. It is when I sensed this that I found myself more than once recovering from moods of sadness to return again to exhilaration.

The finest of these scenes is the final journey of Michael Ondaatje's grandmother, to death, as she is carried high through the town of Nuwara Eliya, in 1947, not by pall bearers in a lifted coffin but by the great swollen floods of that year. She rages through the town, past the tops of trees, handbag still dangling from hand, past all the familiar landmarks of life, aloft the rushing waters, and comes to a sudden end as she hits the top of a Jacaranda tree, to die in its arms. Ondaatje is contemporary with writers like Italo Calvino, and who can say that this is not the spirit in which his grandmother *should* have lived and died? Such scenes make me think of how in *The Baron in the Trees* Calvino's character Cosimo lived and died, leaving home at eleven to spend the rest of his life, away from his family, in the tops of trees.

There is much darkness too, in the work, particularly towards the end when the author begins to brood over the last lonely days of his father. And then he has to back away from the avant garde spirit of Calvino and summon up an atmosphere from the greatest of the poets. Even though Edgar spares Gloucester the knowledge that he is aware of his father's terrible darkness, Ondaatje longs for the scene that is not there in *The Tragedy of King Lear*, Edgar revealing himself to his father.

317

But in life Ondaatje hadn't even this conjectural possibility because he vanished from Sri Lanka when he was eleven. His sudden recalling of Edgar and Gloucester at a point in his own story makes one wonder whether it is better to have actually "loved and lost," however painfully, or "never to have loved at all," and like Ondaatje be left with only the "mercy of distance" as he calls it, to search for a lost father through the exhausting regeneration of art.

Because he left at the age of eleven and never knew his father afterwards he has succeeded now in creating one for himself; not only that, but he has invested the father with a dignity and proportion that are possible only in art. He does this in two ways. First, by revealing the father's unique setting in colonial Ceylon in which his destiny was inescapable, he shows the father carrying to extremes the same things that had been running in all the families of the times. The other is by what the author calls writing at the "mercy of distance" which is another way of saying "*outside* of time," a phrase Tennessee Williams used when he talked of Arthur Miller's character Willy Loman, a man who had lost his grip on the forces of life: "contemplation is something that exists *outside* of time, and so is the tragic sense." "Facing Willy Loman across an office desk . . . we would be very likely to glance at our wristwatch and other schedule of appointments" but, "suppose that the meeting with Willy Loman had occurred in a world *outside* of time, say in the theatre. Then I think we would receive him with concern and kindness and even respect . . . a dignity he would not otherwise have in real existence."

Michael Ondaatje had to visit Sri Lanka twice to seek the past in the present. The "foreigner" journeys along with his native sister Gillian to meet people and see places. He finds in the Wilpatta wildlife sanctuary that his piece of Pears Transparent Soap which kept him clean through all "the filthy hostels of Africa" is now missing. He makes no great effort to write his way out, to disguise his anger or "irritation" that the Sinhalese servants have stolen it, as they pay him back in his own fantastic coin saying that the *wal oora* (wild pig) has taken it. Did I find here a tinge of that familiar reaction, even among Westerners possessed of sensitivity, of fury when natives play them out? And in this case it's also ironic: he who writes such fantastic things is struck for the first time by the functional poetic imagination of the poor people of Sri Lanka, when their backs are against the wall. But Ondaatje recovers

318

superbly as he succumbs to the *fait accompli* and outdoes the Sinhalese imagination by extending it in his own — "What does this wild pig want my soap for? Visions began to form of the creature returning to his friends with Pears Transparent Soap" and all the *wal ooras* standing on all their hind legs, dancing in the rain, armpits exposed, and all foaming in lashings and lashings of froth from Pears Transparent Soap, "then moving in Pears fragrance to a dinner of Manikappolu garbage." There is only one other person I knew personally who could have told this same story, as if it were true, without batting an eyelid, and that was Arthur Van Langenberg, Ondaatje's uncle, who first introduced him to the theatre. Definitely it has been running in the family.

Ian Goonetileke shows him photographs of the last verses in Sinhala, and the last drawings, made in charcoal by the youth rebels of April '71 on the walls of Vidiyalankara University, where they were interned. He has come to know well the story of the tragic uprising and that the verses and drawings have now been "whitewashed" away. He ruminates that, as with the Sigiriya verses and frescoes, the artists are anonymous and that "the works seem as great as the Sigiriya frescoes. They too need to be eternal." As I read I had a vision of Sinhalese civilization as it drifted in decline from the original Anuradhapura and Polonnaruva, to the south west, pausing at Dambedeniya, then Sigiriya, then disappearing through Kotte into the long empires of the west and now its first faint reappearance since then, if only lyrically in the age of the superpowers. Romantic? But what else can one do? A good example, to me at least, of how Ondaatje just lightly "touches" something and the rest emerges in the reader.

2) Train:

7 TOES   7 TOES

The train hummed like a low bird over the rails,
Through
while the white desert and pale scrub. and outside.

Inside
Soft air spun and howled in the carriage.
She stood up, moved
moved to the doorless steps and sat,
placing herself as if stored grain
where the wind could beat at her knees.
When they stopped for water, she got off
and sat on the black wrist. thick stones (by the tracks /rails)
The train shuddered, and then wheeled slowly away from her.
She was too tired, even to call.
Tho, come back, she murmured to herself.

The train hummed like a low bird over the rails
through the desert and pale scrub.
Inside air spun [and howled] in the carriages.
She stood up, moved
to the doorless steps, and sat,
placing herself as if stored grain
where the wind could beat at her knees.
When they stopped for water, she got off
and sat by the rails on the wrist. thick stones.
The train shuddered, and then wheeled slowly away from her,
She was too tired, even to call.
Tho, come back, she murmured to herself.

Manuscript page from *the man with seven toes*

Sam Solecki
AN INTERVIEW WITH MICHAEL ONDAATJE (1984)

The second interview was taped at my house in Toronto, in the middle of June 1984. I assumed that it would be easier to do than the first one since I knew more about Ondaatje's work than I had in 1974. Ironically, either because he had grown more reticent or I was too aware of which questions not to ask (because I knew he wouldn't answer them), the interview seemed more difficult than its predecessor. After transcription, we exchanged copies and made additions and deletions.

One of the things I had intended to do before we met for this interview was to look at the one we did in Rune *ten years ago. I didn't get a chance to reread it and, looking back, I remember very little. . .*

Ya, I don't remember much either.

When I looked again at some of the other interviews you've done in White Pelican, Manna, Poetry Canada *and in a couple of books, the thing that was most obvious was that you're one of those people who can talk for pages and still leave me with the impression that ultimately you're very cagey, even evasive — refusing to say anything about certain areas of your life and work. I'm not suggesting that the ideal is Joan Collins telling us how Warren Beatty wouldn't leave her alone and kept dragging her off to bed five times a day, but there is an almost built-in evasiveness in your participation in any of the interviews I've read. And there are not only limits to what you will talk about but I think I sense that interviewers or even people writing articles about you for* Saturday Night *and* Books in Canada *back off from certain areas knowing that they'll never get more than a "yes" or "no" from you.*

Maybe.

Or a "maybe." Let me try to turn all this into a question: do you ever look back to the various media interviews you've done and think of subjects you would like to have had discussed?

Very few people want to talk about architecture.

Architecture? Frank Lloyd Wright and Mies van der Rohe and that sort of thing?

No, just in poems and novels. There has been a great change in what "structure" is in a poem or in a novel. Or "design." Or the "context" of a novel. Where the narrator stands or sits. For example, how do you talk about the architecture in Salman Rushdie's *Midnight's Children?* It is something remarkable.

In what way? In the interplay of fiction and history, or two eras, several languages both implied and present?

More in terms of repeating and building images and so making them more potent. Much of that book seems formless but something happens in the last hundred pages where Rushdie pulls it together — there's that image of people standing outside the train compartment knocking to get in and, at the end, the narrator himself is in that position. Now that's set up much earlier in the novel but we don't understand it at the point. When I'm reading an interview that's the kind of technical question that interests me: how does he get our confidence early on? How does he *persuade* us with the image? It comes down to nuts and bolts and tone. Ford Madox Ford has about five pages somewhere on how he and Conrad worked on the last paragraph of *Heart of Darkness.* Great stuff.

My impression is that it's easy to stick to technical or formal questions if you're writing an essay but it's almost impossible to deal with them in an interview. Imagine trying to discuss the architecture of Rushdie's Shame, *a novel dealing*

322

not just with a fable set in contemporary Pakistan but also with Rushdie himself. As soon as we mention him, even as a "fictional persona," we're already into a set of autobiographical concerns that someone like you tends to swerve away from in interviews. Although I suspect you tend to be interested in them while reading about other writers.

Think of all the times that magnets are mentioned in your work from Billy the Kid *to* Coming Through Slaughter *to* Running in the Family. *In the poem "Bearhug," for example, the embrace between father and son is both a "dark squeeze of death" and "like a magnet of blood," while the mad dogs held by your father in* Running *are "like dark magnets."*

But that's not structure or what I mean by architecture. That's accident.

"A man of genius makes no mistakes. His errors are volitional and are the portals of discovery." In other words, if I can paraphrase Stephen Dedalus's comment in Ulysses, *there are no accidents or coincidences once you have a body of work before you and apply formalist or psychoanalytical critical principles to it.*

When I wrote down the word magnet in the scene about my father the last thing on my mind was to write it or have it read as a mirror to ''Bearhug.''

But, as I said, it's already there in Billy the Kid *and* Slaughter. *So I could see a convincing argument being made about how "Bearhug" and* Running *are part of an intricate and often tacit pattern or undercurrent of meaning. And in this case the structural or architectural level or dimension leads us to more personal questions as well since the short poem and the fictional memoir both use the image when dealing with the problems of a father and son relationship. I guess I also see it as important because the image is there in both the more impersonal and purely fictional earlier work as well as in the later more subjective and autobiographical poetry and prose.*

But, again, that doesn't really seem to me to be the kind of architecture I'm talking about. You're talking about a thematic echo, a psychological echo; what I want is something more physical, something having to do with the placing of a scene in one place and not in another — that kind of thing. How one *composes* a book. How one turns the real everyday object into something more by placing it in exactly the right place, with the right tone. There is an architecture of tone as well as of rhythm. What academics are obsessed with is who won the horse race or what it really means. But if you watch a replay you start discovering form. You don't watch the horse in front anymore — the leading horse representing "content" — but it's the horse in fourth place saving himself. I think that writers think about and are interested in that kind of thing, the undercurrents of shape and tone as opposed to just the meaning. The way Rudy Wiebe says what really makes the Mad Hatter's tea party go is the door mouse!! Now that to me is wonderful and exact. More is said in that remark than in most critical articles.

Like Alice in Wonderland *your own longer works have resisted easy categorization. Nobody quite knows what to call* Billy the Kid *and I don't find it very helpful to have it described as a long poem or a poem in search of a stage, or a mixed-media collage. Similarly* Slaughter *is and isn't a novel just as* Running in the Family *is and isn't a memoir and/or travel book. I remember being at the reading you gave at* A Space *in Toronto to launch* Slaughter *and you introduced it as a "soup." That sounded like an even more desperate attempt at description than any offered by your critics.*

You know, I wanted to call my new book of poems, *Secular Love*, "a novel." I structured it like one. For me its structure and plot are novelistic. Each section deals with a specific time period but the people in them are interrelated. But, of course, they are drawn in a lyric, perceived by a lyric eye.

When you look back at Secular Love *or at any of your longer works can you recall how self-conscious or unconscious you were in making a book in a particular way, shaping it?*

With each of the longer works I was simply doing what I was able to do at the time. I could not have written *Running in the Family* before *Billy* or *Slaughter* although it would seem to come first logically. I was probably too close to *Running* emotionally and I had no idea how to write it or even that it was in me. For one thing, I was unable to be funny about the material; you're much more intense about these things when you're nineteen years old. If I had written that book then it

324

would probably have been a very one-dimensionally miserable book.

There's also another element: if you're writing a novel then you're writing *against* what you know the novel is. At that time the novel was still *Lucky Jim* because that's what we were reading when we were teenagers. Though we also read Salinger and he's quite different from anything at the time. *Franny and Zooey* is a lovely, oddly-weighted book structurally. Do you know *The Old Man and the Sea* came out after *The Catcher in the Rye*? How could it?

By the time I wrote *Slaughter* I guess I was also reacting against myself because I was determined not to put pictures or photographs in — even though the book had a photographer, Bellocq. I didn't want to go back. Although I guess you always do go back and write the same story. The least you can do is try to make it look like something else . . . . I think one tries to start each new book with a new vocabulary, a new set of clothes. Consciously or subconsciously we burn the previous devices which have got us here but which now are only rhetoric. Peter Handke has a great line about the novel's progression. He says "The progress of literature seems to me to consist of the gradual removal of unnecessary fictions. More and more vehicles fall by the wayside, the story becomes superfluous, what matters more is the communication of experiences, linguistic and non-linguistic ones, and for that it is no longer necessary to invent stories."

Whatever else may be involved in the "new set of clothes" in Running in the Family *there's also an emotional difference. There's a greater tenderness with more attention being paid to the emotions in the middle of the scale; there's less of the running to extremes that you have in* Billy *and* Slaughter.

Maybe in the next book some guy will open the door for somebody. I think it also has to do with the landscape. The props. I can't wait to write a book where I have people talking on the telephone. You don't know how frustrating it has been for me to have books set in the desert, the Australian outback, early New Orleans.

Let's switch from writing to editing, something you've been doing for Coach House Press for over a decade. Do you see any connections between what you do as writer and as editor?

Well, most writers exchange work with each other anyway. I reacted to Daphne Marlatt's *Zocalo* and *How Hug a Stone* and she's helped me often with my books.

But what about your actual work on manuscripts? For example, you've handled both of Sharon Thesen's books for Coach House, Artemis Hates Romance *and* Holding the Pose. *How did Coach House get* Artemis?

I read one of her poems in the magazine *N.M.F.G.* and wrote her asking if she had some other work. Later on she sent the poems.

What does your editing consist of once the manuscript is at the press?

Basically you handle the book through the press, watching out for all the usual pitfalls, making sure that it actually comes out. With *Artemis Hates Romance* we also wrote back and forth about the size of the book, individual poems — that kind of thing. *Artemis Hates Romance*, though, was already all there and powerful when I saw it.

What about the suggestions that others make to you about your own new work? Would it be right to assume that these are usually about small details, small changes?

No. I would say that the suggestions are usually quite major. God, no. When I finished the first drafts of *Billy* and *Slaughter* they were twice as long or a third as long. So there's the problem of tightening it, getting some reactions that are objective. I remember in *Running* Daphne Marlatt saw a chapter that was a retelling of a fairy tale and she thought it was awful — so that went. Then once you get it down to the right length you have to start thinking about the right order.

And *Running.* . . *Running* was impossible. I mean, there were lots of third person things that had to come into the first person. But there was no one real editor. In the end I took lots of advice and had to decide for myself. This is of course most difficult of all. The number of conflicting opinions can drive you crazy. One friend, for example, complained that this was another book using a gerund in the title! And all the while you're coming down to the wire.

Is that why you say in the end note that every work is a communal effort?

No, that refers more to the sources and to everybody I talked to, everyone who helped with collecting the story. But as far as the editing went, there was never just one person although we all need somebody who can say with absolute certainty, "Cut out chapters one to eight and you'll have a better book."

At the conference on the long poem, George Bowering was talking about the derivation of the word "order" as coming from "to begin." I don't know if that's true or not but it's interesting that in writing *Running* and *Slaughter* the two pieces I wrote to *order* the book were written last — but went in at the beginning. I'm always preoccupied over what should be left in and what should be left out. I love restructuring things. Then later there's a stage where you just want to make the book *look* as good as you can; and that's why I'm always interested in how a book is designed.

There's also the idea that a good poem or a good book is like a well-made machine — it has no superfluous parts. Victor Coleman would see a poem of twenty lines and be able to say, with all confidence, "Remove lines one to four, and twelve to nineteen, then you'll have something more subtle." I saw the editing he did on Stuart Mackinnon's *The Intervals.* He drew lines and made jumps all over the place but was still really true to the poem, to what was already there. I think Victor was really important to a lot of writers.

Let's shift from editing to reading, or at least to traces of your reading in your recent work. Probably like everyone else who has followed your career with any interest I was surprised by the emotional intensity of Tin Roof as well as the degree of self-revelation in the poem. But probably the most surprising moment for me came when you addressed Rainer Maria Rilke and referred to the Duino Elegies which, I guess, just don't strike me as the kind of poetry — meditative, metaphysical, abstract — that you would be interested in, moved or influenced by. Perhaps a better term would be what P.K. Page refers to somewhere as "nourishment." I think she was discussing her response to Rumi and Jami, two middle Eastern poets.

You know, I'd had Rilke's book for a long time but I hadn't really read it when I was working on *Tin Roof* — or at least I'd only read the first two or three elegies. So I don't think he was as important in any direct way as you imply. But he was very important for the poem. He was a presence.

But not as important as Yeats, Stevens and Auden were to your earlier work?

Everybody talks about Auden's influence on me but I've never read much of his work. As for writers I find nourishing right now, I probably wouldn't know who they are or won't know till later. I don't read as much as you think I do. But in the sixties Yeats *was* important to me; he was a poet I loved when I was at university; with Stevens I read maybe two or three poems a year but because I wrote those poems about him some feel that I was influenced: Stevens interests me as an artist, the way Louis Armstrong does.

The writers I admire are various and many. I suppose I would pick up and read anything by John Berger. Some part of my brain picks up every Modesty Blaise book. The Per Wahloo-Maj Sjowall series of ten books involving Martin Beck excited me so much that a friend and I wrote two sequels, each four pages long. I read most of the books by my peers because I like them and I like their work. We're all making mistakes or stumbling onto something good. I try not to miss any poems by John Newlove. A poem like "The Weather" by him is stunning, so difficult to do and yet it looks so simple.

I raised the question of influence; I guess I'm also trying to suggest ways of placing you, however tentatively, within a tradition or even a series of overlapping traditions within English poetry. In The New Oxford Book of Canadian Verse *Margaret Atwood has described you as a poet who "evades categorization," and one of the traditions or categories critics are going to have difficulty placing you in is the historical tradition of Canadian poetry. You probably don't spend sleepless nights over this but I wonder whether you have any thoughts about this particular version of "tradition and the individual talent?"*

For writers in Canada today, there's so much stuff being written around them that it's almost like being surrounded and locked up. There is that tendency for critics to try to nail writers down within a literary tradition. But really who cares? A true literary tradition has nothing to do with 1850 to 1980. It's not a line like that. And it's not

328

who are the "five most important poets writing today." It's not who are the postmodernists and who are the humanists and who are the documentary poets. The obsession in contemporary criticism of saying the obvious is appalling. We really need a Guy Davenport around us. Instead we get a lot of self-serving essays on all these forms. I think it's very dangerous for a writer to be living in a community obsessed with all these categories. Tradition defined in that narrow, often period sense has more to do with sociology than literature.

Speaking of speaking about literature, do you pay any attention to contemporary critical theory? Do you read Derrida, Barthes and other carriers of the Parisian disease? Or do you just read Kroetsch on them?

Not in any formal way. I rely mostly on rumours of them. I'm so easily persuaded by critical theories and political tracts *en masse* that I tend to avoid both and prefer to muck about in the real world — human nature, commas, that sort of thing. Some of Barthes' writing I like very much. I'm sure I'm influenced by them all in some way. Pollination of the age.

Having mentioned Robert Kroetsch I'm reminded that the issue of Descant *devoted to your work contains excerpts of your script of Kroetsch's* Badlands. *Why did you decide to do a script of that particular novel?*

I was reading *Badlands* because there was a guy called Web in it. Around page forty the group climbs up an embankment and comes smack up against a brass band. Because of the way Kroetsch wrote that scene — the exact sentencing — I saw that scene. I knew how to film it. So I read the rest of the book slowly, slowly, translating it to film in my mind as I went along and it all worked! To me that is one of the few pure movies in our literature. Writing the script didn't take long.

   Anyway that was the first script. I must be one of the few people in the world not to have tried writing a script of *Under the Volcano*. Since then, last year, I wrote a screen version of *Slaughter* for a film company, and I enjoyed doing it. It was long enough since I had written the book to be able to turn to it objectively, introduce new characters, "translate" it. I felt freer doing it as film than as theatre. What became interesting to think about was how to tone down the violence for the film. In one scene I have Bolden throw a goldfish out a second story window

— which is absurd when you write it down, but I worry that seeing it on film will alienate the audience from Bolden for the rest of the movie. One close-up of the gasping creature on the pavement and they wouldn't forgive Robert Redford or Anne Murray.

You haven't made a film since The Clinton Special *almost ten years ago. Are you working on something?*

Not really. I love film, the end product, or editing; but my main image of making movies is still carrying heavy cans of film through railroad stations. Writing is obviously more difficult and complex but at least you decide where to go, what to carry. Someone should work on this whole question of laziness. I hear that William Carlos Williams turned from art to writing because easels were cumbersome.

Nowadays, of course, you see all these writers tethered to their computers.

How do you respond to or deal with the whole question of the value of your work? Do you remember Eliot's comment that "No honest poet can ever quite feel sure of the permanent value of what he has written. He may have wasted his time and messed up his life for nothing." Do you ever wake up in the middle of a Bergman movie haunted by those possibilities?

It's a good quotation. And perfectly true. But I don't really worry about having wasted my life in writing. If everything we write turns out to be totally unfashionable or wrongheaded, the actual writing has still been a private satisfaction. I'm not sure what that satisfaction is but it has something to do with making something and putting it out there when you're finished — like a table or chair that's there and your role ends at that point. A book's like that, and that's why it's so important to me how a book looks — the quality of the paper, the way the words look on the page, the cover. I really feel that the writer is responsible for this as well as for the writing. I can't understand why Rudy Wiebe lets McClelland and Stewart produce such ugly books of his novels. There's pleasure for me in the physical beauty of a book.

But there's also Eliot's emphasis on messing up a life and not just producing an ugly book. Think of Robert Lowell's willingness to sacrifice Elizabeth Hard-

330

wick's feelings by using her private letters in The Dolphin. *Whatever his psychological condition at the time, I think it was in 1972-73, he must have known the pain those poems would cause his ex-wife and daughter. And the closer your own work comes to dealing with your own problems, especially in* Running *and* Tin Roof, *the more you risk messing up not only your own life but the lives of others — maybe not for "nothing," as Eliot puts it, but as a trade-off for poetry.*

Running was very difficult to write. For lots of reasons. One was the question of whether you were betraying somebody. But there was also the problem of writing about people you know really well and are close to but that the reader doesn't know at all — why would anyone be interested in the story of Mervyn Ondaatje, the story of my father? That's why I tested the book on other people — a lot more than I did any of my other books; that's also one of the reasons excerpts from it appeared in the *Capilano Review.* I also sent it to my brother and my sisters, to my aunts and uncles and cousins to see whether it was "right" or "wrong." One aunt in the States read the book and said, "Drinking, drinking, drinking; no one is making love."

Was anyone disturbed by it?

No. My brothers and sisters would have told me if they'd been annoyed by it. In that sense it was certainly a communal book and I was voicing the feelings we as a family felt. But, of course, the major characters weren't around to say anything and that's a real problem. I just had to say to myself that I thought I was writing the book with enough love, that if it was me it would be ok. And that in the end was the final test for me.

One of the book's reviewers remarked that for all your involvement in the story as narrator and actor you were the person about whom we learned the least. Granted that it's ultimately the story of Doris and Mervyn Ondaatje, you still keep a very low profile.

To tell the truth it would have been the easiest thing in the world to pour everything into *Running.* And I did but not in too obvious a way. It was a book about other people, another age. But I think the emo-

331

tional side of the narrator is clear, and it's essential to recognize it.

In retrospect, it now seems inevitable that your next book would be as personal as Tin Roof, *the long lyric sequence that places your own recent life dead centre. All critical and historical hindsight may be 20/20 but I can't help but see* Tin Roof *as bringing to a close the first phase of your writing career. And if I'm right this raises interesting questions about what's next, what direction your writing will take in the future.*

You mean I've painted myself into this corner and now I have to go out and find another room. But, you know, *Tin Roof* was being written during the same time I was working on *Running* so I remember the two works as being together. And also *Tin Roof* is part of another larger book called *Secular Love*. So I see its real place as being part of another house.

Sam Solecki
MICHAEL ONDAATJE:
A PAPER PROMISCUOUS AND OUT OF FORME
WITH SEVERAL INLARGEMENTS
AND UNTUTORED NARRATIVE

> And he went on talking about himself, not realising that this was not as interesting to the others as it was to him.   (Tolstoy, *The Cossacks*)

> "My life," said La Maga. "Even if I were drunk I wouldn't tell you about it."   (Cortazar, *Hopscotch*)

> Besides, when everybody has his portrait published, true distinction lies in not having yours published at all.   (Melville, *Pierre*)

> "You must get this book right," my brother tells me, "you can only write it once."   (Ondaatje, *Running in the Family*)

His brother was both right and wrong. Because Ondaatje doesn't repeat himself (the styles of the books have the same relationship to each other as a person's portraits taken at long intervals) there could only be one *Running in the Family*. On the other hand, the latest book nudges you into reading sections of the earlier work more autobiographically; it offers the reader the temptation of becoming "Webb" searching for the "real" Bolden. The lure of autobiography: to follow "these giant scratches / of pain" toward legends of fathers and sons (and absent mothers): Garrett and Billy (or, more accurately, Garrett-Billy), Livingstone, Hammett, Bolden as father and son yet fatherless himself except for his fathers in art, like Bellocq self-created.

Looking backwards, we can read everything in one of three ways: as a successful swerve away from *Running in the Family* (*the man with seven toes*); as a displaced, condensed, even sublimated tryout of parts of it (sections of *Billy the Kid* and *Coming Through Slaughter*); and as a hesi-

333

tant and always reluctant rehearsal of it ("Letters and Other Worlds," "Light").

Bolden's desire for silence, then, becomes not only a response to an intolerable creative situation in which "making and destroying" come "from the same source, same lust, same surgery his brain was capable of," (CTS, 55) but also an aspect of a refusal to "play" the self in public. We can read the desire for silences in another way as well. To write is to write about tragic fathers, and that expiatory writing is simultaneously celebration and betrayal.

Related to Proust's voluntary and involuntary memory is the equally necessary Nietzschean voluntary and involuntary forgetting which clears the psychological space for metaphor, for a text no longer simply about self and family (the decor, paraphernalia and hangers-on of bourgeois drama) but self and family forgotten, misremembered and recreated. *Running in the Family*, then, as a revelling in and revelation through forgetting — the imagined autobiography which should be read as a displaced novel, a dream without a latent content or (remember the "running") *Alice in Wonderland.*

> Great feelings take with them their own universe, splendid or abject. They light up with their passion an exclusive world in which they recognize their climate. (Camus, *The Myth of Sisyphus*)

He's among the handful of contemporary poets whom you can sense in almost any line of their work. In Canada, only Atwood has as strong a signature — an impress breathing in and through a line — colouring the work and establishing, constituting Camus' "climate." The climate of a world created book by book, never the same season, yet from *The Dainty Monsters* to *Running in the Family* always the same world.

What changes is the creation of the illusion that his "exclusive" world is becoming less "exclusive," that the later work will "shave" the beard in the photo (CTS, 133) and reveal a true "self-portrait." The illusion depends on one of the tricks he's learned to do; he uses valorized words like mother, father, sister, brother to distract the reader from noticing that for him, as for the best poets, "I" is a third-person pronoun, a word whose referents lie in the poem creating it for the occasion. Even *Billy the Kid* and *Coming Through Slaughter* distract the reader with the image of self as other, other as self.

You could almost read the entire body of his work as the reticent

334

swerve away from memory, from self.

Though it's hard to applaud suicide.   (*The Juicy Fruits*)

The swerve away from self-revelation or confession in the rest of his work gives the moments of his stepping into *Coming Through Slaughter* their particular force.

The thin sheaf of information. Why did my senses stop at you? There was the sentence, ' Buddy Bolden who became a legend when he went berserk in a parade. . . . ' What was there in that, before I knew your nation your colour your age that made me push my arm forward and spill it through the front of your mirror and clutch myself? Did not want to pose in your accent but think in your brain and body, and you like a weatherbird arcing round in the middle of your life to exact opposites and burning your brains out so that from June 5, 1907 till 1931 you were dropped into amber in the East Louisiana State Hospital.
(*CTS*, 134)

The desperate clutch through the mirror is a grab after Bolden, after self (after father) and, because Bolden is the artist as suicide, after the only forms of transcendence available in Ondaatje's completely secular and profane world. Ironically — and this is a source of a radical despair — Ondaatje and Bolden cannot think of art without a concomitant imagery of death: the artist as gunman, as spider, as taxidermist, as Audubon, as cage-maker, as necrophiliac, as insurance executive, as collector, as editor, as suicide.

In *Coming Through Slaughter* Ondaatje plays a slightly insincere Marlow to the more authentic Kurtz, the voyeur allowing the other to suffer while he lives and talks and writes off that pain. This is true unless we read him — before *Tin Roof* — as writing autobiographies in the third person.

Yet even in *Tin Roof* there's the reluctance to give anything away. Desolation, despair announced in the first lyric, are kept distant from the speaker, by the generalized "you" until the final lines.

You stand still for three days
for a piece of wisdom
and everything falls to the right place

335

or wrong place

You speak
don't know whether
seraphim or bitch
flutters at your heart

and look through windows
for cue cards
blazing in the sky.

The solution.
This last year I was sure
I was going to die.

Then, within a page, the sequence shifts away protectively into the third person. Even in a "personal" poem the reluctance to be personal. Having offered too much, the poem backs off, retreats into rhetorical feints of "one" and "you" and "we."

We go to the stark places of the earth
And find moral questions everywhere.

But this also seems to him too emotionally exposed as if the scar hasn't formed, the ink hasn't dried so he retracts it (or at least suspends it and prevents us from taking it solemnly) by illustrating the proposition with a half-serious example.

Will John Wayne and Montgomery Clift
take their cattle to Missouri or Kansas?

The answer holds the key to John Ford's *Red River* not to *Tin Roof.* (Besides, as Ed Dorn said looking over New York from the Empire State Building, "Someday this will all be cattle.")

Marx has ruined Nature / For the moment.
(Wallace Stevens, "Botanist on Alp")

And what are poets for in a destitute time?   (Heidegger / Hölderlin)

His answer to Heidegger's question is unHeideggerian: not to create a climate for the return of Being but like Stevens — another weatherman

336

and poet of jungle pastorals — to offer fictions, supreme fictions, which try and fail to redeem life.

He writes about poetics while wearing Stevens' suit (see the cover of Stevens' 1955 *Collected Poems*) but he explores climates and geographies (King Kong's part of the jungle) Stevens entered with reluctance. Compare the hands. Stevens' "weeping burgher" thinking that "in excess, continual / There is cure of sorrow" ends his reflections by noticing "My hands, such sharp imagined things." Ondaatje's "burgher" is Stevens whose "hands drain from his jacket, / pose in the murderer's shadow." The difference is between the surgeon hinted at and the murderer acknowledged. In other poems, Ondaatje takes the necessary next step and connects the two, and then makes this dialectical image synonymous with the artist.

Comparing Stevens and Ondaatje, however, notice also what we don't find in the latter: "Sunday Morning" and the negative annunciation still naming and recalling the renounced terms.

What is divinity if it can come
Only in silent shadows and in dreams?
Shall she not find in comforts of the sun,
In pungent fruit and bright, green wings, or else
In any balm or beauty of the earth,
Things to be cherished like the thought of heaven?

* * *

She hears, upon that water without sound,
A voice that cries, "The tomb in Palestine
Is not the porch of spirits lingering.
It is the grave of Jesus, where he lay."

Ondaatje is already on the other side of Stevens' renunciation. He begins where Stevens ends. The secular and profane are taken as the ground and essence of his vision. Where Stevens still feels the lure of metaphysics and spirit in his "mind," Ondaatje's physiological and material style stops us short with "brain." "Mind" both implies the presence of a psychology and hints at the possibility of soul. "Brain" asserts a radical materialism whose only depth is in metaphor.

Consider the old morphology of regret. / All sorrows can be borne if

337

you put them in a story or write a story about them.
(Wallace Stevens / Isak Dinesen)

(Consider an alternative: All sorrows can be born ...)

The ideal discourse for this story of sorrow would be *Running in the Family* written and sung in Sinhalese.

> I still believe the most beautiful alphabet was created by the Sinhalese. The insect of ink curves into a shape that is almost sickle, spoon, eyelid. The letters are washed blunt glass which betrays no jaggedness ... Moon coconut. The bones of a lover's spine.

In the *Kabbalah* this is the alphabet of the language spoken in the Garden of Eden, under the Tree of Life, when words and things were one. A language of pure presence. In *Running in the Family* it is the forgotten language, betrayed body, original garden. From another point of view, the references to and in it remind us of the book Ondaatje *cannot* write, in which the writing would be as concrete as "clothes hung out to dry on a line" and as evanescent as "musical notation" (*One Hundred Years of Solitude*, 189). Finally, it would be a writing, like Aureliano Segundo's manuscript, in which the stories were without endings.

Ondaatje's reluctance to begin or to offer *a* beginning anticipates his reluctance or hesitation to end: in both cases the result is the same — each of the longer works begins and ends more than once. The books don't so much end as dissolve suggestively back into the author (see the photo and the ambiguous "I" of *Billy the Kid*, the "I" in *Coming Through Slaughter*, the "Last Morning" in *Running in the Family*) and into their successors.

> It's nothing but a rat, a dead rat. Paris is full of rats. There are more rats than people. Yum. Yum. I — I'll save the asshole for you. Rat's asshole with mayonnaise.   (*Last Tango in Paris*)

> We have been given a bath in shit with no reward.   (Norman Mailer)

> If only people were free enough to let everything in, something extraordinary might come of it.   (Francis Bacon)

Crawley's "tail of shit" announces the "tale of shit" (*CTS*, 30) which

338

lets everything in. Crawley points back to Paul/Brando with his shit-covered shoes in a film determined to offer the "bath in shit" as its own "reward" ("There are no prizes," *CTS*, 156). The "shit" and the "rat" are the residue of the bad taste in "Rat Jelly," the title poem (and one of Ondaatje's weakest) in Ondaatje's best single collection. Why didn't he call the book *Spider Blues* or *White Dwarfs* or *Letters and Other Worlds*? Because. The present title is his constant reminder that the "jelly" (read "poem") begins (sometimes? always?) with everything represented by and associated with the rat ("I must write down where all the ladders start / In the foul rat-and-bone show of the fart"?).

The rat is what is lost in a "rational" poem too "scented with pronunciation" ("A bad taste"), when art forgets its anagrammatic connection with rat. Thomas Pynchon's macabre version ("The Dance of the Macabre Mice?") of this is V or Veronica the rat nun of the New York sewers whose "pronunciation" is Christianity (*V*, 105–8). (While looking for Veronica, pause and think about Teledu and his two weeks in a fridge where he lived on "raw eggs and frozen hamburger" (*V*, 350).) Ondaatje's sublimated or pastoral version of the rat is the gull in "the gate in his head," the

    beautiful formed thing caught at the wrong moment
    ...shapeless, awkward
    moving to the clear.

A lesser poem, "A bad taste," reminds us that missing here is the

    ...dirt thought we want as guest
    travelling mad within the poem
    eating up punctuation, who farts
    heat into the line.

Neither *Billy the Kid* nor *Coming Through Slaughter* is "a morality tale" (*CTS*, 5) because the "rat" is given voice but left unjudged. In a very precise sense, this is an art beyond good and evil: the poems and longer texts contain almost no moral judgements and therefore cannot be tragic. Morality, like genre, pattern and order, is something the reader brings into the work. All that Ondaatje promises are the visions within "a jungle sleep" (*Billy the Kid*, 97) and the occasional "midnight rat"

(Running in the Family, 189) within these.

> The daguerreotypes of Morell usually published in American magazines
> are not authentic. This lack of genuine representations of so memorable
> and famous a man cannot be accidental. We may suppose that Morell
> resisted the camera, essentially, so as not to leave behind pointless clues,
> and, at the same time, to foster the mystery that surrounded him.
>
> (Borges, *A Universal History of Infamy*)

Another of his "tricks" is to let the reader supply the details, fill in the background, even, on occasion, choose the ending. A favourite trope, the image looking in at least two directions.

Still another is the verse paragraph beginning with a verb and an indeterminate subject — persona, poet, reader?

The paint-by-numbers poem and the empty or uncaptioned photograph. In *Billy the Kid* these simultaneously reveal and conceal the written text. The reader supplies captions and connections just as he/she fills in Billy's blank/absent opening portrait — the "white dwarf" out of which arise and on which depend text and negative. Both attempt to avoid having any referents beyond the fiction of the book; both invite a reading of spare, reticent surfaces. The "greater detail" has to come from the thoroughly modern and Barthian "blissful" reader puzzled and pleased by the alternating ellipses and lush proliferations of metaphor. All the longer works are indeterminate texts resisting consumption and appropriation, resisting/revealing the author in the text.

A typical, if small, gesture always ends the book: the author's note — another "signature" — telling us what kind of book we have *not* read.

> With these basic sources I have edited, rephrased, and slightly reworked
> the originals. But the emotions belong to their authors. *(Billy the Kid)*

> While I have used real names and characters and historical situations I
> have also used more personal pieces of friends and fathers. There have
> been some date changes, some characters brought together, and some
> facts have been expanded or polished to suit the truth of fiction.
>
> *(Coming Through Slaughter)*

> While all these names may give an air of authenticity, I must confess that
> the book is not a history but a portrait or "gesture." And if those listed

above disapprove of the fictional air I apologize and can only say that in
Sri Lanka a well-told lie is worth a thousand facts.

(Running in the Family)

This is generic ambiguity as literary striptease.

Two generations from now all postmodernist fiction / writing will
be read as autobiography.

> Dancing I like. I'm a pretty good dancer. Fond of music too. There's a
> Canadian group, a sort of orchestra, that is the best. Great. Heard them
> often when I was up there trying to get hold of a man who went by the
> name of Captain P———. Never found him. But that group will be
> remembered a long time.   (Ondaatje, *Billy the Kid*)

This is the book's Canada Council moment. Referring to the Guy
Lombardo of sound poetry, Ondaatje bows in the direction of Canadian
content, reassuring those like John Diefenbaker who doubted his
suitability for Canlit courses. He repeats the gesture of a national
signature in *Coming Through Slaughter* with "Miss Jessie Orloff's
famous incident in a Canadian hotel during her last vacation" (*CTS*,
12).

But there's an important difference between the two references. The
first is part of a network of *hommages* in his writing, a settling of artistic
debts. (Compare Bertolucci's use of Godard's Paris address in *The Con-
formist.*) In *Billy the Kid* as in the Stevens poems this is almost explicit
and formal (see also " 'The gate in his head' " — for Victor Coleman —
and "Henri Rousseau and Friends"). Other stepfathers appear more
inconspicuously. Sergio Leone, for example, hides behind the flies
caught

> ...with my left hand
> bringing the fist to my ear
> hearing the scream grey buzz
> as their legs cramp their
> heads with no air
> so eyes split and release   (*BK*, 58)

Which is not to say that *Billy the Kid* is a spaghetti western — just that
Billy learned the fly-catching trick from Jack Elam in *Once Upon a Time
in the West*. Perhaps Leone was also important in suggesting (and showing) that the western was not a fixed genre or form and that it could be

341

done as differently as *Red River* and *Once Upon a Time* (and *Billy the Kid*).

More pervasive is the early debt to Leonard Cohen which is often as much a matter of attitudes as of images. Ondaatje's short book on Cohen is his only extended piece of critical writing and, ultimately, clarifies his own work as much as it does Cohen's.

> Children show scars like medals. Lovers use them as secrets to reveal. A scar is what happens when the world is made flesh.
>
> A loon went insane in the middle of the lake.
>
> Breavman loves the pictures of Henri Rousseau, the way he stops time.
>
> Breavman gasped at the brightness of the liquid metal. It was the colour gold should be. It was as beautiful as flesh. It was the colour of gold he thought of when he read the word in prayers or poems. It was yellow, alive and screaming. It poured out in an arch with smoke and white sparks.
>
> A rat is more alive than a turtle.   (Cohen, *The Favourite Game*)

Now think of Cohen's hero Breavman as the author of "The Time Around Scars," "Heron Rex," "Henri Rousseau and Friends," "'The gate in his head'" and "Rat Jelly."

Affinity not influence. For influence see the poems in *The Dainty Monsters* which arrive cluttered with tricks borrowed from Yeats.

For affinity, think of Louis Malle reading *Billy the Kid* and deciding to end *Pretty Baby* with a slightly blurred photograph, or Marquez and Ondaatje as fans of Danilo Kis and Joe Cocker (*Mad Dogs and Englishmen*) who also followed the career of Spider Webb, a great American middleweight who couldn't take a punch.

> "It wasn't fever," he lied. "It was the dream about the spider webs again."
> "Almost always I dream that I'm getting tangled up in spider webs."
> (Marquez, *No One Writes to the Colonel*)

If Malle borrows a trick from *Billy the Kid* (as Dante does from Eliot, translating "I had not thought death had undone so many" into "ch'i' non averei creduto / che morta tanta n'avesse disfata"), Marquez borrows the book's mad dogs, which he then returns to Ondaatje in time for *Running in the Family*.

"Help me," she shouted to me. "What they want is to eat his guts."
We locked them up in the stable. Placida Linero later ordered them
taken to some place far off until after the funeral. But toward noon, no
one knew how, they escaped from where they were and burst madly into
the house. Placida Linero, just once lost her grip.
"Those shitty dogs!" she shouted. "Kill them!"
The order was carried out immediately and the house was silent again.
Until then there hadn't been any concern at all for the state of the body.
The face had remained intact, with the same expression it had when he
was singing, and Cristo Bedoya had put the intestines back in place and
wrapped the body with a linen strip.   (*Chronicle of a Death Foretold*)

When a pack of rabid dogs heads in your direction... you should hit the
ground suddenly, face the dangerous, blood-thirsty enemy on all fours,
look him in the eye, even bark at him. If a person is wearing a soft hat or
derby, he should remove it and place it in front of him. This method,
young fellow, has been tested in practice, *in my very own experience*. It is
infallible, extremely efficient.   (Kis, *Garden, Ashes*)

In 1927 he spent a few weeks in a mental home. Then, as his condition
seemed to have improved, he was handed over into the care of his sisters,
who were living in a small village on Lake Balaton. One evening in
November, he ambled down to the railway station where a goods train
was standing, bound for Budapest. As he was approaching the station,
the train slowly began to move. He broke into a run, squeezed through
under the lowered barrier, knelt down at the track, and, as the train was
gathering speed, laid his right arm in between the carriages on the rail.
The arm was later found cleanly severed and thrown at some distance
from the mangled body.
A few days after Attila's death, his family found in his drawer a shirt
from which the right sleeve had been cut off with scissors.
                    (Koestler, *The Invisible Writing*)

Bolden's hand going up into the air
in agony.
His brain driving it up into the
path of the circling fan.

This last movement happens forever and ever in his memory
                                        (*CTS*, 136)

343

Judith Brady
A BIBLIOGRAPHY

Part 1

Works by Michael Ondaatje

A   Books (Poetry, A1-A10; Prose, A11-A12; Criticism, A13; and Books Edited, A14-A16); Broadsides (A17-A19); Films (A20-A22); Dramatic Productions (A23-A25); Editorial Work (A26-A27)

B   Contributions to Periodicals and Books (Articles, B1-B6; and Reviews, B7-B9); and Audio-Visual Material (B10-B32)

Part II

Works on Michael Ondaatje

C   Articles and Sections of Books (C1-C57); Thesis (C58); Interviews (C59-C65); Books (C66).

Part I

Works by Michael Ondaatje

A   Books (Poetry, Prose, Criticism, and Books Edited),

344

Broadsides, Films, Dramatic Productions, Editorial Work.

Poetry

A1   *The Dainty Monsters.* Toronto: Coach House, 1967. 77 pp.

A2   *Aardvark (for the memory of Emma Peel).* Five cent mimeo, No 20.
      Toronto: Ganglia, [1969?]. 4 pp.

A3   *the man with seven toes.* Toronto: Coach House, 1969. 41 pp.

A4   *The Collected Works of Billy the Kid: Left Handed Poems.* New
      York: Norton, 1970. 105 pp.
      ———. Toronto: House of Anansi, 1970. 105 pp.
      ———. New York: Berkeley, 1975. 105 pp.
      ———. Redtail Reprint Series. Berkeley, Cal.: Wingbow,
      1978. 105 pp.
      ———. London, Marion Boyars, 1981. 105 pp.

A5   *Rat Jelly.* Toronto: Coach House, 1973. 71 pp.

A6   *Elimination Dance.* Coldstream. Ilderton, Ont.: Nairn, 1978.
      [16] pp.

A7   *Claude Glass.* Toronto: Coach House, 1979. 5 pp.

A8   *There's a Trick with a Knife I'm Learning to Do: Poems 1963-1978.*
      New York: Norton, 1979. 107 pp.
      ———. Toronto: McClelland and Stewart, 1979. 107 pp.
      Rat Jelly and Other Poems: 1963-78. London: Marion Boyars,
      1980. 107 pp.

A9   *Tin Roof.* Island Writing Series. Lantzville, B.C.: Island, 1982.
      [22] pp.

A10   *Secular Love.* Toronto: Coach House, 1985. 126 pp.

Fiction

A11   *Coming Through Slaughter.* Anansi Fiction Series, No. 36.
      Toronto: House of Anansi, 1976. 156 pp.
      ———. New York: Avon, 1976. 156 pp.

————. New York: Norton, 1976. 148 pp.

————. London: M. Boyars, 1979. 156 pp.

————. New Press Canadian Classics. Toronto: General, 1982. 158 pp.

A12 *Running in the Family.* New York: Norton, 1982. 186 pp.

————. Toronto: McClelland and Stewart, 1982. 244 pp.

Criticism

A13 *Leonard Cohen.* Canadian Writers, No. 5. Toronto: McClelland and Stewart, 1970. 64 pp.

Books Edited

A14 *The Broken Ark: A Book of Beasts.* Illust. Tony Urquhart. Ottawa: Oberon, 1971. 46 pp.

A15 *Personal Fictions: Stories by Munro, Wiebe, Thomas & Blaise.* Toronto: Oxford Univ. Press, 1977. 231 pp.

A16 *The Long Poem Anthology.* Toronto: Coach House, 1979. 343 pp.

Broadsides

A17 *In a Bangalore Stream.* Quarryposters, No. 5. Kingston, Ont.: Quarry [1968?]

A18 *Philoctetes, on the Island.* Unicorn Folio, 3rd ser., No. 1. [A Canadian Folio.[Ed. Alan Brillant. Santa Barbara, Cal.: Unicorn, 1969. [1 leaf.]

A19 *To a Sad Daughter: For Quintin.* Toronto: Coach House, [1980?]

Films

A20 *Sons of Captain Poetry.* Cameraman Robert Fresco. Mongrel Films / Canadian Film-Makers Distribution Centre, 1970. (16mm.; colour; 35 min.)

A21 *Carry on Crime and Punishment.* Mongrel Films, 1972. (16 mm.; 5 min.)

A22   *The Clinton Special.* Cameramen Bob Carney and Robert Fresco. Mongrel Films/Canadian Film-makers Distribution Centre, 1972. (16 mm.; 71 min.; colour.)

Dramatic Productions

A23   *the man with seven toes.* Dir. Ken Livingstone. Prod. The Gallimaufry Repertory Theatre Company. The Vancouver Festival, B.C. 1968.
———. Dir. Paul Thompson. Stratford Workshop. Stratford, Ont. 1969.

A24   *The Collected Works of Billy the Kid.* Dir. John Douglas and Martin Kinch. St. Lawrence Centre, Toronto. 23 April 1971.
    The cast includes Ray Frady, Tedde Moore, Ashleigh Moorehouse, Anthony Palmer, and Mel Tuck.
———. Prod. Young People's Theatre, [Toronto schools]. Nov.–Dec. 1971.
———. Dir. John Wood. Prod. Neptune Theatre. Music Alan Laing. Neptune Theatre, Halifax. 21 Nov.—2 Dec. 1972.
    The cast includes Ivar Brogger, Patricia Collins, and Neil Munro.
———. Dir. John Wood. Music Alan Laing. Third Stage, Stratford, Ont. 10 April 1973–?
    The cast is Nancy Beatty, Cherry Davis, Michael Donaghue, Ted Follows, Art Hindle, P.M. Howard, Marilyn Lightstone, and Neil Munro.
———. Dir. John Dennis. Old Fox Film Studio, Los Angeles. [3-9?] Nov. 1973.
———. Dir. Martin Kinch. Toronto Free Theatre, Toronto 22-29 Oct. 1974, 30 Oct.–5 Dec. 1974.
    The cast includes Arnie Achtman, David Bolt, Chapelle Jaffe, Nick Mancuso, Wendy Thatcher, R.H. Thomson, and William Webster.
———. Theatre London, London, Ont. 14 March–5 April 1975.
———. Frontenac Playhouse, Quebec. 29 July–30 Aug. 1975.
———. Dir. John Wood. Prod. Neptune Theatre. Music Alan Laing. Brooklyn Academy of Music, New York. 13-25 Oct.

1975.
The cast includes Ivar Brogger, P.M. Howard, and others.
———. Dir. John Wood. Walnut Street Theatre, Philadelphia.
[14-22?] Nov. 1975.
The cast includes Ivar Brogger, P.M. Howard, and others.
———. Manitoba Theatre Centre, Warehouse Theatre, Winnipeg, Man. 25 Nov.–13 Dec. 1975.
———. Dir. John Wood. Prod. Neptune Theatre. Music Alan Laing. National Arts Centre, Ottawa. 5-24 Jan. 1976.
The cast includes Ivar Brogger, P.M. Howard, and others.
———. Dir. Gordon McCall. Prod. Simon Fraser Group Theatre. Simon Fraser Univ., Burnaby, B.C. 9-12 March 1977.
The cast includes John Carroll, Jack Crowston, Rochelle Dubetz, Gary Harris, Richard Newman, Rob Tranquilli, and Lynn Woodman.
———. Theatre Three, Edmonton, Alta. 19-30 July 1977.
———. Prod. Dream Spectrum Young Company. Studio Theatre. 4-15 July 1978.
———. Saidye Bronfman Centre, Montreal. March 1982.

A25 *Coming Through Slaughter.* Dir. Paul Thompson, Theatre Passe Muraille. Toronto. 5-27 Jan. 1980.
The cast is Philip Akin, Ardon Bess, Bibi Caspari, Layne Coleman, Bob Dermer, Patricia Idlette, Diana Knight, Robert O'Ree, and Sandi Ross.

Editorial Work

A26 Editor. *Quarry*, 15, No. 1 (Sept. 1965)-16, No. 3 (March.1967).

A27 Editor. Coach House Press, 1977-

B Contributions to Periodicals and Books (Articles and Reviews) and Audio-Visual Material.

Articles

B1 "Roy Kiyooka (Poet and Painter)." *artscanada*, Oct.–Nov. 1968, 45.

B2   "Little Magazine / Small Presses, 1969." *artscanada*, Aug. 1969, 17-18.

B3   "Michael Ondaatje: Peter." In *How Do I Love Thee: Sixty Poets of Canada (and Quebec) Select and Introduce Their Favourite Poems from Their Own Work.* Ed. and preface John Robert Colombo. Edmonton: Hurtig, 1970, p. 149.

B4   "O'Hagan's Rough-Edged Chronicle. *Canadian Literature*, No. 61 (Summer 1974), 24-31.

B5   "Garcia Marquez and the Bus to Aracataca." In *Figures in a Ground: Canadian Essays on Modern Literature Collected in Honour of Sheila Watson.* Ed. Diane Bessai and David Jackel. Saskatoon: Western Producer Prairie, 1978, pp. [19]-31.

B6   "Pillar of Another World." *Toronto Life*, Jan. 1982, 78-79.

Reviews

B7   Rev. of *A Controversy of Poets*, Ed. Paris Leary and Robert Kelly. *Quarry*, 15, No. 2 (Nov. 1965), 44-45.

B8   Rev. of *The Projector*, by M. Vaughan-James. *Open Letter*, Ser. 2, No. 2 (Summer 1972), 85.

B9   Rev. of *A Childhood: The Biography of a Place*, by Harry Crews. *biography*, 3, No. 1 (Winter 1980), 84-86.

Audio-Visual Material

B10   "Elizabeth." Narr. Michael Ondaatje. In "Poets Here, Now and Then." Hostess Phyllis Webb. *Modern Canadian Poetry.* Prod. John Kennedy and Terri Thompson. CBC Television Extension, 23 July 1967.

B11   "A Love Poem." Narr. Michael Ondaatje. In "Poets Here, Now and Then." Hostess Phyllis Webb. *Modern Canadian Poetry.* Prod. John Kennedy and Terri Thompson, CBC Television Extension. 23 July 1967.

B12   " 'Description is a Bird'." Narr. Michael Ondaatje. *Anthology.*

Prod. Terrance Gibbs. Ed. Robert Weaver. CBC Radio, 20 Aug. 1968.

B13 "Dragon." Narr. Michael Ondaatje. *Anthology.* Prod. Terrance Gibbs. Ed. Robert Weaver. CBC Radio, 20 Aug. 1968.

B14 "Henri Rousseau and Friends." Narr. Michael Ondaatje. *Anthology.* Prod. Terrance Gibbs. Ed. Robert Weaver. CBC Radio, 20 Aug. 1968.

B15 "Over the Garden Wall." Narr. Michael Ondaatje. *Anthology.* Prod. Terrance Gibbs. Ed. Robert Weaver. CBC Radio, 20 Aug. 1968.

B16 "Signature." Narr. Michael Ondaatje. *Anthology.* Prod. Terrance Gibbs. Ed. Robert Weaver. CBC Radio, 20 Aug. 1968.

B17 *The Collected Works of Billy the Kid.* Prod. John Reeves. *CBC Stage.* CBC Radio, 5 June 1971.

B18 *The Collected Works of Billy the Kid. CBC Tuesday Night.* Prod. and dir. John Reeves. CBC Radio, 29 Aug. 1972.

B19 *The Collected Works of Billy the Kid. Encore.* Part II. CBC-FM Radio, 7 Sept. 1972.

B20 "Dates." *Anthology.* Prod. Alex Smith. Ed. Robert Weaver. CBC Radio, 28 July 1973.

B21 "Letter to Ann Landers." *Anthology.* Prod. Alex Smith. Ed. Robert Weaver. CBC Radio, 28 July 1973.

B22 "Letters & Other Worlds." *Anthology.* Prod. Alex Smith. Ed. Robert Weaver. CBC Radio, 28 July 1973.

B23 "Philoctetes on the island." *Anthology.* Prod. Alex Smith. Ed. Robert Weaver. CBC Radio, 28 July 1973.

B24 "White Dwarfs." *Anthology.* Prod. Alex Smith. Ed. Robert Weaver. CBC Radio, 28 July 1973.

B25 "A bad taste: For Bob." *Anthology.* Prod. Alex Smith. Ed.

Robert Weaver. CBC Radio, 4 Aug. 1973.

B26 "Burning Hills: For Chris and Fred." *Anthology*. Prod. Alex Smith. Ed. Robert Weaver. CBC Radio, 4 Aug. 1973.

B27 "Rat Poems." *Anthology*. Prod. Alex Smith. Ed. Robert Weaver. CBC Radio, 4 Aug. 1973.

B28 "Letters & Other Worlds." In "Poetry and the Microphone." *Anthology: International Festival of Poetry, Oct. 26–Nov. 1, Hart House*. Host Kildare Dobbs. Prod. Patrick Hynan. Ed. Robert Weaver. CBC Radio, 15 Nov. 1975.

B29 *Coming Through Slaughter. Once More from the Top*. CBC Radio, 3 May 1979.

B30 *Anthology*. Prod. Howard Engel. CBC Radio, [Summer 1979?].

B31 "Sweet Like a Crow." In *Poetry in Motion*. Prod. Ron Mann. Sphinx, 1982.

B32 "The Passions of Lalla." *Anthology*. Exec. prod. Howard Engel. CBC Radio, 6 Nov. 1982.

Part II

Works on Michael Ondaatje

C   Articles and Sections of Books, Thesis, Interviews.

Articles and Sections of Books

C1   Story, Norah, "Poetry in English." In her *The Oxford Companion to Canadian History and Literature*. Toronto: Oxford Univ. Press, 1967, p. 651.

C2   Dudek, Louis. "Poetry in English." *Canadian Literature*, No. 41 (Summer 1969), 117, 119.

C3   Geddes, Gary, and Phyllis Bruce. "Michael Ondaatje." In *15*

Canadian Poets. Ed. and preface Gary Geddes and Phyllis Bruce. Toronto: Oxford Univ. Press, 1970, pp. 287-89. Rpt. in *15 Canadian Poets Plus 5.* Ed. and preface Gary Geddes and Phyllis Bruce. Toronto: Oxford Univ. Press, 1978, pp. 402-03.

C4   Gustafson, Ralph. "Ondaatje, (Philip) Michael." In *Contemporary Poets of the English Language.* Ed. Rosalie Murphy. New York: St. Martin's, 1970, pp. 820-22.
      In addition to biographical data, Gustafson notes that Ondaatje's poetics indicate "a choice counter to the standard derivation" of that which is based on William Carlos Williams and the Black Mountain school.

C5   Rodriguez, Elizabeth. "A Report on the Poets at Festival 70 (Bishop's University)." *The Fiddlehead*, No. 84. (March–April 1970), 124-25.

C6   Barbour, Douglas. "The Young Poets and the Little Presses." *Dalhousie Review*, 50 (Spring 1970), 124.
      The Dainty Monsters "remains one of the finest books of the past decade."

C7   Sharp, Daryl L. *Commentator*, 15 (March 1971), 13-14.
      Sharp admires Ondaatje's "immense creative talent," finding there is nothing to match [*Billy the Kid*] in terms of conception and sheer writing skill, since Leonard Cohen's *Beautiful Losers.*

C8   Atwood, Margaret. *Survival: A Thematic Guide to Canadian Literature.* Toronto: House of Anansi, 1972, pp. 76, 84.

C9   Scobie, Stephen. "Two Authors in Search of a Character." *Canadian Literature*, No. 54 (Autumn 1972), 37-55.

C10   Watson, Sheila. "Michael Ondaatje: The Mechanization of Death." *White Pelican*, 2, No. 4 (Fall 1972), 56-64. Rpt. in *Open Letter*, Ser. 3, No. 1 (Winter 1974-75), 158-66.

C11   G[eddes]., G[ary]. "Ondaatje, Michael (1943–   )." In *Supplement to The Oxford Companion to Canadian History and Literature.* Ed. William Toye. Toronto: Oxford Univ. Press, 1973, pp. 238-39.

C12 Gnarowski, Michael. "Ondaatje, Michael, 1943– ." In his *A Concise Bibliography of English Canadian Literature.* Toronto: McClelland and Stewart, 1973, pp. 89-90. Rev. ed., 1978, p. 105.
Bibliographical data.

C13 Waterston, Elizabeth. *Survey: A Short History of Canadian Literature.* Methuen Canadian Literature Series. Toronto: Methuen, 1973, pp. 88, 139.

C14 Atwood, Margaret. "Mathews and Misrepresentation." *This Magazine*, 7, No. 1 (May–June 1973), 30. Rpt. in *Second Words: Selected Critical Prose.* By Margaret Atwood. Toronto: House of Anansi, 1982, p. 142.
Atwood argues that the poetry of Ondaatje and others was omitted from her *Survival: A Thematic Guide to Canadian Literature* because "It seems to me dangerous to talk about 'Canadian' patterns of sensibility in the work of people who entered and/or entered-and-left the country at a developmentally late stage of their lives." See C8.

C15 Barbour, Douglas. "Three West Coast Poets and One from the East." *The Lakehead University Review* (Fall–Winter 1973), 240-45.
Barbour finds *Rat Jelly* "an incredibly rich book of poetry," citing in particular, "Billboards," "Burning Hills," "Letters & Other Worlds," "We're at the graveyard," and "White Dwarfs."

C16 Davey, Frank. "Michael Ondaatje (1943–)." In his *From There to Here: A Guide to English Canadian Literature since 1960.* Vol. II of *Our Nature — Our Voices.* Erin, Ont.: Porcepic, 1974, pp. 222-27.
"Ondaatje has a thoroughly disconcerting talent for presenting the ordinary in an extraordinary way." He is "a deliberate craftsman, firmly controlling the pace of his lyric poems, and totally manipulating the structure and characterization of his longer narratives." His poems "reverberate with exotic violence," contain "a strong photographic element," and employ an "openly subjective and symbolic treatment of history

and document." In his long narrative poems, Ondaatje attempts "radical experiments in writing technique . . . . The narrative voice switches without overt signal . . . . In his own defence Ondaatje manipulates and watches, not only surviving, but creating a superbly tense, multicolour, explosive, macabre work . . . ."

C17 "Ondaatje, Michael 1943–   ." In *Contemporary Authors: A Bio-Bibliographical Guide to Current Writers in Fiction, General Nonfiction, Poetry, Journalism, Drama, Motion Pictures, Television, and Other Fields.* Ed. Frances Carol Locher. Vols. LXXVII-LXXX. Detroit: Gale, 1974, p. 406.

C18 David, Jack. "Michael Ondaatje's *The Collected Works of Billy the Kid." Canadian Notes & Queries,* No. 13 (June 1974), 11-12.
    David suggests that *The Collected Works of Billy the Kid: Left Handed Poems* was influenced by the American poet Jack Spicer's poem, "Billy the Kid," which Ondaatje had favourably reviewed in *Quarry.*

C19 Kertzer, J.M. "On Death and Dying: *The Collected Works of Billy the Kid." English Studies in Canada,* 1 (Spring 1975), 86-96.
    Kertzer provides a detailed analysis of the text to substantiate the argument that the work is "based not on logic, but on insistence, on a continual repetition with variation of the facts and details and circumstances of death" using "imagery drawn from the Wild West, where life was stripped to primitive conditions."

C20 Bowering, George. "Modernism Could not Last Forever." *Canadian Fiction Magazine,* Nos. 32-33 (1979-80), 5, 8. Rpt. in *The Mask in Place: Essays on Fiction in North America.* By George Bowering. Winnipeg: Turnstone, 1982, pp. 78, 81-82.
    In a general discussion of the Canadian critical unwillingness to accept Post-Realism, Bowering notes that "There are [however] signs" that Ondaatje and others are being viewed "as something other than oddities." Ondaatje's "portraits of Buddy Bolden & Billy Bonney resemble his photo portraits of Canadian writers."

C21   Lee, Dennis. *Savage Fields: An Essay in Literature and Cosmology.*
      Toronto: House of Anansi, 1977, pp. 4, 15-60, 115-22.

C22   Solecki, Sam. "Nets and Chaos: The Poetry of Michael
      Ondaatje." *Studies in Canadian Literature*, 2 (Winter 1977),
      36-48. Rpt. in *Brave New Wave.* Ed. Jack David. Windsor,
      Ont.: Black Moss, 1978, pp. 24-50.

C23   Bowering, George. "The Painted Window: Notes on Post-
      Realist Fiction." *The University of Windsor Review*, 13, No. 2
      (Spring–Summer 1978), 28. Rpt. in *The Mask in Place: Essays on
      Fiction in North America.* By George Bowering. Winnipeg: Turn-
      stone, 1982, p. 118.
          Ondaatje's *Coming Through Slaughter* is given as an example of
      Post-Realism's concentration on "linguistic activity," which
      allows "you to feel as if you have attended the action...,"
      rather than on removed character portraits.

C24   Blott, Anne. "Stories to Finish: *The Collected Works of Billy the
      Kid.*" *Studies in Canadian Literature*, 2 (Summer 1977), 188-202.
          In an analysis of language, rhythm, and structure, Blott illus-
      trates that "the richness of Ondaatje's vision" is a "montage of
      techniques designed to catch and to record the process of
      recollection" and the "disintegration of living things."

C25   Whitten, Mark. "Billy, Buddy, and Michael: The Collected
      Writings of Michael Ondaatje Are a Composite Portrait of the
      Artist as Private 'I.'" *Books in Canada*, June–July 1977, 9-10,
      12-13.
          Whitten furnishes background about Ondaatje's research and
      personal involvement in the shaping of *Coming Through
      Slaughter*, and his personal interest in films and audience response
      to *Billy the Kid.*

C26   Mathews, Robin. *Canadian Literature: Surrender or Revolution.*
      Ed. Gail Dexter. Toronto: Steel Rail, 1978, pp. 158-59.
          Mathews sees significance in the choice of *The Collected Works
      of Billy the Kid: Left Handed Poems* for a Canadian Governor
      General's Award ("the choice by a Canadian of a U.S. folk hero
      for a major poem") and finds Ondaatje one of the poets who

355

"believe that certain forms of non-political violence and rejection of what they take to be the values of capitalism constitute some kind of radicalism."

C27   Stevens, Peter. "Ondaatje, Michael (1943–   )." In his *Modern English Canadian Poetry: A Guide to Informational Sources.* Vol. XV of *American Literature, English Literature and World Literatures in English.* Detroit: Gale, 1978, pp. 37, 41, 185-87.

C28   Kroetsch, Robert. "Contemporary Standards in the Canadian Novel." Calgary Conference on the Canadian Novel, Univ. of Calgary. Feb. 1978. Printed in *Essays on Canadian Writing*, No. 20 (Winter 1980-81), 15. Rpt. in *Taking Stock: The Calgary Conference on the Canadian Novel.* Ed. Charles R. Steele. Downsview, Ont.: ECW, 1982, p. 17.
    Kroetsch cites Ondaatje's "fear of fact" and links him with Rudy Wiebe in their "subsumed eroticism." "Both furiously engaged with the language that at once announces and subdues their fear. Both, curiously, tempted by the myth of reality as it adheres in story."

C29   Mandel, Eli. "The Regional Novel: Borderline Art." Calgary Conference on the Canadian Novel, Univ. of Calgary. Feb. 1978. Printed in *Taking Stock: The Calgary Conference on the Canadian Novel.* Ed. Charles R. Steele. Downsview, Ont.: ECW, 1982, pp. 103-04, 116.
    Mandel links lines from "White Dwarfs" and *Coming Through Slaughter*, both of which speak of those " 'who sail to that perfect edge....' " The "moral paradoxes of the spirit speak in both" Rudy Wiebe and Ondaatje.

C30   Scobie, Stephen. "His Legend a Jungle Sleep: Michael Ondaatje and Henri Rousseau." *Canadian Literature*, No. 76 (Spring 1978), 6-21.

C31   Scobie, Stephen. "*Coming Through Slaughter*: Fictional Magnets and Spider's Webbs." *Essays on Canadian Writing*, No.12 (Fall 1978), 5-23.
    Scobie notes a "poetic" unity between *Coming Through Slaughter* and such earlier works as *Rat Jelly* ("White Dwarfs"

section) and *The Collected Works of Billy the Kid: Left Handed Poems*. The subject of *Coming Through Slaughter* is defined as "the experience of a certain kind of artist," "Beset by fame, obsessed by problems of equilibrium, and ultimately self-destructive."

C32   Solecki, Sam. "Making and Destroying: Michael Ondaatje's *Coming Through Slaughter* and Extremist Art." *Essays on Canadian Writing* No. 12 (Fall 1978), 24-47.

C33   Marshall, Tom. *Harsh and Lovely Land: The Major Canadian Poets and the Making of a Canadian Tradition*. Vancouver: Univ. of British Columbia Press, 1979.
        Ondaatje is cited among poets of the "fourth stage" in Canadian literature, who assimilate "process of language and consciousness and finished work." He is among those poet-novelists who have "extended the thematic, formal, and expressive possibilities of fiction in Canada" and who recently "seek to depict in fiction rather than in epic verse a world of primal psychic conflict, a dark underground of the soul in which the horror that accompanies the world's glory insists on itself."

C34   Pacey, Desmond. "The Course of Canadian Criticism." In *Literary History of Canada: Canadian Literature in English*. Gen. ed. and introd. Carl F. Klinck. 2nd Ed. Toronto: Univ. of Toronto Press, 1979. Vol. III, p. 28.
        Ondaatje's *Leonard Cohen* "is full of brilliant aperçus."

C35   Ripley, John. "Drama and Theatre." In *Literary History of Canada: Canadian Literature in English*. Gen. ed. and introd. Carl F. Klinck. 2nd ed. Toronto: Univ. of Toronto Press, 1979. Vol. III, p. 224.
        "Michael Ondaatje's dramatization of his *Collected Works of Billy the Kid* (St. Lawrence Centre, 1971) has been revived several times to critical acclaim."

C36   Woodcock, George, "Poetry." In *Literary History of Canada: Canadian Literature in English*. Gen. ed. and introd. Carl F. Klinck. 2nd ed. Toronto: Univ. of Toronto Press, 1979. Vol. III.

Ondaatje is listed among those who have made a rapid reputation and who are "fine poets by any standard of excellence, fine in vision and craft alike."

C37   Thesen, Sharon. Introduction. *The Capilano Review*, Nos. 16-17 (Feb.-March 1979), 2-3.

C38   Dragland, S.L. "Questions of Form in Contemporary Canadian Writing." *TICS* [Univ. of Western Ontario], 1, No. 1 (March 1979), 6, 22.
      Coming Through Slaughter and *Personal Fictions: Stories by Munro, Wiebe, Thomas & Blaise* are among other works cited as "experimental."

C39   Hutcheon, Linda. "'Snow Storm of Paper': The Act of Reading in Self-Reflexive Canadian Verse." *Dalhousie Review*, 59 (Spring 1979), 116-17.
      Among other "self-reflexive" writers mentioned, Ondaatje uses "black/white imagery" in his *The Collected Works of Billy the Kid: Left Handed Poems* to represent ink on paper and light on a negative.

C40   Gallager, Noel. "Ondaatje Still Part of London Literary Community." *The London Free Press*, 6 April 1979, Sec. D. p. D6.

C41   Abley, Mark. "Home is Where the Hurt Is." *Maclean's*, 23 April 1979, p. 62.
      Abley gives brief biographical information and notes that Ondaatje retreats to a farm in Eastern Ontario where he writes at a table in the barn. His novel, *Coming Through Slaughter*, was "edited in the dining car of a CP train going west." Ondaatje is "soft-spoken and witty" and has "a courtesy and gentleness of manner that seem to belie the ferocity of his art." Ondaatje says, "I try not to talk about the writing. There's so much ego involved. Writers who are personalities drive me up the wall." Abley quotes Ondaatje as once writing, "Nothing is more irritating than to have your work translated by your life."

C42   Freedman, Adele. "From Gunslingers to Jazz Musicians." *The Globe and Mail* [Toronto], 22 Dec. 1979, Sec. Entertainment,

p. 1.

In this profile, based on an interview, Freedman notes that Ondaatje has "the courage of his obsessions": "gunfighters," "jazz musicians," and "Scaramouche." Ondaatje admires another artist fascinated by gunslingers, Sergio Leone. Ondaatje's *The Collected Works of Billy the Kid: Left Handed Poems* was inspired by films (Roy Rogers) and a subscription to *Frontier News*. Ondaatje learned "about jazz through films (*The Glenn Miller Story* and *Young Man with a Horn*) and saw an editorial in a London, Ontario, newspaper which " 'hooked me' . . . to find anything related to Bolden in the New Orleans Jazz Archives and the Jazz Archives in Tulane." Ondaatje "writes sequences, puts them away and doesn't look at them again — sometimes not before years have passed." He worked on *Coming Through Slaughter* for two years. " 'I put myself into the characters' situations for a long period of time. . . . A lot of my own world gets into their stories. It's probably a major illness.' " Freedman discusses Ondaatje's Governor General's Award for *The Collected Works of Billy the Kid: Left Handed Poems* and the staging of that play at Stratford and Theatre Passe Muraille.

C43 Smith, Patricia Keeney. "Michael Ondaatje: A Poet Sets the Stage." *Performing Arts in Canada*, 7, No. 1 (Spring 1980), 30-33.

Comparing the stage adaptations for both *Billy the Kid* and *Coming Through Slaughter*, Smith highlights the more powerful adaptation.

C44 Solecki, Sam. "Point Blank: Narrative in Michael Ondaatje's *the man with seven toes*." *Canadian Poetry: Studies, Documents, Reviews*, No. 6 (Spring–Summer 1980), 14-24.

C45 Nodelman, Perry. "The Collected Photographs of Billy the Kid." *Canadian Literature*, No. 87 (Winter 1980), 68-79.

C46 Kroetsch, Robert. "The Exploding Porcupine: Violence of Form in English-Canadian Fiction." In *Violence in the Canadian Novel since 1960/dans le roman canadien depuis 1960*. Ed. Terry Goldie and Virginia Harger-Grinling. St. John's: Memorial

Univ., [1981], pp. 194-99.
Ondaatje and Audrey Thomas "anticipate a group of emerging Canadian writers who are . . . the gangsters of love."

C47 Mathews, Robin. "Private Indulgence and Public Discipline: Violence in the English Canadian Novel since 1960." In *Violence in the Canadian Novel since 1960/dans le roman canadien depuis 1960*. Ed. Terry Goldie and Virginia Harger-Grinling. St. John's: Memorial Univ., [1981], pp. 40, 41, 42-43.
Ondaatje is cited as one of a group of writers who "came out of a tradition of individualism — a tradition that celebrates the writer's alienation and isolation." *Coming Through Slaughter* is presented "as a carefully researched piece of documentary fiction that becomes increasingly the personal history of its author. . . . It is almost unmotivated violence and so can be celebrated as a part of individual peculiarity, and, perhaps, the cult of Michael Ondaatje."

C48 Moss, John. *A Reader's Guide to the Canadian Novel.* Toronto: McClelland and Stewart, 1981, pp. 223-24, 355, 360, 363, 365.
Coming Through Slaughter is "not really about Buddy Bolden," but "about Michael Ondaatje: Bolden just provides the facts, the mythology of his style and times. . . . [I]t is the artist's soul that is being offered up."

C49 MacLulich, T.D. "Ondaatje's Mechanical Boy: Portrait of the Artist as Photographer." *Mosaic: A Journal for the Comparative Study of Literature and Ideas*, 14, No. 2 (Spring 1981), 107-19.
MacLulich analyzes the special relationship of photography "both literal and metaphoric" in *The Collected Works of Billy the Kid: Left Handed Poems.*

C50 Goldie, Terry. "For Sheila Watson." Rev. of *Figures in a Ground: Canadian Essays on Modern Literature Collected in Honour of Sheila Watson,* Ed. Diane Bessai and David Jackel. *Canadian Literature*, No. 90 (Autumn 1981), 146.
Ondaatje's "Garcia Marquez and the Bus to Aracataca" "simply shows the way that the influence of someone like Marquez can lead even an excellent writer to confusion."

C51   Atwood, Margaret. Introduction. In *The New Oxford Book of Canadian Verse: In English.* Ed. Margaret Atwood. Toronto: Oxford Univ. Press, 1982, pp. xxiii, xxxviii.
    Although Ondaatje's work "evades categorization," his "exotic imagery and violent mini-plots have gained him a reputation as one of the most vital and inventive of the younger poets."

C52   Blodgett, E.D. "The Canadian Literatures as a Literary Problem." In his *Configuration: Essays in the Canadian Literatures.* Downsview, Ont.: ECW, 1982, pp. 34, 37n.
    In a discussion of "pluralism" in Canadian writing, Blodgett notes Ondaatje's essay on Gabriel Garcia Marquez and suggests that his prose can be "traced" from Marquez.

C53   Blott, Anne. "Michael Ondaatje 1943–   ." In *Canadian Poetry.* Ed. Jack David and Robert Lecker. Introd. George Woodcock. New Press Canadian Classics. Toronto/Downsview, Ont.: General/ECW, 1982. Vol. II, 317-18.

C54   Ratner, Rochelle, "Voices of the Underdog." *CV/II,* 6, Nos. 1-2 (Winter 1982), 105-08.
    Ratner discusses Ondaatje's development of surreal images, his "poems in persona," his "animalistic sense of humor," and his movement "away from the lyric and into a more narrative, prosaic line."

C55   Cooley, Dennis. "An Interview with Don Gutteridge." *CV/II,* 6, No. 4 (Aug. 1982), 41-42.
    Gutteridge notes the direct influence of *The Collected Works of Billy the Kid: Left Handed Poems* on his own *Tecumseh.* Reference in particular is made to the "necklace of blood" — "one of the most powerful lines in Billy . . . and I wanted to use it." Ondaatje is "very quiet and shy . . . . [H]e's got that Ceylon jungle in his imagination. . . ."Gutteridge "got to know him in the late '60s in London and went to his first reading."

C56   [Levenson, Christopher.] "Editorial: The Long Poem in Canada." *arc* [Carleton Univ.], No. 7 (Autumn 1982), 5-6.
    In a discussion of the form of the long poem, Levenson questions Ondaatje's quotation from Jack Spicer in the Introduction

to *The Long Poem Anthology* "espousing the concept that all a poet's work (is) one continuing poem which must be never fully realized (confined) within the boundaries of one poem." In this "concept of inclusiveness" the "emphasis is displaced from artifact to artificer, trivia are accorded quasi-mystical significance," and those who "think of the poet as a *Maker*, find most of the products of this attitude to poetry slipshod, haphazard, self-indulgent and lacking in structure or direction."

C57   Oughton, John. "Sane Assassin: The Double Life of Michael Ondaatje, Mild-Mannered Professor of English Literature and Risk-Taking Celebrator of Madmen." *Books in Canada*, June–July 1983, pp. 7-10.

Thesis

C58   McColm, Sheila Clare. "Metaphorical Style and Thought in the Poetry of Margaret Avison and Michael Ondaatje." M.A. Thesis Western Ontario 1981.
      Both Avison and Ondaatje "share an interest in the innovative use of figurative language." McColm examines "the way that metaphor is thought of and used" by these two writers. The poems analyzed "display stylistic innovations that are, to a large extent, dependent upon metaphorical strategies...." Both poets venture "into unexplored lands of thought," and their language strives "to render the new forms of consciousness ...." Chapter iv, which concentrates on Ondaatje, examines metaphor that creates the place " 'where the raw of feelings exist.' "

Interviews

C59   Barbour, Douglas, and Stephen Scobie. "A Conversation with Michael Ondaatje." *White Pelican*, 1, No. 2 (Spring 1971), 6-15.
      Ondaatje discusses the reasons for *Sons of Captain Poetry*'s emphasis on sound poetry, the limitations of the film medium in portraying word-play and "particular" works, and the reasons for producing this "fantasy documentary." Ondaatje discusses "organic" forms in traditional and concrete poetry, although he

does not feel very qualified in discussing concrete. Although Nichol found "traces of concrete poetry" in *the man with seven toes*, Ondaatje experiments more with collage, than concrete, especially when there is a "lack of reality in words." The film is a "moving collage." Ondaatje notes the influence his wife's paintings have had on him. He discusses the process of selecting Nichol's works and the co-operative viewpoint which was presented. Robert Fresco, the cameraman, is also discussed. Because "So much depends on accident" in film, Ondaatje was not intentionally influenced by any director, and the co-operative experience is very different from writing. Ondaatje discusses the filming done in Captain George's Memory Lane. Both Ondaatje and Nichol are "very Hollywoodish" and are "arch-romantics." An important link for Nichol is being a "romantic and an anarchist simultaneously." Ondaatje discusses potential further involvement in the film media as interesting, but not highly likely at the present. He notes that there is not enough silence in the film and that it is really modelled on *The Joker is Wild*. As with Nichol's *The Martyrology*, Ondaatje had little sense of where *The Collected Works of Billy the Kid: Left Handed Poems* was going, or whether it would be good or bad, until it was finished.

C60 Interview (by mail) with Michael Ondaatje by an Anonymous Correspondent. *Manna*, No. 1 (March 1972), 19-22.

Ondaatje comments on early writing, imagery, myth in *The Dainty Monsters* and *The Collected Works of Billy the Kid: Left Handed Poems*, and his interest and involvement in films and film-making. The identity of the photographed child in a corduroy outfit at the back of the book is claimed as "me in Ceylon in a cowboy outfit . . . about the age of seven."

C61 "The Charm of Kingston." *CBC Tuesday Night.* CBC Radio, 11 Dec. 1973.

This interview includes comments by Ondaatje regarding the "interpenetration of landscape and city," the area near Kingston, and a reading of his "We're at the graveyard." Ondaatje also comments on the true landscape of Kingston "where the sense of history lives for me" — old houses, people, limestones, graveyards, evidences of the past. Kim Ondaatje, artist and wife of the author, talks about Blue Roof Farm where they live and where she began to paint.

C62 Solecki, Sam. "An Interview with Michael Ondaatje." *Rune* [St. Michael's College, Univ. of Toronto], No. 2 (Spring 1975), 39-54.

C63 Pierce, Gretchen. "Canada Gives Writer 'Sense of Place' Author of 'Billy' Keeps Low Profile." *Halifax Chronicle Herald*, 10 Oct. 1975, p. 30.

Pierce interviews Ondaatje in the office of the Neptune Theatre where *Billy the Kid* was in rehearsal. Ondaatje discusses the "selfish" act of writing and how the play is not "a western." Of the adaptation, he says " 'I always felt it was a play. It's a mixture of prose, poetry, and scenes from a life. *Billy* grew out of my obsession with that dark side of our nature; most people have it at certain times . . . . I started writing at 20 not knowing I really wanted to be a writer. It was the effect the Canadian landscape had on me . . . . The play doesn't try to explain why he [Billy] was that way or preach about good or evil, it presents him as a person and leaves it up to the listener to judge. . . . Maybe some will be offended by the language. . . . It wasn't written to offend, I have too much respect for the audience. Writing *Billy* was a catharsis and I learned more about myself.' "

C64 Pearce, Jon. "Moving to the Clear: Michael Ondaatje." In his *Twelve Voices: Interviews with Canadian Poets.* Introd. Jon Pearce. Ottawa: Borealis, 1980, pp. [129]-43.

Pearce provides brief biographical data. Ondaatje discusses when he began to write, who his influences were, and his editing and writing processes. He notes that poems and books have organic structures and comments on his involvement with a character and the need to move beyond thematics to "style, technique, the method and movement of the poem." Ondaatje needs a balance of "gentleness and violence" in his works to articulate "a very real world." Billy and Bolden are both artists, yet it is difficult to generalize them into statements of the artist in society. For Ondaatje, "morality" is what is "human." The "artist" needs to be connected with "the real world" and not elevated above it. Pearce does not often receive detailed replies to his questions involving the interpretation of Ondaatje's poems. When questioned about the poet's responsiblity to his poem, Ondaatje says it is "to remain silent after he's written the poem." Because the meaning is as much in the structure as in the content, paraphrase "can only destroy a poem." Pearce comments on the thin line between form and chaos that Ondaatje straddles to be able to communicate the live event. Ondaatje comments on the continuity of a writer's works and the poem as a process of clarifying, discovering, and "more." Neither Billy nor Bolden come to "pessimistic" ends, though the books are "not *joyous*."

C65 [Whiten, Clifton.] "PCR Interview with Michael Ondaatje." *Poetry Canada Review*, 2, No. 2 (Winter 1980-81), 6.
Ondaatje speaks about the role of an editor from his experience as poetry editor for *Quarry*, the symbolism of the covers of *There's a Trick with a Knife I'm Learning to Do: Poems 1963-1978* and *Rat Jelly*, the influence of "poetry from other countries," and "fine" Canadian writers, of whom he mentions Roy Kiyooka, Colleen Thibodeau, Sharon Thesen, Christopher Dewdney, Phyllis Webb, and David Donnell.

C66 Mundwiler, Leslie. *Michael Ondaatje: Word, Image, Imagination.* Vancouver: Talonbooks, 1985.

ACKNOWLEDGMENTS

Some of the following interviews, articles and reviews first appeared in these journals: "An Interview with Michael Ondaatje," *Rune*, No. 2 (Spring 1975), 39-54; "Let There Be Commerce Between Us: The Poetry of Michael Ondaatje," *Descant*, 42 (Fall 1982), 89-98; "His Legend a Jungle Sleep: Michael Ondaatje and Henri Rousseau," *Canadian Literature*, 76 (Spring 1978), 6-21; "Nets and Chaos: The Poetry of Michael Ondaatje," *Studies in Canadian Literature*, 2 (Winter 1977), 36-48; "Controlling the Jungle," *Canadian Literature*, 36 (Spring 1968), 86-88; "A Bitter Aspic," *Books in Canada*, April-May-June 1973, 17; "Review of *There's a Trick with a Knife I'm Learning to Do*," *The Fiddlehead*, 129 (Spring 1981), 100-102; "All That Poetry Should Be," *The Canadian Forum*, 690 (June-July 1979), 34; "Coming Through," *The Canadian Forum*, 745 (January 1985), 32-36; "Point Blank: Narrative in *the man with seven toes*," *Canadian Poetry*, 6 (Spring-Summer 1980), 14-24; "Dream as History; *the man with seven toes*," *The Fiddlehead*, 86 (August-September-October 1970) 158-62; "Michael Ondaatje: The Mechanization of Death," *White Pelican*, 2, No. 4 (Fall 1972) 56-64; "Savage Fields: *The Collected Works of Billy the Kid*," is excerpted from *Savage Fields: An Essay in Literature and Cosmology* (Toronto: House of Anansi, 1977); "Two Authors in Search of a Character: bp Nichol and Michael Ondaatje," *Canadian Literature*, 54 (Autumn 1972), 37-55; "Making and Destroying: Michael Ondaatje's *Coming Through Slaughter* and Extremist Art," *Essays on Canadian Writing*, 12 (Fall 1978) 24-47; "The Poet Novelist" was originally an untitled review of *Coming Through Slaughter* in "Letters in Canada: 1976. Fiction: II," *University of Toronto Quarterly*, Vol. XLVI, 4 (Summer 1977) 350; "The Blurred Photo" was originally an untitled review of *Coming Throught Slaughter* in *The Fiddlehead*, 113 (Spring 1977) 126-9; "Michael Ondaatje: A Paper Promiscuous and Out of Forme with Several Inlargements and Untutored Narrative,"*Descant*, 42 (Fall 1982) 77-88; "Michael Ondaatje: A Bibliography," is a radically shortened version of Judith Brady's "Michael Ondaatje: An

Annotated Bibliography'' which will be published as part of ECW's *The Annotated Bibliographies of Canada's Major Authors*; all the other essays were commissioned for this volume.

The editor thanks everyone who delivered on time, Michael Ondaatje for tolerating questions and requests, and Audrey McDonagh who helped with typewriter, encouragement and just by being there.

CONTRIBUTORS

J.E. Chamberlin is a member of the Department of English at the University of Toronto; *Stephen Scobie* is a member of the Department of English at the University of Victoria; poet and critic *George Bowering* teaches at Simon Fraser University; poet *Susan Glickman* lives in Toronto; *Tom Marshall* is a poet, critic, novelist teaching English literature at Queen's University; *Sam Solecki* is a member of the Department of English at the University of Toronto; *Douglas Barbour* teaches in the Department of English at the University of Alberta; poet *Bert Almon* teaches at the University of Alberta; *M. Travis Lane* is a member of the Department of English at the University of New Brunswick; novelist and short story writer *Sheila Watson* lives in Nanaimo, B.C.; poet, critic and editor *Dennis Lee* lives in Toronto; *Dennis Cooley* teaches in the Department of English at the University of Manitoba; poet *David Donnell* lives in Toronto; *Constance Rooke* is a member of the Department of English at the University of Victoria; *R.P. Bilan* is a freelance writer living in Toronto; *Jon Kertzer* teaches in the Department of English at the University of Calgary; *Linda Hutcheon* is a member of the Department of English at McMaster University; *Ernest MacIntyre* is a Sri Lankan playwright living in Australia; *Judith Brady* lives in Toronto.